BLUE & GRAY
in
BLACK & WHITE

Also by Brayton Harris

The Age of the Battleship: 1890-1922 (1965)

Johann Gutenberg and the Invention of Printing (1970)

The Navy Times Book of Submarines: A Political, Social and Military History (1997)

With Jerome Kirschenbaum:

The U.S. Navy Diving Manual (1972)

SAFE BOAT: The Most Comprehensive Book on Boating Safety (1990)

BLUE & GRAY in BLACK & WHITE

Newspapers in the Civil War

BRAYTON HARRIS

BRASSEY'S

An Imprint of Batsford Brassey, Inc.
Washington · London

Library of Congress Cataloging-in-Publication Data

Harris, Brayton, 1932–
    Blue & gray in black & white : newspapers in the Civil War / Brayton Harris.
—1st ed.
      p. cm.
    Includes bibliographical references and index.
    1. United States—History—Civil War, 1861–1865—Press coverage. 2. United States—History—Civil War, 1861–1865—Journalists. 3. United States—History—Civil War, 1861–1865—Journalism, Military. 4. American newspapers—History—19th century. 5. Journalism—United States—History—19th century. I. Title. II. Title: Blue and gray in black and white.
E609.H37 1999   99-29906
070.4'499737—dc21   CIP

ISBN 1-57488-165-5 (alk. paper)

Printed in the United States of America on acid-free paper that meets the American National Standards Institute Z39-48 Standard.

Batsford Brassey, Inc.
22883 Quicksilver Drive
Dulles, Va. 20166

First Edition

10 9 8 7 6 5 4 3 2 1

TO THE ARMY CORRESPONDENTS and Artists, 1861–
1865 Whose Toils Cheered the Camps,
Thrilled the Fireside, Educated Provinces of Rustics Into a
Bright Nation of Readers and
Gave Incentive to Narrate Distant Wars and Explore Dark Lands.

> O Wondrous youth
> Through this grand ruth
> Runs my boy's life its thread.
> The General's name, the battle's fame,
> The rolls of maimed and dead
> I bear, with my thrilled soul astir,
> And lonely thoughts and fears,
> And am but history's courier
> To bind the conquering years—
> A battle ray through ages gray
> To light to deeds sublime,
> And flash the lustre of my day
> Down all the aisles of time.

Inscription on a memorial arch erected on the South Mountain battlefield in Maryland long after the war, bearing the names of perhaps one-third of the writers and artists who served—both sides—during the war. The verse was presumably written by the war correspondent who was responsible for creation of this monument to his brethren, George Alfred Townsend.

Contents

List of Illustrations / viii

Preface / ix

1   Introduction: The War Correspondent / 1
2   State of the Art / 3
3   Rehearsals / 19
4   Sumter / 41
5   An Age of Innocence / 51
6   A Battle Too Soon / 67
7   Bull Run Russell / 89
8   Sedition and Suppression: North / 97
9   Sedition and Suppression: South / 109
10 Modus Scribendi / 119
11 Washington / 137
12 Command and Control / 149
13 The Summer of '62 / 161
14 A Matter of Color / 187
15 The Press Reports a Battle: Fredericksburg, I / 205
16 The Press Reports a Battle: Fredericksburg, II / 223
17 The Other War / 239
18 Transitions, 1863 / 253
19 The Poet as Historian, I / 267
20 Watershed / 277
21 The Poet as Historian, II / 287
22 Endgame / 303
23 Coda / 317

Notes and Sources / 325
Selected Bibliography / 347
Index / 355

Illustrations

The Hoe "Lightning" printing press / 10
A basic woodcut map from the New York *Times* / 12
A Vigilence Committee in Memphis admiring the work of
    Harper's artist, Theodore Davis / 36
The bombardment of Fort Sumter / 42
Field Marshal Horace Greeley / 59
Printers among the Union's soldiery / 114
McClellan at Frederick, Md. / 178
Burnside assumes command / 206
Assault on Fredericksburg / 214
Bridgebuilding at Fredericksburg / 217
Federal troops looting Fredericksburg / 219
New York *Times* map of Fredericksburg / 225
Thomas Nast panorama of action at Fredericksburg / 226–27
Confederate perspective of an assault on Marye's Heights / 229
Burying Federal dead at Fredericksburg / 236
Burnside's "mud march" / 255
Ulysses S. Grant / 261
Barbara Frietchie / 268
Sheridan's ride / 288
Winslow Homer's "Sharpshooter" / 292
Winslow Homer self-portrait / 306
Harper's schizophrenic depiction of blacks / 322

Preface

ON AVERAGE, there has been one book about the Civil War published every day since the shooting ended, 134 years ago—histories, biographies, diaries, collections, and reprints of any and all of the above. However, aside from a few postwar memoirs by journalists themselves, and outside of a chapter or two in histories of journalism in general or in corporate histories of newspapers in specific, only a handful of authors have dealt with the single most important element in creating the public record of the war—the popular press.

The intersecting technologies of the mid-nineteenth century put newspapers at the forefront of social activity; a town as small as Vicksburg, Mississippi, population 4,500, had six independent newspapers at the start of the war. The telegraph had wired much of the continent; the steam-powered rotary press allowed the larger metropolitan newspapers to turn out thousands of copies per hour; the railroad linked major cities with travel times not much different from those of today and provided timely distribution of the product. The telegraphed report of an afternoon event in Chicago could be set in type in New York by supper time, roll off the presses by midnight, and be in the White House before noon. A report of the president's reaction could appear in an edition, a bit later in the day, anywhere in the nation. The report of a battle could be flashed around the nation while the guns were still firing—provided that the reporter had access to a telegraph line, and that the "authorities," whether military or civil, allowed the material to be sent.

This is not a history of the Civil War, only a guided tour of highlights as covered by, and at times influenced by, the press. As with any tour, the guide has selected the route and picked the points of interest. There is much that must be left out: the total wartime journalistic output was more than 100 million words; on average, 50,000 words per day were filed from

Washington, DC, alone. The book you now hold includes about 130,000 words. Obviously, we have not only been selective, but also ruthless. We look at few battles, we review little of strategy, we examine but a few of the colorful personalities who shaped the course of the war. We devote little time to the self-reported exploits of journalists; they may make good drama, but not necessarily good history. We barely mention the navy—and yet, in the broad scheme of things, the Union navy perhaps rendered the more valuable service in the war, slowly choking the Confederacy with a 3,500-mile-long blockade. But then, the navy was not much covered by war correspondents. The navy was a tough assignment for a journalist; it was hard to get aboard a ship without actually joining the navy, hard to file any copy except under the total control of the commanding officer, and then only when there was access to dry land, and hard to find anything interesting about which to write.

We *do* study the political philosophies of major daily and weekly newspapers; the partisan coloration of the news ("objectivity" was not an operative philosophy); the impact of newspapers on the war and of the war on newspapers; government censorship; official suppression, and unofficial destruction, of "disloyal" newspapers; relations between the journalists and the army; relationships among the journalists themselves; and, above all, the quality of the reporting. Most of the nation's knowledge of the war then, and much of it yet today, started with something published in a newspaper.

Most of that came from the special correspondents. There were some 350 for the North, about 150 for the South. Most, but not all, were male, and most were young—on average, in their late twenties. They led a difficult life in the field alongside the men of the army whose dangers and hardships they shared. Some were *in* the army, "war correspondents" in a literal sense.

As observers of the war and the human condition, they were often trite but sometimes brilliant; as interpreters of battlefield tactics or grand strategy, they were frequently wrong, and often wrong-headed. As eyewitnesses to one of the most memorable conflicts in the history of mankind, they left a record, North and South, filled with trial, triumph, and pain; a record not as complete as, but more alive than, the official version, and although often in error, not as self-serving as the multitudinous postwar biographies of participants. It is a record that deserves to be studied on its merits, to be enjoyed for its content, and that, for too long, has been overlooked.

This book grew out of an assignment by the Civil War Society to prepare a study on the subject for its official magazine, *Civil War*. That study was published in December 1988, as volume 15. I am indebted for that assignment to my long-time colleague Garrison Ellis—founder of the society—and Christopher Curran, then and still publisher of the magazine. Because space limitations were more severe than those imposed by a book format, we were able only to scratch the surface of most topics, and Don McKeon at Batsford Brassey encouraged this expanded, and basically all new, version.

However, much of this material was written long ago by other people: the special correspondents, editors, historians, general officers, legislators, cabinet members, and presidents, North and South, who created the record from which I have drawn. I stand in awe of the skill, intelligence, and dedication exhibited by most, but offer this warning: because of the historical relevance of the language of some, I have not bowdlerized the text of any. Beware of gross and unpleasant racial slurs and epithets.

On a less controversial note, because much of the spelling, punctuation, and capitalization was inconsistent *then* and does not match standards *today*, those largely have been brought into contemporary practice; the names of newspapers have been normalized with the city in Roman typeface, the *name* in italics; emphasis, when shown, was always in the original.

1 / Introduction: The War Correspondent

THE ORIGIN of the "war correspondent," like the origin of any species, is shrouded by imperfect history. We know it happened, but we do not know when and how.

There have been writers on war, whether as participant or historian, as long as there have been war and writing, and in cultures lacking the latter, the former has been recorded in pictures. The term *war correspondent* was early and easily attached to anyone who sent letters from a war zone to a newspaper, whether as a working newsman or merely a literate member of an armed force.

There were, however, two preconditions: there had to be a newspaper to which the correspondence might be sent, and "newspapers," as we know them, did not begin to appear in appreciable numbers until the 1840s. And there had to be a war.

Thus, the first professional war correspondent may have been George Kendall, one of five or six otherwise anonymous American journalists attending the Mexican War of 1846–48. Kendall was covering for the New Orleans *Picayune* (of which he was cofounder and editor), and the group, which worked in close cooperation, included a representative of the New Orleans *Delta* and at least one journalist on the payroll of the New York *Herald*. Building on a *Herald* experiment of 1845, using horseback messengers across the plains, steamboats on the rivers, and the first newly installed telegraph lines for the last leg of the journey, they managed to get copies of their dispatches to Washington well before any army reports, and into print before any official government announcements. They thus demonstrated the sort of enterprise that was to be a major feature of Civil War reporting, but they otherwise seem to have had so little impact that many histories of that war—or of journalism—fail to mention their effort.

A few years later, another small group of journalists went to war, but with more measurable effect. Edwin Lawrence Godkin of the London

Daily News, Thomas Chenery and William Howard Russell of the London *Times*, and Richard C. McCormick of the New York *Evening Post* were witnesses to the Crimean War, 1854–56. They demonstrated a different sort of basic truth, one which has held in every war since: an unfettered, honest journalist is a burden to an army in the field, anathema at the seat of government, and vital to a democratic society.

The British correspondents had a significant impact on both the war and the government. Because of their reports citing deplorable conditions at the Crimean front—a grossly inadequate supply system, bone-headed leadership, and a grotesque shortage of medical staff and facilities—they were blamed for the downfall of a British government and indirectly held responsible for the death (from poor health aggravated by shame) of the British commander, Lord Raglan. The government tried to counter the criticism with carefully staged photographs of happy, healthy soldiers in the battle zone. The effort failed; Florence Nightingale's pioneering ministrations came in direct response to reports of the shabby treatment of British wounded.

Russell was the standout, a careful, thorough reporter who took nothing for granted, who assembled widely separated points of view into a coherent whole, and who wrote in a readable, swinging style. He went on to establish a reputation as the world's leading war correspondent. Russell brought his professionalism to the American Civil War, where he proved that his reputation was well-deserved—but, as we shall see, his efforts may be more appreciated in *our* time than they were in *his*.

This book is not about Russell, but through the early period of the war he was important as both a reporter and a subject of the news, and must be given his due. However, he was but one of perhaps five hundred journalists assigned by newspapers—North, South, and international—to participate in the first truly public war. This book is an exploration of their individual and collective efforts.

2 / State of the Art

The brilliant mission of the newspaper is . . . to be, the high priest of
history, the vitalizer of society, the world's great informer,
the earth's high censor, the medium of public thought and opinion,
and the circulating life blood of the whole human mind.
It is the great enemy of tyrants and the right arm of liberty, and is
destined, more than any other agency, to melt and mold the jarring and
contending nations of the world into . . . one great brotherhood. . . .

—Samuel Bowles, editor-publisher of the
Springfield *Republican*, 1851 [1]

THE TYPICAL AMERICAN NEWSPAPER in the early years of the
nineteenth century was a journal of opinion, a cheerleader for politicians,
and a vehicle for cultured discourse and cultural pretension. It was not,
however, much of a *news* paper. Few editors made an effort to leave the
office to gather information, and much of what they did publish about the
world outside came to them in the mail: letters from subscribers; copies of
speeches which may or may not have been delivered; and copies of other
newspapers, part of an informal system of exchange, from which interesting items could freely be appropriated.

However, within the space of a very few years, advancing technologies,
increasing literacy, and journalistic enterprise would change the American
newspaper forever. The metamorphosis perhaps began in 1828, when a
man named David Hale bought the New York *Journal of Commerce* and
demonstrated the commercial value of enlightened competition. At that
time, most New York newspapers obtained news from Europe—of interest
to businessmen throughout the city—by picking up copies of foreign news-

papers from newly arrived ships. Hale found a better way: he purchased a fast schooner and stationed it outside the entrance to New York harbor to meet incoming ships, gather up copies of the European newspapers, and head for port under full sail. By the time the newcomers were tied up or anchored and ready to receive visitors, the *Journal of Commerce* would already have posted the news on an increasingly popular public bulletin board. Then, because the ships from Europe might arrive at any time during the day, Hale began issuing an afternoon edition of his morning paper—an "extra" edition, if you will, thus launching a peculiarity of American journalism that would burst into full flower during the Civil War.

Hale's next innovation was a "pony express" to gather state news (especially on election day). One of Hale's editors soon learned *this* trade, and split off to start his own newspaper. In 1830, his Boston *Atlas* was able to publish returns from every town in Massachusetts by nine o'clock of the morning after the election. Other competitors got the message, and by 1833 there were at least two pony express routes between New York and Washington, D.C. (Within a few years, they would be replaced by a newly established railroad.)

One of those enlightened by Hale's success was a thirty-nine-year-old immigrant from Scotland, James Gordon Bennett. In 1835, with ten years of newspaper experience and a largely borrowed stake of five hundred dollars, he rented a basement office and invented the modern newspaper—the New York *Herald*. He was to set the style and tone of much of what subsequently would pass for American journalism; he offered the following editorial prescription in the first edition of the *Herald*:

> What is to prevent a daily newspaper from being made the greatest organ of social life? Books have had their day—the theaters have had their day—the temple of religion has had its day. A newspaper can be made to take the lead of all these in the great movements of human thought and of human civilization. A newspaper can send more souls to Heaven, and save more from Hell, than all the churches or chapels in New York—besides making money at the same time. [2]

It would be hard to verify the accuracy of the first part of the final sentence, but the rest was prophetic: the *Herald* funded its coverage of the Civil War at a level of more than $100,000 per year and Bennett was able to refuse a postwar purchase offer of $2 million.

The *Herald* was filled with crime and scandal—and innovation. In 1836, Bennett published what was probably the first newspaper "interview" (with the madam of a house of ill repute in which an inmate had been murdered), but he also gets credit for establishing the Wall Street report as a regular newspaper feature, and engineered a change in the rules of Congress to allow attendance by journalists representing papers published outside of the District of Columbia. He made his newspaper, well, *interesting*. The New Orleans *Picayune* had him dead to rights: "The *Herald* may be said to represent, in one particular, the genius of the universal Yankee nation—that is, in its supreme regard for what is vulgarly called the main chance." [3]

Horace Greeley was to join Bennett as one of the most influential newspapermen of the age, if not of all time. Greeley started as a printer's apprentice, and in the 1830s moved on to become an editor and writer of political tracts for the conservative Whig Party. In 1841, he founded the New York *Tribune*.

If Bennett intended to be a sort of benign Pied Piper and to make money, Greeley's announced intention was "to advance the interests of the people, and to promote their Moral, Political and Social well-being." He promised that "the immoral and degrading Police Reports, Advertisements, and other matter which have been allowed to disgrace the columns of our leading Penny Papers, will be carefully excluded from this, and no exertion will be spared to render it worthy of the virtuous and refined, and a welcome visitant at the family fireside." [4]

The *Tribune* was launched as a Whig daily, but in 1854, disenchanted with that party's ambivalence toward slavery, Greeley helped to organize, and shifted his editorial allegiance to, the Republican Party. He thenceforth became the self-anointed messiah of abolition, sent forth with his newspaper to savage the forces of slavery and to salvage mankind.

The *Herald* and the *Tribune* were not the only innovative newspapers in the nation, but their efforts were representative and their influence was transcendent. Newspapers began to shift from a limited local focus to coverage of a broader scene. The *Herald* established a European bureau in 1838; by 1850, the *Tribune* had at least sixteen designated "correspondents" writing letters under contract, with three full-time correspondents in Washington and part-time stringers in California, Philadelphia, Baltimore, and Boston, and nine in other countries.

Another major factor in Civil War journalism was Henry J. Raymond, who spent the first nine years of his adult life working for Horace Greeley. The two men became increasingly disenchanted with each other, and Raymond split off in 1848 to pursue what was to become a dual career. He was elected to the New York State legislature in 1849, elected speaker in 1851, and launched the New York *Times* that same year. It was *his* vision that a good newspaper might fall somewhere between the *Herald* and the *Tribune*. In his first editorial, he pledged that the *Times* would uphold "every just effort to reform society, to infuse higher elements of well-being into our political and social organizations, and to improve the condition and character of our fellow men." [5]

Raymond's strained relationship with Greeley was irrevocably broken in 1854 when Greeley sought the party's nomination for lieutenant governor of New York—and Raymond won, not only the nomination but also the office. Raymond would hold other elective offices during the Civil War, while at the same time running his newspaper. Greeley ran his newspaper during the Civil War, while at the same time trying to gain elective office. When New York senator William H. Seward—who had been an unsuccessful candidate for the 1860 Republican presidential nomination—was given a cabinet post as secretary of state, Greeley asked President Abraham Lincoln to support *his* candidacy for the senate seat; the president gently declined. Greeley also was himself to be a candidate (unsuccessful) for president in 1872. As one of his associates once remarked, "Mr. Greeley would be the greatest journalist in America if he did not aim to be one of the leading politicians in America." [6]

The year the *Herald* was founded was a seminal year in the history of communications. The world's first news agency began operations, linking London and Paris by carrier pigeon; the number of miles of operational railroad track in the United States passed the one-thousand mark; and Samuel F. B. Morse created his code for reducing written letters into an audible or visible series of dots and dashes. Two years later, Isaac Pitman introduced a different sort of code, a method of quick, or "shorthand," writing by which newspapers were able to offer verbatim reports of public and political speeches—much to the distress of the speakers, who preferred to leave a written copy of their remarks with favored journals.

Then, in 1844, came the technological breakthrough that would help free journalism forever from the constraints of the mailbag. Morse transmitted the first public telegraph message—"What hath God wrought"—by sending electrical impulses over wires strung between Baltimore and Washington, D.C. The electromagnetic telegraph was not a new idea, but Morse made it practical. However, because the term *telegraph* (from the Greek words for distance and writing) already was applied to various forms of signaling devices, his invention was for some years differentiated in the press by the adjective, *magnetic*.

The telegraph was a mixed blessing, providing rapid transmission of the news, but at considerable cost. The Washington-to-New York tariff for a typical two-thousand-word newspaper column was about $100; from New Orleans to New York, perhaps $450; this, at a time when the man writing the column might have earned less than $10 for his effort. To reduce telegraphic charges, the correspondents frequently eliminated prepositions, conjunctions, and unnecessary words to a point where intelligibility disappeared. Here, an example that was offered in the April 18, 1863, Savannah *Daily News*:

> Jackson, April 17—Eight boats passed Vicksburg last night; one burnt two disabled five succeeded. Rumor canal Milliken's Bend reach Mississippi near New Carthage believed construction Batteries opposite Vicksburg paid burn bridge Big Black Vicksburg attacked within ten 10 days all officers absent ordered report opposite Vicksburg sixty-four 64 steamers left Memphis for Vicksburg soldiers niggers nor papers allowed below Cairo Yankees fortifying Rolla RR north Memphis Bulleting argus suppressed editors arrested.

In the early days of the telegraph, the more affluent papers quickly learned how to use wealth to competitive advantage on fast-breaking news, by plugging up the wire with a wad of dummy copy to prevent transmission of a rival's dispatch. One common tactic was for the reporter to rush to the telegraph office before he had even written his own story, and hand the telegrapher a pocket Bible open to the first page, with the instruction, "Start sending at Genesis and don't stop 'til I say so." He could then polish his copy, to be sent when ready, while exasperated competitors could only wait.

To forestall such ungentlemanly behavior and impose some fairness, the telegraph companies established the "fifteen minute system," whereby each customer was allowed to send material in blocks of fifteen minutes. The telegrapher would send copy until the allotted time had expired, then shift to the copy of another for fifteen minutes, and so on, until returning to the first customer for another fifteen minutes of glory.

This, however, satisfied none of the newspapermen. Hale suggested to Bennett that they pool their interests. They did—along with those of the *Tribune*, the *Sun*, the *Express*, and the *Courier and Enquirer* to form the New York Associated Press early in 1849. (The *Times* was added after it began publication in 1851.) Subscribing newspapers around the nation were permitted to copy any given report, providing that they paid a share of the telegraphic costs, thus substantially reducing the price for everyone. The New York Associated Press quickly grew into a major business enterprise on its own, with additional bureaus in Washington and Albany, a staff of fifty agents culling news from local papers for retransmission to members, and favorable contracts with the American Telegraph Company and Western Union.

As the war intruded, a Southern Associated Press tried to fill in the gaps, but midway through the war, when editors complained of high prices and poor service, a rival Press Association of the Confederate States of America was established, with headquarters in Atlanta and about twenty correspondents in the field. Members could count on a weekly report of about 3,500 words for a flat rate of twelve dollars, ten cents per word for additional material. The Press Association made a special effort to ensure objectivity, but in this was not entirely successful. Some newspapers complained that they were being forced to pay telegraph charges for editorials and speculation.

By 1860—only a dozen or so years after Kendall's pioneering effort at war correspondence—the telegraph had become a fifty-thousand-mile network, Kansas to the Atlantic seaboard, and a San Francisco to New York telegraph line was opened in 1861. (A transatlantic cable had been put into service in 1858; the cable handled 750 messages, until the insulation failed after a week's operation. The wartime replacement: fast boats and tight scheduling. For the North, copy was sent to New York or Boston and put aboard the earliest transatlantic packet. Near the coast of Ireland, the dispatches were placed in a phosphorescent floating buoy and tossed overboard, to be retrieved by a local boat and hustled to the nearest city with a telegraph for transmission to London and retransmission to the rest of Europe. Dispatches from the South were carried in returning blockade runners or by diplomatic pouch from the French consulate at Richmond.)

Publishing news received by telegraph became as much a marketing ploy as a journalistic service, highlighted in special columns headed "News from the Magnetic Telegraph." Not everyone, however, appreciated the benefits of the telegraph. Outgoing president James Buchanan shared his concerns in a December 1860 letter to James Gordon Bennett:

> I do not know whether the great commercial and social advantages of the telegraph are not counterbalanced by its political evils. No one can judge of this so well as myself. The public mind throughout the interior is kept in a constant state of excitement by what are called "telegrams." They are short and spicy, and can easily be inserted in the country newspapers. In the city journals they can be contradicted the next day; but the case is different throughout the country. [7]

Six weeks later, the editor of the Philadelphia *Morning Pennsylvanian* offered this caution to his readers:

> Every day's experience and observation more and more convinces us that that great institution, the magnetic telegraph, instead of be-

ing a blessing, is a curse to the country. . . . We warn the people to beware of this new power in our midst. . . .

And beware also, the editor wrote, the motives of the telegraph company:

Its whole stock in trade consists in the perpetual excitement of the community—in a morbid appetite for startling news and a monomania for extravagant and almost incredible rumors; because this diseased condition of the public mind furnishes a market for the sale of improved "extras" and "sensation" newspapers—bringing grist to two mills—the telegraph and the printing office.

That sounds a bit like "sour grapes." Perhaps the *Morning Pennsylvanian* could not much afford the use of the telegraph. [8]

Coupled with the growth of a literate population—the literacy rate among Northern whites reached 89 percent in 1850—the number of active newspapers in the United States quadrupled between 1825 and 1860. There were almost 2,500 on the eve of the Civil War (twice as many in the North as in the South, and with four times the circulation). At least 373 of these were published daily, perhaps 80 of which were in the South. New York alone supported 17 daily newspapers, and, thanks to convenient rail service, the *Herald*, *Tribune*, and *Times* offered same-day home delivery in Washington. (Washington entered the war with three dailies of its own, none of which could compete with the New York papers in style, size, or timeliness; Richmond had four.) The *Herald* had been publishing a Sunday edition for some twenty years, and was joined in 1860 by the New York *Tribune*, the New York *Times*, the Chicago *Tribune*, and the Boston *Herald*. Railroads laid on special "Sunday expresses" to speed delivery. Some papers began publishing both morning and evening editions. (One wag commented, "They issue those evening editions to contradict the lies that they tell in the morning.") [9]

For most of the nation's newspapers, the basics of production had not much changed in four hundred years. The pressman would lay a single sheet of paper on top of the inked typeform in the bed of the press, bring down the pressure platen, release it, and carefully pull the sheet away. The impression of two pages would be left on the sheet and after the ink had dried it would be flipped over and put back in the press, whereby two pages would be printed on the other side. When folded, this produced a four-page newspaper—the size of most papers in the nation, other than a few of the New York papers, which published eight-page editions.

The Hoe press at the New York *Tribune.*

New printing technology was entering the marketplace, but initially only the major New York newspapers could afford the investment. First came the Hoe Lightning rotary steam-powered printing press, thirty-four-feet high, fed by eight sheet-handlers, which could spit forth twenty thousand impressions per hour. Then, by April 1861, the *Tribune* had developed the stereotype process, a technique for casting lead printing cylinders from a papier-ma [ché mold of the type. Presses could be run faster, and duplicate cylinders could quickly be made and mounted on other presses to increase the run for special editions. Within four months, both the *Herald* and the *Times* had mastered the process. (Espionage, we presume, was not limited to military affairs.) In 1863, the Philadelphia *Inquirer* installed a press that could print both sides of the paper—now fed from a roll—at the same time.

The public's appetite for illustration was as great as that for information, and by 1860, more than two hundred printmakers—of which the firm of Currier & Ives was perhaps the best known—were turning out lithographs and copperplate engravings celebrating everything from country courtship to warehouse fires. Newspaper publishers, eager to capitalize on this public enthusiasm, were faced with a practical limitation: the most energetic printmakers could not turn out more than about three hundred copies per day. Photography, just then coming into widespread use, certainly had promise and already was providing reference images for artists, but no method had yet been devised for directly converting a photograph into a printing plate.

Newspapers found an interim solution in the revival of an ancient form of printed illustration, predating even the fifteenth century invention of movable type: the woodcut. A drawing (or photographic image) was transferred to the surface of a block of hard-grained wood and transformed into a relief printing surface under the hands of a skilled craftsman who cut away whatever was to be "white" in the printed illustration. The block was then mounted in the printing frame along with the type. Even today, schoolchildren use the technique to transform linoleum-faced blocks (soft, and, therefore, easily carved) into printed greeting cards. In a later refinement, an electrotype shell was made of the engraving, which, when properly mounted, became the printing surface; this allowed the engravers much greater control, as they now could cut away what was to be "black" in the printed version, creating illustrations very similar to ink drawings.

The first "illustrated newspaper" may have been the London *Illustrated News*, founded in 1842. The first American version was launched a dozen years later, bankrolled in part by the showman P. T. Barnum. It proved to be a failure, barely making expenses, and soon was abandoned. However, Barnum's head engraver went off on his own in 1855 with the eponymous *Frank Leslie's Illustrated Newspaper*. Leslie found the right balance of artistic style and newsworthy content, and by 1860 was selling an average 100,000 copies per issue. One edition, featuring a championship prize fight in England (the blocks for which had been engraved on the passage home), sold 347,000 copies.

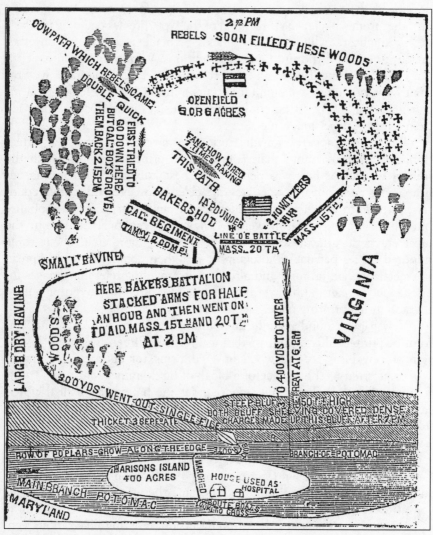

A very basic woodcut map from the New York *Times*. The illustrated newspapers did a markedly better job.

In 1857, the Harper Brothers, who operated a book publishing house and knew a good thing when they saw it, began a competing weekly, which they grandly named *Harper's Weekly Journal of Civilization*. A third New York production, the *Illustrated News*, had a moment in the sun but did not survive past the middle years of the war. A Confederate counter-part, the *Southern Illustrated News*—inaugurated when the war intruded on delivery of the Northern weeklies—stumbled along with limited success for twenty-five months.

While the printing rate of the wooden block was acceptable, the carving rate was snail-paced, especially for larger illustrations. The need for timely material and the demands of weekly deadlines led to the development of a multiple-block system, whereby a large drawing was divided among blocks of perhaps four by five inches. These could be locked together in a frame while the drawing was laid down; then, separated, each block was carved by a different engraver, all to be reunited when ready for the press. At first, these fragmented illustrations were crudely executed, with the block-lines starkly evident. Later refinements, including the appointment of a "master engraver" to cut the lines that crossed the edges, led to some of the finest examples of the wood engraver's art ever produced. Still later, as the stereotype process became more generally available, more easily-produced copperplate engravings began to displace the woodcut.

By the start of the Civil War, the larger newspapers had become big business; for example, the *Tribune* of 1861 was a corporation with a board of directors and 212 employees, 28 of whom were editors. On most large papers, the editor in chief set the policy but otherwise stayed out of the way and let a managing editor actually run the newspaper. A reporter offered an apt analogy, when he wrote:

> The modern newspaper is a sort of intellectual iron-clad, upon which, while the Editorial Captain makes out the reports to his chief, the public, and entertains the guests in his elegant cabin, [which is known as] the leading column, and receives the credit for every broadside of type and every paper bullet of the brain poured into the enemy, back out of sight is an Executive Officer, with little popular fame, who keeps the ship all right from hold to maintop, looks to every detail with sleepless vigilance, and whose life is a daily miracle of hard work. [10]

There was little popular fame, but a handsome level of compensation. Frederick Hudson, who occupied the position of "executive officer" at the *Herald*, was the highest-paid newsman in the nation, with an annual salary of $10,000—at a time when the salary of a member of the president's cabinet was $8,000. Bennett, who spent a great deal of time in Europe (at one point in the 1850s he remained abroad for eleven months), turned more and more of the management over to Hudson. By 1861, Bennett rarely went to the office.

Hudson's counterpart as managing editor of the *Tribune* was Charles A. Dana. Given that post in 1849, Dana would grow to exercise so much control over the editorial content of the paper that, near the end of March 1862, Greeley issued an ultimatum to the *Tribune* company board of directors: either Dana must go, or he would quit. That left the members of the board with a dilemma, beause Dana owned about one-third more of the company stock than Greeley and could provoke a messy confrontation. However, when Dana heard of this meeting, he simply left the office, never to return. His post as managing editor went to Sidney Gay, more of an administrator and less of an activist. Dana soon was given a job as a special investigator for the War Department, and in 1864 was appointed assistant secretary of war. He became editor and part owner of the New York *Sun* in 1868, and gave tepid support to Greeley's candidacy in the 1872 campaign.

As the newspaper's horizons expanded, so grew the profession of newspaper correspondent. Who were they? Although biographical data is limited for most, and what can be studied is not statistically significant, it is nonetheless useful. Of seventy-eight Northern war correspondents for whom the data is relatively complete, four out of five had been in newspaper work before the war. More than half had been born in a city. Three women reported from Washington. There was at least one black correspondent: Thomas Morris Chester of the Philadelphia *Press*. There was a smattering of lawyers and schoolteachers. One journalist was a professional mariner. At least two had served a prison term. Their average age was late twenties; half a dozen were nineteen or younger when the war started—Joe Robinson of the Philadelphia *Inquirer* was sixteen. Some were immigrants, such as nineteen-year-old Joe McCullagh from Ireland, eight years in America, or twenty-six-year-old Bavarian Henry Villard. (Born Ferdinand Heinrich Gustav Hilgard, Villard had left his native land in 1853 to escape service in the army; he borrowed the name of a former schoolmate for camouflage.) Of the fifty about whom educational background is known, nearly half had attended college. [11] Notable among the artists: Thomas Nast was twenty, Winslow Homer twenty-four.

The pay was adequate. When the war began, a New York–based staffer for the *Tribune* earned about as much as a captain in the Union army, roughly $27 per week; space-rates for free-lance writers began at $7.50 per column. A presumed glamour—travel, meeting famous people—may have drawn some to the job; and for many, that journey began with a few unsolicited letters to a newspaper. However, most papers received far more letters than could ever be printed, and rather than an offer of encouragement, the editor's response was more likely to be along the lines suggested in one reporter's postwar memoir: "My Dear Sir—Your article has unquestionable merit; but by the imperative pressure of important news upon our columns, we are very reluctantly compelled . . . etc." [12] Of course, many new reporting jobs opened up when the war began—but any presumed glamour quickly evaporated at the first sight of mangled dead.

By general policy, few reporters were allowed to write under their full names. Some were permitted to use initials, but most articles in most papers were published unsigned or under fanciful nicknames: Whitelaw Reid of the Cincinnati *Gazette* was "Agate," Franc Wilkie of the New York *Times* was "Galway." Richmond correspondent George W. Bagby covered for newspapers in South Carolina, Alabama, Louisiana, and Georgia under the pseudonyms, respectively, Hermes, Gamma, Malou, and Pan.

Bennett had long insisted on anonymity for *Herald* reporters; Sam Wilkeson, while the New York *Tribune* Washington bureau chief, advised *his* editor, "The anonymous greatly favors freedom and boldness in newspaper correspondence. I will not allow *any* letter writer to attach his initials to his communications, unless he was a widely known & influential man like Greeley or Bayard Taylor. . . . Besides the responsibility it fastens on a correspondent, the signature inevitably detracts from the powerful impersonality of a journal." [13]

Such considerations did not apply to the country weeklies—the only newspapers seen by a large portion of the population—or to the less affluent city dailies, which could not afford to hire reporters or pay telegraph tolls. Editorial opinion remained their own, but most "news" was clipped from the big city exchange papers and set in a section under a heading such as "THE LATEST INFORMATION."

The census of 1860 classified 80 percent of U.S. newspapers (including all 373 dailies) as "political in their character." Many were supported almost entirely by officeholders or office seekers, subsidized by "honoraria" or local government printing contracts in exchange for well-positioned coverage. James Gordon Bennett offered an 1862 editorial slap at "country editors" who enjoyed "free paper, pens and ink, free drinks and chewing tobacco, free board at the hotels, free travel by railroad." [14]

The modern concept of "balanced reporting" was unknown; this made for a lively press, but left an uncertain historical record. Reporters usually, although not always, slanted their copy to match the political coloration of their newspapers, which fell roughly into one of four categories. On the far right—in today's lexicon—were the Radical Republicans, for whom the only cause for going to war was the abolition of slavery; the *Tribunes* of New York and Chicago and the Philadelphia *Inquirer* were at the head of that pack. Slightly to the left were the moderate Republicans, who supported abolition but saw the war more as a struggle to preserve the Union: representative were the New York *Times*, Cincinnati *Commer-*

cial, and Boston *Journal*. The middle ground was held by the Independents, such as the New York *Herald*, although it often acted more like a member of the next group, the Democrats.

Northern Democrats knew that the party could not regain political power in a heavily Republican North unless the breach was healed and the party was reunited with the more populous Southern Democrats. Thus, the aim of many, if not most, of the Northern Democrats was settlement, not conquest; ending slavery was not a goal, but an impediment; the path to peace was seen as enlightened discourse, not battlefield victory. (This position aroused deep suspicion among the Radicals, who assumed that Democrats serving in the army were not committed to victory.) The more militant faction called themselves the Peace Democrats, although the opposition tagged them with the pejorative label "Copperhead," borrowed from the venomous snake of the same name. At some point during the first year or so of the war, some Peace Democrats began wearing copper Indian head pennies as a badge of identification (or defiance).

The most strident of the Democratic newspapers were the Chicago *Times*, the Cincinnati *Enquirer*, and the New York *World*. The *Times* was vitriolic on general principles. The *Enquirer* reflected the economic concerns of readers along the Ohio Valley, largely farmers, who had lost access to their normal markets in the South and were forced to ship their wares on high-priced railroads to the east. Business was bad, taxes were high, banks were failing, and there was an undercurrent of fear among the working classes that they were about to be overrun with an onslaught of cheap labor by former slaves—an ethnic group they didn't know, didn't understand, and didn't particularly like.

The constituency of the New York *World* included brokers, merchants, and shippers who had lost business because of the war, and recent immigrant Irish workingmen, who, like the Ohio farmers, were "poisonously suspicious of the Negro." [15] The *World* began as a religious journal of balanced opinion but fell on hard times in the first winter of the war, to be rescued, and transformed, by a syndicate of Democrats.

Many Democratic newspapers were clearly identified as such by their title, although the Missouri *Democrat* was a Republican paper and the Missouri *Republican* was an organ of the Democrats. Most Southern papers were Democratic; a few were Whig, the philosophical predecessor of the Republican Party, which had largely ceased to exist in the North and was barely noticed in the South. As noted below (Chapter 9), most Southern papers, of whatever political persuasion, quickly fell in line behind the cause of secession—or went out of business.

All Democrats—North and South—saw the war as a "Black Republican" plot led by a "demented despot" (Lincoln) to overthrow civil liberties and the rule of law (i.e., take lawful property away from slaveholders) and force full racial equality on the nation. It is not an exaggeration to say that, as a rule, where the Republican press celebrated the rustic wisdom and sweet humanity of blacks, the Democratic press portrayed them as degraded and inferior beings, unfit for participation in a society as complex as that of the United States.

In 1841, Charles Dickens, then the world's most popular author, visited the United States, where he spoke out vigorously against the lack of copyright protection in America. His visit was not treated well by the American press, some portions of which enjoyed the benefits of that lack of copyright. Dickens returned fire (and boosted sales of the monthly installments of his current project *Martin Chuzzlewit* as well) by satirizing American newspapers under such names as the *Sewer*, the *Stabber*, the *Family Spy*, the *Private Listener*, the *Peeper*, the *Keyhole Reporter*, and the *Rowdy Journal*. [16]

Satire—but not too far off the mark, then or now. A Dickensian newsboy hawks his wares, offering the "exclusive account of a flagrant act of dishonesty committed by the Secretary of State when he was eight years old; now communicated, at great expense, by his own nurse." As Colonel Driver, the quasi-fictional editor of the *Rowdy Journal*, explained, "It is in such enlightened means . . . that the bubbling passions of my country find a vent."

"Quasi-fictional." The portrayal of Driver clearly was drawn from Bennett:

> Colonel Driver, in the security of his strong position, and in his perfect understanding of the public sentiment, cared very little what [anybody] thought of him. His high-spiced wares were made to sell, and they sold; and his thousands of readers could as rationally charge their delight in filth upon him, as a glutton can shift upon his cook the responsibility of his beastly excess.

The portrait also had a modest dash of Hale: "The colonel occasionally boards packet-ships, I have heard, to glean the latest information for his journal. . . ." Greeley, well known for a penchant for heavy-handed editorials, also took a shot: "We are a busy people, sir," said the captain of one of those packet ships, "and have no time for reading mere notions [although] We don't mind 'em if they come to us in newspapers. . . ."

Dickens's running argument with the American press was not aided when *Chuzzlewit* arrived on American shores. "I have been given to understand by some authorities," the author wrote in the Introduction to the later, 1844, edition, "that there are American scenes in these pages which are violent exaggerations . . . beyond all bounds of belief." He acknowledged that he had focused on "the ludicrous side of the American character" but pointed out that much of what he wrote was a literal paraphrase of some newspaper reports of June and July 1843, "at about the time when I was engaged in writing those parts of the book."

Dickens appears to have invented, or at the least first put into print, the term *war correspondent*, several years before any professional journalist seems actually to have filled the role. Colonel Driver introduced an assistant as "My war correspondent, sir, Mr. Jefferson Brick."

The author, however, offered no explanation of Mr. Brick's duties.

Read on.

3 / Rehearsals

It is impossible to condemn too strongly the pestiferous inventions
and exaggerations of reckless political gossips and paid letter-writers,
whom the times have hatched into being.
The moral influence they are wielding, perhaps without being
fully conscious of it themselves, is dangerous to the last degree.

—Newark (New Jersey) *Daily Advertiser*, January 12, 1861

AS THE TELEGRAPH began to replace the mailbag as the link to
distant news, and the public appetite for more timely reports grew apace,
the "special correspondent" was born. Here was a reporter sent off to discover and cover the news, at any time to any place, where—under the
twin pressures of competition from their peers and "guidance" from their
editors—they learned how to deliver prompt, readable, but not necessarily accurate, copy.

For some papers—notably, but not exclusively, the New York *Tribune*—
a correspondent on a mission was expected to be a "missionary." During the
Free State struggles in Kansas (1855–56), the abolition bias of one *Tribune*
reporter turned a raid on Lawrence by a mob of drunken proslavery hood-
lums into "a pyramid of fire." Fleeing women and children were "disarmed,
robbed, plundered, and shot down," the town was left "in ashes and many
of its inhabitants butchered." The actual score: two accidental casualties,
an empty hotel burned, and the newspaper office destroyed. Twenty-one-
year-old James Redpath, covering affairs in Kansas for three radical Republican papers (the *Missouri Democrat*, the Chicago *Tribune*, and the New
York *Tribune*), was so passionately committed that he would admit, a few
years later, that he did more than "report" the news. He believed that,
properly manipulated, "Kansas" could lead to a civil war and a nationwide

slave insurrection. I "went to Kansas," he wrote, "and endeavored, personally and by my own pen, to precipitate a revolution." [1]

There was another seminal event in the middle of October 1859: the trial and execution of John Brown. This ultimate consequence of Brown's failed raid on the Federal arsenal at Harper's Ferry attracted a gaggle of correspondents to the county seat at Charles Town. *Harper's Weekly* was represented by a man who would soon become a Confederate officer; he saw Brown as a fanatic and his men as scurrilous assassins. The artist for *Leslie's Illustrated Newspaper* was suspected of being a *Tribune* man and was asked to leave town; he did. The real *Tribune* reporters pretended to be something else, while lamenting the fate of a mistaken, "broken and bewildered old man," and poking fun at the country bumpkins of Charles Town, population 1,700. [2]

While most papers were transfixed with content, the *Herald* demonstrated a skill for process that soon would put it at the forefront of Civil War reporting. *Herald* correspondents in New York, Washington, Baltimore, and Richmond were brought into the story. Some were dispatched to Harper's Ferry, others were sent out to get reaction from leading abolitionists, public officials, military leaders, scholars, the proverbial "man in the street," and even free blacks. One *Herald* reporter, a local man, displayed admirable enterprise by signing on as a jailhouse guard; he then arranged to be assigned as driver of the wagon that took Brown to (and from) the gallows. Another *Herald* man managed to put a question to the defendant: "I do not wish to annoy you; but if you have anything further to say I will report it." Brown's answer:

> I wish to say . . . that you had better—all of you people at the South—prepare yourselves for a settlement of that question that must come up for settlement sooner than you are prepared for it. The sooner you are prepared the better. You may dispose of me very easily. I am nearly disposed of now; but this question is still to be settled—this Negro question I mean; the end of this is not yet." [3]

Not yet, almost 140 years later.

Editorial attitudes toward blacks in general and slavery in particular were divided along regional or party lines, although this topic was not much discussed in the South. One exception: an article on "Slavery among the Indians" in the February 1860 issue of the *Southern Literary Messenger* held that turning laboring and domestic chores over to slaves enabled the enslavers to become civilized. A house advertisement in the same issue proclaimed the *Messenger* to be "alone among the monthly periodicals of America in defense of the Peculiar Institutions of the Southern Country."

The New York *Tribune* provided a constant supply of articles, letters, observations, and editorials to vividly describe what that paper saw as the realities of slavery: the corporal punishment of sluggish or recalcitrant workers, the not-so-secret sexual motives displayed by purchasers at slave auctions ("nearly white" young women on the block: "not likely they were bought for purposes of toil.") [4], and the wrenching family separations. One item reported the pleading of "Jeffrey," whose ownership had just been changed and who hoped his new master could buy his companion as well:

> "I loves Dorcas, young mas'r, I loves her well an' true; she says she loves me; and I know she does; de good Lord knows I loves her better than I loves any one in de wide world—never can love another woman half so well. Please buy Dorcas, mas'r. We're be good sarvants to you as long as we live. . . . We loves each other a heap—do, really, true, mas'r." [5]

The purchaser could not, however, afford the pair. Were these tales accurate? Some descriptions—notably, this tale of Jeffrey and Dorcas—were suspiciously similar to sections of Harriet Beecher Stowe's *Uncle Tom's Cabin* (published in 1852), and one historian has suggested that "they may have been visioned from a perspective no better than that afforded by the windows of the bustling Manhattan offices of the paper. . . . The line between reporter and propagandist was almost invisible, and the propaganda was aimed at an audience that believed unhesitatingly in its sermons, and wept over the death of Little Eva." [6]

The *Herald* took the opposite view: slavery was a boon to the slaves and free blacks were a menace. The slaves at an auction in Alabama were "happier and less concerned about their situations than three-fourths of the white people clustered about them . . . fugitive slaves go into Canada as beggars, and the mass of them commit larceny and lay in jail until they become lowered and debased, and ready for worse crimes." A *Herald* reporter filed stories from Mauritius, where the natives were "not one half so well clothed as the slaves that I have seen in our Southern States"; and from Panama, where the local blacks were "incurably lazy, lying and thievish." And, for any reader who believed in the enfranchisement of free blacks, there was a warning from Nicaragua: a local election was decided by "a crowd of the worst looking Negroes human eyes ever gazed on, all fresh from the grog shops, armed with cudgels, whooping and yelling in the most unearthly strains, and thrusting their votes in the faces of the inspectors." [7]

The Civil War did not start with the bombardment and surrender of Fort Sumter—that was merely a ceremonial flourish. There had been rumblings for perhaps thirty years, and on June 16, 1858, while (unsuccessfully) campaigning for the Senate seat held by Stephen A. Douglas, Abraham Lincoln had set the stage for much of what was to follow: "A house divided against itself cannot stand," he said in debate at Springfield, Illinois. The phrase was not new, but the application was:

I believe this government cannot endure, permanently half *slave* and half *free*.

I do not expect the Union will be dissolved—I do not expect the house to *fall*—but I *do* expect it will cease to be divided.

It will become *all* one thing, or *all* the other.

Either the *opponents* of slavery, will arrest the further spread of it, and place it where the public mind shall rest in the belief that it is in course of ultimate extinction; or its *advocates* will push it forward, till it shall become alike lawful in *all* the States, *old* as well as *new*— *North* as well as *South*. [8]

It was clear that Lincoln did not expect the *advocates* to win the argument. Two years later, his nomination as the Republican candidate for president was taken as a signal: the cause of abolition must soon become like a runaway train, headed toward an inevitable conclusion. More than just a "signal," actually—the Richmond *Enquirer* cited evidence: "Not the least significant feature in the present canvass is the organization of Black Republican Clubs in the Northern States into military companies under command of marshals, captains, and sub-officers, some of whom have distinguished themselves in the Mexican war, and all of whom are selected with reference to superior qualifications as martial men." The so-called Wide Awakes were said to number 400,000 men, thoroughly drilled, "and ready for any service which their leaders may demand at their hands." The *Enquirer* inquired:

Is there no significancy in these things? Our Northern friends are men of action, not of words; they organize, drill, march, and die, while we speak and talk—they do privately and by voluntary associations, what we debate in deliberative bodies, and hesitatingly perform, if at all, by legislative action. Their organizations are not yet *armed*, it is true, at least not that outsiders are aware of, but they are *drilled, uniformed, and provided with rails, overcoats, and torches ready for marching!* [9]

The Baltimore *American*, however, dismissed the idea:

Some philosopher has said that mankind suffers more from the ap-
prehension of troubles than they do from any actual evils of their
lot. . . . the South has been taught to believe that the election of
any but an ultra Southern man to the Presidency would irrevocably
injure its property in slaves and lead the way to the overthrow of
slave institutions. Yet though no ultra Southern man has ever been
elected President, slave property has steadily increased in value, and
the two strongest things on the Continent at this moment are the
Union and slavery. Whilst both North and South are eaten up with
imaginary horrors of mutual aggression, neither was ever as strong,
thriving and prosperous as now since the foundation of the Government. [10]

Election day came, and as if to validate the *Enquirer*'s suspicion, the
Harrisburg *Telegraph* proclaimed: "We have received returns enough to indicate that the Republicans have achieved one of the most brilliant victories ever gained, by any party, in this country." Even at midnight, the
editor noted, jubilant Republicans made "the welkin ring with cheers, and
the reports roll in over the magnetic wire from every direction, bringing
the glorious intelligence that State after State has gone for Lincoln. . . .
The Wide-Awakes are parading the streets, in uniform, with much and
brightly burning torches, cheering enthusiastically as they pass through
the city on their triumphal march." [11]

South Carolina was the first Southern state to declare that it would
not wait for the inevitable, and two days after the election the legislature
announced an intention to secede. The editor of the *Telegraph* was not
impressed. "Let the chivalry amuse themselves," he wrote on November
10, "the farce will soon be 'played out.'" Two days later, however, he ap-
provingly reprinted the suggestion of "a sensible Kentucky editor," to let
them go their own way, after all.

Their absence would be an incalculable and invaluable relief to the
balance of the people of these United States. We should escape
large quantities of quadrennial gas and noise and confusion and
stuff. . . . Every four years these Southern Quixotes swell up with
bad whiskey and worse logic, and tell the balance of the people if
they don't do so and so, that they—the Quixotes—will secede. Let
them secede and be—blessed. We are tired of their gasconade, their
terrific threats, and of their bloody prophesies. They were never cal-

culated for any higher destiny than that of frightening old women and young children. . . . Their bombast is absolutely sickening. [12]

The Chicago *Democrat* agreed: "The chivalry will eat dirt. They will back out. They never had any spunk anyhow. The best they could do was to bully, and brag, and bluster. . . . They are wonderful hands at bragging and telling fantastical lies; but when it comes to action, count them out." [13]

The editor of the Sandusky (Ohio) *Daily Commercial Register* wished that South Carolina would get on with it, if secession was its true wish, but—perhaps not having given a close enough reading to all of his exchanges—also predicted that the state "will not do anything of the kind." He blamed the whole issue on newspaper hype: "The rage of the day, the sensation, the excitement, the panic, or whatever else is generally uppermost in the public mind on the streets, in the shops, in the hotels, on the cars, or wherever men are to be found, inevitably becomes the leading staple of the newspapers. . . . For weeks past, since South Carolina has become rampant . . . nothing can get into the popular ear but secession, disunion and division." [14]

"I never thought I should witness such time," a businessman in Charleston wrote to friends at the Boston *Journal*:

We are in the midst of a revolution,. Every man is enrolled—all kinds of business at a stand—no shipping in port—all Northern communication cut off—Custom House officers resigned their office—no cotton coming in. I have ten hands walking about, doing nothing—I have them to feed. There are twelve hundred drays in the city—not ten of a day get one load. All the banks stopped—our State notes out of the State not worth one cent. We are in a state of starvation—no meat to eat, even at twenty-five cents a pound.

I am in hopes the Abolitionists of the North will be paid in their own coin. There will be no compromise—it is out of the question. [15]

He was right. The secession of South Carolina was celebrated on December 20 by the firing of one hundred guns and dancing in the streets in cities throughout the South. A different kind of train became the runaway, and Southern papers that had been loyal to the Union were already rushing to climb on board. The Montgomery *Confederation*, which before the election labeled talk of secession as "treason," announced: "We earnestly hope that the day is not far distant when we shall have withdrawn from such an obnoxious and oppressive government, and established a confederacy of the whole of the Slaveholding States." On November 10, the Memphis *Daily Appeal* urged that its readers give Lincoln a chance; a month later, the paper declared that the Union clearly was ended, and the "irrepressible conflict" could never be reconciled. [16]

On October 5, the New Orleans *Bee* was steadfast to the Union "under every conceivable circumstance"; on December 4, the editor dismissed as an "idle abstraction" any debate on the legality of secession; by December 14, the metamorphosis was complete. "The North and the South are heterogeneous and are better apart. . . ." The *Bee* cautioned, "With what shadow of reason could Southern men be advised to submit and await the possible events of the future when abolitionism had swept every Northern Commonwealth, and had even displayed unexpected and growing power in some of the slaveholding States themselves?" [17]

The November 1860 issue of the *Southern Literary Messenger* let readers know exactly how the editors felt about their neighbors to the north: "Not a breeze that blows from the Northern hills but bears upon its wings taints of crime and vice, to reek and stink, stink and reek upon our Southern plains." The December issue asserted, "When loyalty to the Union is loyalty to Lincoln . . . then is loyalty . . . dishonorable, shameful. . . .Virginia must speak. All states wait to hear her."

A December series of editorials in the Richmond *Examiner* took up that general theme, "Why should Virginia continue to grovel at the feet of Seward, the children of Andrew Jackson clutch tremblingly the knees of Andrew Johnson? . . ." On Christmas Day, the Richmond *Enquirer* predicted that, "if Virginia and Maryland do not adopt measures to prevent Mr. Lincoln's inauguration at Washington, their discretion will be as much a subject of ridicule as their submission will be of contempt." [18]

Prevent the inauguration? Certainly, said the January edition of the *Southern Literary Messenger*, "even if Governor Wise and his minute men have to take the place by storm." This was a theme widely discussed, which prompted the exasperated editor of the Newark (New Jersey) *Daily Advertiser* to declare:

> It is impossible to condemn too strongly the pestiferous inventions and exaggerations of reckless political gossips and paid letter-writers, whom the times have hatched into being. The moral influence they are wielding, perhaps without being fully conscious of it themselves, is dangerous to the last degree. . . . Who can measure the mischief of seriously discussing the rumored intended invasion of the Capitol by the crack-brained Wise, and thus beginning a civil war in trying to prevent the regular inauguration of President Lincoln? . . . It would be an ineffectual and absurd project, because the President may qualify himself for the office by taking the oath of allegiance before any magistrate authorized to administer one at any other place as well as Washington. [19]

The inauguration was held on schedule, but with heavy physical security and great emotional insecurity. Washington was a divided city. A Southern city, characterized by the *Herald* as "the abode of a very slow and respectable people, who cool themselves during the hot weather by the delightful remembrance that they are of gentle blood." [20] A city filled with rumors of secessionist current running just below the surface, or, perhaps, *on* the surface, as when the Washington *Constitution* joined in calling for armed force to prevent the inauguration.

In the middle of March, a Confederate delegation (which included John Forsyth, editor of the Mobile *Register*) journeyed to Washington, hoping to arrange diplomatic relations between the two "nations." Secretary of State Seward refused to see them, asserting that "the whole policy of the Government is put forth in the President's inaugural, from which there will be no deviation." The president's inaugural reaffirmed his position to preserve the Union, pledged his allegiance to the Constitution, and asserted that the Southerners had nothing to fear from him unless they themselves were the aggressors. He appealed to "the better angels of our nature," a lucidly poetic turn of phrase that was characterized in the Richmond *Enquirer* March 5, 1861, as "the cool, unimpassioned, deliberate language of the fanatic. . . ." [21]

Politics and philosophies aside, newspaper readers in the North long had been eager for "news" from the South, and from late summer of 1860 until the middle of April 1861, a contingent of Northern reporters had been at work in that region—most, undercover or in disguise. These included at the least one representative each from the Boston *Post*, the New York *Post*, and the New York *World*; there were several working for the New York *Times*, and more than eight for the *Tribune*. The *Herald* had at least four reporters in the Southern field, but they operated openly, given confidence by the paper's acknowledged Southern leanings.

Most of the stories that flowed North were for the Republican press, and, to avoid inspection by unfriendly eyes, most were sent by mail or express rather than by telegraph. They often were addressed to blind mail drops rather than newspaper offices, and some were written in private code. Most advanced the Radical agenda with a vengeance, to the collective exasperation of the Democratic papers:

Take any New York paper, and read about the "barbarity of the people of the South." Northern men expelled because of their political opinions, or of a preacher, hung, "for no other offense than preaching the gospel." Or, from a Chicago paper, "that a printer was *invited* to leave Charleston, South Carolina, simply because he had worked in the N. York *Tribune* office. Will any sensible man believe all these things?" The answer would be "no," if the country were ruled by sensible men. It is not. [22]

Already have the Abolition journals commenced the system of hor-
rifying the public by tales of Southern outrages and Southern barbarity, for the purpose of maddening people and rendering a
peaceful solution of our difficulties impossible. . . . The ears of the
public are besieged with the recitals of the most inhuman monstros-
ities of "men barreled up alive and rolled into the Mississippi river
for having voted for Lincoln." . . . We have a list of exchanges that
covers every State from Maine to Texas. They are daily examined in
this office, and we unhesitatingly assert and believe that no man has
been put in jeopardy of life or limb in the Southern States, by reason
of his vote or opinions. [23]

Every possible phase of the crisis furnishes capital to the sensation
writer, and he is consequently in his glory now. If no new and startling development is on hand, he has the happy ability to manufacture one to satisfy the craving appetite which he has done so much
to create. [24]

Much of the so called "special correspondence" is entirely *bogus*.
The largest portion of it is *manufactured*, and palmed upon the cred-
ulous as veritable "news from Washington." It is the work of prolific
imaginations, bent upon creating a "sensation"—or rather, a demand for the papers. [25]

In truth, many newspapers, North and South, agreed that "manufactured" was the operative word and dismissed much of this Southern correspondence and most of the *Tribune*'s as editorial figments. In large
measure, they were not.

George Forrester Williams of the New York *Times* toured the major
Southern cities from late summer until mid-April, pretending to be an
English tourist. Williams began his journey in Haiti, where he acquired
appropriate British clothing and accessories, and entered the South
through the port of Galveston. He carried out his assignment with skill
and a reasonably authentic British accent, but eventually came under
suspicion in Charleston, where every citizen seems to have been set to
ferret out Northern reporters. He escaped one close call in a tavern
through a combination of wit and pocket change; when accused by a suspicious drunk of being a "Damned Lincoln spy," he dropped a pair of British sovereigns on the bar. This established his bona fides long enough to
pay for drinks for the house and to allow him to slip away unnoticed. He
headed North, and was about to be exposed in Richmond when a strang-
er gave him warning. "Don't notice me, sir!" he said, "I'm a Union man
You are suspected of being a Yankee newspaper correspondent. Get out of
town as quick as you can." He did. [26]

The *Tribune*'s Charles Brigham was under cover in Charleston from November until mid-February, when he was arrested on suspicion of being a Federal spy. He was tried in a makeshift court, and, while not denying the specific charges, admitted nothing specific, assuming that it was probably less hazardous to be a spy than a *Tribune* correspondent. Eventually, a lawyer advised him that, "under the circumstances, it will be necessary for you to leave the South at once." Brigham offered a mild demurrer (he had "done nothing improper") but raised no further objection when advised "it is not a question for argument."

The matter thus being settled, the lawyer brought forth a bottle of wine, that they both might end this experience on a pleasant note. After some time, the lawyer asked, "By the way, do you know who is writing the letters from here to The Tribune?"

"Why, no," Brigham answered. "I haven't seen a copy of that paper for six months." He affirmed his understanding that there really was no such person, as "I had read in your journals that the letters were purely fictitious." He was allowed to catch the next train north. [27]

Just at this point, Albert Deane Richardson was assigned to the *Tribune*'s Southern traveling beat for as long "as the excitement lasts." [28] He spent a memorable two months, mid-February to mid-April, contributing a remarkable series of articles, especially from New Orleans.

Richardson had a knack for spotting the ironic and absurd, and made great sport of everything he saw. He described the triumphant welcome that New Orleans gave to septuagenarian Maj. Gen. David E. Twiggs, viewed in the North as a coward and traitor, but on March 6, 1861, honored in New Orleans as a hero. Twiggs had been the senior Federal commander in Texas who, a few weeks earlier, readily turned all government property in the state over to the Rebels. In truth, Twiggs had sought guidance from Washington but was given none, and asked to be relieved of his command. A firm Southern sympathizer, he believed that his action was appropriate under the circumstances; had he *not* "surrendered," the war might well have started in Texas in February, rather than in South Carolina in April.

Richardson gleefully remembered,

This is the same Twiggs in whose name the popular hair-color nostrum, "Twiggs Hair Dye" has been for some years offered to an eager public. As the story is told, during the Mexican War, Twiggs, wounded in the head, discovered that an unguent being applied to the injury restored his hair to its natural color—or close enough for the sake of vanity. An enterprising vendor seized upon the opportunity and the rest, as they say, is history, particularly as preserved in the lines of Dr. [Oliver Wendell] Holmes:

> How many a youthful head we've seen put on its silver
>   crown!
> What sudden changes back again, to youth's empurpled
>   brown!
> But how to tell what's old or young—the tap root from
>   the sprigs,
> Since Florida revealed her fount to Ponce de Leon
>   Twiggs? [29]

Richardson asserted that efforts to develop indigenous industries in New Orleans were a sham. He reported that much of the product of a furniture factory was actually shipped in from the North and brought in the back door under cover of darkness, and the only thing Southern about the "Southern Shoe Factory" was the name:

> I strolled homeward, reflecting upon the *Southern* Shoe Factory. It was admirably calculated to appeal to local patriotism, and demonstrate the feasibility of southern manufacturing. Its northern machinery, run by northern workmen, under a northern superintendent, turned out brogans of northern leather, fastened with northern pegs, and packed in cases of northern pine, at an advance of only about one hundred per cent upon northern prices! [30]

Most of his reports were not so benign, offering blunt descriptions of slave auctions (heart-wrenching), character studies of civic leaders (framed, of course, to demonstrate a lack of character), and assessments (negative) of local military preparations. His efforts prompted this advice in the New Orleans *Crescent*, directed at "correspondents of northern papers, who indite *real falsehoods and lies* as coolly as they would eat a dinner at the St. Charles":

> We have for a long time thought that no man ought to be allowed to write for the northern Press, unless he has passed at least two years of his existence in the Slave States of the South, doing nothing but studying southern institutions, southern society, and the character and sentiments of the southern people. [31]

Richardson recited his experiences in such light-hearted banter that he reinforced the common suspicion that the dangers of the South were a bit of journalistic hype, but his life may well have been as much in danger as his editors earnestly suggested. Some weeks after his journey had ended, the correspondent was approached by a refugee businessman who told Richardson that, under suspicion of being "the *Tribune* man" he had been kept in a Memphis jail for some fifty days.

More to the point: Richardson and fellow *Tribune* reporter Junius Browne were to become prisoners of war in May 1863, held in the most notorious of camps for more than a year and a half and never released or exchanged by the Confederates precisely because of their *Tribune* affiliation. Throughout the war, captured reporters for other papers were released, some rather quickly, but not *Tribune* men. While held, Richardson learned of the death, first, of his young wife and then of their daughter, but nonetheless was given no "humanitarian" relief. As the Confederate commissioner of exchange wrote when turning down one of a continuing series of requests for their release, "Such men as the *Tribune* correspondents have had more share even than your soldiery in bringing rapine, pillage and desolation to our homes. . . . They are the worst and most obnoxious of all non-combatants." [32]

Richardson and Browne finally managed to escape; see page [339].

Planting journalistic spies in the other camp was not limited to Northern papers. On January 30, 1861, the editor of the Charleston *Mercury* advised his man in Washington:

I consider your connection with the Washington correspondence, as strictly confidential. No one in South Carolina, outside of the *Mercury* office, knows your name, and if you will be as discrete [*sic*] as I will, no one shall ever know. The wisdom and consequent usefulness of your letters will depend entirely upon this. If you are known, it is impossible to criticize and use names as you otherwise can do, to the great benefit of the Southern cause. . . . Crandall was my correspondent for some time, and was very useful in exposing the intrigues of sundry would-be fireaters . . . until he, through imprudence, allowed them to ferret him out. After that, he was of no account. Jones of New York has just been exposed, either through his own indiscretion, or the treachery of some telegraph operator. . . . [33]

One journalistic tourist who did not have to resort to disguise or stratagem was William Howard Russell. The London *Times* had been represented in the United States since 1854 by Bancroft Davis, a New York lawyer, son of a former senator from Massachusetts, nephew of historian (and former secretary of the Navy) George Bancroft. However, Davis was an avowed Republican who did not keep his personal opinions out of his weekly letters. Toward the end of February 1861, he was advised that the paper was sending someone over for a fresh look, someone "who has not been mixed up with your domestic politics, and whose sympathies are not engaged in the struggle now going on." [34] That "someone" was Russell, who was then struggling to make ends meet as editor and part owner of

the one-year-old *Army and Navy Gazette*. The *Times* offered a salary of
£1200, plus expenses. Russell also negotiated a £750 advance on a book
(which was published in London in 1863 and in an abridged edition a few
months later in Boston, as *My Diary North and South*). As soon as he was
satisfied that his family was well settled into the home of a friend, he was
on the next boat to te United States.

Russell arrived in New York March 17, 1861, and immediately became immersed in the New York version of national politics and journalism—a baptism that began at his hotel, the Clarendon. "In what is called
'the bar,'" he wrote in the *Diary*, "I met several gentlemen, one of whom
said, 'the majority of the people of New York, and all the respectable people,' were disgusted at the election of such a fellow as Lincoln to be President, and would back the Southern States, if it came to a split." [35]

For the next week, Russell dined with former and present elected and
appointed officials, ministers, members of the cabinet, and most of the
leading editors and journalists of the day. "The men I have met," he
wrote in a private letter to his editor on March 26, "do not much impress
me." He offered stinging comment on two of the three leading "journalists" of New York. "Gordon Bennett is so palpably a rogue—it comes out
so strongly in the air around him, in his eyes & words & smell & voice
that one pities the cause which finds in him a protagonist"; and "Horace
Greeley is the nastiest form of narrow minded sectarian philanthropy,
who would gladly roast all the whites of South Carolina in order that he
might satisfy what he supposes is a conscience but which is only an auto-
cratic ambition. . . ." [36]

He was a great deal more circumspect in the *Diary*, which, after all,
was intended as a public, not private communication. There was an
oblique reference to Bennett in the entry for March 19, as a comment
from an acquaintance: ". . . the fact is, no one minds what the man
writes of any one, his game is to abuse every respectable man in the
country in order to take his revenge on them for his social exclusion, and
at the same time to please the ignorant masses who delight in vitu-
peration and scandal." The *Diary* description of Russell's meeting with
Greeley was limited to three sentences: "I paid a visit to Mr. Horace
Greeley, and had a long conversation with him. He expressed great pleasure at the intelligence that I was going to visit the Southern States. 'Be
sure you examine the slave-pens. *They* will be afraid to refuse you, and
you can tell the truth.'" [37]

In some respects, Dickens was no match for Russell when it came to
comment on the newspapers of New York. Dickens claimed to be writing
fiction; Russell did not have to bother. "The journals," he wrote, "are
more engaged now in abusing each other, and in small party aggressive
warfare, than in the performance of the duties of a patriotic press, whose
mission at such a time is beyond all question the resignation of little dif-

ferences for the sake of the whole country. . . . the New York people must have their intellectual drams every morning, and it matters little what the course of the Government may be, so long as the aristocratic democrat can be amused by ridicule of the Great Rail Splitter. . . ." [38]

Politics aside, he added, "It is strange, too, to see in journals which profess to represent the civilization and intelligence of the most enlightened and highly educated people on the face of the earth, advertisements of sorcerers, wizards, and fortune-tellers by the score—'wonderful clairvoyants,' 'the seventh child of a seventh child,' 'mesmeristic necromancers,' and the like, who can tell your thoughts as soon as you enter a room, can secure the affections you prize, give lucky numbers in lotteries, and make everybody's fortunes but their own." Later, in a private letter, Russell noted that "I find that no one of any weight in society attaches the least importance to the opinions or leaders of such a paper as the N.Y. Herald for example tho' they read it for the news." [39]

Russell shifted his base to Washington on March 26, and contacted the principal members of the administration. His first meeting with Abraham Lincoln was cordial:

> Mr. Lincoln put out his hand in a very friendly manner, and said, "Mr. Russell, I am very glad to make your acquaintance, and to see you in this country. The London *Times* is one of the greatest powers in the world—in fact, I don't know anything which has much more power—except perhaps the Mississippi." . . . Conversation ensued for some minutes, which the President enlivened by two or three peculiar little sallies, and I left agreeably impressed with his shrewdness, humor, and natural sagacity. [40]

Russell's comments on the first lady were less admiring: "The impression of homeliness produced by Mrs. Lincoln on first sight, is not diminished by closer acquaintance." [41]

Secretary of State Seward—still hoping, in March, for a rational solution to the crisis—seems to have been living in a world of fantasy. As he explained to Russell,

> We are all—all have been—secessionists. Me, my brothers and sisters and friends . . . all seceded from home when we were young, struck off on our own, full of ourselves. But we all went back home sooner or later. The bonds were simply too strong. The Southern States will all return. We can forgive them for the moment, for they are much like any other adolescents. On the one hand, they mistake idle extravagance for elegant luxury; on the other, they universally harbor an in-

flated image of themselves. The Southern States are in that state of industrialization—development—socialization—through which New York passed sixty or seventy years ago. They will catch up. We only need to be patient. [42]

On April 13, Russell headed out on an ambitious and thorough ten-week journey through the South. As *the* representative of *the* leading newspaper of *the* most important international customer for cotton, Russell was most happily entertained by governors, mayors, other politicians, and businessmen. They assumed that he at the least would favor British recognition of the Confederacy, and at best favor British intervention—lest the mills of England be forced to shut down for lack of raw material.

His eager hosts were to be disappointed, however—Russell was not to serve as advocate or messenger. For the *Times,* and in the *Diary,* he reported what he saw and heard; if his editors had been hoping for a less partisan flavor than that offered by Davis, they, too, were to be disappointed. Russell clearly favored the North, and, while he approached the Southern part of his assignment with pen in check, he did so with tongue in cheek. On the governor of Mississippi: "'Well, sir,' he said "dropping a portentous plug of tobacco just outside the spittoon, with the air of a man who wished to show he could have hit the center if he liked. . . ." Or, Gideon Pillow at Memphis: "The Major-General, in fact, is an attorney-at-law, or has been so, and was partner with Mr. Polk [James K., President, 1844–48], who, probably for some of the reasons which determine the actions of partners to each other, sent Mr. Pillow to the Mexican War, where he nearly lost him, owing to severe wounds received in action." [43]

Russell spent several days in the company of General Pillow, and was told by another officer that Pillow "had made himself ludicrously celebrated in Mexico for having undertaken to throw up a battery which, when completed, was found to face the wrong way so that the guns were exposed to the enemy." [44] The same level of engineering incompetence seemed to have overtaken his efforts at Memphis, where the general had now spent some five weeks directing his troops in building "a series of curious entrenchments," which looked like an assemblage of dams constructed by "mad beavers."

In a word, they are so complicated that they would prove exceedingly troublesome to the troops engaged in their defense, and it would require very steady, experienced regulars to man them so as to give proper support to each other. The maze of breastworks, of flanking parapets, of parapets for field pieces, is overdone. Several of them might prove useful to an attacking force. [45]

A formal inspection of troops was arranged. "The General addressed the men . . . and said what generals usually say on such occasions—compliments for the past, encouragement for the future. 'When the hour of danger comes I will be with you.' They did not seem to care much whether he was nor not. . . ." [46]

Not all of Russell's observations were offered as wit or whimsy; his reputation as the world's leading war correspondent, after all, had been earned, not granted. Thus, as in this *Diary* comment on the volunteer forces at Memphis on June 18, the journalist demonstrated more insight than many of the military professionals who were trying to shape the armies, North and South.

The officers were plain, farmerly planters, merchants, lawyers, and the like—energetic, determined men, but utterly ignorant of the most rudimentary parts of military science. It is this want of knowledge on the part of the officer which renders it so difficult to arrive at a tolerable condition of discipline among volunteers, as the privates are quite well aware they know as much of soldiering as the great majority of their officers. [47]

In Montgomery, the temporary capital of the Confederacy, he wandered into a slave auction. He was appalled:

I am neither sentimentalist nor Black Republican, nor Negro worshipper, but I confess the sight caused a thrill through my heart. I tried in vain to make myself familiar with the fact that I could, for the sum of $975, become as absolutely the owner of that mass of blood, bones, sinew, flesh, and brains as of the horse which stood by my side. There was no sophistry which could persuade me the man was not a man—he was, indeed, by no means my brother, but assuredly he was a fellow creature.

After a moment's reflection, he added, "Perhaps these impressions may wear off, for I meet many English people who are the most strenuous advocates of the slave system, although it is true that their perceptions may be quickened to recognize its beauties by their participation in the profits." [48]

It was during his visit to Charleston, the epicenter of the Rebellion, that Russell discovered how deep ran the enmity between portions of the North and South. "There is nothing in the dark caves of human passion," he wrote in his letter of April 30, "so cruel and deadly as the hatred the South Carolinians profess for the Yankees." The state of South Carolina, he was told, was "founded by gentlemen," New England, by fanatics:

The New Englander must have something to persecute, and as he has hunted down all his Indians, burnt all his witches, and persecuted all his opponents to the death, he invented Abolitionism as the sole resource left to him for the gratification of his favorite passion. Next to this motive principle is his desire to make money dishonestly, trickily, meanly, and shabbily. He has acted on it in all his relations with the South, and has cheated and plundered her in all his dealings. . . .

"Anything on earth! [he was told] . . . Any form of government, any tyranny or despotism you will; but"—and here is an appeal more terrible than the adjuration of all the Gods—"nothing on earth shall ever induce us to submit to any union with the brutal, bigoted blackguards of the New England States, who neither comprehend nor regard the feelings of gentlemen! Man, woman and child, we'll die first." Imagine these and an infinite variety of similar sentiments uttered by courtly, well-educated men, who set great store on a nice observance of the usages of society, and who are only moved to extreme bitterness and anger when they speak of the North, and you [even so] will fail to conceive the intensity of the dislike of the South Carolinian for the free States." [49]

Russell was lectured on Southern politics and instructed in the intersection between Southern economics and culture. "We do not," he was told by an otherwise unidentified member of an influential political family, "cast able men aside at the caprices of a mob or in obedience to some low party intrigue, and hence we are sure of the best men, and are served by gentlemen conversant with public affairs, far superior in every way to the ignorant clowns who are sent to Congress by the North." [50]

That anonymous informant was Edmund Rhett, son of the founder and brother of the editor of the Charleston *Mercury*. Rhett also told Russell that "We have a system which enables us to reap the fruits of the earth by a race which we save from barbarism in restoring them to their real place in the world as laborers, whilst we are enabled to cultivate the arts, the graces, the accomplishment of life, to develop science, to apply ourselves to the duties of government, and to understand the affairs of the country." [51]

A version of the same conversation, published in the London *Times*, was softer, offering Russell's compliments to the "well-bred, courteous, and hospitable" gentlemen of the South, affirming them as a "genuine aristocracy" with "time to cultivate their minds, to apply themselves to politics and the guidance of public affairs." For this, Russell was roundly scored in *Harper's Weekly* for a "taste for the flavor of aristocracy. He found it . . . at the South; he enjoyed it, and he reported it. The tone of admiration and confidence in his first letters undoubtedly helped the rebellion in the public opinion of England." *Harper's* overlooked the frequent caveats by which Russell had urged his readers to read between the lines: "In my next letter I shall give a brief account of a visit to some of the planters, as far as it can be made consistent with the obligations which the rites of hospitality impose on the guest as well as upon the host." [52]

Of course, *Harper's* was not privy to a comment in the private letter Russell sent to his editor, July 16, in which his ethnocentric British bias came to the fore: "There is do you know a real & prodigious energy in this people in spite of all their bunkum, but they are so very French I can not cotton to them. I wish I cd. have remained in the South, but the place was not fit for me." [53]

"Our artist, Mr. Davis, met with an unpleasant adventure on his return from New Orleans. On his arrival at Memphis, Tennessee, he was waited upon by the Vigilence Committee, who inquired, after the fashion of these bodies, who he was, where he came from, what he was doing, where he was going, and whether he didn't need any hanging. Having obtained answers to these various queries, the Committee then proceeded to inspect Mr. Davis's trunk, which they overhauled with commendable thoroughness. Finding at the bottom of the trunk a number of sketches made for us, they examined them minutely, and each member, by way of remembering Mr. Davis, pocketed two or three of the most striking." —*Harper's Weekly*

Harper's attitude likely was influenced by a recent ("recent," as in the previous issue) public disagreement with the British journalist. For a portion of his journey in the South, Russell had been accompanied by Theodore Davis, an artist for the newspaper. It is possible that Mr. Davis may have been allowed to join Russell's party under false pretenses, having introduced himself, according to Russell, as an artist for the London *Illustrated News*. (In the published version of the *Diary*, Russell misrecorded his name as "Mr. Deodore F. Moses.") Russell claimed to have been warned of the deception while in Mobile. John Forsyth—who Russell had met earlier when he was one of the Southern commissioners sent to Washington to negotiate an accommodation—was now fully occupied not only as principal editor and proprietor of the Mobile *Register*, but also as the mayor of the city and head of the Vigilance Committee.

Forsyth showed Russell an announcement from *Harper's*: "The proprietors have dispatched an artist to the South in company with Mr. Russell, correspondent of the London *Times*." Forsyth was not pleased with the idea that he had been extending hospitality to a Northern press spy, nor was Russell, who—in his own account—confronted "the young gentleman, who was very pale and agitated on being shown the advertisement and sketch, declared that he had renounced all connection with Harper's, that he was sketching for the *Illustrated London News*, and that the advertisement was contrary to fact, and utterly unknown to him. . . ." [54]

Russell sent an exculpatory letter to editor Forsyth for publication in the *Register* of May 13, in which he firmly stated that he was "a neutral . . . employed on a mission that requires the utmost impartiality" and affirmed the parallel impartiality of Mr. Davis, "a young artist, who is taking sketches for the *Illustrated London News*, and who assures me that he is not engaged by or connected with *Harper's Weekly*, though he formerly sent sketches to that periodical."

Davis continued the masquerade—again, according to Russell—until after they had parted company in New Orleans, where Davis had appeared "in great agitation to say his life was in danger, in consequence of his former connection with an abolition paper of New York, and that he had been threatened with death. . . ." At Russell's request, British consul William Mure offered to take Davis "to the authorities of the town, who would, no doubt, protect him, as he was merely engaged in making sketches for an English periodical," but at this point, the artist was only interested in getting back to the North. He asked, as a form of protection, if he might carry any "letters of an official character for Washington." Mure and Russell each gave him some correspondence. "He started off North in the evening," Russell wrote on May 24, "and I saw him no more." [55]

That did not, however, end their relationship. Another sketch, attributed to "our artist who has been traveling with W. H. Russell, LL.D., Barrister at Law," appeared in the May 15 issue of *Harper's*. That provoked a letter of complaint from Russell, in which he enclosed a copy of his letter to the *Register*. This most certainly had not yet been received at *Harper's* when the June 22 issue was put to bed, containing a Davis portrait of Russell along with the complimentary note:

> In his personal intercourse, Dr. Russell unites the charms of experiences, genius, and sincerity. A willing conversationalist, he rushes into a discussion with the fearlessness of conviction and the generosity of one who feels that he has ideas and knowledge to spare. As an observer, while endowed with a keen relish for enjoyment, nothing seems to escape him.

With Russell's complaint in hand, *Harper's* rounded up letters for the July 20 edition to demonstrate that, for once, his powers of observation (or memory) had failed. The letters came from Theodore Davis (Russell knew who he was, he said, and had urged him to "Tell the editor of *Harper's Weekly* that I am very happy to have a pleasant companion on my journey"); from Russell's other traveling companion and secretary Samuel Ward (a "recommendation" for his "talented and prudent young friend" Davis); and from Benjamin Perley Poore (of the Boston *Journal*, now doubling as a major of Massachusetts volunteers in the capital, who affirmed that "It was announced last spring in the . . . papers . . . that Mr. Davis, your correspondent, was about to accompany Mr. Russell southward").

Other newspapers joined in the dispute. The New York *Times* published a letter from Russell's secretary Ward claiming that *Harper's* had taken his comment out of context (*Harper's* asserted, August 3, that the letter had been published as received) and the *Tribune* charged *Harper's* with maligning "Mr. Russell with treachery to our cause." The *Tribune*, however, probably came nearest the mark with a July 21 hint that "The *social habits* of the *Times* correspondent . . . have been matters of general discussion. Grant that *the drinking* and smoking a journalist does is stimulus to intellectual exercise. . . ." [56]

Politics, personalities, and personal habits aside, Russell had been welcomed everywhere in the South on the assumption that Great Britain would soon support the Confederacy; his hosts, he noted, acted as if the Lord High Chancellor and the British crown both sat atop a cotton bale. "The dependence of such a large proportion of the English people on this sole article of American cotton," he wrote in his *Diary* on April 16, "is fraught with the utmost danger." [57]

The Southern leaders clearly believed that this gave them the power to control policies in Great Britain. The governor of Mississippi reminded Russell, "England is no doubt a great country, and has got fleets and the like of that, and may have a good deal to do in Eu-*rope*; but the sovereign State of Mississippi can do a great deal better without England than England can do without her." "Why, sir," said one citizen of Charleston, "we have only to shut off your supply of cotton for a few weeks, and we can create a revolution in Great Britain." [58]

Or, as explained with somewhat more subtlety by a resident of Wilmington, North Carolina: "The Yankees ain't such cussed fools as to think they can come here and whip us, let alone the British."

"What have the British got to do with it?"

"They are bound to take our part; if they don't we'll just give them a hint about the cotton. . . ." [59]

4 / Sumter

Is there to be no limit to the *Herald's* open advocacy of treason and rebellion? That print has done everything in its power to encourage and stimulate the secession movement. It has vilified the Government, belied the people of the Northern States, scattered broadcast throughout the South the most infamous falsehoods concerning the public sentiment in this City, and done everything in its power to incite the South to the open war into which they have at last plunged the country. . . .

—New York *Times*, April 15, 1861

THE NEW YORK *HERALD* had long been seen as the Northern champion of the South, and just before the election had been lauded as such by the Richmond *Enquirer*: "Impartial justice demands the need of Southern gratitude for its manly and bold assaults upon the sectional enemies of the Union with which the 'Herald' is surrounded. . . . the 'Herald' has, for months, devoted the best energies of its talents, influence and power to open the eyes of the North to the impending danger which now threatens alike the North and the South." [1]

The *Herald* was not the only Northern supporter of secession. However, as the Buffalo *Commercial Advertiser* noted, "Of this class of newspapers, we are happy to say, the list is but small, and we doubt not that an indignant public will soon make it still smaller." In addition to the *Herald*, the editor cited "among this band of Judases of the press," the *Journal of Commerce*, the New York *Express*, *Day Book*, and *News*, and the Cincinnati *Enquirer*. "Whether the Southern circulation of these prints will serve profitable enough to enable them to brave the obloquy and scorn of their indignant fellow citizens time alone will determine. . . ." [2]

Since the Harper Brothers were well known to be militant Unionists, an assignment to sketch the bombardment of Fort Sumter would have been hazardous duty; thus this *Harper's* artist imagined his coverage. This engraving shows a group of spectators watching from rooftop, the women weeping—for what? The loss of the Union? Actually, watching the bombardment of Fort Sumter was a most popular sport, with thousands of people thronging into Charleston by train and buggy to cheer.

This was one of the earlier large, muti-block engravings; the lack of skill is clearly evident.

The *Advertiser* might have added the Bedford (Pennsylvania) *Gazette*:

The so-called "peace policy" of the Lincoln Administration has all at once been turned into one of blood and horror. . . . when the cruel ferocity of the liberated slave shall bring fire and rapine to the homes of the North, as well as to the plantations of the South; when this lovely land, ere while an Eden of love and peace, shall have been turned into a very hell of hate and strife; Mr. Lincoln and his partisans may learn to pray that the curse placed upon their political sins may be removed. . . . [3]

Through the middle of April 1861, the *Herald*'s editorial position remained patently clear. On April 9, "a vicious, imbecile, demoralized Administration" was about to force a civil war upon the country. "Far better that the Union should be dismembered forever," the editors wrote, "than that fraternal hands should be turned against one another, to disfigure the land by slaughter and carnage." April 10, the editors called for "the over-throw of the demoralizing, disorganizing and destructive sectional party, of which 'Honest Abe Lincoln' is the pliable instrument." The next day's edition brought a dark prediction:

The feverish excitement of the last few days, will probably have given place, before the lapse of many hours, to that stunned sensation of horror, which follows every terrible, irreparable catastrophe. . . . The stupendous treason . . . is at length consummated. [4]

Within a matter of hours—at 4:27 A.M. on Friday April 12, 1861—the irreparable catastrophe was at hand, as the shore batteries in Charleston began shelling the Federal's island garrison of Fort Sumter. By the time the bombardment ended at two o'clock in the afternoon of the next day, almost four thousand shells had been fired, to the delight of Charleston throngs, who viewed the event as great sport.

The telegraph was closed to reporters; trains were held in town. Roving bands of armed men went looking for reporters; they found one, George Salter of the *Times*. Salter, who wrote under the name of "Jasper," was so well known for his sympathy toward the South that Northern readers had urged that he be fired. To no avail; he was arrested shortly after the bombardment began, thrown in jail for twenty-four hours, and put in fear of his life when he heard policemen on the street outside speculating on the possibility of a sunrise hanging. When released, he was taken to the railroad station and told to leave the city on the next train.

Even New York *Herald* correspondents were harassed—one of their men in Charleston was arrested at least three times, the Pensacola representative escaped only by assuming a disguise, and there was an unsubstantiated report that a mob with a rope was looking for the Richmond correspondent.

The *Herald*'s coverage on April 12—"The War Has Begun"—was accompanied by a cut of the new Confederate flag. War, the editor suggested, was more easily started than stopped, and might last twenty years; "oceans of blood, and millions of treasure will be wasted, with no other imaginable end than to leave the country exhausted, impoverished and wretched, and, worse than all, despoiled of the freedom purchased at such cost by our forefathers."

The editions of April 14 carried the first full dispatch from the *Herald*'s chief Charleston correspondent, Felix Gregory De Fontaine—one who was *not* arrested, as he was a close friend of the Confederate officer in charge of the affair, Brig. Gen. P. G. T. Beauregard.

Dateline 3:00 p.m. April 12:

Civil War *has* at last begun. A terrible fight is at this moment going on between Fort Sumter and the fortifications by which it is surrounded. . . . The excitement in the community is indescribable. With the very first boom of the gun, thousands rushed from their beds to the harbor front, and all day every available place has been thronged by ladies and gentlemen, viewing the solemn spectacle through their glasses.

Fort Sumter commander Maj. Robert Anderson surrendered on the morning of April 14. By that evening, the *Herald* had run off an extra edition of 135,600 copies, bragging that this was "the largest issue of any newspaper that has ever been printed." Crowds surged around the *Herald* building through much of the evening and into the night, searching the bulletin boards for new postings.

The next morning, the citizens of New York learned that President Lincoln had called up the militia, "to the aggregate number of 75,000," to suppress the rebellion and "to cause the laws to be duly executed." The New York *Times* celebrated patriotism: "Not for fifty years has such a spectacle been seen, as that glorious uprising of American loyalty which greeted the news that open war had been commenced upon the Constitution and Government of the United States. . . . Millions of freemen rally with exulting hearts, around our country's standard." [5]

The *Tribune* called for unity: "It seems but yesterday that at least two-thirds of the journals of this city were the virtual allies of the Secessionists, their apologists, their champions. The roar of the great circle of batteries pouring their iron hail upon devoted Sumter has struck them all dumb. . . . They would evidently like to justify and encourage the traitors further, but they dare not. . . ." [6]

The *Tribune*'s editors seem not yet to have read that day's *Herald*. Editor Bennett did acknowledge that, "At all events, the reduction of Fort Sumter and this manifesto of President Lincoln are equivalent to a declaration of war on both sides. . . ." but called for conciliation, a "peace meeting" to oppose this "causeless and senseless appeal to arms." His editorial concluded, "Earnestly laboring in behalf of peace, from the beginning of these sectional troubles down to this day, and for the maintenance of the Union through mutual concessions, we do not even yet utterly despair of arresting this civil war before it shall have passed beyond the reach of reason." [7]

The response in the *Times* was scathing—"Is there to be no limit to the *Herald*'s open advocacy of treason and rebellion?"—and offered this suggestion to James Gordon Bennett:

> The *Herald* announces a meeting in the Park to declare against coercion. It is rather late in the day to stigmatize the effort of the Government to protect itself from destruction as coercion. And when the *Herald* succeeds in getting together a public meeting in this City to protest against taking any steps to redress the outrage of Fort Sumpter [*sic*] . . . we trust Mr. Bennett will consent to make the opening speech in person. He will receive such a greeting as will probably discourage his oratory, if it does not cure his treason." [8]

The mood of the crowds milling about the *Herald* building turned ugly; the formerly curious became an angry mob, threatening violence to the property and all within unless the *Herald* showed some tangible sign of national unity. A timely display of the "Stars and Stripes" was loudly and frequently suggested. As it turned out, there was not a single American flag in the building (although an unsubstantiated rumor later printed in the *Tribune* asserted that the *Herald*, perhaps anticipating a different outcome, was prepared with a healthy supply of secessionist flags). An office boy was sent out to buy a proper flag, which finally, at four thirty, was flung from an upper-story window. Not too much later, according to one account, it was joined by enough flags to equip the color bearers of a division. The mob appeared to be satisfied. The lurking presence of thirty New York City policemen, assigned to protect the property, perhaps had some influence; the announcement that another five hundred were on call, and could be summoned on ten minutes' notice, was also of interest. Then, too, the *Herald*'s chief engineer let it be known that water pipes had been rigged to spray boiling water in the hallways, should anyone force entry.

As insurance against future incidents, the *Herald* laid in a supply of small arms and ammunition, concealed behind movable panels at strategic points throughout the building. As insurance against future economic impact, Bennett wasted no time in shifting, in both style and substance, the *Herald*'s coverage of the crisis. On April 16, the lead editorial agreed that "the actual presence of war cuts short all debate. . . . there will now be but one party, one question, one issue, one purpose in the Northern States—that of sustaining the government." The *Tribune*'s flag charge was branded as "false, mean, and malicious. . . . In regard to the display of the American flag, no one asked us to do so. It was unnecessary to take that trouble. The glorious flag of the Union is our flag, and long may it wave."

Bennett asked one of his correspondents, Henry Villard—who had given candidate Abraham Lincoln some of his earliest national press coverage—personally to convey this message to the president: that the *Herald* would "energetically and unconditionally support the Government in putting down the Secessionists' rebellion by force of arms." [9] Bennett also asked Villard to volunteer his son's sailing yacht *Rebecca*—along with the professional services of his twenty-year-old namesake—for the duration. (James Gordon Bennett Jr. indeed was commissioned in the Revenue Service and assigned as lieutenant commanding his own yacht.)

The mob that had threatened the *Herald* moved off to visit other recalcitrant newspapers: the *Daily News*, the *Journal of Commerce*, and *Day Book & Express*. All managed to find and display the Stars and Stripes. All continued to be reluctant to support the Union.

Newspapers in New York City were not the only mob targets of that day; a similar throng marched through the streets of Trenton, New Jersey, and, according to the next day's *Tribune*, an "excited" crowd in Philadelphia moved from one newspaper office to the next "ordering that the flag should be displayed." They were about to demolish the printing plant of an advertising sheet called the *Palmetto Flag*, when they discovered that the same office also issued a paper called the *Stars and Stripes*. Attempting to capitalize on their confusion, Philadelphia's mayor called for patriotic reason: ". . . stand by your flag and protect it at all hazards . . . [but] remember the rights due your fellow citizens and their private party." The *Tribune* reported "immense cheering" but noted that rather than "going to their respective places of abode" as urged by the mayor, the crowd "marched in a body up Market street [and] at all points on the route, well-known Union men were obliged to make all haste to borrow, beg or steal something red, white, and blue, to protect their property. . . ." [10]

Petty disputes with the *Herald* aside, the *Tribune* deplored the mob actions: "The cause of the Union is the cause of Law and Order. . . . The true way to deal with these disloyal sheets," the paper affirmed, "is to let them alone. If all good citizens would cease to buy them they would be suppressed much more effectually than by mob violence, which only tends to give them notoriety and to excite sympathy for them by natural reaction in favor of the freedom of the press." [11]

On April 17, the *Tribune* announced that it would thenceforth also publish an evening edition. The *Herald* went one (or three) better, announcing that afternoon editions would thenceforth be issued at one thirty, three, and four thirty. The New York *Evening Day Book* remained defiant:

> Let us look at this Fort Sumter matter stripped of all its disguise. We have no doubt, and all the circumstances prove, that it was a cunningly devised scheme, contrived with all due attention to scenic display and intended to arouse, and, if possible, exasperate the northern people against the South. . . . They wished to arouse the Democrats of the North, and the *Tribune*, the next day after the fall of Sumter, thus coolly chuckles:
>
> "We have lost Fort Sumter, but we have gained a united North."
>
> We venture to say a more gigantic conspiracy against the principle of human liberty and freedom has never been concocted. Who but a fiend could have thought of sacrificing the Gallant Major Anderson and his little band in order to carry out a political game? [12]

Also on April 17, Virginia's legislature voted to join the Confederacy. Albert Deane Richardson was on a train headed back home when, while passing through Wilmington, North Carolina, the passengers were electrified by that news. "Sitting alone at one end of the car," Richardson reported, "I observed three fellow-passengers . . . conferring earnestly. Their frequent glances toward me indicated the subject of the conversation." One of them approached, and said, "We just have news that Virginia has seceded."

Richardson had earlier determined the appropriate course of action in such a situation: "I remembered the injunction of the immortal Pickwick: 'it is always best on these occasions to do what the mob do!' 'But,' suggested Mr. Snodgrass, 'suppose there are two mobs?' 'Shout with the largest,' replied Mr. Pickwick." Richardson therefore replied to the suspicious passenger, "with considerable emphasis: 'Good! That will give us all the border States.'" The man returned to his companions, satisfied, and Richardson, perhaps offering a prayer to Charles Dickens, returned to the relative safety of the North. [13]

In a public forum at Montgomery on April 12, the Confederate secretary of war had prophesied that the Confederate flag, which that day flew in the breeze in Alabama, would "float over the dome of the old Capitol at

Washington before the first of May." The newspapers of the South, which had not had much impact on the inauguration, returned to a verbal attack. Richmond *Enquirer*: "Nothing is more probable than that President Davis will soon march an army through North Carolina and Virginia to Washington." Vicksburg *Whig*: "Major Ben McCullough [*sic*] has organized a force of five thousand men to seize the Federal Capital the instant the first blood is spilled." [14]

The exhortations to overwhelm the Federal capital had no effect in the South, but terrified the residents of a virtually unprotected Washington. Richardson would note that "twenty-five hundred well-officered, resolute men could undoubtedly have captured the city." [15] Militia units, quickly routed from Northern cities to Washington, created the semblance, but not the reality, of a military presence. Most of the Northern militia, at this point, were not qualified for any real service; men had joined as they would join a social club, for the camaraderie and the parade. Many had no knowledge of, or experience in, the field—their summer encampments had been supported by professional caterers. On the other hand, some, at least, knew something about fighting—although more in the barroom than battlefield sense. The Fire Zouaves, recruited from New York's volunteer fire departments, were rowdy, tough, and undisciplined. They picked fights with other soldiers, they terrorized merchants, and they destroyed property. The Washington *Star* called them "Pet Lambs" and reported their antics with amusement.

It was at this time that the Federal government took the first steps toward telegraphic censorship, although this at first had not been the intention. Col. Charles P. Stone, chief of security for the District of Columbia, believed he had uncovered a conspiracy to ship flour from Washington docks to the rebels, and asked the War Department to suspend use of the telegraph and thus forestall any conspiratory communications until he could round up the perpetrators.

His timing was unfortunate. The first regiment from the North to reach Washington, the Sixth Massachusetts, had been attacked by a mob of Southern sympathizers as it passed through Baltimore on April 19. When reporters rushed to send off the story, they found the Washington telegraph office under the control of armed guards and assumed that the government was trying to suppress news of the Baltimore riots. [16]

Next, with troop passage through Baltimore temporarily denied, an alternate route was established by ship to the port of Annapolis, then by rail to Washington. However, a stretch of about twenty miles of track had been torn up by the rebels, and Thomas A. Scott, vice president of the Pennsylvania Railroad, was brought in to supervise repairs and organize traffic. Scott brought along a team of his railroad telegraph operators, and the War Department took charge of the telegraph. This was not—as the newsmen then (and some historians, later) assumed—to censor embarrassing dispatches, but to coordinate transport on the rails. Censorship per se was not in Scott's portfolio, but because so much news copy referred to troop movements, he took on the responsibility of removing what he deemed to be "sensitive" material from the reporters' copy.

However, because no one in Washington had any experience with formal censorship, it is no surprise that the men Scott assigned to review news dispatches were singularly unqualified. At first, they would deny transmission to an entire dispatch if it contained one small censorable fact. Next—a slight improvement—they would delete the offending material and let the rest of the dispatch go through, but they did not let the authors review the chopped up copy for sense and logic, both of which often had been removed as well. As summed up by the New York *Times*, "A more stupidly, ill-judged proceeding could scarcely be imagined. . . ." [17]

Censorship was more easily implemented in the South, and more readily accepted. A censorship of sorts had long been in place in some Southern states, where the press was forbidden to publish, for example, any material advocating the abolition of slavery. More directly to the point, the South was largely unified behind the Confederate movement, and had the most to lose through newspaper indiscretion. The Southern papers certainly thought so. As the Virginia *Sentinel* affirmed:

> The plans of our Government are, of course, not suitable matter of public proclamation. Our military boards must keep their own counsels, as it is obviously proper they should do so. The people should patriotically abstain from even the attempt to unriddle them, for the wisest plans are often baffled by disclosure, however made. Let us trust with a generous confidence those to whose hands we have committed the conduct of affairs, and prepare ourselves to sustain them with all the power of a united and courageous people. [18]

The Richmond *Whig* added, "We beg to suggest to all Southern papers the propriety of omitting all mention of the movement of troops within our borders. A word to the wise." [19]

"The caution is a good one," agreed the New Orleans *Picayune*, "and might well be extended to correspondents, both private and public, by telegraph and by mail. The caution is the more necessary, because of our large daily correspondence with the people of the North, with whom we are unfortunately at war." [20]

That "daily correspondence" included reading each others' newspapers, which spread military information freely across the borders. This also led to some convenient plagiarizing as well: there is an unmistakable similarity between the following two items. The first is from the Richmond *Whig*, April 22, 1861:

> A gentleman of Richmond, Va., was in New York. The scene which he witnessed in the streets reminded him of the descriptions of the Reign of Terror in Paris—desperadoes of that great city are now in the ascendant. At present, they are animated by very bloody designs against the South. They have been persuaded, or urged by hunger, to believe that by enlisting for the war they will win bread and honor and riches. By-and-by, they may come to reflect there is an abundance of meat and bread, and inexhaustible supplies of money all around them—in the banks, the palatial residences, in the fireproof safes of the princely merchants a wealth of treasure and good things all around them—to be had for the taking.

The second was published just over a week later in the New York *Times*, May 1, 1861:

> A gentleman from Richmond . . . gives some information of the feeling prevalent there. He represents it as a perfect reign of terror, and an excitement that he never saw paralleled. . . . [A man] who was organizing a corps of infantry, told them they had nothing to do but to march to glory and wealth. "What," said he, "could a Northern army do on our sterile hills—they would starve to death. But you," he continued, "have but to march to Washington, and lay that in ashes—then to Philadelphia, which is rich in all kinds of wealth—from that through all the North; there is a village every five miles, and every village has a bank, every bank has a vault of specie, and you have but to help yourselves."

The Charleston *Courier* suggested that Southern newspapers voluntarily adopt some reasonable guidelines: do not discuss the number or position, or announce the arrival or departure, of Confederate forces; do not describe likely enemy objectives or rebel plans; when describing a battle, do not reveal too many details and write only about completed actions.

The Confederate congress authorized telegraphic censorship in May, with little opposition. The congress itself exercised censorship at the source by closing sessions at which military matters were discussed.

5 / An Age of Innocence

From the mountain tops and valleys to the shores of the sea there is one wild shout of fierce resolve to capture Washington city at all and every human hazard. The filthy cage of unclean birds must and will assuredly be purified by fire. . . . many indeed will be the carcasses of dogs and caitiffs that will blacken the air upon the gallows, before the great work is accomplished.

—Richmond *Examiner,* April 23, 1861

FOR THE TIME BEING, it was to be a war of bombast, not of bombs.

New Orleans *Bee,* April 27, 1861: "Sectional prejudice . . . has been roused to active demonstration by the fiendish tactics of Black Republican journals. These have so mingled the most violent denunciation of the South and its institutions with frantic appeals in behalf of the Union and the American flag, as to stir up the ignorant masses to a pitch of uncontrollable excitement and to fill them with vindictive and malignant hostility. . . ."

Peoria *Daily Transcript,* May 8, 1861: "The high-bred and chivalrous 'Southron' of whom we have all heard so much, and read so much, and seen so little, is an absolute and universal humbug." We of the North, the editor suggested, dependent on our own labor for survival, may be a bit rough about the edges; we recognize our social inferiority to the "Southron," who is full of the "grace and polish of a courtly and imperial race fed by the labor of slaves" and therefore "able to devote an elegant leisure to self-culture."

Albany *Evening Journal,* May 10, 1861: "The Dictionaries are exhausted in the demand for epithets expressive of their [the Southern papers] contempt, their hatred, their loathing of us. . . . 'Black hordes,' 'Northern barbarians,' 'Goths and Vandals,' 'brutal mercenaries,' 'besotted hirelings,' 'hogs,' and 'cattle,' 'frowzy fanatics,' and 'imbecile ruffians' are a few of the more popular titles with which they honor us when they happen to be in their more playful moods. The language of their sterner moments . . . are quite too expressive to be repeated in these decorous columns."

Some newspapers, North and South, affirmed that secession merely validated what was common knowledge: the North and the South already were separate and distinct. Russell had recorded a conversation with Edmund Rhett (page [51]), which outlined differences between South Carolina and New England. An item in the Rhett-owned Charleston *Mercury* the next day clearly reflected the same conversation:

> We are socially and politically as distinct a people from the North, as from France or England. The people of the two sections have ever hated each other, not merely because their laws, customs, manners, and institutions are different; but more still, because their races, their blood, their ancestry, were different. The people of the South belong to the brave, impulsive, hospitable, and generous Celtic race; the people of the North to the cold, phlegmatic Teutonic race. . . . We wish to make peace with them as soon as possible and to keep peace with them, by having in the future nothing to do with them. [1]

They agreed with the theme, although not with the detail. "We are not a homogenous people. We never have been so." American civilization, the editor suggested, had developed in two parallel streams, flowing from Plymouth Rock and Jamestown. "These two great currents of civilization were radically different from the start. Plymouth Rock had little sympathy with Jamestown. The plain, stern, reverent Puritan could not fraternize with the extravagant, profligate and courtly planter of the 'old Dominion.'" In the present contest, the editor asked, which brand of civilization would prevail? An obvious answer: "Which is toughest, most tenacious— has the most vigor and the greater power of resistance? As God reigns Virginia must come to Massachusetts, and there shall be *one people*." [2]

More than a year later, this same argument appeared in the Mobile *Telegraph*, but with a Southern spin:

> In the settlement of this country, two great streams of civilization poured out. One had its head at Jamestown, and one at Plymouth Rock. The canting, witch-hanging, nasal-twanging, money-worship-

ping, curiosity-loving, meddling, fanatical, "ism"-breeding followers of Cromwell, spread over the greater part of the North and West. Jamestown stock chiefly peopled the South, and small sections of the North-west territory, which, with Kentucky, belonged to Virginia. . . . Extreme religious bigotry indulged for more than two centuries, and constant intermarriage have impoverished the Yankee blood. . . . On the contrary, though, the South has preserved its great English features, a healthy admixture of the blood of other races has kept it from degeneration. [3]

To the common Southern boast that any rebel soldier counted at least as two Yankees, one New Orleans paper suggested, not wholly in jest, that the war be decided by a set-piece battle, 50,000 "of the Chivalry" against 100,000 Yankees. Other papers raised the ante: "one Southerner is, on an average, a match for at least three Northerners," asserted one; another predicted that for each Southern soldier lost, "a dozen of the dastardly marauders will be made to bite the dust." [4]

The Southern claim to superiority in things martial rested, in part, on the knowledge that the South had provided the overwhelming portion of soldiers for America's two previous wars. That was true: 155,000 Americans served in the War of 1812, two-thirds from the South, which had half the population of the Northern states; for the Mexican War, 66,000 served, of whom, again, two-thirds were from the South.

This argument, however, did not impress the London *News*:

It is the boast of the South that the force for the Mexican war was furnished chiefly by that section; and the assertion is ratified by the Northern boast that the free States supplied a very small force to that atrocious war, and that that contingent consisted mainly of the adventurer class, who are always sent away to a distance with great alacrity.

When we hear of the military genius of the South, we naturally turn to what we know. We know something of the Mexican war, of which they make their boast. We know what a miserable enemy they had there; and we know what a miserable hand they made of several of the enterprises of the campaign. . . . the commanders were at their wits' end to get their troops out and home again, and what to do with them while abroad. [5]

The *News* predicted a short and tepid war, and cited four reasons: one, there was strong Union sentiment through much of the South; two, there was a serious deficiency of food throughout the South; three, blacks, North and South, were eager "to use the opportunity for putting an end to the captivity of their race"; and four, the quality of the Southern army was questionable.

In his London *Times* letter of April 30, written in Charleston, Russell suggested a fifth reason: a questionable *quantity* of warriors:

> They entertain very exaggerated ideas of the military strength of their little community, although one may do full justice to its military spirit. Out of their whole population [South Carolina] they cannot reckon more than 60,000 adult men by any arithmetic, and as there are nearly 30,000 plantations, which must be, according to law, superintended by white men, a considerable number of these adults cannot be spared from the state for service in the open field. The planters boast that they can raise their crops without an inconvenience by the labor of their Negroes, and they seem confident that the Negroes will work without superintendence. But the experiment is rather dangerous, and it will only be tried in the last extremity.

"Our ablest journals," Richardson would later note, "were fond of contrasting the resources of the two sections, and demonstrating therefrom, with mathematical precision, that the war could not last long; that the superiority of the North in men and money would make subjugation of the South a short and easy task." [6]

The New York *Times* bragged: "We have only to send a column of 25,000 men across the Potomac to Richmond, burn out the rats there; another column of 25,000 to Cairo, seizing the cotton ports of the Mississippi; and retaining the remaining 25,000, included in Mr. Lincoln's call for 75,000, men, at Washington, not because there is need for them here, but because we do not require their services elsewhere." The Chicago *Tribune* suggested that "Illinois can whip the South by herself" in "two or three months at the furthest." The Philadelphia *Press* predicted victory in one month; against the "simply invincible" people of the North, the rebels—"a mere band of ragamuffins"—would fly like "chaff before the wind." [7]

In the editorial middle ground of largely Democratic Northern papers, which continued to espouse the Southern cause, comment ranged from the mild reproof of the Utica (New York) *Observer*, "Of all the wars which have disgraced the human race, it has been reserved for our own enlightened nation to be involved in the most useless and foolish one," to the rhetorical flourish of the Bangor *Union*: "Democrats of Maine! . . . Those who have inaugurated this unholy and unjustifiable war are no friends of yours, nor friends of Democratic Liberty.'"

The Baltimore *Sun* called for compromise: recognize the independence of the Confederate States and end the strife. The New York *Express* warned that "the cold-blooded, heartless demagogues, who started this civil war" would find their account "if not at the hands of an indignant people, then in the tears of widows and orphans. . . ." The New York *Day Book* entered a pleading against "these destroyers of our country—these worse than madmen, who talk about preserving the Union by fighting for it! Are they crazy?" [April 17, 1861]

The Concord (New Hampshire) *Democratic Standard* reported rumor as fact: "Our Southern papers are filled with heart-sickening accounts of the murders and robberies which individuals in Old Abe's Mob are perpetrating on the Southern people. Innocent women and children are shot on their own doorsteps. . . . "

When Virginia announced its intention to join the Confederacy, April 17, the editorial clamor to invade Washington became almost universal. From North Carolina, April 24: "Washington city will soon be too hot to hold Abraham Lincoln and his Government." From Alabama, April 25: "seize the old Federal capital and take old Lincoln and his Cabinet prisoners of war." From Georgia, April 30: "The government of the Confederate States must possess the city of Washington." [8]

The New Orleans *Picayune* suggested on May 3, "A Southern victory at Washington would not only strike terror . . . but go far towards releasing the good and estimable people of the North from a thralldom which has become as terrible as it is degrading. We hope to have the pleasure, ere many days, of chronicling the glorious achievement." [9]

On May 22, the Richmond *Whig* urged Jeff Davis and friends to "keep themselves in readiness to dislodge at a moment's notice" for a move into Washington, but assured its readers that Jeff Davis and friends "do not need this warning at our hands. They must know that the measure of their iniquities is full, and the patience of outraged freedom is exhausted. Among all the brave men from the Rio Grande to the Potomac, and stretching over into insulted, indignant and infuriated Maryland, there is but one word on every lip: 'Washington'; and one sentiment on every heart: vengeance on the tyrants who pollute the Capital of the Republic!"

On May 24, as a defensive move against such a rebel attack on Washington, Federal forces shifted across the Potomac River into Virginia and occupied Alexandria. Leading Southern papers shifted—with no acknowledgment of any inconsistency—from aggression to outrage. The Richmond *Examiner* was shrill: "That horde of thieves, robbers, and assassins in the pay of Abraham Lincoln, commonly known as the army of the United States, have rushed into the peaceful streets of a quiet city of the State, and stained the hearth of Virginia homes with the blood of her sons." The Richmond *Enquirer* was grim: "The 'bloody and brutal' purposes of the Abolitionists, to subjugate and exterminate the Southern people, stands confessed by the flagrant outrage upon Virginia soil. . . . Virginians, arise in your strength and welcome the invader with 'bloody hands to hospitable graves.'" [10]

It was during this incursion that Col. Ephraim Ellsworth, personal friend of President Lincoln and organizer and colonel of the New York Fire Zouaves, was shot and killed for ripping a Confederate flag from the Marshall House hotel in Alexandria. The killer—proprietor James T. Jackson—was, in turn, killed by one of Ellsworth's men.

This sparked an interesting debate: what standing, in law, did either man have? It depended, of course, on which side of the law stood your sentiments. To the Southern press, Ellsworth was an intruder and his killer was a hero. As the editor of the Richmond *Examiner* noted, "The slayer of Colonel Ellsworth was branded, in the North, as an 'assassin.' The justice of history does not permit such a term to be applied to a man who defended his country's flag and the integrity of his home with his life, distinctly and fearlessly offered up to such objects of honor: it gives him the name . . . of 'martyr.'" Russell, reflecting the sentiment in the North, wrote: "As it seems to me, Colonel Ellsworth, however injudicious he may have been, was actually in the performance of his duty when taking down the flag of the enemy." [11]

In one grand irony—of uncounted ironies of the war—on the day that Virginia left the Union, the New York *Tribune* made the argument for *rebel* action and Federal patience. "It is a plain case that they must hurry matters or succumb, and that they must make an immediate dash at our weakest point, the Federal Metropolis. If Jeff. Davis and Beauregard are not on the Potomac within sixty days, their rebellion will stand exposed a miserable failure. . . . *They cannot wait; we can. . . .*" [12] A grand irony, because the *Tribune* was to become an increasingly militant agent for precipitate action on the part of the Federals.

The *Tribune* entry for April 22 warned the administration to pay attention: "If good Uncle Abe wants to read the Secessionists another essay proving that he never meant them any harm, or Gov. Seward has another oration to deliver to them on the glories and blessings of the Union, let the performances come off by all means, but this will have to be before Jeff. Davis and Wise capture Washington." [13] On April 25, after Governor Hicks of Maryland had asked the administration not to send any more troops through Baltimore, en route to the capital, and the administration agreed, the *Tribune* turned outrage into aggression: "Let troops be poured down upon Baltimore, and if need be, raze it to the ground." Governor Hicks—a "snivelling, whiffling traitor" of "the plug-ugliest State south of Mason and Dixon's line"—should be advised, the North would "go through her and over her, in every direction, through every acre."

On April 26, the editors expressed frustration: "How much longer shall we wait? . . . How much more disgrace shall we suffer? Before the Government shall seem to begin to suspect that we are involved in a war where desperation of treason on one side is to be met by the desperation of loyalty on the other?"

All of the above was little better than errant musing, compared with what came a month later. Fitz-Henry Warren, an experienced newsman, politician, and former government official (as first assistant postmaster general in the Taylor administration) had looked for appointment in the Lincoln administration as postmaster general. When offered only his old job, he converted his disappointment into an angry energy, which he took to the *Tribune* as the new Washington bureau chief. Warren was obsessive: he felt that Sumter must be avenged, and *now*! His first significant contribution, dateline May 27:

TO RICHMOND! TO RICHMOND ONWARD. . . . Mr. President, Lieutenant-General Scott, Messieurs Secretaries, when shall the bayonet flash to the "Forward" of the Centurion of the conquering line? "Celebrate the Fourth of July there." Ah, God bless you and Amen, gentlemen, for the words. . . .
　　On to Richmond, then is the voice of the people. . . . Again, we repeat, On to Richmond! . . . Let her still sowing of the wind, have a generous harvest of the whirlwind, and let it be *now*. . . . To Richmond! To Richmond!

On June 10, there was a small action near Norfolk. It was called "Big Bethel" and was treated by the newspapers of both sides as a battle, although it was more of a confused skirmish. The Federals suffered seventy-one casualties and the rebels, only eight. This led, naturally, to Southern newspaper accounts of a "glorious victory," as indeed it was, as a matter of proportion. However, as a small footnote to this bit of history, one Southern paper gave away the news that one reason for the low Confederate casualty count was the poor aim of the anxious and unseasoned Yankee infantry—they were largely shooting over the heads of their enemy. Whether the Federal officers noted the error, or read about it in the newspaper, makes little difference: that problem was soon fixed.

In the meantime, the Confederates had been gathering in force at Manassas Junction, a railroad center some thirty miles west-southwest of the capital city. The Memphis *Appeal* predicted:

The next few days will witness the most momentous developments in the history of the continent. . . . we infer, from the proclamation of General Beauregard, issued from Manassas Junction, that an early offensive movement is contemplated, which the South desires, and will support. . . . But whatever may be the conclusions . . . of one result we feel assured, and that is, of the final success of our great and glorious cause, and of the eventual defeat and humiliation of our vaunting enemies. Our people are not discouraged—our troops are brave, anxious, and hopeful, and the God of battles will defend the right and carry our standard to victory. . . . [14]

The referenced "proclamation," issued on June 5 and printed in the Richmond *Enquirer*, was addressed "to the People of the Counties of Loudon, Fairfax, and Prince William." General Beauregard decried the acts of the "reckless and unprincipled tyrant," Abraham Lincoln, who "has thrown his Abolition hosts among you, who are murdering and imprisoning your citizens, confiscating and destroying your property, and committing other acts of violence and outrage, too shocking and revolting to humanity to be enumerated." The war cry of the Federals, he wrote, "is 'BEAUTY AND BOOTY.' All that is dear to man—your honor and that of your wives and daughters—your fortunes and your lives, are involved in this momentous contest." Therefore, in the name of the "constituted authorities of the Confederate States—in the sacred cause of constitutional liberty and self-government—in behalf of civilization itself," General Beauregard called on all "by every means in your power, compatible with honorable warfare, to drive back and expel the invaders from your land." [15]

This sparked a June 18 response from the Baltimore *American*: "The most objectionable of all the pronunciamentos of the Secessionists that has come under our notice, since the beginning of the contest, is the proclamation of General Beauregard to certain 'good people' in Virginia. How any man of his standing could put his name to such a production we are at a loss to conceive. . . . Can *any* intelligent community in the South be thus cheated into madness? Surely if they can be, they are to be pitied. . . ." [16]

Fitz-Henry Warren's *Tribune* letter of June 21 suggested a Northern madness of a different sort. He had been talking to the troops: "Our soldiers have been requested to fire blank cartridges in all engagements with Southern forces," he wrote, without explaining the source of the "request." His submission of June 22 expanded on that idea:

Shall I tell you, frankly and honestly, what I hear all around me and abroad? It is, that there is no intention to press this suppression of the rebellion—that the patience of the people is to be worn out by delay—that the soldier is to have his spirit wasted in the torpor and inaction of the camp, and when, at length, the nation are disgusted and outraged to a proper point, then we are to run after the old harlot of a compromise.

FIELD-MARSHAL GREELEY, THE MISCHIEF-MAKER.
"Forward to Richmond," by Way of Bull's Run!!!

Harper's Weekly delighted in poking fun at its competitor, Horace Greeley.

Secretary of War Simon Cameron denied that charge; Warren suggested that if the administration were to "break up the camps on the other side of the river, for an advance to Richmond . . . the country will believe him, and discredit us." [17] The next day, and every day for a week through the Fourth of July, the *Tribune*'s editorial page took up and amplified Warren's theme with a vengeance:

THE NATION'S WAR-CRY
Forward to Richmond! Forward to Richmond!
The Rebel Congress must not be allowed
to meet there on the 20th of July!
BY THAT DATE
THE PLACE MUST BE HELD
BY THE NATIONAL ARMY!

There was no particular danger, the *Tribune* assured its readers on no discernable evidence, because the Confederate armies "dare not meet the Unionists in fair and open battle."

On June 28, Warren was called to the White House where, apparently, the president told him that his wish was about to be granted. It is interesting to note that the president did not meet with his staff even to discuss a move against the rebels until the next day.

At that meeting. Lt. Gen. Winfield Scott, infirm but not a fool at seventy-five, urged caution. Two months earlier, he had proposed a plan of encirclement, a land and water blockade to keep the South from getting any supplies and materials—and then, to wait for the inevitable strangulation of the Confederacy. The press, in no mood to wait for anything, derisively tagged the proposal the "Anaconda" plan, and hinted that the real reason behind such a passive effort was Scott's reluctance to invade his native state of Virginia.

Brig. Gen. Irwin McDowell, a staff officer with no command experience who was assigned as commander in the field, planned to use his Washington-area force of 35,000 to attack the Confederates (then some 20,000 in number) at Manassas. A corollary Federal force of 15,000 troops near Harper's Ferry, commanded by a recalled sixty-nine-year-old veteran of the War of 1812, Robert Patterson, was expected to keep another 12,000 Confederates, led by Gen. Joseph Johnston, from joining Beauregard.

McDowell asked for a delay so that the newer additions to his force might be trained. Quartermaster General Montgomery Meigs recommended immediate action, arguing that a fight then, in the relatively benign Northern Virginia countryside was better than a fight later in the miasmic swamps of the deep South. Hanging over the meeting was the knowledge that the enlistments of many Federal troops—men who had signed on for only ninety days—were about to expire.

Lincoln, perhaps on the assumption that newly enlisted Southern forces were in no better condition than McDowell's men, said, in effect, "move out—but quickly." He would not have known about the report that was to be published three weeks later in the Philadelphia *Press* about Colonel Gregg's South Carolina regiment, although it would have made his point. Their term of service had expired, and they had reached Richmond on their way home from Manassas. The colonel tried to get them to reenlist and go back—where a battle was in the offing—but only sixteen out of the whole regiment were willing. "The men were nearly all mechanics [artisans]," the *Press* noted, "and were dissatisfied with the service." [18]

Not every Northern paper had been urging an immediate advance on Richmond, nor did every Southern paper celebrate a presumed military superiority. Some, on both sides, reported shortcomings that would have been, or *should* have been, patently obvious. Russell offered a sobering assessment of the troops around Washington, "this horde of battalion companies—unofficered, clad in all kinds of different uniform, diversely equipped, perfectly ignorant of the principles of military obedience and concerted action. . . ." The Washington *Star* seconded the notion: "Of soldiers the country is full. Give us organizers and commanders. We have men, let us have leaders. We have confusion, let us have order. . . ." [19]

The Charleston *Mercury* suggested:

Let us not commit the mistake of underrating our enemy, or of supposing that, in modern warfare, it is only the courage of a people and the relative military talent of their field-officers that decide the issues of war. Ability in combinations and bravery in executing them may fail of success where the material is wanting or deficient. An hour's delay of a corps of reserve lost the battle of Waterloo; and Napoleon fought the battle with the best troops in the world. They were cut to pieces. [20]

Six weeks later, the *Mercury* offered a more pungent observation:

The Sixteenth Regiment S. C. M., comprising eight beat companies, were on the Green yesterday for inspection (?). A more ridiculous farce could not possibly have been enacted than that gone through with yesterday—that is, if regarded in a military point of view. If six hundred citizens, drawn up in two ranks, without arms or equipments, un-uniformed, and ignorant of the first principles of a soldier's duty, can be called a regiment, this was a regiment.

We forego [sic] further comment, only remarking, that what is a farce now, to be enjoyed by idle juveniles, may be at no distant day a tragedy. . . ." [21]

A tragedy, at no distant day. On June 30, 1861, the Richmond correspondent of the Charleston *Courier* had written that all eyes "are directed towards Manassas, and it is not improbable that by the time these lines reach your readers, the telegraph will have preceded me with the details of a great battle." The Northern press, he noted, offered daily reports on the Federal moves to strengthen outposts and position troops; in contrast, the Southern press was "discreetly silent." However, he continued, "unless the good Lord creates a modern Babel at Manassas and Alexandria, or drops down between the armies a veil of Cimmerian darkness, nature, personal gravitation, and animal magnetism will as certainly conspire to produce a collision as the multiplication table tells the truth." [22]

The Richmond *Dispatch* offered a less scientific but equally prophetic comment: "Gen. Scott desired to delay an advance . . . till his army was fully organized. But [the Lincoln press] could not brook the whole delay recommended by the only General in their ranks that deserves the name. . . . They will discover before long that it would have been well for them to take his counsel." [23]

They would, indeed.

In the meantime, the governments, North and South, were beginning to understand that unfettered freedom of the newspapers was a distinct liability, as the buildup of forces on both sides was being chronicled with the accuracy of a railroad timetable. On April 27, the Richmond *Enquirer* reported, "The rebel army stationed at Richmond numbers three thousand and seventy-two men. . . ." For the May 4 issue of the New Orleans *Delta*, special correspondent "A. W." submitted a complete list of the forces of General Bragg at Pensacola, with an exact count for each unit ("Captain Carr's Jackson artillery, 63 . . . Captain Tull's Vicksburg Artillery company, 60") to a grand total of 6,708, some of whom, A. W. confessed, "are quite deficient in the drill." On May 5, the Charleston *Mercury* noted that "Raleigh, North Carolina, is alive with soldiers. . . . Sixteen companies, comprising twelve hundred men, rank and file, are encamped at the Fair Grounds, and there are several more quartered in other parts of the city."

The New York *Tribune* did its part to inform the Confederates: "A regiment left New York for Fortress Monroe; 350 men left New York to join the 69th Regiment at Washington; two regiments of Ohio volunteers, numbering altogether eighteen hundred men, reach Washington." So did the New York *Times*, when it reported the movement of 13,000 men into Virginia, "each man having sixty rounds of ball cartridge." [24]

Natural pride, naiveté, or stupidity prompted the *National Intelligencer* to brag, "The big guns were planted at Cairo, Ill[inois], and the first thirty-two pound ball was sent booming down the Mississippi, a warning to all traitors to keep at a respectable distance. . . . a whole regiment of nearly a thousand men . . . sprang to . . . the work of completing the breastworks." As if that were not specific enough, the Chicago *Tribune* filled in the blanks: "Our forces at Bird's Point now consist of the following regiments:

Colonel Wallace's Eleventh Illinois Regiment, Colonel Lawler's Eighteenth Illinois Regiment, and Colonel Dougherty's Twenty-second Illinois Regiment; also, 17 pieces of artillery, consisting of six 24 pound siege guns, three 24 pound howitzers, two 12 pound howitzers and six 6 pound brass pieces. [25]

The Mobile *Register* complained about its fellow journals of the South, "No regiment has ever passed Lynchburg that Lincoln has not had the fullest notice of. There is not a battery in the country that has not been as fully described by correspondents as Frank Leslie's or Harper's artist could have done. They keep old Scott as well posted about the strength of our forces at every point . . . as if he were present at every dress parade and heard the morning orders read." On the other hand, Confederate secretary of war LeRoy Pope Walker applauded "the great amount of valuable information obtained by us from the enterprising journals of the North," one of which, *Frank Leslie's*, acknowledged the compliment by printing his remarks. [26]

As a result of these and other disclosures, both sides began to examine unresolved issues of military-media relations. With the censorship law already on the books, the South asked for—and in large degree obtained—voluntary restraint, as noted in the Savannah *Republican:* "We are requested by the military authorities of the Confederate States to urge upon our brethren of the press . . . the importance of abstaining from all specific allusions to the movement of troops. The very wisest plans of the Government may be thwarted by an untimely or otherwise injudicious exposure." To which, the Washington *National Intelligencer* offered wistful comment that a directly opposite policy appeared to prevail in the North—where every movement of the Federal troops was heralded with lightning speed in the "sensation press" and some news gatherers, with ready access to the plans of the War Department, rushed to proclaim every plan and purpose. [27]

An open letter, addressed to the press by the Confederate secretary of war, appeared in the Richmond *Enquirer* on July 1. "It must be obvious that statements of strength, or of weakness, at any of the points in the vicinity of the enemy, when reproduced in the North, as they would be in spite of all the vigilance in our power, would warn them of danger to themselves, or invite an attack upon us; and, in like manner, any statements of the magnitude of batteries, of the quantity and quality of arms, or of ammunition, of movements in progress or in supposed contemplation, or the condition of troops, of the Commissariat, &c., might be fraught with essential injury to the service."

Meanwhile, the North was groping for a policy. Maj. Gen. Benjamin F. Butler told Murat Halstead of the Cincinnati *Commercial* that "the Government would not accomplish much until it had hanged . . . half a dozen spies, and at least one newspaper reporter." Two weeks later, the Cincinnati *Enquirer* noted that Winfield Scott would prefer a hundred spies in camp to one reporter. When the Washington *Star* reported that the Federals would probably move off toward Manassas within a week—and justified the disclosure on the grounds that other papers had already broken the story—General Scott issued the following barely enforceable order: "Henceforth the telegraph will convey no dispatches concerning the operations of the Army not permitted by the Commanding general." The order was barely enforceable because the commanding general and his staff could not run the army while at the same time reading all the copy that all the newsmen wished to send on the telegraph. As this became apparent, Scott backed away from the impractical and met with a group of reporters to establish ground rules. [28]

As reported in the New York *World* on July 11, "The Executive Government of the United States and correspondents arrived at a full understanding . . . regarding the transmission of telegraphic dispatches giving information as to movements of the army. So, hereafter, it will be necessary for the distant public to await the arrival of the mails before knowing what advances of troops have been made, as also what reinforcements have arrived. The Government alleges that it has been greatly embarrassed in its movements by the Washington correspondents of the New York press, and patriotically called upon them to co-operate in not publishing any movements prematurely. Should a battle occur, the Government will probably permit the official accounts to be transmitted."

Russell entered this appraisal in his *Diary*: "The Government have been coerced, as they say, by the safety of the Republic, to destroy the liberty of the press." He viewed it as a wary arrangement, with the government agreeing to make timely "official accounts" of all actions and the correspondents reserving the right to decide what details to include or leave out of their dispatches. "They will break this agreement if they can," he correctly predicted, "and the Government will not observe their part of the bargain." He also flagged what always has been the most controversial aspect of the Constitutional guarantee: "The freedom of the press, as I take it, does not include the right to publish news hostile to the course of the country in which it is published. . . ." [29]

Tom Scott's office had been taken off censor duty in June; now, General Scott appointed George H. Burns, the Washington supervisor of the Associated Press, as the telegraphic gatekeeper. It was a curious anomaly of the system, however, that whatever censorship Burns might exercise would apply only to *telegraphic* reports. Letters sent in the mail, carried away in person, or—strangest of all—published in the local Washington papers, were not subject to review. A clever reporter for a New York paper could arrange to have a touchy item planted in a Washington paper, which would then be borrowed with impunity. This ploy may have avoided the censor's scissors, but did little to bolster relationships with the War Department; this loophole finally was plugged on August 14, in the aftermath of the Battle of Bull Run.

In his earlier rather sarcastic comment on the press, General Butler was operating more on instinct than experience. Soon he would have sufficient reason for complaint, and the press, operating on instinct, not logic, would rise to the defense. The Cincinnati *Commercial* revealed that a Federal steamer on the James River had been armed in secrecy, in hopes that a marauding enemy tugboat might be lured into combat. Butler, the area commander, issued a stern edict, not unreasonable, forbidding publication of any information relating to planning or discussion of future efforts. The New York *Tribune* carried the fight for the newspapers, with managing editor Charles Dana wielding the pen:

> Whose fault is this? Is the Major General such an old lady that he cannot hold his tongue? . . . Do reporters, eluding the sentinels, attend his councils of war in feminine disguise? . . . If officers, in violation of military law and personal confidence, are weak enough to tattle, shoot them or hang them, we do not care which; but to suppose that paid men, sent expressly to obtain information, will not use it when obtained, is to exhibit a fatuity unworthy of a Major General. We profess to print a newspaper. [30]

Dana was making an argument, commonly restated throughout the war, that any information a newsman might uncover, was just as easily—and more likely—to have come into enemy hands, and that publication, therefore, was in the public, not the enemy, interest. On the same day, the same argument was being advanced by the editor of the Charleston *Mercury*:

> It does not seem to me, any army intelligence published in Charleston can be harmful. Scott has his own agents throughout Virginia. *The Mercury is not sent to any place or portion of the North.* Letters from Manassas take several days to reach Charleston. From here, after publication the intelligence takes several days more to reach Virginia or Kentucky. So that, if news contained in the Mercury *was* sent North and not *already known*, in Washington through other channels, it would at least be stale and *behind the times*. [31]

However, Dana took the argument to the bizarre, when he ended his piece with this unique interpretation of the responsibilities of the press:

> Millions of men and women, fathers, mothers, children, wives, sweethearts, who have sent those dearer than life to these wars, look every day at this journal . . . and turn pages with hands made unsteady by emotion. It is quite as important that . . . their apprehensions should be allayed, that these tortures of suspense should be averted, as that Gen. Benjamin F. Butler should keep secret any expedition which he is likely to undertake.

There was, as yet, no reality to the "war."

6 / A Battle Too Soon

We have sent into Virginia the best appointed division of our
Grand Army and we have fought the greatest battle ever fought
on this continent, and we have not only been beaten, but our army has
been routed and many of its best regiments wholly demoralized.
The narrative of this disaster will be my duty;
you may make your own conclusions and solve the terrible political
problem it presents to the American people. . . .
—Philadelphia *Press*, July 23, 1861

To NORTHERNERS, who tended to name military actions after the nearest geographic feature, it was the First Battle of Bull Run. To the South, following a lexicology based on political boundaries, it was First Manassas. To the historian, it was the end of innocence, the last battle of amateurs in the first modern war. It was a battle that signaled also the end of innocence for the gentlemen of the press, the opening skirmish in the neverending war between the U.S. military and the media.

The Federal forces began their move on July 16, more than two weeks after the move had been approved. It was neither soon enough nor quick enough to prevent the Confederates from shifting reinforcements in from the Shenandoah Valley, where a too-timid General Patterson had failed in his blocking mission. Gen. Joseph Johnston's troops traveled fifty-five miles by foot and rail to the junction at Manassas, leaving the day after the Federals began their march into the Virginia countryside.

However, our present focus is not the strategy or battlefield tactics of Bull Run/First Manassas—that story has been told in exquisite detail in hundreds of books. Our focus is on the baptism of American war correspondence, and on the greatest war correspondent of the day, and how he came to be known, ever after, as "Bull Run Russell."

As the army began streaming out of Alexandria, William Howard Russell bumped into General McDowell, who said: "You are aware I have advanced? No! Well, you have just come in time, and I shall be happy, indeed, to take you with me." Russell, having just returned to Washington and still working over his notes, was not quite ready. McDowell assured him that he would be welcome, anytime. "I have made arrangements for the correspondents of our papers to take the field under certain regulations," he said, adding with what he must have assumed was a touch of whimsy, "and I have suggested to them they should wear a white uniform, to indicate the purity of their character." [1]

"Certain regulations" included a suggestion that the reporters stay together, as a group, out of the way. Some did—few, if any, costumed in white. More than two dozen were observing on the Union side, and perhaps two among them had ever seen a battle: Henry Raymond of the *Times*, in the 1859 Austro-Italian War, and the *Post*'s Richard McCormick in the Crimea. To the rest of the Northern specials, it was an excursion, a lark. As E. C. Stedman of the *World* wrote to his wife on July 17, 1861: "We had a perfectly magnificent time to-day. I never enjoyed a day so much in my life. Was in the van throughout, at the head of the army, and it was exciting and dramatic beyond measure." [2]

The July 18 letter of "G. P. R." to the Boston *Transcript* affirmed the honor: "It was a glorious sight, and a rarely interesting privilege, to witness the moving of the advance of General McDowell's vast column of troops towards the 'land o' Dixie,' on Wednesday morning [July 17]; and I send you the following details, devoid of all attempts at sensation news, directly from the seat of war. . . ." Among those details:

> The troops on foot started off as joyfully as if they were bound upon a New England picnic, or a clambake; and not the slightest exhibition of fear or uneasiness, even, as to what might possibly be in store for the brave fellows, (thus really setting out upon an expedition from which, in all human probability, hundreds of them will never return!) seemed for an instant to occupy any part of their thoughts or their anticipations.

A cannon shot warned the rebels of the Federal advance on Fairfax, and, as G. P. R. noted, "before ten o'clock the town of Fairfax was evacuated by the cowardly rascals, who fled. . . ."

The *Herald*'s first report was in agreement: "The enemy ran as soon as the first shot was fired. . . . tangible evidence of the hurry in which the rebels had retreated was found, in the shape of a large number of blankets, pistols, guns, canteens, &c., &c., that had been indiscriminately thrown away, and were immediately appropriated by our soldiers." Henry Raymond ("H. J. R.") sent a note to the *Times*: "The discovery of these abandoned camps afforded a splendid opportunity for our troops to replenish their slender stock of camp furniture. They rushed to the plunder with a degree of enthusiasm which I only hope will be equaled when they come to fight." [3]

Some troops also rushed to break into the homes of local folk, prompting an appalled General McDowell to issue General Order 18: "It is with the deepest mortification the general commanding finds it necessary to reiterate his orders for the preservation of . . . property. . . ." [4]

The ease with which the Federals moved into Fairfax encouraged the *Tribune*'s editors to assert, "We do not believe that the thousands forced into the rebel armies by conscription or terror of mob violence will choose to sacrifice their lives for a cause they abhor." [5]

The first real contact came on July 18, another skirmish elevated to the status of a battle, with at least one newspaper—the New Orleans *Picayune*, a bit tardy on July 28—setting Yankee casualties between four and five thousand. The actual tally: sixty-three for the Confederates, perhaps double that for the Federals.

G. P. R.'s July 18 report in the Boston *Transcript* concluded:

The fever's up, and our bold troops ask only to be led, and listen earnestly for the thrilling order—"forward!" . . . There will be no yielding, no parley, no compromises now. The march is *onward*, and the willing host who have thus taken their lives in their hands for liberty, the Constitution, and the laws, will halt no more, it is believed, until the back of this unholy rebellion is effectually broken. They meet the issue manfully, cheerfully, boldly, and their watchwords now are—
"God and the Right!
Richmond, and Victory!"

Secretary of War Simon Cameron, a former Pennsylvania printer and newspaper publisher, watched out for the interests of his friends. On July 20, he penned a brief note to McDowell, "The young gentleman who hands you this is connected with Forney's *Press* in Philadelphia. . . .[I] will esteem it a personal favor if your will turn him over to one of the Brigadiers, who will extend to him the hospitalities of his military family. You will also direct the quartermaster to furnish Mr. Young a horse and equipments." John Russell Young was twenty. McDowell handed him off to a brigadier. [6]

That night—the eve of the battle–Henry Raymond was caught up in the romance. "This is one of the most beautiful nights that the imagination can conceive," he wrote for the *Times*.

The sky is perfectly clear, the moon is full and bright, and the air as still as if it were not within a few hours to be disturbed by the roar of cannon and the shouts of contending men. . . . the scene . . . seemed a picture of enchantment. The bright moon cast the woods which bound the field into deep shadows, through which the camp-fires shed a clear and brilliant glow. On the extreme right, in the neighborhood of the Fire Zouaves, a party were singing the "Star-Spangled Banner," and from the left rose the sweet strains of a magnificent band, intermingling operatic airs . . . with the patriotic bursts of "Hail Columbia" and "Yankee Doodle.". . . [7]

War, as romance—and spectator sport. Sunday morning dawned bright and clear and warm, and a stream of civilian buggies headed from Washington toward Manassas, many bearing members of Congress demonstrating their conscientious stewardship of the national interest, accompanied by socially prominent ladies out for a lark.

The night before, Russell had arranged his own transportation, in the form of a horse, buggy, and driver, with a saddle horse and rider to follow along. By that time, the faint rumble of artillery could be heard in the distance. Rumors of a great battle were flying around Washington, and the livery stable operators were suddenly reluctant to risk their stock-in-trade to the vagaries of war. Russell tried to parse the conflicting reports: "I can assure you, Sir," he was told by one passing gentleman, "that the troops had fifteen hundred killed and wounded; I know it." He went off to army headquarters and there was told by General Scott's aide that General Mc-Dowell's official report gave six killed and thirty-seven wounded. The livery keepers were happier with the higher figures, as Russell later noted, because "the greater number of *hors de combat* the higher the tariff for the hire of quadrupeds . . . I had to enter into an agreement with the owner to pay him for horses and buggy if they were captured or injured by the enemy." [8] The liveryman requested no indemnity against injury to the driver or the boy who rode the saddle horse.

Russell had invited Frederick Warre, secretary to the British ministry, to join him, although their planned predawn start was delayed by Mr. Warre's difficulty with early rising. They were on the road before nine o'clock, however, and soon ran into a regiment headed east, away from the battle. The men all seemed to be in good spirits, but with a puzzling air that Russell could not understand. He asked an officer "Where are your men going, sir?"

"Well, we're going home, sir, I reckon, to Pennsylvania."

"I suppose there is severe work going on behind you, judging from the firing?"

"Well, I reckon, sir, there is." He paused and then added, by way of explanation, "We're going home because the men's time is up. We've had three months of work."

Russell wondered "on the feelings of a General who sees half a brigade walk quietly away on the very morning of an action . . . because the letter of their engagement bound them no further." [8]

Russell's landlady had prepared a light lunch—chicken sandwiches—and Russell added a flask of brandy and a bottle of Bordeaux. It was lunch-time when they arrived at Centreville; they stopped to feed the horses, and themselves as well. "On a hill beside me," Russell noted in the *Diary*, "there was a crowd of civilians. . . . A few officers and some soldiers, who had straggled from the regiments in reserve, moved about among the spectators, and pretended to explain the movements of the troops below, of which they were profoundly ignorant. . . . The spectators were all excited, and a lady with an opera-glass who was near me was quite beside herself when an unusually heavy discharge roused the current in her blood—'That is splendid. Oh, my! Is that not first-rate? I guess we will be in Richmond this time to-morrow.'"

An officer rode up, waving his cap and shouting at the top of his voice, "We've whipped them on all points." Russell sat back and took a nap. At not quite three o'clock, Mr. Warre, the driver, and the boy returned to Washington. The world's leading war correspondent mounted the saddle horse and set forth to find the war. [9]

To this point, things were going very well for the Federals; Beauregard almost ordered a retreat. At three thirty, the *Herald*'s William Shaw sent the following from the nearest telegraph station: "Hudson, Herald—I am en route to Washington with details of a great battle. We have carried the day. The rebels accepted battle in strength, but are totally routed. . . ." McDowell dispatched a report for General Scott: "The enemy accepted battle in full force. A great battle was fought and a victory won. The rout of the enemy was complete." The censor's office in Washington released McDowell's message to the national wires at 5:30 P.M. [10]

In New York, the "extras" hit the streets and newsboys hailed a great victory. A headline in the *Herald* celebrated the "HEROISM OF THE UNION FORCES . . . THEY KNOW NO SUCH WORD AS FAIL." The *Tribune* reported:

A great battle was fought yesterday at Bull's Run. . . . The Rebels had every advantage—position, numbers, and perfect knowledge of the ground over which the Unionists advanced to engage them. Yet all did not avail against the enthusiasm and well-directed valor of the national forces. The Rebel Batteries were ultimately silenced, and their ranks forced back inch by inch, until they were driven from Bull's Run, leaving their dead on the field and the National troops undisputed victors. . . . [11]

Henry Raymond sent a hasty wire to New York, and the coverage in the *Times* was every bit as wrong as that in the *Herald* and the *Tribune*:

CRUSHING REBELLION
The Greatest Battle Ever Fought
on this Continent

The Whole Rebel Army of
Manassas Engaged
Fearful Carnage on Both Sides

The Rebels Routed and Driven
Behind the Manassas Lines

The report was filled with bits and pieces, some from Raymond in the field, some from Washington. The copy admitted to some confusion, but was unequivocal in celebrating a victory:

This morning a general engagement took place along the entire line. After a terrific fight, with great slaughter on both sides, each and every battery was taken. . . . This news is corroborated by dispatches now before President Lincoln, Gen Scott and Gen Mansfield. Gen Mansfield says the enemy's guns and equipment are in the hands of our forces.
Now on to Richmond! [12]

At Manassas, however, the world had turned upside down. Beauregard pushed forward, the Federals fell back, and in many Federal units, order and discipline were shattered and retreat became a rout. This was the scene that greeted Russell as he approached the battlefield:

Suddenly there arose a tumult in front of me at a small bridge across the road, and then I perceived the drivers of a set of wagons with the horses turned towards me, who were endeavoring to force their way against the stream of vehicles setting in the other direction. By the side of the new set of wagons there were a number of commissariat men and soldiers, whom at first sight I took to be the baggage guard. They looked excited and alarmed, and were running by the side of the horses—in front the dust quite obscured the view. At the bridge the currents met in wild disorder. "Turn back! Retreat!" shouted the men from the front, "We're whipped, we're whipped!" They cursed and tugged at the horses' heads, and struggled with frenzy to get past. Running by me on foot was a man with the shoulder-straps of an officer. "Pray what is the matter, sir?" "It means we're pretty badly whipped, and that's a fact," he blurted out in puffs, and continued his career. I observed that he carried no sword. The teamsters of the advancing wagons now caught up the cry. "Turn back—turn your horses" was the shout up the whole line, and, backing, plunging, rearing, and kicking, the horses which had been proceeding down the road reversed front and went off towards Centreville. Those behind them went madly rushing on, the drivers being quite indifferent whether glory or disgrace led the way, provided they could find it. [13]

The World—when the press reports would later catch up with reality—would tell much the same story: "The retreat, the panic, the hideous headlong confusion, were now beyond a hope. . . . I saw officers with leaves and eagles on their shoulder-straps, majors and colonels, who had deserted their commands, pass me galloping as if for dear life." The Tribune's follow-on was every bit as critical: "From the distant hills, our troops, disorganized, scattered, pallid with a terror which had not just cause, came pouring in among us, trampling down some, and spreading the contagion of their fear among all. . . . Every impediment to flight was cast aside. Rifles, bayonets, pistols, haversacks, cartridge-boxes, canteens, blankets, belts, and overcoats lined the road. . . . All was lost to that American army, even its honor." [14]

There are reports—enough of them to be credible—that civilian observers, including some reporters and some members of Congress, tried to intervene. Uriah Painter of the Philadelphia Inquirer described the scene as Stedman of the World grabbed the flag of a Massachusetts outfit, "waving it over him and pleading for the men to rally around him but it was in vain," and with the Herald's Villard "trying to pacify the men, telling them it was only a panic." The World reported that, with two exceptions, "all efforts made to check the panic . . . were confined to civilians. I saw a man in citizen's dress, who had thrown off his coat, seized a musket, and was trying to rally the soldiers who came by at the point of a bayonet." When asked by the reporter, he gave his name as "Washburne . . . the member by that name from Illinois. The Hon. Mr. Kellogg made a similar effort." [15]

Russell, by his own account, ". . . ventured to speak to some officers whom I overtook, and said, 'If these runaways are not stopped the whole of the posts and pickets into Washington will fly also!' One of them, without saying a word, spurred his horse and dashed out in front. I do not know whether he ordered the movement or not, but the van of the fugitives was now suddenly checked. . . ." A week or so after the battle, an army correspondent of the Cincinnati *Daily Gazette* took exception to those reports: "Among the humorous phases of the affair are the 'you-tickle-me-and-I'll-tickle-you' statements made by some of these redoubtable individuals, as to the strenuous efforts of each other and certain Senators and Congressmen to rally the retreating troops. The idea of panic struck troops rallying at the appeals of gentlemen in white linen coats whom they never saw before is rather amusing to say the least." [16]

About six o'clock in the evening, news of the panic reached official Washington. Secretary of State Seward passed the word, "Tell no one," and the War Department gave the same guidance to the chief censor. When the *Herald*'s Shaw reached the Washington telegraph office about eight o'clock, unaware of the debacle behind him, he expanded his initial bulletin, to the effect, "the rebels are flying." The censor let it pass. The Associated Press had prepared a victory dispatch based on the initial reports; conflicting information that arrived about nine o'clock was tacked on to the end of the copy. The censor passed the original story and deleted the addition. The Washington bureau chief of the *World* was picking up details from haggard troops rushing back into the city. The censor allowed him to make an ambiguous release: "There are ten thousand rumors prevailing . . . of such a contradictory character that it would be idle to transmit them." [17]

Henry Raymond, who had been caught up in the melee soon after filing his own "victory" announcement, reached the capital about midnight. When he tried to file a correction, the censor declined. Raymond asked, what about the wrong, the "victory" dispatches? "It is too late," the censor replied, "to countermand dispatches already sent," and closed the office for the night. [18]

The other correspondents straggled in from the field, where they had been threatened by friend and foe alike, assaulted by thunderstorms, and undone by the first sight of mangled dead and wounded. "It was a strange ride through a country now still as death," Russell wrote, "the white road shining like a river in the moonlight, the trees black as ebony in the shade; now and then a figure flitting by into the forest or across the road—frightened friend or lurking foe, who could say?" [19]

Painter of the *Inquirer* and Stedman of the *World* arrived together, about five o'clock in the morning. They planned to take the morning train north to Philadelphia and New York, respectively, that they might deliver their copy without benefit of the censor's hand. Painter caught the train, but Stedman, who had collapsed into bed, slept a solid twelve hours. He ended up on the night train instead, writing his piece as he traveled northward through the night, wondering if he would still have a job after having been so roundly beaten by the competition,.

In the meantime, the Associated Press had taken advantage of the loophole in the censorship scheme and arranged for the story to be published in the Monday morning *National Republican*. When the telegraph office reopened, it was besieged by reporters. The censor on duty asked for guidance. The new stories were released.

Henry Villard filed a six-hundred-word dispatch, and the *Herald* had an extra on the streets of New York within the hour—an extra that the public regarded for some time as a fraud. The *Herald* had not yet recovered from its reputation as a Southern sympathizer and, in fact, when Villard's extended treatment was received later in the day, the editors removed comments that were highly critical of the performance of some New York regiments. The *Herald* wanted no more angry crowds at the doorstep.

When Painter reached the *Inquirer* office in Philadelphia, his editors were puzzled: why was he not on the way to Richmond? The explanation came easily, and to the *Inquirer* goes credit for publishing the first complete account of the battle—but the paper then had to deal with its own disbelieving, angry crowds.

The London *Times* man in New York, Bancroft Davis, described the atmosphere in that city in his letter of July 23:

> The morning papers have been issued in the usual "sensation" style, with half a column of the largest type, giving the details of a supposed victory over General Beauregard, and nine-tenths of New York, not taking the trouble to read the details with care, believed it. About 11 o'clock came the first news of defeat in the form of a telegram from Washington, to the effect that General M'Dowell was retreating on Washington in good order. By common consent all business was suspended, men gathered in crowds about the various newspaper offices, and as fast as news was received from Washington "extras" were issued and short condensed bulletins were posted.

Davis added a reasonable conjecture: "Not a man among the multitude that congregated about the corners of the streets and stood patiently at the newspaper offices for hours thought of yielding or dreamt of peace; or, if he did, he kept his thoughts and dreams to himself."

Over at the *World*, Stedman's editors were so delighted with his story that they forgave him for being tardy and offered this editorial salute:

Our special correspondent's graphic account of the Battle of Manassas which we published yesterday morning was the most complete and comprehensive description of that affair, by an eye witness, from the beginning of the march, through all the varying fortunes of the day to the end of the retreat which the public had had. . . .

We had previously published the extended and often conflicting telegraphic accounts of the occurrences of the day, but the demand for this authentic and clear narrative was so great that our ten-cylinder press running from morning til night was unable fully to supply it.

His letter is reprinted in our weekly and semiweekly editions and may be had singly, in wrappers, or by the hundred at the counter. [20]

The Confederate side was supported by fewer reporters, but had a better story to tell: "Glory to God in the highest!" began the account in the Savannah *Republican*. "A great battle has been fought and a victory won!" [21]

The Confederate war department had issued passes to perhaps thirty reporters, each of whom, according to the Mobile *Register*, was required to sign a rather peculiar pledge: "upon his honor as a man that he will not communicate in writing or verbally for publication *any fact ascertained by him*." However, as the day of battle approached, General Beauregard had ordered that all civilians not resident in the area clear at least four miles from his camp, blocked the use of the telegraph for any "private" messages, and laid an embargo "on the railroad, so far as the passage of citizens is concerned, the entire services of the road being necessary for the transportation of men and munitions of war." [22] A handful of reporters already in the area (or who managed to slip through) headed toward the battlefield early Sunday morning, totally unprepared. Some of them would walk as many as twenty miles through that hot July day, so naïve that they had only one cracker between them and no other provisions.

Southern reports of the key element of the day were just as clear as those of the North. The New Orleans *True Delta* exulted, "Our men were perfectly frantic. Regiment after regiment ran up the hill in the wild excitement of pursuit. They were only stopped about two miles this side of Centreville by Gen. Bonham, who saw, I presume, that in the confusion they might be led into a trap. The men shouted, 'to Washington,' 'to Baltimore,' &c &c, and I believe, if left to themselves they would have neared the first point, for the enemy were in perfect rout." The New Orleans *Picayune* agreed: "Such a rout of such an army—so large, so equipped, and so commanded—was never known before in the wars on this continent. . . . a mighty body of disciplined men converted into a panic-stricken mob.. . ." [23]

Much of the Southern press thought that the war was now over; Forsyth's Mobile *Register* invoked a comparison with the English defeat of the Spanish armada. Others returned to the "on to Washington" theme—a theme that played well in newspapers but not in the field, where Beauregard well understood the shortcomings of his under-equipped army.

Southern reporting carried more than its share of errors, however, including gross exaggerations of the number of troops that had been engaged, and in the number of casualties on both sides. Under the rubric of "official information" from the Confederate government, the newspapers bragged of 15,000 Confederates whipping 35,000 Yankees and inflicting 15,000 casualties with as few as 1,500 killed, wounded, and missing on their own side. "The enemy fought bravely and well," admitted the Charleston *Courier*, "but their valor could not resist the courage of men under the inspiration of a grand and holy cause, and they have been utterly routed by half their number." [24] Actual casualties were about equal: 625 Confederates were killed or died of wounds, somewhat fewer than 1,400 were otherwise wounded; for the Union, 625 were killed or died of wounds, 950 otherwise wounded, and 1,200 were captured. The captured included at least one of the sight-seeing congressmen, Alfred Ely. In a very real sense, he was the first politician to make good on the "Forward to Richmond" scheme, as he was held prisoner there until being released in December.

President Jefferson Davis arrived at Manassas just in time to view the Federal retreat; some early accounts gave him more credit than he deserved. The New Orleans *Crescent* cheered, "That the President of the Confederate States was himself in the thickest of the fight, exposed to all the perils of the battle-field, is another circumstance that adds to the joy of our triumph, and swells our triumphant note of exultation." [25] The Richmond *Dispatch* gave Davis full credit for the victory. General Beauregard, we may presume, was not pleased, but, according to Richmond journalist Edward Pollard (of the *Examiner*), the president never forgave Beauregard for winning the battle before he himself had arrived. The *Dispatch* quickly recovered, and apologized, in effect, for error:

No newspaper does or can be expected to vouch for the entire accuracy of every item that appears in its columns. Its conductors have no power to summon their informants before them, and put them on oath, subject to the pains and penalties of perjury. The most they are bound to do is to sift as fairly and accurately as they can the mass of matter before them and conscientiously suppress what they honestly believe to be untrue in itself or unjust to any individual. This duty they perform, as far as we know, about as honestly as the world at large discharges any of its obligations. . . . The real wonder is that so many of the multitudinous items of information in a daily journal should be as correct as they are. [26]

The South had bragging rights, however, and out of the newspaper accounts was to come perhaps the most lasting result of the battle: the nicknaming of Thomas J. Jackson. As reported in the Charleston *Mercury*, a mortally wounded Lt. Col. Barnard Bee, his brigade reduced to a handful, had ridden up to General Jackson to report that his troops were being beaten back. Jackson, so the story went, replied, "Sir, we'll give them the bayonet," whereupon Bee returned to rally his troops with the cry, "There is Jackson standing like a stone wall. Let us determine to die here, and we will conquer. Follow me." The London *Times* had it, "Look at Jackson's men; they stand like a stone wall!" Or, according to *The Civil War Dictionary*, he may have said, "Yonder stands Jackson like a stone wall; let's go to his assistance." [27]

And the story followed Jackson into history, although there have been at least two more versions. One, from the Boston *Journal*, may be discarded: "Gen. Jackson is admittedly the best and bravest commander in the rebel service. His sobriquet 'Stonewall' is said to have been given him after the battle of Bull Run. During that affair Gen. Lee asked him 'if his brigade had not better retire under the heavy fire they were sustaining.' 'No, sir,' said Gen. Jackson, 'we will stand here like a stonewall!'" [28]. The other version, unsubstantiated but credible, holds that Bee's comment was more to the effect that Jackson was standing "like a stone wall" rather than coming to the aid of his brigade, then under heavy attack. In any event, Bee's reward was a posthumous promotion to brigadier general.

William Howard Russell was about to be enshrined in the history of the American Civil War as well, but in less admiring fashion. On his return from the battlefield, he, too, at first had collapsed into sleep. When he arose, he sat down and set forth "to give an account—not of the action of yesterday, but of what I saw with my own eyes. . . ." He acknowledged that he had not seen the battle, only the retreat, but he had seen enough.

Now, he wrote, "Washington . . . is crowded with soldiers without officers, who have fled from Centreville, and with 'three months' men,' who are going home. . . . The streets, in spite of the rain, are crowded with people with anxious faces, and groups of wavering politicians are assembled at the corners, in the hotel passages, and the bars." Washington, he asserted, was wide open to capture, and unless the North put "its best men into the battle . . . she will inevitably fall before the energy, the personal hatred, and the superior fighting powers of her antagonist." Then, displaying a constitutional inability to remain aloof, he took a very broad swing at the Northern press:

> In my letters, as in my conversation, I have endeavored to show that the task which the Unionists have set themselves is one of no ordinary difficulty, but in the state of arrogance and supercilious confidence, either real or affected to conceal a sense of weakness, one might as well have preached to the Pyramid of Cheops. Indeed, one may form some notion of the condition of the public mind by observing that journals conducted avowedly by men of disgraceful personal character—the bewhipped and be-kicked and unrecognized pariahs of society in New York are, nevertheless, in the very midst of repulse and defeat, permitted to indulge in ridiculous rhodomontade towards the nations of Europe, and to move our laughter by impotently malignant attacks on "our rotten old monarchy," while the stones of their brand new republic are tumbling about their ears. It will be amusing to observe the change of tone, for we can afford to observe and to be amused at the same time. [29]

Finished, he sent his letter off to New York to catch a ship for England, and went on about his business of observing the American scene. He had lit the fuse on a bomb that would later blow him out of America.

The Northern newspapers began steering a convoluted course, finding excuses on the one hand and villains on the other, in an unresolved game of scapegoating. There must be *reasons* for the defeat. There was talk of the damage done by Confederate "masked batteries"—artillery that remained hidden behind earthworks or some natural feature until brought into action—as if this were an underhanded form of warfare; how could the "chivalry" be so unchivalrous? The major ingredient, however, was the supposition that the Federals were greatly outnumbered. New York *Tribune*: "In numbers and in tactics the enemy proved themselves our superiors." *World*: "the enemy's forces had been largely underrated, and nearly doubled our own in number. . . ." New York *Evening Post*: the rebels had "between eighty-five and ninety thousand men to oppose our troops, which number less than fifty thousand." Providence *Journal*: "Overwhelming numbers have repulsed our army, after it had conquered an equal force entrenched behind earthworks and masked batteries." [30]

The Boston *Journal* played Pollyanna: "In the valor of our outnumbered and exposed troops, we see assurances which immeasurably overshadow the incidental mishap which followed." The *World* was less sanguine: ". . . a grand army, retreating before superior numbers, was never more disgracefully disrupted, and blotted, as it were, out of existence in a single day. This is the truth, and why should it not be recorded?"[31]

As for "truth," McDowell had 35,000 men; Beauregard had 22,000, reinforced by Johnston's 12,000. Thus, despite the newsmen's claims of "overpowering" force, the Federals actually outnumbered the rebels.

Dana set down an editorial for the *Tribune*, demanding resignation of the entire cabinet, as if *they* were responsible. Elsewhere, the role of the press—especially the *Tribune*—came under bitter scrutiny. John Russell Young of the Philadelphia *Press* offered perhaps the most balanced appraisal: "We have sent into Virginia the best appointed division of our Grand Army and we have fought the greatest battle ever fought on this continent, and we have not only been beaten, but our army has been routed and many of its best regiments wholly demoralized. The narrative of this disaster will be my duty; you may make your own conclusions and solve the terrible political problem it presents to the American people. . . ." He summarized, with amazing insight for a twenty-year-old:

> The causes of our defeat appear to be these: a premature advance on the enemy without sufficient force, which may be attributed to the clamors of politicians and newspapers like the New York *Tribune*; the negligence of General Patterson in not intercepting General Johnston at Winchester and preventing him from joining Beauregard at Manassas; the want of an efficient force of artillery to answer their masked batteries; the inefficiency of many of the officers; the want of proper discipline among the volunteers, and the general panic which seized upon our forces in the latter part of the action. [32]

Judicious appraisals came from other papers. The Boston *Post* noted that ". . . all along, here at the North, there has been a continuous deprecation of the numbers, the resources, and the quality of the Confederate army; and the press that have kept on this strain, especially the sensation press of New York, have been insanely urging a forward movement to Richmond. . . . The result is before the astounded country." [33] *Harper's Weekly* offered:

If we are true to ourselves, the disaster of the 21st July will prove a benefit rather than an injury. It will teach us in the first place, and not only us, but those also who have in charge the national interests at this crisis, that this war must be prosecuted on scientific principles, and that popular clamor must not be suffered to override the dictates of experience and the rules of strategy. We have the best evidence to prove that the march to Bull Run, and the fight there, were both undertaken against the judgement of Lieutenant General Scott, and solely in deference to the popular craving for action which owed its origin and main virulence to the New York Tribune. The wretched result must serve as a warning for the future. [34]

Fitz-Henry Warren sent a letter to Greeley, apologized, resigned, and went off to the war; he became a brigade commander. Greeley did not print the letter, but for the *Tribune* of July 24 tried to escape responsibility for the disaster, while at the same time affirming responsibility for anything and everything that appeared in his newspaper. It would have been a neat trick.

An individual's griefs or wrongs may be of little account to others; but when the gravest public interests are imperiled through personal attacks and the coarsest implications of base motives, the assailed, however humble, owes duties to others which can not be disregarded. . . .

I am charged with what is called "opposing the administration . . ." and various paragraphs which have from time to time appeared in the Tribune are quoted to sustain this inculpation. The simple fact that not one of these paragraphs was either written or in any wise suggested by me suffices for that charge. . . . It is true that I hold and have urged that this war can not, must not, be a long one; that it must be prosecuted with the utmost energy, promptness and vigor, or it will prove a failure. . . . But the watchword, "Forward to Richmond," is not mine. . . . So with regard to the late article urging a change in the Cabinet. . . .

I wish to be distinctly understood as not seeking to be relieved from any responsibility for urging the advance of the Union grand army into Virginia. . . . I thought that that army, one hundred thousand strong, might have been in the rebel capital on or before the twentieth instant. . . . And now, if any one imagine that I, or any one connected with the Tribune, ever commanded or imagined such strategy as the launching of barely thirty thousand . . . against ninety thousand rebels enveloped in a labyrinth of strong entrenchments and unreconnoitered masked batteries, then demonstration would be lost in his closed ear. . . .

If I am needed as a scapegoat for all the military blunders of the last month, so be it. Individuals must die that the nation may live. If I can serve her best in that capacity, I do not shrink from the ordeal.

Henceforth I bar all criticism in these columns on army movements. . . . Henceforth it shall be the Tribune's sole vocation to rouse and animate the American people for the terrible ordeal which has befallen them. . . .

The journal which is made the conduit of the most violent of these personal assaults on me attributes the course of the Tribune to resentment "against those who have ever committed the inexplicable offense of thwarting Mr. Greeley's raging and unsatiated thirst of office."

I think this justifies me in saying that there is no office in the gift of the government or of the people which I either hope, wish or expect ever to hold. . . .

Now let the wolves howl on . . . .

The Baltimore *American* was reasonably restrained: "'Onward to Richmond!' has been the senseless battle-cry which has stunned the ears of the nation for weeks past, and the authorities at Washington may consider themselves fortunate that the case for them is no worse." [35]

Russell tried a light touch: "The battle having been duly fought and lost, the Federals are employing their minds to find out why it was fought at all. The convulsions into which the New York press have been thrown by the inquiry, resemble those produced on a dead frog by the wire of Galvani. 'Who cried 'On to Richmond?' *'Not I, 'pon my honor. It was shouted out by some one in my house, but I don't know who. I never gave him authority. I won't shout anything any more.' 'Who urged general Scott to fight the battle, and never gave anybody any peace till he was ordered to do it?' 'Nobody!' 'It was that other fellow' 'Please, sir, it wasn't me.'"* [36]

But the Albany *Evening Journal* was brutal: "With a presumption and insolence unheard of, a leading journal, assuming command of the army, issued and reiterated the order, 'On to Richmond.' . . . 'The rebels will not fight!' 'The cowards will run!' &c., &c., appeared in flaming capitals over flash paragraphs. The whole popular mind was swayed by these frenzied appeals. A movement upon Manassas was universally and blindly demanded. . . . The New York *Tribune* was educating millions to distrust the wisdom of the administration and the fidelity of the commanding generals. . . . The 'on to Richmond' dictators have added another year to the war, an hundred millions of dollars to its cost, and opened graves for fifteen or twenty thousand more soldiers. . . ." [37]

By July 29, Greeley could stand the howling no longer and had taken to his bed, feverish, almost deranged. He wrote to the president "in the strictest confidence, and . . . for your eye alone" proposing a truce with the Confederacy:

> If the Union is irrevocably gone, an armistice for thirty, sixty, ninety, one hundred and twenty days, better still for a year, ought at once to be proposed with a view to a peaceful adjustment. . . . It is best for the country and for mankind that we make peace with the rebels at once, and on their own terms, do not shrink even from that. . . . [38]

He signed the letter, "Yours, in the depth of bitterness," and thrashed about in the throes of what his doctor diagnosed as "brain fever." Rationality returned in mid-August, and Greeley set about trying to rebuild the reputation of his paper. Circulation had fallen; the daily average was only about half that of the *Herald*, and Greeley suspended the Sunday edition for lack of advertising. The *Herald*, which was by then running some editions of twelve pages, boasted, "We can't resist poking our slow coach contemporaries in the ribs, now and then, in contrasting their scanty columns of subscriptions and advertising with our heavy battalions." [39]

Fitz-Henry Warren finally entered the debate. In a letter published in the St. Louis *Republican* on August 8, he denied creating the phrase "Forward to Richmond" and defended his efforts to bring rationality to the preparations—or, as he saw it, the lack thereof—for war:

> There was no order and no system. Troops came in, and marched in review before the President, and went supperless to bed. They were stowed away in public buildings and private halls, with no regard to health or the modified comfort of a soldier's life. They were neither instructed in the art of war nor made to understand the discipline of the camp. . . . But what shall I say of sending 25,000 men into the massacre of Bull Run? . . . No one knew the force of the position. There was no reconnaissance. Men marched into bloody graves as they walked into the doors of the homestead. Batteries blazed out at their feet, of which none but the enemy had the slightest knowledge. One half of the men engaged had nothing to eat after supper of the night previous. Many of them marched at double-quick for ten miles, and were under fire for hour after hour, so exhausted by hunger that they could hardly stand. . . . Do you wish more of this damning testimony to imbecility? If you do, you can have it. [40]

He had a point, and was not alone. Even the *Tribune* had admitted as much, back on July 23: "The majority of our generals were ignorant of their duty, and incapable of performing it even when it was laid down before them." The *World* agreed: ". . . many of our leaders displayed a lamentable want of military knowledge. There was little real generalship in the field. . . ." So did the Baltimore *American*: "Without assuming any of that profound knowledge of strategy, and of military matters general, which has made the New York major-general of the printing-offices so famous, it strikes us that such leadership as has thus been exhibited is not what soldiers would expect. . . ." [41]

The Albany *Evening Journal* suggested that "Effective troops, however excellent the material, cannot be found in workshops, the cornfields, or the cities. They must have military training, without which every 'On to Richmond' movement will prove a failure." [42]

Harper's Weekly cited a problem not otherwise much discussed:

> The detailed accounts of the retreat from Bull Run prove that a very large proportion of our militia officers failed in their duty on that occasion. This is no matter of surprise. In selecting company and even field officers, our militiamen often attach more weight to wealth and political or social influence than to bravery or soldierly aptitude. Very many commissions are won by intrigue. It was to be expected that they would rather lead than check a panic. This radical flaw in our military system must be corrected. Bull Run must rid us of cowardly or imbecile colonels, majors and captains. Better offend a thousand ambitious candidates for military rank than have another flight led by colonels, majors and captains. [43]

To the Manchester (England) *Examiner*, "The great question is, Whom shall we hang? Of course a victim will be found, even if justice itself expires in the effort. . . . The gentleman who is likeliest to figure as culprit-in-chief is Gen. Patterson, who commanded the troops at Harper's Ferry. . . . We trust our Northern friends will not copy the Carthaginians, by crucifying a general just because he is unsuccessful." [44]

It was not, however, General Patterson who took the fall—he was simply released from active duty. McDowell became the villain, as most Northern newspapers now called for new leadership. The Baltimore *American*: "It is evident enough, from proofs afforded on all hands, that in the late contest, the Federal troops may be said to have been without a general, in fact." The *World*: "We must discover the executive leader whose genius shall oppose new modes of subduing a novel, and thus far successful, method of warfare, and whose alert action shall carry his devices into resistless effect." [45]

Well, there was nothing "novel" about the forces or tactics at Bull Run; the "masked battery" ploy simply had the newspapers confused.

However, the desired "executive leader" was brought forward a few days later. McDowell was replaced on July 27 by George Brinton McClellan, West Point Class of 1846. McClellan left the army in 1857 to accept appointments, first, with the Illinois Central Railroad and, then, in 1860, as president of the Ohio & Mississippi. According to comment passed on to Russell and published in his *Diary*, McClellan the railroad executive seemed at times to be more interested in playing soldier, covering the floor of his Illinois Central office with military maps as he followed the course of the Franco-Austrian War (1859).

Back in the army in 1861, McClellan had achieved enough success in operations in western Virginia in June to mark him as the next commanding general. One newspaper, possibly the *Tribune*, dubbed the thirty-five-year-old McClellan "the young Napoleon," and the name, poetic but a bit inaccurate, caught the public fancy. No one seemed to care that McClellan was already seven years older than Napoleon had been when he first made his mark. In truth, by the time Napoleon was thirty-five, he was emperor of France.

General McClellan got off to a good start with the press. Within a week, he struck a gentleman's agreement with twelve newspapermen in behalf of "all newspapers in the loyal states" to refrain from publishing "either as editorial or correspondence, any description, from any point of view, of any matter that might furnish aid and comfort to the enemy." Someone suggested "that the pictorial papers should be severely talked to for giving representations of our military works and operations." As reported in the Washington *Star*, McClellan "seemed to think that they could be safely left alone, as quite as likely to confound as to instruct the enemy." [46]

The guidance may have seemed like a good idea, but the guidelines were too broad. Few newsmen ever agreed with McClellan's idea of what was or was not suitable matter and the gentleman's agreement did not bind those newspapers that were not represented at the meeting and had not, therefore, agreed.

The War Department favored a more direct approach. On August 26, it took a fifty-five-year-old article of war, which provided penalties up to and including death for passing military information to an enemy, and stretched it to cover information printed in newspapers. The result was published as General Order 67:

> By the fifty-seventh article of the act of Congress entitled "An act for establishing rules and articles for the government of the armies of the United States, approved April 10, 1806, holding correspondence with or giving intelligence to the enemy, either directly or indirectly," is made punishable by death, or such other punishment as

shall be ordered by the sentence of a court-martial. Public safety requires strict enforcement of this article. It is therefore ordered that all correspondence and communication, verbally or by writing, printing, or telegraphing, respecting operations of the army, or military movements on land or water, or respecting the troops, camps, arsenals, intrenchments, or military affairs, within the several military districts, by which intelligence shall be, directly or indirectly, given to the enemy, without the authority and sanction of the General in command, be, and the same are, absolutely prohibited, and from and after the date of this order persons violating the same will be proceeded against under the fifty-seventh Article of War. [47]

Any intercourse with the enemy was prohibited, unless under a recognized "flag of truce" or by special permit. This was interpreted by the judge advocate general even to include the "Personals" column of the newspapers, whereby citizens North or South would exchange inquiries about such items as the fate of missing relatives.

McClellan's place in then-western Virginia was assumed by Brig. Gen. William Rosecrans, who also asked for cooperation from the journalists. From his headquarters at Clarksburg, he invited "the aid of the press to prevent the enemy from learning, through it, the position, strength, and movements of the troops under his command. Such information is of the greatest service to the enemy, and deprives the commander of our own forces of all the advantages which arise from the secrecy of coordination and surprise. These advantages are constantly enjoyed by the rebels, whose press never betrays them." [48] An exasperated reporter for the Cincinnati *Press* responded:

General Rosecrans is a humorist. . . . General Rosecrans invites. It is time he did something more than invite. He and his superiors and predecessors should have commanded, and enforced obedience, from the day that active operations began. Except the rebellion itself, there has been no engine of mischief to our course, that will bear a comparison to the newspaper press. We have put ourselves to trouble about spies, arrested men that looked suspicious, and let them go again; had visions of individuals that were seeking the rebel posts with letters written in cipher in their pockets, or women with plans of camps hidden away in their stockings, while a thousand newspapers from Boston to St. Louis have been each doing the work of an hundred spies—furnishing daily to the enemy the latest possible information of every movement, the size and position of every regiment and detachment, and the actual or probable policy and designs of its commanding officers. . . . What have the rebels wanted of spies, when they could find daily in the columns of a New York, Philadelphia, or Cincinnati newspaper more reliable intelligence of the very things they wanted to know than hundreds of spies could collect and transmit?

Yet these things have been tolerated; nay, they have been encouraged. Every officer from Commanding General to Corporal, has seemed to think it desirable to have the correspondent of a newspaper at his elbow, to sing his praises, put him right with the public, and be the convenient vehicle to transmit to the world a knowledge of his exploits. The very Commander-in-Chief of the army invites the editor of a New York journal to dinner, and develops to him the entire plan of a campaign, which, on the next day, makes its appearance in print, semi-editorially and semi-officially, without an suspicion of breach of confidence. . . .

The author then sharpened his point: "These things are profitable to the newspapers that have embarked in it. It is *enterprise*; and enterprise always meets with reward. The people want news more than they want victories." [49]

7 / Bull Run Russell

My unpopularity is certainly spreading upwards and downwards
at the same time, and all because I could not turn the battle of
Bull's Run into a Federal victory, because I would not pander to the
vanity of the people, and, least of all, because I will not bow my knee
to the degraded creatures who have made the very name
of a free press odious to honorable men.

—William Howard Russell, *My Diary, North and South,*
September 8, 1861 [1]

RUSSELL'S BULL RUN LETTER slowly moved its way to London, to be published in the *Times* edition of August 6, and then sailed slowly back across the Atlantic. It burst on the American public in the New York *Times* on August 18:

> Let the American journals tell the story their own way [he ended his account]. I have told mine as I know it. . . . if the Federal Government perseveres in its design to make Union by force it may prepare for a struggle the result of which will leave the Union very little to fight for. . . . the records, such as they are, of this extraordinary repulse must command attention. It is impossible to exaggerate their importance. No man can predict the results or pretend to guess at them.

It was not well received. It was one thing for American writers to question the leadership, bravery, and skill of American forces on the field of battle; it was a different thing altogether for a foreigner—of a country itself an enemy within the lifetimes of many Americans—to offer unsolicited (and insufferable) advice, admonition, and criticism during a time of national peril. The London *Morning Star* chided Russell for "deliberately and recklessly pouring vinegar and vitriol into the wounds of the national pride and sensibility. . . . if decency did not restrain us from laughing aloud at the fears of the brave and the errors of the great—surely prudence should teach us not to provoke the bitter resentment of a people of eighteen millions, by scoffing at their momentary humiliation." [2]

Men who had watched the *Times* reporter in action came forward to dispute portions of his testimony. A correspondent for the Chicago *Tribune*, who had "enjoyed the privilege of riding . . . with Mr. Russell," asserted that his version of events "in that portion of his narrative with which we are immediately concerned" did not at all square with observed facts. The *Tribune* man decided that, therefore, Russell had not been a witness to anything. "The truth is probably this: The imaginative correspondent left the battle-ground before any confusion occurred, and when the retrograde movement was ordered. Hearing the exaggerated stories of what came to be a flight, after he got to Washington on Monday, while the excitement was at its height, he wove them into his letter as facts of his own observation. The rout was disgraceful enough . . . but it was not what Mr. Russell describes. As we asserted, he did not see it." [3]

"We have lost the day," another witness wrote for the *Knickerbocker* magazine,

> after a sturdy fight of nine hours against the great odds of a superior force . . . and after an actual victory, have fallen back at the last moment, and a part of one wing, with the wagons and outsiders, have started from the field in a sudden and unaccountable panic. . . . leading the van, was a solitary horseman of different aspect: figure somewhat stout, face round and broad, gentlemanly in aspect, but somewhat flushed and impatient, not to say anxious, in expression. Under a broad-brimmed hat a silk handkerchief screened his neck like a Havelock. He rode a fine horse, still in good condition, and his motto seemed to be "onward"—whether in personal alarm or not it would be impertinent to say. His identity was apparent at a glance. . . .

The writer reported the panic as but a brief event, quickly controlled, but not before Russell had galloped off "to write the worst account of the disorder." [4]

As if some unseen hand had drafted a plan to discredit Russell, a flurry of letters to editors stated and reinforced the same theme: "By his own account," a writer signing his letter "Union" told the Washington *Star*, "he saw nothing of the battle. He arrived at a late hour of the conflict at

Centreville; saw not a shot fired; saw not one solider of the rebel army, horse or foot, but was a spectator merely of the panic and the rout." How dare Mr. Russell, the writer continued, even if his observations were accurate, heap "derogatory comments upon the character of the conflict he did not witness at all, and upon the behavior of our troops, successfully engaged for hours before and up to the time of his arrival. . . ." [5]

"W. E. H" wrote to the Providence *Journal*: "Mr. Russell, who occupies so large a space in the London *Times* in giving a description of 'What he saw' at the repulse of 'Bull Run,' was at no time within three miles of the battle-field, and was at no time within sight or musket-shot of the enemy." [6]

Another letter to the *Journal* expanded on that theme: "As your correspondent, W. E. H. . . . says, 'He was at no time within three miles of the battle-field,' and consequently was no better informed upon the subject than you were, Mr. Editor, sitting in your sanctum. Therefore the earlier struggles of the day—the hard won successes of the Union troops—receive but passing notice, because *he did not see them*—he only saw the rout." [7]

The trickle of ridicule became a torrent; in one forum or another, the world's leading war correspondent became London Stout Russell, Bombast Russell, Dr. Bull Run Russell, the battle was Russell's Run; his reporting became John Bull Russell's Bull Run romance. The whole affair was given a poetic flip:

> Tell the tale of the flight, but no word of the fight;
> How is it—all over the inquiry chimes—
> Only one-half the story fell under his sight?
> But a reason exists why the battle's chief brunt
> Brought no sight to his eye, and no sound to his ear,—
> A strict army rule held him back from the front,
> For the old women always are kept in the rear. [8]

What happened next? You can follow the thread in Russell's diary:

August 22. A general officer said to me, "Of course you will never remain when once all the press are down upon you. I would not take a million dollars to be in your place." "But is what I've written untrue?" "God bless you! Do you know, in this country, if you can get enough of people to start a lie about any man, he would be ruined, if the Evangelists came forward to swear the story was false. There are thousands of people who this moment believe that McDowell, who never tasted anything stronger than a watermelon in all his life, was helplessly drunk at Bull's Run. Mind what I say; they'll run you into a mudhole as sure as you live." [9]

August 26. General Sherman, whom I met for the first time, said, "Mr. Russell, I can endorse every word you wrote; your statements about the battle, which you say you did not witness, are equally correct." [10]

September 1. Took a ride early this morning over the Long Bridge. As I was passing out of the earthwork called a fort on the hill, a dirty German soldier called out from the parapet, "Pull-Run Russell! you shall never write Pull's Runs again," and at the same time cocked his piece, and leveled it at me. I immediately rode round into the fort, the fellow still presenting his firelock, and asked him what he meant, at the same time calling for the sergeant of the guard, who came at once, and, at my request, arrested the man, who recovered arms, and said, "It was a choake-I vant to freeken Pull-Run Russell." However, as his rifle was capped and loaded, and on full cock, with his finger on the trigger, I did not quite see the fun of it. . . . On reflection, I resolved it was best to let the matter drop; the joke might spread. . . . [11]

September 8. Going home, I met Mr. and Mrs. Lincoln in their new open carriage. The President was not so good-humored, nor Mrs. Lincoln so affable, in their return to my salutation as usual. [12]

About two months later, the storm of opprobrium had passed and the New York *Times* sought to put Russell's role in the proper context:

The correspondent of the London Times, who was the historian of the war in the Crimea, and the reporter of the Indian campaign, has become to European ears the great chronicler of a mightier event— the American Rebellion. As a popular historian, he is himself a public, if not a historic character. The importance of the position he now occupies can hardly be exaggerated. . . . He is, at this time, the people's historian for Europe. Public opinion is probably more affected by him, as it respects the character of our struggle and the materiel of our armies, than by any other living man. . . . it should be remembered that in this day of the world's history it is opinion, not force, which determines great struggles. . . .

Now that the general howl, which certain portions of the Press raised against Mr. Russell, has subsided, it may not be useless to direct attention to his letters as indispensable to a thorough and just appreciation of the progress of events. His criticisms upon our army, his observations on military movements, his notes of our defects and shortcomings in various ways, may be made exceedingly serviceable, if we are not too proud to learn at all, or too prejudiced to learn from him. [13]

Through this period, Russell continued to send letters to his paper and to record his observations of the American scene. On November 14, at dinner with "Mr. Seward, Mr. Raymond, of New York, and two or three gentlemen," the president stopped by. "Here, Mr. President," someone said, "We have the two Times—of New York and of London—if they would only do what is right and what we want, all will go well." "Yes," said Mr. Lincoln, "if the bad Times would go where we want them, good Times would be sure to follow." Two weeks later, Russell had a conversation with Secretary of War Cameron, who "once worked as a printer in the city of Washington, at ten dollars a week, and twenty cents an hour for extra work at the case on Sundays. . . . He says the press rules America, and that no one can face it and live. . . ." [14]

Soon thereafter, Russell fell victim to typhoid fever and went to Canada to recuperate. A two-month absence from the war did not sit well with the foreign manager of the *Times*, who wrote: "You must either go to the front or come home. . . . up to the beginning of this year you did well, but since then you seem to have lost heart and to have thrown us overboard." [15]

Russell returned to Washington on March 1, 1862, to learn that, "In place of Mr. Cameron, an Ohio lawyer named Stanton has been appointed Secretary of War." Stanton appeared to welcome Russell, but actually gave him a bit of a runaround. Russell was hoping for permission to draw rations when with troops in the field, but Secretary Stanton had other ideas. Too many of the American correspondents might demand the same privileges.

"Now this is undoubtedly honest on Mr. Stanton's part," Russell acknowledged, "for he knows he might render himself popular by granting what they ask; but he is excessively vain and aspires to be considered a rude, rough, vigorous Oliver Cromwell sort of man, mistaking some of the disagreeable attributes and the accidents of the external husk of the Great Protector for the brain and head of a statesman and a soldier." [16]

For a man who desperately needed to cement a friendly relationship with the one man who held the key to his future, Russell was marvelously obtuse. In his proximate letter to the London *Times*, he made so bold as to expose Stanton's dislike of the press to international scrutiny:

Here is Mr. Stanton—the man of an hour, the lawyer of yesterday; the hippodamos, the press-tamer of today! How he has grown, almost in a moment, into life and power! . . . There is no one in Congress, there is not in Senate, in House of Representatives, in pulpit, or stump, or in the forum, a man who has a word to say in this year of grace 1862 against a war against the press compared with which there has been nothing known. . . . And the American people are very glad of it; leastways, they don't appear at all dissatisfied. Here are billiard-table keepers and whiskey-drinkers getting up at public meetings, and all sorts of interests moving against taxation, but not a man cries out "murder," or even "robbery," far less "fire" at the visible extinction of all life in the Press in its function of giving news. . . . When an American is content to do without news in his newspaper he has exhausted submission and forbearance, and made his sacrifice.

My next letter will be from the neighborhood of Fortress Monroe. [17]

The forbearance of Mr. Stanton, it would appear, was soon exhausted, but it was Russell who became the sacrifice. Denied permission to travel, he remained in Washington for his "next," and the few following letters from America.

McClellan was preparing to move his army to the peninsula formed where the Chesapeake Bay meets the James River, for the first major Federal offensive in the East since Bull Run. Secretary Stanton issued instructions that no passes would be granted to headquarters at Fortress Monroe, "unless to officers and soldiers going on duty, or to persons in the service of the United States." [18]

Russell tried to see the secretary, but was handed only a note: "Mr. Stanton informs Mr. Russell no passes to Fortress Monroe can be given at present, unless to officers in the United States service." Russell tried to arrange transportation with the navy, ostensibly to visit the British H.M.S. *Rinaldo*, then at Norfolk. Permission denied. The assistant secretary of war told him that approval for journalists to accompany the army had been vested in General McClellan. Russell was delighted, and immediately approached McClellan, who not only granted permission, but also offered "any assistance in his power." [19]

With pass in hand, Russell was allowed to board a transport at the Washington Navy Yard. However, Stanton found out shortly before the ship was to sail, and Russell was asked to leave. He made one more attempt to see Stanton, calling "at his house on his reception night, the door was opened by his brother-in-law, who said, the Secretary was attending a sick child and could not see any person that evening." He later heard that when Stanton learned about McClellan's pass, he "flew out into a coarse passion against General McClellan because he had dared to invite or to take anyone without his permission." [20]

Russell explained his situation to the readers of the *Times* in his letter of April 3:

Before I proceed to write the last letter, in all probability, which I shall have occasion to date from the United States of America, it will be necessary to state the circumstances under which I am compelled to abandon the post to which I have been so long faithful, under an ordeal the severity of which can be known to none but myself. . . . I bore the attacks upon me in silence . . . and from time to time my patience was rewarded by unexpected marks of sympathy and by tokens of friendship and goodwill which I shall always cherish. But now a power is brought to bear against me which I cannot resist or evade. The Government of the United States of America not merely refuses me permission to accompany its armies in the field; it . . . gives me orders not to do so. . . . [21]

Russell had not quite abandoned the fight. He sent a note to the president, who in response asked for more details, which Russell quickly furnished. However, Russell next heard from a member of the White House staff, who wrote that the president "directs me to say that, with every disposition to oblige you, he is disinclined to overrule a decision of the Secretary of War, founded on what appear to the Secretary considerations of high public importance. To do so in your case alone would seem to all others an invidious distinction." [22]

The order prohibiting transportation to nongovernment civilians had been directed to all members of the press corps, but about the same time that Russell was reading the note from the White House, Stanton notified the newspapers that the prohibition was only intended for agents of "foreign journals" and would not affect any of their correspondents, all of whom now scrambled to catch up with the expedition. Russell noted in the *Diary*:

I am led to believe that Mr. Stanton was actuated by a desire to show his power in a manner which might at once gain him the approbation of certain journals in the North, and at the same time make General McClellan feel his subordinate position; and, if the same authorities do not err, he is influenced by the jealousy which has been openly attributed to him of that officer on political and personal grounds. [23]

Russell gave a more direct appraisal to the foreign manager of the *Times*: Stanton "is a coarse vigorous ill tempered dyspeptic of the most inordinate vanity & ambition & his jealousy of McClellan is almost a mania for he thinks he sees in him ye next Presdt. . . ." [24]

The final *Diary* entry for Russell's American adventure was dated April 9, 1862:

It was plain I now had but one course left. . . . I went to America to witness and describe the operations of the great army before Washington in the field, and when I was forbidden by the proper authorities to do so, my mission terminated at once. . . . I arrived in New York late on Tuesday evening, and next day I saw the shores receding into a dim grey fog, and ere the night fell was tossing about once more on the stormy Atlantic, with the head of our good ship pointing, thank Heaven, towards Europe. [25]

And the next day's New York *Times* offered a literary obituary of sorts:

Mr. W. H. Russell, Special Correspondent of the London Times, was among the passengers by the China, which sailed for Liverpool yesterday. Mr. Russell's stay in the United States had extended over more than a year of our eventful times, during which time he has contributed letters of a varying merit to the leading London journal. Some of his earlier descriptive letters were characterized by all his brilliant and unrivaled power in that style of writing; but he was less happy, and sometimes extremely unhappy, in his speculative and philosophical essays, and thus incurred the odium of many who were, perhaps, not always willing to make due allowance for the extreme difficulty and delicacy of his task. . . . It will be a matter of regret to Mr. R Russell's many friends that he leaves the United States with the feeling that his career here has been in great degree a failure. He leaves without having had an opportunity to see a single battle, at a time when battles are in progress that match the greatest that history records. [26]

Russell's days as a war correspondent, however, were not ended; he went on to cover the Austro-Prussian War (1866), the Franco-Prussian War (1870–71), and the Zulu War (1879–80). He was awarded a knighthood in 1895. Artist Frank Vizetelly of the *Illustrated London News*, the only other "foreign" journalist refused permission to go to Fortress Monroe as a result of Stanton's order, went South, providing sketches from the Confederate side for the rest of the war. Many were intercepted and printed in *Harper's Weekly*.

8 / Sedition and Suppression: North

Men and presses who are to-day preaching "Compromise" and "Peace,"
are doing more to cripple the Government and help treason than
the rebel armies themselves. We would hang a spy who should be caught
prowling about our camp to obtain information to be used against us;
but we must tolerate if not respect these loyal traitors who labor in the
rostrum and through the press to aid the enemy!
—Albany *Journal*, August 20, 1861

SOON AFTER THE DEBACLE at Bull Run, the Federals lost a battle at Wilson's Creek, Missouri, and a week after that, Russell's London
Times letter was splashed across the nation. The Federal government,
shaken to the core, tried to bring the roiling press under better control.
There were McClellan's voluntary rules for the loyal and severe sanctions—legal and otherwise—for the unruly.

A small but aggressive peace faction was arguing, in public meetings
and sympathetic newspapers, to let the South go. The government, however, was not willing to allow "sedition" to masquerade (in its opinion) as
"freedom of the press." The *Missouri State Journal*, was suppressed July 12,
the St. Louis *Ear Bulletin* and the *Missourian* were closed down August
14, and a company of Federal troops took possession of the Savannah
(Missouri) *Northwest Democrat* on August 18. U.S. marshals seized the
type, paper, and other appurtenances of the Philadelphia *Christian Observer*, August 22; according to the next day's issue of the Philadelphia
Press, this forestalled a more dramatic public assault on account of "The
indignation of the people against this sheet . . . a matter of which the authorities were cognizant." [1]

Mail privileges were denied to several papers: The New York *Daily News* and the New York *Evening Day Book* on August 22, the New York *Journal of Commerce*, *Freeman's Journal*, and the Brooklyn *Eagle* on August 25, followed on September 12 by the Baltimore *Exchange*—a paper the New York *World* branded "the worst secession sheet in America."[2] The editor, F. Key Howard, was arrested along with a number of members of the Maryland legislature, the Baltimore city legislature, and Thomas J. Hall Jr., editor of the Baltimore *South*, all under orders from the War Department.

Howard was an unabashed rebel sympathizer and proud to be a martyr in the cause of constitutional liberty. The *Exchange* took the position—in print the morning after his arrest—that the right of a newspaper to discuss and condemn government policy was identical to the freedom of the "people" to do the same thing. Howard refused to appear in court (an "irresponsible tribunal") and would not accept a discharge offered on the condition that he keep his opinions to himself. He was released.

Most actions against newspapers were carried on under color of the law. A Westchester County (New York) grand jury returned presentments on September 7 against the Yonkers *Herald*, the Highland *Democrat*, the *Eastern State Journal*, the *Staats Zeitung*, and the *National Zeitung* "as disseminators of doctrines which, in the existing state of things, tend to give aid and comfort to the enemies of the Government. . . ." On September 25, a grand jury at Trenton, New Jersey, returned presentments against the Newark *Evening Journal*, the Warren *Journal*, the Hunterdon *Democrat*, the New Brunswick *Times*, and the Plainfield *Gazette*, for "persistently denouncing and libeling those to whom the great duty of National defense is necessarily intrusted . . . in a war for the life of a nation, the Press, as well as individuals, should uphold the existing Government or be treated as enemies." This grand jury proposed no legal sanctions, rather, suggested that the cited newspapers be left "to the wholesome action of public opinion." [3]

The grand jury may have had in mind the sort of "wholesome action" that then was being practiced throughout the North. The crowds that had gathered outside the *Herald* building after the fall of Fort Sumter had been restless but restrained. The mobs that visited the offices of unpopular newspapers in the heat of August were violent. Some offices were totally destroyed, the type and presses smashed, the records burned: the Bangor (Maine) *Democrat*, August 11; the Easton (Pennsylvania) *Sentinel*, August 19; the West Chester (Pennsylvania) *Jeffersonian*, August 20; the Cumberland (Virginia) *Alleghanian*, August 23; the Canton (Ohio) *Stark County Democrat*, August 23; and the Mauch Chunk (Pennsylvania) *Carbon Democrat*, August 31, 1861.

The office of the Bridgeport (Connecticut) *Advertiser and Farmer* was demolished on Saturday, August 24; and on Sunday, the New Haven *Palladium* sent a reporter "to gain such facts as possible regarding the deplorable events." The *Palladium* report of Monday described a "Peace Meeting" in the village of Stepney that had turned into a "regular Union meeting" through the aggressive intervention of a crowd from nearby Bridgeport. That crowd included many of the volunteer soldiers who had just returned from Bull Run and Phineas T. Barnum—sometime newspaper publisher and full-time showman—who took over the platform. "Pistols were . . . drawn by the secessionists," the *Palladium* duly noted, "and threats were made that if Mr. Barnum spoke he would be shot. He was immediately surrounded by a number of returned volunteers, who with revolvers in hand, promised death to any one who should fire at the platform." Barnum invited any of the scheduled secessionist speakers to join him, "promising them in the name of the Union men a fair hearing, provided they uttered nothing treasonable." None accepted the invitation. At that point, another local celebrity, inventor of the sewing machine Elias Howe Jr., was elected chairman of an ad hoc Union meeting, P. T. Barnum, secretary.

There was some scuffling and a few threats of greater violence, but none materialized until the Bridgeport Unionists returned home "apparently ready for any desperate enterprise." When someone shouted, "To the *Farmer* office," perhaps five hundred men, with a couple of thousand trailing spectators, moved to the building housing the *Advertiser and Farmer* newspaper and job printing office. There, the *Palladium* reporter was told "a scene of destruction occurred that almost passes description. The invaders, maddened by the obstinately and unnaturally disloyal and traitorous course of the doomed sheet, left nothing whole that could be disposed of. Type, job presses, ink, paper, books, all the paraphernalia of a printing establishment were thrown into the street, and two presses, too large to get through the windows, were broken in pieces by aid of a large and heavy lever."

The next morning "the streets were thronged . . . by excited groups of men, and Nathan F. Morse, the junior partner in the concern, was vigorously groaned when he appeared on the street." [4]

The Stepney meeting was but one of several contested "peace flag" raisings held around the state that weekend, at which the white flag of the peace faction was forcefully replaced with the Stars and Stripes. One meeting turned bloody, when a peace group at New Fairfield was attacked by men from Danbury wielding pitchforks and axes. At least two men were killed.

A group of Bull Run veterans demonstrated their own version of "wholesome action" when they paid an angry visit to the offices of the

Concord (New Hampshire) *Democratic Standard*. Members of the 1st New Hampshire had just returned from service with General Patterson at Harper's Ferry and demanded a "retraction" for an unflattering article about "a certain Northern New England regiment" that the *Standard* had accused of mutiny "against the abolition Colonel who commands it. . . ." Apparently, the colonel refused to grant a weekend furlough to a number of his men, whereupon they formed into line and charged him with bayonets mounted. The colonel ran for cover, followed by "shouts of derisive laughter, and 'three cheers for Jeff. Davis.'" The men got the weekend off.

The response of the Palmer brothers—editors and proprietors of the *Standard*—was not so wholesome: they fired four shots into the mob, wounding two soldiers. The office was immediately stripped, and the materials burned in the street. The Palmers took refuge in the attic, from which they were rescued by city authorities. [5]

The regiment's war record was nothing to brag about: one skirmish with the rebels, during which they lost six men captured. Their most arduous duty, according to the Philadelphia *Bulletin* of August 5, had been marching. "The regiment," the *Bulletin* also noted, "had twenty ladies with them."

The Unionist mobs—the Buffalo *Courier* preferred to call them "volunteers"—did not always destroy property; some merely sought a "pledge of allegiance." The New York *Herald* reported that Ambrose L. Kimball, editor of the Haverhill (Massachusetts) *Essex County Democrat*, was "forcibly taken from his house by an excited mob, and, refusing information, was covered with a coat of tar and feathers, and ridden on a rail through the town." No fool, "Mr. K. promised to keep his pen dry in aid of rebellion, and was liberated. . . . [he] made the following affirmation on his knees: 'I am sorry that I have published what I have, and I promise that I will never again write or publish articles against the North and in favor of secession, so help me God.'" To their credit, Haverhill officials and many residents as well had tried, unsuccessfully, to interfere. [6]

Residents of Scranton (Pennsylvania) directed their wrath against William Halsey, a subscription agent for the New York *Day Book*. He was challenged to leave town, or be ridden out on a rail. He left. The editor of the Indianapolis *Sentinel* was induced to swear allegiance to the U.S. Government.

In September, the Louisville *Courier* was excluded from the mail "until further orders" for "having been found to be an advocate of treasonable hostility to the Government and authorities of the United States." The office was taken over by the U.S. marshal, and several associates (including a former governor) were arrested on charges of treason or complicity with treason. A few months earlier, the *Tribune*'s Richardson had noted that the *Courier* was openly urging readers to take up arms against the government. In contrast, and at the same time, the Louisville *Journal*—published across the street—was advising Union men to arm themselves. For his readers who might not be versed in the small-arms trade, *Journal* editor George D. Prentice hinted that first-class revolvers might be obtained through his office. Prentice appeared to be a late convert to the cause, having earlier denounced Lincoln's first call for troops with "mingled amazement and indignation." However, as he assured Richardson—he did so because "we know our own people. They require very tender handling." [7]

Suppression at times crossed over the line from controlling sedition to punishing honest criticism. An action at Lexington, Missouri, toward the end of September resulted in the capture of a Federal garrison and the temporary closing of a newspaper that blamed the area commander (Maj. Gen. John Charles Frémont) for not having rescued his troops.

The world-renowned "Pathfinder" of Western exploration and the first presidential candidate (1856) of the Republican Party, Frémont demonstrated a penchant for substituting image for reality. Missouri, Kansas, and Arkansas were in turmoil, with well-armed groups of rebels moving through the territory, but Frémont's energies were devoted to supplying (with contracts of questionable legality) and creating an imperial headquarters in St. Louis. He even established a 150-man personal mounted guard, all Hungarian mercenaries with perfectly matched horses, "enlisted" without legal authority.

Lexington, with a garrison of Chicago Irish under command of Col. James A. Mulligan, was put under siege by a Confederate force led by the former governor of Missouri, Sterling Price. The Federals were in an untenable position, soon cut off from any source of water; Frémont did in fact send a relief column, under Brig. Gen. Sam Sturgis, but Sturgis balked at crossing the Missouri River into rebel-occupied Lexington and abandoned the effort.

General Frémont was challenged in print by the St. Louis *Evening News*. "Lexington is fallen!" wrote editor Charles G. Ramsay. "We write it with sorrow; for it is a heavy reverse to our arms in Missouri—the twin disaster to the reverse in Springfield [Wilson's Creek] and, like that reverse, easily avoidable, had prompt steps been take to avoid it." His complaint: the Federal garrison and "its heroic Irish commander . . . ought to have been supported, by a department that has hundreds and thousands of tons of shot, shell, powder, cannon, artillery, muskets and rifles, and that has command of all the rivers, all the railroads, and all the steamboats in the State, for the speedy transportation of men and material to any point of danger." [8]

Frémont overreacted, arrested the editor, suppressed the paper, and had the building seized. The suspension was lifted after a couple of days when Ramsay—who, after all, *had* been in error, because a relief effort had been made—agreed that he would, first, make sure of his facts before publishing any reports of military activities and, second, "not publish anything injurious to the interests of the National Government." [9]

The *Evening News*, however, was not the only paper to attack Frémont. Newspapers that had been supporters—the New York *Herald*, *Times*, and *World*, the Philadelphia *Press*, the Washington *Star*, and the Chicago *Tribune*—now turned against him, demanding his removal not only for failing to rescue Mulligan, but also because they now knew that he had basically failed to do anything useful during his tenure. The New York *Tribune*, however, remained his champion; "I believe in him and love him," St. Louis-based Richardson assured Greeley. [10]

Frémont, sensing a personal defeat unless he achieved a military victory, any victory, took bold corrective action and announced, "I am taking the field myself." He began to assemble his forces near Jefferson City, accompanied by a press contingent large enough to prompt comment in the St. Louis *Democrat*:

> If it be true that "the pen is mightier than the sword," [General] Price
> has shown admirable discretion and tact in getting out of the way of
> our army as fast as possible, for the number of army correspondents
> going forward . . . would be enough to annihilate him. [11]

Some in that press corps seemed determined to use the pen against their own side; one of the New York *Tribune* contingent described Frémont's force of fifteen thousand troops, assembled sixty miles west of Jefferson City, as "waiting for the remainder of the army to join them." It would have been an invitation to attack, had General Price not been in such a hurry to head South. [12]

Just at this point, Secretary of War Cameron and Adj. Gen. Lorenzo Thomas went to St. Louis to investigate reports about what appeared to be the total military incompetence of, and tolerance of fraud by, Major General Frémont. In fact, Cameron carried a letter from the president that would dismiss Frémont, but was told that he could deliver or withhold the letter, at his discretion. He held off when Frémont promised that there would be action, soon.

"Soon" became not soon enough and the dilatory general was relieved of his command on November 2. The New York *Tribune*, by way of A. D.

Richardson's pen, offered a sad and sympathetic portrayal of his return to St. Louis: the troops, waiting en masse at the train station; the procession back to headquarters; serenades by regimental bands; threats of resignation; and "Universal gloom" throughout the camps. [13]

By the end of 1861, most efforts to close down opposition papers had dwindled—possibly because the number of papers in opposition had dwindled. Four newspapers were banned from the U.S. mail on February 16, 1862, for giving aid and comfort to an enemy and for advocating the overthrow of the U.S. government: the *Mississippian*, the *Oregon Democrat*, the *Los Angelos*, and the *California Star*. The Baltimore *South* was suppressed (for the second time) on February 17, 1862, and the next day the editor and the publisher were arrested (for the second time) and taken to Fort McHenry.

In May 1862, Maj. Gen. Benjamin Butler was trying to bring the restless population of New Orleans under Federal control. The city had been captured on April 25, 1862, and by May 1, Military Governor Butler declared martial law for "as long as in the judgment of the U.S. authorities it may be necessary." He set forth "the rules and regulations under which the laws of the United States will be for the present and during the state of war enforced and maintained, for the plain guidance of all good citizens of the United States, as well as others, who may heretofore have been in rebellion against their authority." His guidance for the instruction of the press was clear:

> No publication, newspaper, pamphlet, or hand-bill, giving accounts of the movements of the soldiers of the United States within this Department, reflecting in any way upon the United States, or tending in any way to influence the public mind against the Government of the United States will be permitted.
>
> All articles of war news, editorial comments, or correspondence making comments upon the movements of the armies of the United States, must be submitted to the examination of an officer, who will be detailed for that purpose from these headquarters.
>
> The transmission of all communications by telegraph will be under the charge of an officer from these headquarters. [14]

For instruction of the rest of the citizens of New Orleans, General Butler affirmed that "the American ensign, the emblem of the United States, must be treated with the utmost respect by all persons, under pain of severe punishment." Citizen William B. Mumford learned, to his terminal distress, that this was not an idle threat. Mumford was convicted of treason "in tearing down the United States flag from a public building of the United States [the Customs House], for the purpose of inciting other evil-minded persons to further resistance to the laws and arms of the United States. . . ." Just before he was hanged on May 8—from a temporary gallows erected at the scene of the crime—he told the New Orleans *Delta* that "the offence for which he was condemned to die was committed under excitement," and that he thought the punishment was unjust. [15]

The execution—legal, but extreme—had the intended effect on the rebellious citizens and no more flags were ripped from public buildings. However, Butler's next action—the one for which he is better known—backfired: the infamous "Order 28" of May 15:

> As officers and soldiers of the United States have been subject to re-
> peated insults from women calling themselves ladies, of New-
> Orleans, in return for the most scrupulous non-interference and
> courtesy on our part, it is ordered hereafter, when any female shall by
> mere gesture or movement insult, or show contempt for any officers
> or soldiers of the United States, she shall be regarded and held liable
> to be treated as a woman about town plying her avocation. [16]

Most of the "insults" were relatively benign—crossing the street or leaving a room to avoid sharing the space with a Yankee, making derisive comments, some spitting—although one woman had emptied a chamber-pot on navy captain David Farragut just after he had taken control of the city. The women may have been trying to provoke some overt retaliatory acts by the Federals on the assumption that the men of New Orleans would rise up in anger.

Whether or not Butler fully understood that the treatment of Southern women was such a tender subject, he came under immediate and immortal attack and became known—then and still today—as "Beast Butler." The newspapers of New Orleans at first refused to publish the order, whereupon Butler ordered them all to be closed. The *True Delta* was the first to give in and print Order 28; the others soon followed suit. General Beauregard (at this time directing the defense of Corinth, Mississippi) used Order 28 as the platform from which to launch another call to arms: "Men of the South, shall our mothers, wives, daughters and sisters be thus outraged by the ruffianly soldiers of the North, to whom is given the right to treat at their pleasure the ladies of the South as common harlots? Arouse, friends, and drive back from our soil these infamous invaders of our homes. . . ." [17]

There was a flurry of more permanent closings of newspapers in New Orleans: the *Crescent* (the owner "now in arms against the government of the United States"), May 12; the *Bee* and the *Delta* on May 16 for printing information prohibited by the order of May 1. The *Delta* was taken over by the Federals; the *Bee* was allowed to resume independent operations on May 30, 1862.

Butler was not a bad administrator; he gave captured food to the poor, cleaned up the streets, and kept law and order. The "Unionized" *Delta* offered compliments: "In the memory of the 'oldest inhabitant,' our city was never more healthy at this season of the year. For this great blessing we are greatly indebted to Gen. Butler's idea of relieving the poor, and at the same time getting said poor to clean up the streets. . . . The result is, that our city is a model of cleanliness." [18]

However, there were some charges of modest corruption, and Butler's effectiveness as governor diminished. He was reassigned in December.

On July 17, 1862, Congress passed what became known as the "treason" act, targeted at individuals who gave aid and comfort to the enemy "through the expression of disloyal statements." In this context, some government officials believed that newspaper editors could be counted as "individuals," and a few editors were charged with resisting the draft or counseling draft resistance. The editors and publishers of the Harrisburg *Patriot and Union* were arrested August 6, 1862, for issuing antirecruiting posters. D. A. Mahoney, editor of the Dubuque (Iowa) *Herald*, was charged with discouraging enlistments and arrested by the U.S. marshal August 14, 1862. Two years later, editor and proprietor of the New York *Metropolitan Record* John Mullaly was brought to trial for advocating resistance of the draft, but his case was discharged on a technicality. However, as part of the proceeding, the U.S. commissioner affirmed the right of citizens to criticize the government. [19]. It does not appear that any case brought against an editor actually resulted in a conviction.

There were, incidentally, a few civil actions brought against newspapers during the war—for libel, for example—but without much effect. It was too easy for the newspapers to cloud ownership and shift assets, leaving no clear target for a suit or source of funds for an award. [20]

The *Maryland News Sheet* was suppressed on August 14. (The paper changed its name but apparently not its politics. Now the *Gazette*, it was suspended from September 28 to October 7, 1862.) A party of Federal soldiers demolished the office of the *Constitutional Gazetteer* in Marysville, Kansas, on August 17, 1862. After the Federal defeat at Second Manassas (August 29, 1962), the provost marshal sent squads of soldiers through New York City to rip down the bulletins posted outside the newspaper offices. The New York *Tribune* printed a rumor that the president had denounced McClellan as a traitor and removed him from command. That issue of the paper was suppressed in Philadelphia.

There were only a few acts of aggression against newspapers in 1863. A group of soldiers destroyed the offices of the Columbus (Ohio) *Crisis* on March 5, 1863. On May 10, 1863, the Department of Missouri prohibited sale or distribution of New York's *Freeman's Journal* and *Caucasian*, the Jerseyville (New Jersey) *Democratic Journal*, the Chicago *Times*, and the Dubuque (Iowa) *Herald*. On June 2, 1863, Gen. Ambrose E. Burnside suppressed the Chicago *Times* and banned the New York *World* from the Department of the Ohio because "repeated expressions of disloyal and incendiary sentiments" were "calculated to exert a pernicious and treasonable influence."

The Illinois delegation in the House of Representatives called Burnside's move an act of military despotism and a violation of state sovereignty. Horace Greeley—no friend of either paper—agreed, and called a meeting of his fellow editors in New York. They considered "the rights and duties of the public press in the present crisis" and acknowledged a duty to the Constitution, the government, and the laws; they affirmed that treason and rebellion are crimes, and especially so in a republic, where every man has a voice in the administration. However, they noted, while journalists have no right to incite or aid rebellion or treason, they do have the right freely and fearlessly to criticize the acts of public officers. "Any limitation of this right created by the necessities of war," they said, "should be confined to localities wherein hostilities actually exist or are imminently threatened." They denied the right of any military officer "to suppress the issue or forbid the general circulation of journals printed far away from the seat of the war." [21]

The supression order was revoked.

In May 1864, Joseph Howard, former New York *Times* reporter, gadfly, and journalistic hack fallen on hard times, hoped to make a killing on the gold market with a phony presidential proclamation. He teamed with another out-of-favor journalist and drafted a text disguised as an Associated Press dispatch that acknowledged recent military failures, called for a day of national fasting, humiliation, and prayer, and announced a draft call for 400,000 more men. Copies were to the New York papers about three o'clock in the morning, after the close of the normal business of the day and while the final type forms were being locked up. There were, however, enough errors in style and presentation that most of the papers were at least skeptical and at best convinced that it was a hoax. Most, that is, except for the *World* and *Journal of Commerce*.

The bogus story appeared in the editions of May 18, 1864, and in the normal course of business, was picked up and put on the wire by the New

York headquarters of the Associated Press. In the normal course of business, gold rose 10 percent. Also in the normal course of business, New York military commander Gen. John Dix asked Washington for verification and the Associated Press general agent in New York sent a query to the Washington bureau: How had they missed such an important story? Quick action by the government blocked transport of the papers on a ship just about to sail for Europe, and timely bulletins published in most papers knocked the story back down, along with the price of gold.

On the presumption that the *World* and *Journal* were responsible for the fraud, General Dix was sent to seize the offenders, an action that sparked an unexpected fight. Under what authority, local officials and newspaper editors asked, was the army shutting down newspapers in a city that was not under martial law? The Democratic governor of New York, Horatio Seymour, brought charges against the general for usurping state authority. General Dix's defense was clear—he had acted on a lawful order from the president—and he was acquitted. The source of the hoax was soon tracked to Howard and his friend, who each spent a few months in jail as a consequence.

Meanwhile, in Washington, the president had quietly postponed issuing a real proclamation—which he had signed at almost the same moment that the counterfeit was being written—that called for a new draft of 300,000 men.

9 / Sedition and Suppression: South

After the Hon. Jeff. Davis had stated in Richmond, in a conversation
relative to my paper, that he would not live in a Government that did
not tolerate the freedom of the press . . . and after the entire press
of the South had come down in their thunder tones upon the Federal
Government for suppressing the Louisville Courier, and the
New York Daybook, and other secession journals, I did expect the
utmost liberty to be allowed to one small sheet, whose errors
could be combated by the entire Southern press!
—William G. Brownlow, editor, Knoxville *Whig*, October 26, 1861

THERE WERE FEW ACTIONS against dissident newspapers in the
South because the South had few dissident newspapers. Most of those
that had been strong for the Union in 1860 quickly fell in line, as did the
Alexandria (Louisiana) *Constitutional*: "We have all embarked on the
same ship. No matter how much we may be dissatisfied with her commanders, her equipments or the manner of her launching, *we are on
board. . . .*" [1]

For some papers, a change in management brought about the same
result—the antisecession editor of the Richmond *Whig* was forced out of
his job the day after Sumter surrendered. The proprietor of the staunchly
Union Greensboro *Alabama Beacon* read the auguries and sold his paper
to a man who would better reflect the views of the readers. Some, like A.
B. Hendren of the Athena (Alabama) *Union Banner*, simply quit: "I
would with pleasure be willing to continue an unrelenting warfare against
the spirit of secession if my subsequent labors could promise the least encouragement to our cause, but being *the only press* now in Alabama that

'shows its hand' in that particular, I cannot of course expect to survive the mighty powers brought against me." [2]

There were a few holdouts, but not many, and not for long. The offices of the Galveston *Union* were trashed by a mob in January 1861, sending a signal to others. The editor was not even an abolitionist, but had merely suggested caution. A sister Unionist paper in Galveston, the *Civilian and Gazette*, was so fearful of a similar attack that it did not even report the incident.

James P. Newcomb, editor of the San Antonio *Alamo Express*, spoke his mind on February 8: "Is this still a land where liberty loves to dwell? Where freedom is allowed to opinions and not denied utterance? Where men are not to be persecuted for opinion's sake? If it is, it would be well for those who differ with us to remember it." On April 17, he chided the men of Charleston for starting a war "upon the question of supplying sixty men [at Ft. Sumter] . . . with pork and beans for a few days." Not quite a month later, an item that made sport of local rebels prompted a nocturnal call by the Knights of the Golden Circle and the Confederate Rangers. "The morning light," Newcomb later recalled, "displayed the charred ruins of the *Alamo Express*, the last Union paper in Texas." [3]

In March 1862, General Winder, provost marshal in Richmond, threatened the *Examiner* with suspension for publishing articles offensive to the police and arrested the editor of the *Whig* over an "unpatriotic" article. But there were few other aggressions.

In fact, while most papers in the South wholeheartedly supported secession and the war, many continued to be as openly critical of the government as any in the North and did so largely without interference. At the head of this class stood the Richmond *Examiner*. "In the midst of revolution," the editor wrote on February 4, 1862, "no greater calamity can befall a people, than for their affairs to pass into the control of men who could not understand it in the beginning, and are incapable of appreciating the demands of the crisis as they arise." A year later, he chided Davis for being "affable, kind and subservient to his enemies" and "haughty, austere and unbending to his friends." [4]

There were others of like mind; the Mobile *Daily Tribune* affirmed that "Mr. Davis's cabinet is composed of a set of old fogy broken down politicians. . . ." and the Mobile *Daily Advertiser and Register* expressed regret that Davis possessed "the absurd ambition of getting all power and never using it." [5]

On the other hand, many editors exercised a self-imposed political censorship. In November 1861, R. B. Rhett Jr., of the Charleston *Mercury*, notified his Richmond correspondent George W. Bagby that "in light of the shaky condition of public morale" and because of their "despondent and fault finding tone," he had not published Bagby's last three letters. [6] The following April he sent Bagby another advisory:

You have perceived that I have struck out of your letters many hits against Davis. However true and necessary to a knowledge of his real character, they savor too much of personal dislike, in the opinion of the public, to effect the object. I would never attack him, except upon public matters, and with infallible proofs. People will not tolerate the expression of mere opinions derogatory to this great little head of a great country. . . . Be therefore, I suggest, as amiable as consistent with truth, and give the dear weakly public as much as possible of the bright side of things. The *Courier* here flourishes on flattering every thing and everybody out of which any thing is to be made. [7]

One historian suggested that "no newspaper was ever suppressed by state or Confederate authority throughout the war. . . ." [8] However, he missed one: the Knoxville (Tennessee) *Whig*, edited by William G. Brownlow, a former Methodist minister widely known as "Parson." A public man all his life, Brownlow sought nomination for a seat in Congress in 1843, losing out to Andrew Johnson, and became editor of the *Whig* in 1849.

He was proslavery, but militantly antisecession. Alabama politician William L. Yancey—unsuccessful suitor for the role of Confederate president—predicted that Brownlow would be hanged. The editor's response: "come what may, through weal or woe, in peace or war, no earthly power shall keep me from denouncing the enemies of my country." When invited to become the chaplain of a volunteer brigade being raised by General Pillow, Brownlow replied, "When I shall have made up my mind to go to hell, I will cut my throat, and go direct, and not travel round by way of the Southern Confederacy." The Charleston *Mercury* suggested that "It is not necessary that the 'Reverend Gentleman' should cut his throat and go to the place he mentions, as it is pretty evident he is making there direct without any such operation." [9]

He was clearly charting his own course. The Chicago *Journal* reported that "The house of the celebrated, bold-hearten, and outspoken Parson Brownlow, is the only one in Knoxville, Tenn., over which the Stars and Stripes are floating." The *Journal* said that two men showed up at the house at six o'clock one morning in May, to be confronted by Brownlow's twenty-three-year-old daughter, who "demanded their business. They replied they had come to 'Take down them d-m Stars and Stripes.' She instantly drew a revolver from her side, and presenting it, said, 'Go on! I'm good for one of you, and I think for both!'" The men backed off but returned some hours later with an armed mob—to find the house filled with a throng of "gallant men, armed to the teeth. . . ." "When our informant left Knoxville," the *Journal* concluded, "the Stars and Stripes still floated over Parson Brownlow's house. Long may they wave." [10]

Brownlow was accused of treason for publishing items such as the wry description of a man in April 1861, "swaggering and swearing in every crowd he enters, that he will go out of the Union because he can't get his rights, by having the privilege guaranteed to take slaves in the Territories, when, in fact, he does not own a Negro in the world, never did, and never will; and withal can't get credit in any store in the country where he lives, for a wool hat or a pair of brogans!" [11]

His case was not helped in August, when he poked fun at General Pillow. The general hoped to blockade the Mississippi at Memphis with a huge chain cable, stretched over a series of buoys moored in the riverbed, at a cost of about $30,000. The cable and the buoys all were swept away by the first surge of river-borne trees, logs, and driftwood, "as any flat-boat captain would have informed the Confederate authorities would certainly be the case." [12]

As the pressure increased, Brownlow backed down—a bit. Asserting that he was not a "candidate for martyrdom, or imprisonment" he promised to moderate his stand. "I conduct the only Union paper left in the Southern Confederacy," he affirmed, and "most respectfully decline the honors and hazards of so brave and independent a course."

"We are," he continued, "in the midst of a fearful revolution—that the civil law has given way to the military rule—and that, if [anyone] is fool enough to attempt such a course, the military authorities in the South are not fools enough to tolerate it. I come down from my extreme position, not of choice, but of necessity, and I frankly confess that I have not the courage to meet, in open combat, unarmed as I am, eleven States in arms and in full uniform." Henceforth, he would concentrate on "literary, Agricultural and Miscellaneous matter, including the war news of the day." [13]

That concession did not serve him for long. Brownlow was given an opportunity to escape prosecution by admitting his errors and swearing loyalty to the Confederacy. The Union flag, still flying over his home, stood for his response. His charge sheet was expanded with specious allegations that he had been involved in acts of sabotage. He gave up, and suspended publication on October 26: "This issue of the Whig must necessarily be the last for some time to come—I am unable to say how long. The Confederate authorities have determined upon my arrest, and I am to be indicted before the 'Grand Jury of the Confederate Court' meeting at Nashville. . . . The real object of my arrest, and contemplated imprisonment, is, to dry up, break down, silence, and destroy the last and only Union paper left in the eleven seceded States. . . ."

He was to be sent to jail, Brownlow continued, "because I have failed to recognize the hand of God in the work of breaking up the American government, and the inauguration of the most wicked, cruel, unnatural, and uncalled for war, ever recorded in history." He pledged, if it was ever within his power, to make good on his obligation to his subscribers, and tried to get away. He was caught in North Carolina, returned to Knoxville, and put in jail, where he contracted typhoid fever. His confinement was shifted to house arrest; then, still in poor health, he was released and banished to the North on March 3, 1863.

The Knoxville *Register* called his banishment a great blunder, not for any journalistic skill he would take to the North, but because he might become a potent guerrilla leader:

Let him but once reach the confines of Kentucky, with his knowledge of the geography and population of East-Tennessee, and our section will soon feel the effect of his hard blows. From his own old partisan and religious sectarian parasites he will find men who will obey him with the fanatical alacrity of those who followed Peter the Hermit in the first crusade. . . .let us not underrate Brownlow. [14]

However, Brownlow went on the stump, not on an armed crusade, writing and giving lectures in the North. When Knoxville was occupied by the Federals in December 1863, he returned and reopened the paper, which he then called the Knoxville *Whig and Rebel Ventilator*. Brownlow was elected governor of Tennessee in 1865 and 1867, and U.S. senator in 1869, at which time he sold the *Whig*. However, when his senate term ended, he purchased a controlling interest in the *Whig* and returned to journalism until his death in 1877.

The war itself was the major intrusion on the business of newspapering, and Southern papers were steadily closed or taken over by the Yankees. A group of printers serving with the First Iowa Infantry operated the Macon (Missouri) *Register* for a few days in June 1861, the secessionist editor having left town. They turned out at least one edition of a newspaper they called *Our Whole Union*, and offered, in print, a "Valedictory" to the editor, "wherever you are . . . remember us. We sat at your table; we stole from your 'Dictionary of Latin Quotations'; we wrote Union articles with your pen, your ink, on your paper. We printed them on your press. . . . We even drank some poor whiskey out of your bottle. . . ." [15]

Printers among the Union's soldiery returned to their trade whenever possible: here, putting out the first issue of *The Loyal Georgian*.

In March 1862, the Newbern (North Carolina) *Progress* announced a change in management:

> We come before the people of North-Carolina in an earnest advocate of that glorious Union which her patriotic ancestry so nobly aided to cement and establish. . . . The Progress has been heretofore one of the most virulent and bitter opposers to the Government in the South, and its former proprietor, not satisfied with treason already committed, has filled his cup of bitterness by openly taking up arms against the Union which so long fostered and nourished him. [16]

On June 17, 1862, Gen. Lew Wallace sent a note and two newsmen to educate the proprietors of the Memphis *Argus* concerning their proper role in a Federal environment: "As the closing of your offices might be injurious to you pecuniarily," he wrote, "I send Messrs. Richardson, of the New York *Tribune*, and Knox, of the New York *Herald*—two gentlemen of ample experience—to take charge of the editorial department of your paper. The business and management will be left to you." [17] While teaming men from the *Tribune* and the *Herald* might seem akin to a shotgun marriage, Richardson and Knox were good friends, and before the war had been partners as publishers of a short-lived newspaper in Colorado.

By February 1864, the number of daily Southern papers had dwindled from about eighty to thirty-five, and was steadily decreasing. Some papers held out, in a manner of speaking, by shifting their base of operations just ahead of the Federals—the Memphis *Appeal* was published in at least five cities before the war ended—but some papers could not get out of the way. General Sherman's forces destroyed the offices of the Fayetteville *Telegraph* and *Observer* in April 1865. There was a report in at least one Southern newspaper that his troops had offered a $10,000 reward for E. J. Hale, senior editor of the Fayetteville *Observer*—dead or alive—but this is unverified and reasonably improbable.

Politics and Federal encroachment aside, many Southern papers were forced to close or reduce operations because too many subscribers or printers volunteered for military service—some even before the war had begun. Half the staff of the Harrisonburg (Virginia) *Rockingham Register and Advertiser* "deserted . . . and joined the standard of its country." "Our partner, our son, and our pressman, have gone to the war," wrote the editor of the Wadesborough (North Carolina) *Argus*. The Hillsborough (North Carolina) *Recorder* complained of the absence of "Editors or workmen, or both," which had forced seven neighboring journals to cease publication. Some papers went out of business because there was not enough business—perhaps forty papers in Virginia and fifty in Texas closed down during the first year of the war. [18]

A year into the war, the Confederate congress began to offset a growing shortage of military manpower with conscription. All able-bodied men between the ages of eighteen and thirty-five were liable for three years of service, and all one-year volunteers were liable for a mandatory two-year extension. By September 1862, the upper age limit had been raised to forty-five; in February 1864, the full range was extended to cover men between the ages of seventeen and fifty.

Some states moved to exempt newspapermen; "Resolved," said the Executive Council of South Carolina,

That the editors and owners of newspapers in this State be informed, that if any of their employees shall fall under the conscription, the Adjutant and Inspector-General will be instructed to withhold from Confederate service such of said conscripts as the editor or owner of such newspaper shall declare by affidavit to be absolutely necessary to carry on their respective establishments, and that the work cannot be done by workmen within their command or other wise exempt: Provided, the number withheld shall not exceed seven for the Charleston daily papers, five for the Columbia daily papers, and two for each country paper. . . .

Employees thus privileged were subject to such "local and special duty as may not seriously interfere with the business of their respective offices." Virginia exempted "one editor of each newspaper now being published, and such employees as the editor or proprietor may certify on honor to be indispensable for conducting the publication of the newspaper so long as the same is regularly published at least once a week." [19]

Not quite a year later, the Confederate congress debated a bill for ending the exemptions. Congressman Charles M. Conrad of Louisiana argued that a man more than forty-five years old could very well edit a newspaper, so why should anyone younger be exempt? For that matter, he suggested that the South could do without newspapers altogether for at least six months and, anyway, newspapers had done more harm than good to the cause. [20]

Southern printers continued to go off to war, drafted or otherwise. In 1863, about eight hundred were actively employed at newspapers; by June 1864, three-quarters of them had seen army service.

In the midst of a dimishing press, one new publication was launched in September 1862. The first issue of the *Southern Illustrated News* offered a goal and a critique:

> By the aid of pen and pencil [to] present more vividly to the reader the grand and imposing events that are happening around us. . . . The illustrations we shall furnish will be honestly and faithfully drawn and engraved by competent and experienced artists. We cannot engage or give pictures to victories that were never won, or to sketch the taking of capitals that never surrendered, as have the illustrated weeklies of Yankeedom. Nor shall we ever attempt to make one engraved head serve as a portrait [for many] passing off the likeness of a British orator for an American divine, and bringing it out again, upon occasion, for a new Major General.

The editors promised to "present engravings of battles as they actually occurred, and not fancy sketches originating only in the brain of our artists—also maps showing the localities and positions occupied by the contending armies, which will prove invaluable to the general reader. . . ." [21] Those proved to be virtually invisible to any reader. In twenty-five months of publication, the *Southern Illustrated News* printed not a single battlefield scene, and only one map.

The paper did feature a running series of head-and-shoulders portraits of "distinguished men connected with the present struggle. . . ." However, the Savannah *Republican* called the portraits "miserable daubs." The *Southern Illustrated News* rushed to the defense: "Abuse cannot harm us. . . . We shall continue to print the best and most popular paper in the Confederacy, without regard to the sensibilities of persons laboring under hepatic derangement, and whose opinion of pictures, as of everything else, will continue to be jaundiced, until they consent to the mollifying influence of a course of blue pills." [22]

There indeed had been a rush of initial success—the paper claimed to be making money at a rate of $50,000 per year right from the start, but the *Southern Literary Messenger* offered this caution in April 1863:

> We wish its Editors would pay less attention to the Theatre and more to the illustrations. . . . in a professedly illustrated paper the literary matters should be subordinate to the pictures. The best articles of the best writers will not insure success half so quickly or so certainly as a plenty of even mediocre pictures.

Three months later, a house advertisement in the *Southern Illustrated News* indicated one reason for the lack of illustrations: "Engravers wanted. Desirous, if possible, of illustrating the "NEWS" in a style not inferior to the "London Illustrated News," we offer the *highest salaries* ever paid in this country for *good* engravers." [23]

The paper struggled along for another fourteen months; the last issue appeared on October 29, 1864, with one cartoon, no portraits, and no illustrated news.

Politics, Yankee occupation, poor editorial judgment, and manpower issues aside, Southern newspapers faced another serious problem: an increasingly acute shortage of supplies. This did not necessarily force the closing of any paper, but certainly challenged the ingenuity of the surviving printers. Shoe polish was a poor substitute for printing ink and, whatever else may have been needed, their products were called news*papers* for a reason. However, at the beginning of the war the paper mills of the South accounted for only 5 percent of the total national production of newsprint, and as time passed—and as most of those mills came under Federal control—the South became home to the shrinking newspaper. The usual four-page folio was reduced to one sheet, and that in diminished size.

Much has been made of the fact that some of the Southern journals were forced to resort to printing on scraps of recycled paper, most notably wallpaper. That is true, but be advised: anyone with a letterpress print shop, a modestly-stocked typecase, and rolls of old wallpaper could have created a plausible counterfeit at any time since the war. There are probably more copies of the wallpaper version of the *Vicksburg Times* offered in roadside antique shops *today* than were printed *then*.

10 / Modus Scribendi

The energy, enterprise, and lavish expenditure of money by the
representatives of the press with the army, for the furtherance of the
single object of getting news, and *getting it first*, too, would astonish
people, were even only the half told. Probably in no business in existence
is the competition so hard as between the leading newspapers
of New York and their representatives in the field.
—"The Army Correspondent," *Harper's New Monthly Magazine*,
October 1863 [1]

MOST OF THOSE who covered the war at the beginning already
were working newsmen and artists. As the months became years, they
were joined by men of less experience but perhaps no less enthusiasm,
and by war's end, some five hundred had served as "special correspondents." However, only a handful of the pioneers were still in the field in
1865. Along the way, a few died—victims of a combat in which they were
unlucky spectators. One, six feet away from General Grant, had his head
taken away by a cannon ball. A few were killed by accident—drowning,
or victims of a fallen horse. Perhaps fifty were held, for some period of
time, as prisoners of war. Some were promoted to the editor's chair; some
were fired for incompetence. Some were banished by the army for palpable indiscretion. Most just wore out.

It was not an easy job. "Virginia wastes, where only desolation
dwells," wrote a special for the New York *Tribune*, "arid with summer
heats, and now four weeks without a sprinkle of rain. The sky is brass,
heated to a white fervor . . . you boil; you pant; you thirst; your temples
throb with thrills of mighty pain . . . you wish yourself anywhere—

anywhere, out of such torment." There was always the reality of war: to properly report battles, one special acknowledged, a reporter must be "*so closely observant of them as to be in danger of being killed.*" A *Herald* man challenged his readers, "Those who suppose that the labor of a news gatherer upon the battle field is facile and rapid, should stroll, as I have, over the ground where the dead yet lie unburied, and the survivors expect momentarily to resume the conflict." There was the obvious lack of amenities: "A man is forced to seek his epistolary comfort," noted the Charleston *Courier*, ". . . at the crumbling end of a lead pencil with a shady tree or its equivalent for a sanctum, and fence rail for his writing desk. . . . It is an ignominious rostrum from which to talk to twenty thousand people." [2]

The correspondents shared the weather and battlefield and "amenities" with the common soldiers—although some of the better-supported correspondents might, from time to time, enjoy horses for transport, convivial libations, perhaps (for some) servants—former slaves—to handle the cooking and washing. Some—but not all. In a letter to his editor, Sam Wilkeson of the New York *Tribune* described his efforts in managing a team in the field:

Colston came to me yesterday with his lifeless drawling whine about the impossibility of getting "accommodations" and buying forage for his horse. Soon he asked me for money (I have furnished him $25 in all) and announced his purpose of going to [retrieve from the mail] a box of summer clothing and of comforts sent to him by his wife. The mention of the word "comforts" by a newspaper man in the field enraged me. He has no more right to them than private soldiers have. . . .

The work needs *first Class men*: men of physical courage, intelligence, tact, patience, endurance, DEVOTION.

To enlarge on this—while my hand is in. I wear four shirts a week when I am at home. The flannel shirt I have on I have worn five weeks. It is abominable, certainly. But it is not unendurable. . . . Rails make my bed. . . . My jackknife is my spoon, knife, fork, and toothpick. . . . My horse (the Tribune's) don't starve & by God! he shan't starve. I have burst open a planter's store room, and taken the hominy corn hidden for his family's food, and shelled half a bushel of it with my fingers, and fed it to "Bayard" out of my pocket handkerchief—running the risk of the Provost Marshal. That pocket handkerchief—certainly, I have washed it ten times. Washing! It has not cost me 80 cents since I left Washington. He must be damned helpless who cant wash clothes. [3]

The soldier's schedule was provided. The correspondent not only had to discover and follow that schedule, if he wanted to follow the action, but also had to find time to write his copy and then find a way to get it to the home office. Then, underlying all, the correspondent often was not welcome with the army and rarely given credit for his effort. Let this comment by a reporter for the Richmond *Dispatch* stand for all:

> The duties of newspaper correspondent are much more difficult than many are inclined to believe. He is obliged to know everything, hear everything, and do everything at the same time—in fact, he is expected to be ubiquitous. If anything escapes his eye, up jumps somebody and accuses [him] of a willful omission of facts to the prejudice of another; if he is led into error by the statements of others, he is accused of falsification; whether he blame severely, makes what he believes a plain statement of events, or praises but feebly, it is all the same. Somebody is dissatisfied. What wonder the band of young fellows who began with this war and wrote such pleasant, interesting, and gossipy letters for the Southern papers, has dwindled down to one or two? Who can blame them for leaving a labor that met with little true reward—the appreciation of the country? To have accomplished the task expected of them would have required the fabled lamps of Aladdin; and even then I have my doubts— while the vast public look to the pen of the correspondent for news, and for the daily record of events, few individuals are willing to assist him in his search after the truth. On the contrary, there are many who will rather place falsehoods in his way in order to mislead him into error. While endeavoring to do justice to everybody, to state the truth, and nothing but the truth, it is not surprising that he should sometimes be wrong, and should make some erroneous statements, either through haste in writing or on the responsibility of friends. [4]

Salaries varied widely. Henry Timrod signed on with the Charleston *Mercury* in 1862 for $6 a day plus traveling expenses. Winslow Homer's drawings in *Harper's Weekly* earned him $60 a page. Samuel Chester Reid was receiving $25 a week from the New Orleans *Picayune* in 1862; by the end of 1863 the Mobile *Tribune* was paying him $100 a week, plus horse allowance. Some were granted an "allowance" of a different sort: a senior artillery officer rewarded the *World*'s Stedman for some published laudatory comment. As Stedman wrote to his wife, "If ever a man needed $50, it is I. . . . Of course he expects me to keep a lookout for his guns hereafter, and I believe I can do so with a clear conscience." [5]

Income was likely to be a function of the number of masters a reporter might serve at the same time. In 1861, George W. Bagby was paid $3–$5 an article by the Richmond *Whig*, while contributing to at least four other newspapers. George W. "Shad" Adams, who was the Washington representative for three largely opposition papers, the Boston *Herald*, Chicago *Times*, and New York *World*, enjoyed an annual income at least equal to that of the New York *Herald*'s managing editor, on the order of $10,000. Adams's net worth was enhanced when he learned that a friend was about to be arrested for treason. He warned the friend, who begged him to buy his house, certain to be confiscated otherwise. Adams demurred—he could not assemble more than $2,000; his friend exclaimed, "That is better than losing it entirely." Thus, Adams acquired a house, which soon was worth more than thirty thousand dollars. [6]

Other correspondents took advantage of "opportunities" to deal in scarce commodities. Franc Wilkie of the New York *Times* was to accuse Albert Deane Richardson of the *Tribune* of having "interest" in a contract to sell two thousand mules to the army at St. Louis. "The public have a right to know," Wilkie wrote, "whether the reports provided by correspondents from this Department have been of that disinterested character which should entitle them to credence, or whether they have simply been those that one would naturally expect from the paid hirelings of knavish contractors." Sam Wilkeson, who accompanied Secretary of War Cameron on his visit to Frémont's headquarters in St. Louis, heard the same story and dropped a note to his (and Richardson's) employer, Horace Greeley. "Richardson," he wrote, "your special St. Louis correspondent was along—interested in Wheeler's contract for 2000 mules." The note has been preserved; Greeley's reaction is unknown. [7]

Truth to tell, both Wilkie and Wilkeson also seem to have been among those correspondents who used their position to gain financial advantage. Wilkie earned a $100 "fee" from a knavish contractor who needed an army permit to ship cotton from Memphis. Abandoned on the docks in the wake of the advancing Federal army, cotton had become lucrative fair game for anyone who could invent some claim to possession and manage to get his prize to the mills in New England, which were spinning their wheels, so to speak, with nothing to spin. The contractor asked Wilkie for help, Wilkie asked Grant, who granted the request. A few hours later, Wilkie was handed $200 by another cotton speculator who asked only for the name of the man to whom the permit had been issued. (Cotton trading allowed Albert H. Bodman of the Chicago *Tribune*—on a salary of $16 a week—to buy a house for $22,000 in cash.) Wilkeson was to be accused by the *Herald* (misnamed as "Wilkinson"), along with two other members of the *Tribune* Washington bureau, of participation in a contract for 25,000 muskets. The *Tribune* denied any improprieties; Wilkeson admitted only to "disinterested kindness" in assisting the manufacturer with the bureaucracy. [8]

Junius Browne—who contributed to the *Missouri Republican* as well as to the *Tribune*—was accused of "living at the expense of the government" in exchange for "advocating" Frémont. Browne responded, in the *Republican*, that he "asked no courtesies whatever, and received none except those invariably accorded to all correspondents and shared alike by all those with the Army in Missouri." Regarding any alleged relationship with General Frémont, he noted, "I have no personal acquaintance whatever, never having exchanged a syllable with him in all my life . . ." [9] Browne challenged anyone to call him before a court of inquiry. No one bothered.

Market speculation was a constant temptation. As already noted, Joseph Howard tried to manipulate the gold market, and someone circulated an untrue, but credible, rumor that Russell had profited on gold by leaking government intelligence. Uriah Painter, while chief Washington correspondent of the Philadelphia *Inquirer*, clearly had an arrangement with the trader who sent him the following on April 13, 1863:

> Your dispatch was *ahead* of all the others but one day behind the papers. How was this! I never was so disappointed in my life. Certainly it would have made for you at least $5000—had you sent it sooner.
>
> Allow me to assure you that I am depending on you, and will make you *a pile* if you can get the news in advance when the market is not excited by the same news. [10]

Not all profiteering was illegal or immoral; some was merely high enterprise, like that of a fourteen-year-old Washington newsboy who managed to sell about four hundred papers a day, a level of effort that required the services of a full-time assistant. He bought his papers in Washington for a cent and a half apiece and peddled them to the soldiers for a dime, clearing about thirty two dollars a day.

Some reporters had two jobs—government and newspaper—which provided two sources of income, with the added bonus that one served as a source of information for the other. Some were full-time military officers with prior newspaper experience and continuing connections. Others may have sought additional glory as "war correspondents" by responding to invitations such as that issued by the Charleston *Mercury*: ". . . the officers of the army and navy of the Confederate States, and captains sailing under letters of marque, will greatly oblige the proprietors . . . by furnishing sketches and incidents of the expected conflict between our gallant soldiers and their enemies. . . .When supplied exclusively, a liberal compensation will be allowed." [11] Both *Harper's* and *Leslie's* advertised for sketch artists with the army, offering free subscriptions to anyone who would at least send in a trial drawing; by war's end, each had arrangements with about fifty army artists, but their contributions were minimal.

Some specials were part-time volunteers to the military and full-time paid newspapermen— a category necessarily operated with the sufferance or collusion of senior officers, and which saw a marked expansion in the spring of 1862 after authorities on both sides tried to keep reporters from traveling with the armies. The "volunteer" route was a natural haven, favored throughout the war—favored, that is, by the newsmen, but not necessarily by the senior officers. In July 1861, covering activities in western Virginia, William Swinton of the New York *Times* and the *Tribune's* Richardson applied to Brig. Gen. Jacob F. Cox for appointment as "volunteer aides" with military rank, privileges of the general's mess, and freedom from censorship or review of their reports. Cox, an attorney and politician with no significant military experience, had been left in charge of an operation already in progress, by the sudden transfer of his superior, McClellan. He may have been inexperienced, but he was not a fool, and he refused this rather overreaching demand. However, he obviously did not *understand* (as the Chicago *Times* would later note) that a special correspondent

> is a very important personage, and must be treated with becoming consideration by all with whom he comes in contact, and especially be patronized by the superior officers, who are expected to furnish him with a horse and detail a servant to take care of it. All plans of battles and general movements should be submitted to his inspection. He should be admitted to all military councils, and be furnished in advance with a copy of every order, general or special. . . . "Our correspondent" holds a rod of terror suspended over the heads of all officers, whom he threatens with a severe writing down if they fail to pay him due deference. [12]

Swinton's "writing down" appeared in the New York *Times*, August 2, 1861:

> I cannot close this letter, already too long, without saying a few words concerning this division of the Grand Army of the Union. The men have no confidence whatever in their leader, and are already in a state of insubordination. . . . Last night our men were encamped between two high hills, and most of them compelled to

sleep on the bare ground, although their tents were in wagons hard by. If [Confederate General] Wise had attacked us last night with five hundred men, our rout would have been complete. *Not a picket was thrown out.* This system of carrying on a war in an enemy's country, and especially when the enemy is thought to be only a few miles in advance, is certainly a novel one, and original with Brig.-Gen. Cox.

Richardson's version, published on the same day in the *Tribune*:

General Cox's brigade is in a wretched condition. Insubordination, disorganization, inefficiency and incompetency are so palpable that it would be wrong to pass them over in silence. . . . The camp last night was in a locality affording neither comfort nor safety. The precaution of throwing out pickets was neglected in some directions and five hundred resolute, disciplined men could have routed the command. . . . The only safety of our troops lies in the fact that the Rebels are even worse disorganized than they, and dare not attack. . . .

Those twin contributions to the journalistic record, published just a few days after McClellan's gentleman's agreement, helped spur the resurrection of the Fifty-Seventh Article of War. General Cox's later wartime contribution's transcended such early notices, and, after the war, he was elected governor of Ohio and then served as secretary of the interior.

The rich Northern papers in New York, Philadelphia, Boston, Cincinnati, and Chicago sent most of the men into the field. Even the unabashed Copperhead Chicago *Times* would brag: "There is not an important point in the country where we do not now maintain one or more special correspondents. We employ the magnetic telegraph at a cost of more than a thousand dollars annually, special messengers at a heavy outlay, and the express and mails only as they can be made useful." [13] The New York *Tribune* had perhaps twenty-nine specials on assignment at the end of the war.

In this, however, no paper could compete with the New York *Herald*. By 1862, the *Herald* had thirty specials in the field at a cost of more than $2,000 per week, and by the end of the war had been maintaining a corps of sixty-three—according to an 1867 magazine article by *Herald* reporter William Shanks—"of the most enterprising, though by no means the most learned . . ." correspondents. The conditions of employment were simple: "Promptness in action, not perspicuity in English; a clear head not a concise style; and common-sense, not a college education." [14] Every man who signed on with the *Herald* was handed this guidance:

> In no instance, and under no circumstances, must you be beaten. . . . You will have energetic and watchful men to compete with. Eternal industry is the price of success. You must be active—very active. To be beaten is to be open to great censure. . . . Remember that your correspondence is seen by half a million persons daily and that the readers of the Herald *must* have the earliest news. . . . Again bear in mind that *the Herald must never be beaten.* [15]

This fifteen-hundred word circular included instructions for handling various items—maps, plans, Southern newspapers—and came with the admonition, "You will reveal [the] contents to no one—not even to anybody claiming to be a Herald correspondent."

"The successful correspondent did as he pleased," Shanks continued, "his wishes were consulted, his advice asked, his requests granted, his accounts unquestioned, his salary advanced unsolicited." The unsuccessful were put on notice. . . . *if* they held on to their jobs. [16]

Another *Herald* reporter, George Alfred Townsend, described most of his coworkers as not "fit to describe a fire. . . . the usual run of forward, uneducated, flimsy-headed, often middle-aged, misplaced people, who had mysteriously gotten on a newspaper. They were capable of plenty of endurance, and would ride up and down, and talk with great confidence, and be familiar with everybody, and then not know how to relate what they saw." [17]

However, the *Herald*'s skill at deploying the staff—flimsy-headed or otherwise—was unmatched. For example, in the fall of 1862, while the *Tribune* had five men (who shared one horse, one messenger, and not enough of anything else) covering the Army of the Potomac, the *Herald* fielded sixteen men with wagons, tents, boats, horses, money, and whatever supplies might be needed. To cover a minor excursion down the Potomac the *Herald* had one man riding a navy ship, one hanging around Navy Department headquarters to catch a look at any official dispatches, and one standing by at the navy yard to interview the officers when they returned.

The managing editor of the New York *Tribune* offered a bit of his own competitive guidance to at least one sluggish field correspondent, Thomas Butler Gunn:

> My Dear Sir— . . . Your sketch of ye battle-ground of the 16th came just *eight* days after ye battle. Of course it was useless. The corr. of ye Philadelphia *Inquirer* had sent one to that paper, which it had

engraved & published, which I had also engraved &published, three days before yours reached me. I pray you remember ye *Tribune* is a *daily* news-paper—or meant to be,—and not a historical record of past events. Correspondents to be of any value must be prompt, fresh, & full of facts. I know how difficult it is, under ye censor-ship to write, but there must be facts enough of general interest all about you to make a daily letter. . . . I should like you to write daily, if only a half, a quarter column, so that ye report of all you may tell be continuous. The curiosity & anxiety about Yorktown is feverish, & ye public like ye paper best that is always giving something. If there is absolutely *nothing* to write about, drop a line and tell me that. The *Herald* is constantly ahead of us with Yorktown news. The battle of ye 16th we were compelled to copy from it. [April 28, 1862]

Gunn scribbled some notes on the back of the letter, and then lost it. This "private" communication of the *Tribune* appeared in the New York *Herald* on May 16, 1862, with the comment that it had been discovered after the evacuation of Yorktown:

One of our correspondents—who see everything, hear everything, and find everything—fished this unique epistle out of a pile of rebel documents. . . . We do not know the name of the *Tribune* reporter to whom it is addressed, but his notes in pencil are on the back of the original letter. . . . Thank you, Mr. Gay. But why not acknowledge this openly in your editorial columns, and not clandestinely in letters to your reporters?

The next day's *Tribune* claimed that one of their correspondents had reported the loss of a horse and saddlebags, alleging therefore that the thief must have been a *Herald* man. By acknowledging this much, the *Tribune* as much as authenticated the contents of the letter. This must have preyed on Greeley's mind, because eight months later the *Tribune* warned that the material that the *Herald* had published from the letter, which it "caused to have stolen is a FORGERY." [18]

The spirit and drive of competition, thus mandated all around, produced a great deal of suspect behavior. The *Herald* was not the only newspaper in the race, but, almost always, took first place. For example, the "fifteen-minute" rule of the telegraph disappeared on the establishment of the Associated Press, and government appropriation of the lines imposed a discipline on content, but not on tactics. The old "first come, served-until-finished" rule seems to have been revived, because the Bible ploy—"Start at Genesis and don't stop 'til I say so"—was back in fashion. In this, the goal was usually to buy enough time for the correspondent to finish his own dispatch before his competitors could file theirs, not to tie up the line forever; few newspapers could have afforded the charges.

Except for the *Herald*. During the battle at Gettysburg, correspondent Frank Chapman used his pocket Bible to maintain an exclusive hold on the telegraph line out of Baltimore until a *Herald* extra could hit the streets. Then, he purchased an effective monopoly by sending 5,000 to 10,000 words a day, buying the loyalty of the operators who told other correspondents, without shame, that "the *Herald* has control of the line, as long as they choose to use it." Chapman also seems freely to have appropriated the copy of others—bought, borrowed, or stolen from the telegrapher's desk—for his own use. "I note in yesterday's N.Y. *Herald* a short dispatch I left in telegraph office on Sunday night," J. H. Taggart of the Philadelphia *Inquirer* wrote to an associate, with the suspicion that "it was sold to Chapman here, by the operator, or he was permitted to copy it from the dispatch I left in the office." [19]

On another occasion, Chapman stole some sheets of copy from the pocket of New York *Tribune* correspondent Francis C. Long while the two men were seated together on a train headed toward Washington—and then reported Long to the train guards as a suspicious person. Long was taken off the train at an intermediate stop, and by the time he had established his identity, the train had left. The purloined dispatch, in part verbatim, appeared in the next day's *Herald*. Long had a chance to get back at Chapman a few weeks later, again meeting him on a train. Chapman, who had nothing useful to send to his paper that day, offered Long $250 just to let him read a dispatch Long was carrying. Long refused, but then pretended to be polishing his copy—knowing that Chapman was looking over his shoulder. Long wrote a completely spurious account, including a list of fictional general officer casualties. The story was published in the *Herald* on December 4, 1863.

Chapman may best be described in the words of a Confederate reporter, who met him during a prisoner exchange late in 1861: "the gassiest deadhead of all was a chap named Chapman representing himself as a reporter and correspondent extraordinary for the New York *Herald*. He was successively social and impudently inquisitive, relating, unasked, his many wonderful experiences. . . ." [20]

Another special who maneuvered for unfair advantage—in at least one recorded incident—was Albert Dean Richardson. In September 1861, Franc Wilkie had joined Brig. Gen. Samuel Sturgis in the aborted effort to rescue Colonel Mulligan and his men from the besieging rebels at Lexington, Missouri. When Sturgis determined that crossing the Missouri river into rebel-held territory was not practical, Wilkie managed to get drunk enough to imagine himself invincible, caught a ferry across the river, and immediately fell into rebel hands.

The next morning, nursing a hangover and the sober realization that he was in real danger of being hung as a spy, Wilkie convinced rebel general Sterling Price that his intentions were honorable—to write a sympathetic article for the New York *Times*. The general, perhaps thinking that no spy would be dumb enough to get as drunk as Wilkie had been, wrote out a bemused pass:

> The bearer, Franc B. Wilkie, newspaper correspondent, is hereby authorized to observe operations of this Army at Lexington, Mo. Treat him courteously, but keep an eye on him. He is a Yankee.

Wilkie spent four days with the Confederates, interviewed Colonel Mulligan and other Federals after the surrender, and then quietly headed back across the river and on to St. Louis, writing one of the war's most unusual eyewitness scoops as he went. He arrived penniless, having lost his wallet during a fracas with another band of rebels, and sought out a friend—Thomas Knox of the *Herald*—from whom he might borrow some money. Knox was away, and the *Tribune*'s Richardson answered Wilkie's knock on the hotel room door. Wilkie asked if he could to borrow $10. Richardson was noncommittal until he learned that Wilkie had been on the inside at Lexington, whereupon he offered to buy the story for the *Tribune* for $125 in gold—about four times what Wilkie could expect in payment from the *Times*.

Wilkie said, "It belongs to the *Times*."

Richardson said, "But you can write another for the *Times*."

Wilkie declined, and Richardson declined to loan him any money. "All right Mister Richardson," Wilkie said. "This is going to be a long war." [21]

When *Times* editor Henry Raymond heard about Wilkie's loyalty, he arranged for a generous bonus, shifted the reporter from space rates to a weekly salary and expenses, and published the report with great pleasure and a rather disingenuous salute:

> We do not believe any instance can be cited of similar courage and devotion on the part of a newspaper correspondent; and we respectfully commend it to those who are so glib in their censure of a class of men who will compare most favorably with any others, not excepting officers in the Army, for the zeal, resolution and self-denying enterprise which they bring to the performance of their arduous and responsible duties. [22]

The pressure of competition pushed many into deception. A letter to the editor of the Cincinnati *Commercial* complained of specials who never went near the battlefield:

With what pleasant assurance they date their letters at these "head-quarters" and on that "gunboat," while themselves wrapt in soothing sloth, far from enemies at the St. Charles [hotel in Cairo] or Gayoso [hotel in Memphis], button-hole from straggling soldiers and dyspeptic officers their fragmentary falsehoods for tomorrow's mails. The worthy rogues are too lazy even to individualize their own bosh, and by mutual interchange of lies, present the same brazen surface in all their letters. [23]

The *Herald*'s Tom Knox would fall victim to similar deceit. Knox, as the only New York special on hand at the Battle of Pea Ridge (Missouri, March 7–8, 1862), felt no sense of urgency in writing and sending his letter. However, Junius Browne of the New York *Tribune* and Richard Colburn of the *World* learned of the battle, got as close as they could—the railhead at Rolla, about 195 miles from the battlefield—and, from telegraph reports and interviews with a local man who was familiar with Pea Ridge, wrote such plausible "eyewitness" reports that the London *Times* saluted that which appeared in the *Tribune* as "the ablest and best battle account which had been written during the American war." Eyewitness, and ear-witness: "Even now," "remembered" Browne, "while I attempt to collect my blurred and dis-connected thoughts, the sound of booming cannon and the crack of the rifle rings in my ears, while visions of carnage and the flames of battle hover before my sight. Three days of constant watching, without food or sleep, and the excitements of the struggle, have quite unstrung my nerves." [24]

In another context, the pressure of competition (or a lack of decency; or both) led to some rather bizarre behavior. Three examples stand out, all following the Union capture of Fort Donelson, Tennessee: one, about a newspaper artist who kept Confederate general Buckner locked in a room until he could complete a pencil sketch; another, which held that a special threatened to reveal Confederate general Bushrod Johnson's past indiscretions—forgery—unless granted an interview; and the third, which concerned a representative of a New York journal who confronted a dying officer of some distinction with a request to "hold on" until his last words might be captured and polished for the readers of his "widely circulated and highly influential" newspaper. When the officer's friends forced the overzealous fool from the scene, he expressed a departing hope that they would remember who it was made the first request and would not permit "any other member of the Press" to capture the dying officer's sentiments, "no matter what inducements might be offered." [25]

What was the result—in terms of literary merit—of all the jockeying for position, of the flattery and cajolery, of the squabbles with the censors and the enmity of the military, of the harassment by editors, and, always, of the inevitable pressure from writing under a deadline? Putting aside the obvious limitations imposed by political bias and a continuing problem with accuracy, the specials produced a lot of good writing, indeed, some very great writing, much of which may be lost, or moldering in some deep unfathomed archive.

There also was a lot of very bad writing. The style of much mid-nineteenth-century newspaper writing was, on balance, *dense*—a series of generally-related clauses strung together like, and about as swiftly moving as, the joints of a caterpillar. The lead sentence of one report of the battle at Missionary Ridge contained 174 words. We repeat the plea lodged in the October 23, 1864, edition of the Mobile *Daily Register and Advertiser*:

> Let our correspondents . . . condense their logic, leave out their rhetoric entirely, and in their recapitulations take *some* things for granted. Are they writing from the front; let them bear in mind that all our soldiers are heroes, and not dwell too much on the gallantry of Major This or Colonel That, or even of Private So and So—that will keep (if it is worth keeping) till the war is over.
>
> Did any of our correspondents ever take the trouble of reading one of Cicero's orations by a watch? If they will they will find some of the best of them less than half an hour long. . . . The intellectual fault of our age and nation is verbiage; the times admonish us to correct it. . . . If an idea can be stated in four words instead of five, we implore them to strike out the fifth . . . and, as a general rule, to omit their comments and permit the reader to make them instead. We could say more, but our theme admonishes us to desist.

Many correspondents were not very good at their craft and had a difficult time capturing the flair and flavor of combat; there are too many examples of atrocious writing to merit extended attention, so let one sample from the Knoxville *Daily Register*, May 7, 1863, suffice:

> The alarm was sounded, and when the boats had gained a point where they were within range of our uppermost batteries, a ten-inch Columbiad welcomed them with an iron messenger in the shape of a shell. In less time than it takes to relate it, five transports, heavily laden with provisions, and one gunboat were receiving the fire of these death-dealing monsters that grin defiance from the hills overlooking the Mississippi. At this juncture, it was fearfully grand and

awfully sublime to see the flaming metal gushing forth from the mouths of our blackthroated defenders, which had been aroused and angered by the insolence and audacity of the foe in venturing within their dominions.

It is more interesting—and infinitely more rewarding—to review some of the better contributions to the journalistic record, such as this, by Maj. Robert Henry Glass, writing for the Lynchburg *Republican*, September 5, 1961:

As we rode through the field this morning, the enemy's bullets could be heard cutting through the corn and whistling by your ears as thick as hail, and yet but few of our men were touched. The calculation recently made by some one, that it takes seven hundred balls to kill one man, is really true, though the calculation is not of much consolation to the poor fellow who gets the fatal shot.

Or this, from a report of the battle at Perryville, in the Atlanta *Daily Southern Confederacy*, November 13, 1862:

All my conceptions of the hurrah and din and dust of a battle were confounded by the cool, business-like operations going on before me. . . .Those badly clothed, some shoeless dirty and ragged-looking men walked into the harvest of death before them with all the composure and much less of the bustle than a merchant would exhibit in walking to his counting-room after breakfast.

And this from William Swinton of the New York *Times*, two weeks before the battle of Fredericksburg:

The men go hulking and shuffling along. . . . I cannot doubt that there is among our men plenty of high and patriotic feeling; but the soldier-habits do not encourage its expression. . . . men march to death and to exploits that live in history, frivolous, light-hearted, jocular or morose as their personal moods and idiosyncrasies may be. [26]

In our own time—when television news first brought war into our living rooms—the news was given the credit, or the blame, for turning public opinion against the American effort in Vietnam. In reality, television news showed more of politics and protest than it did of combat, and all of the news media adhered to a set of ground rules they worked out among themselves, including an agreement not to show grievous casualties or recognizable dead. The following bits illustrate just how graphic was much of the coverage for the Civil War:

> In the ditch around the works, the dead and wounded, white and black, were literally piled together. Blood, mud, water, brains and human hair matted together—men lying in every conceivable attitude, with every conceivable expression on their countenances, their limbs bent into unnatural shapes by the fall of twenty or more feet, the fingers rigid and outstretched, as if they had clutched at the earth to save themselves—pale, beseeching faces, looking out from among the ghastly corpses, with moans and cries for help and water, and dying gasps and death struggles. [27]

Frank W. Reilly reported for the Cincinnati *Times*: "I hope my eyes may never again look upon such sights. Men with their entrails protruding, others with bullets in their breasts or shoulders, and one poor wretch I found whose eyes had been shot entirely away. . . ." Charles Anderson Page, the editor of a small Iowa weekly wanted a *real* newspaper job, and got one with the *Tribune*. He arrived just in time for an action at Mechanicsville, Virginia, on June 27, 1862: "During the stampede, for a moment the attention of hundreds was attracted to a horse galloping around carrying a man's leg in the stirrup—the left leg, booted and spurred. It was a splendid horse, gaily caparisoned." [28]

While the correspondents were sent into the field specifically to report on battles, the time devoted to combat, in any war, is but a fraction of the whole. The specials filled their time and their letters with comment on the world through which they passed, providing a truly unique view and loads of grist for any modern writer's mill. The Richmond *Daily Dispatch* of April 29, 1862, offered this description of Southern soldiery in the western theater:

> Troops from Louisiana are small, wiry, quick as squirrels in their motions and thoroughly Gallic in their habits and associations. The men of Alabama and Mississippi are taller, as a general thing less cosmopolized, yet full of Southern fire. . . . Here you see the well dressed gentleman with nothing to mark the soldier but the cartridge box, body belt and shot gun. There is a group of Mississippi boatmen in their slouched hats, red shirts, heavy pants, and cowhide boots coming up to the knee. Again you encounter the bushwhackers of Arkansas, Texas and Missouri, large bearded, hard handed, tough, muscular fellows, who eat victuals with their bowie knives and sleep on the butts of their guns. Some have rifles which have come down to them as heirlooms from an untainted ancestry

and are historic with the bloody records of bar fights and wild cat adventures; thousands have nothing but an ordinary shotgun, but all, more or less, go armed with the inevitable knife and revolver. Many ride poor Rosinantes of beasts, sometimes a horse, but as frequently a mule; and thus equipped, go forth looking like dilapidated Don Quixotes, but acting like very devils when they smell blood.

In February 1863, a special from the Columbus *Sun* was "hungry as a wolf" when he spotted a welcome sign:

Those great golden letters above the door—restaurant—tell of good things within that make a soldier think of home. . . . the smiling individual who meets you at the door evidently understands his business. Dinner for one? Yes, sir, what will you have? What have you got? Coffee, real Rio—this is always mentioned first, for everybody likes real Rio—beef mutton, pork, potatoes, butter and bread. A hungry man eats everything with pleasure, but this coffee certainly has a strong smell of villainous rye; and the beef is poor enough to have fasted ever since it left the verdant plains of Texas; and the butter smells as if it had made a trip from Texas too, or had even run the blockade from some foreign country across the deep blue sea. There is, however, no use in grumbling about what one has eaten, and, after all, this dinner is so much better than camp fare, that you feel good and pull out your pocket book with the air of a man who has been benefitted and wished to compensate his benefactor. What do I owe you, sir? Two dollars and a half. Two dollars and a half! You are exor— And before you can finish the sentence your accommodating host begins talking in such an excited manner about paying forty cents a pound for flour, fifty cents for pork, three dollars for butter, five dollars for coffee, so much for wood, house rent &c &c that you feel ashamed that you have said anything and are glad to beat a hasty retreat. [29]

The menu during the Siege of Vicksburg, as reported in the Augusta *Daily Constitutionalist*, July 26, 1863, was somewhat more exotic:

I told you we would stay until starved out. Well, rats are a luxury. Small fishes sell at twenty dollars. Chickens at ten dollars each. Corn meal has sold at one hundred and sixty dollars per bushel. Mule meat has sold readily at two dollars per pound, in market, and I eat it once a week. The soldiers have had only one meal a day for ten days, and then one man does not get what a child should have.

We close this sampler with a haunting vision of an October Missouri, from the New York *Times*, November 4, 1861:

This, our first night on the open prairie, gave us a foretaste of Winter. The night was intensely cold, and this morning there was a heavy frost, accompanied by an east wind that cut one to the very marrow. Winter is nearly upon us—the woods have lost their rich variety of Autumn tints and now present only a dull, dead expanse of faded brown. The leaves go whirling crazily to the ground or rattle like skeletons in the mournful winds. I dread the march over these gloomy mountains. . . . a few ragged boys, overgrown girls, pale women and fever-wasted men gaze enviously at us from the doors of their log shanties as we pass by, headed, as they assume, for warmth and home and family. The country through which we pass seems weighted down by something like a nightmare or Puritan Sunday—or as if half the State were dead and the balance had just returned from attending the funeral.

11 / Washington

If there are any men in Washington who lead dog's lives,
they are the correspondents of the daily papers. From morning to
midnight they are on watch for items, or "points," to use a
common term among them, resting not from one week's end
to the other, in their weary round of duties, and scarcely able to call
one day in the seven their own, indeed, not at all if they are the
victims of a Sunday edition.
—Cincinnati *Daily Commercial*, December 29, 1862 [1]

WHILE MOST OF THE ACTION, of course, was in the field, covering armies on the move (or otherwise), much of the material for the North was focused by the lens of "Washington." It was there that official reports were parsed, government leaders pursued, and rumors amplified. On any given day, perhaps thirty specials made regular daily rounds of congressional and department offices, military headquarters, nearby army camps, the railroad station, hotels, bars, and restaurants—sending their copy to New York "in wads" by the telegraph:

> They hang about the Department offices; they button-hole the unhappy ushers; they besiege goers and comers; they read physiognomies; they absorb the contents of all leaky vessels like a sponge; they study hotel registers as faithfully as a monk his breviary; they "spot" "distinguished arrivals" as quickly as a detective, and pursue them like Death in the Apocalypse. And if these resources fail, there is a bank that never fails, a supply that never gives out, in their fertile imaginations. [2]

Sam Wilkeson had been sent to Washington to replace Fitz-Henry Warren—who had resigned in the wake of the Bull Run debacle—as bureau chief for the New York *Tribune*. Wilkeson quickly earned his pay. The War Department, under the direction of Secretary Cameron, was awarding contracts to men whose only qualification seems to have been their close personal relationships with the secretary, and Wilkeson pretended not to notice. "Secretary Cameron gives day and night service to the service of his country" he wrote after only a week on the job. "The contracts made by him will defy the most unfriendly scrutiny. . . ." To ensure that his good deed would not pass unnoticed, he sent a clipping to the secretary, with a note, "The satisfaction of doing justice to a wronged statesman, is not equaled by the pleasure with which I sincerely pay a tribute of respect to a maligned good man." [3]

Three weeks into the job, Wilkeson could boast: "Three of the Departments here are about secured to us. It will take me a week longer to finish the conquest. Then I shall advance on two others, and by detail & in time get them all. Then the Herald and the Times will be smilingly defied to a competition." [4] Along the way, he assumed additional duties working *for* Cameron as a sort of one-man U.S. Information Agency, writing War Department dispatches for European distribution. When Cameron went to St. Louis to "investigate" General Frémont, Wilkeson not only gained a berth as part of the secretary's party, but also was assigned to write the official report.

Tangible evidence of Wilkeson's success is preserved in a note dated October 5, Cameron to chief censor H. E. Thayer: "My Dear Sir—It is my wish that you neither suppress nor alter the telegrams of Mr. Samuel Wilkeson. Please send them as they are written and signed by him." The note is preserved because it was reprinted in the *Herald* of March 23, 1862, and the Cincinnati *Commercial* of March 27, 1862. On that same day in October, the *Herald*'s chief Washington correspondent made a private arrangement with the censor to allow *his* personal, ostensibly not-for-publication, telegrams to pass unmolested. The *Herald* did not mention this exclusive exception.

Wilkeson's special relationship with Cameron did not pass unnoticed. The New York *Times* of October 29, 1861, reprinted one of Wilkeson's *Tribune* items with the explanation, "The confidential relations which the *Tribune*'s Washington correspondent is understood to sustain to the Secretary of War give this letter more importance than it would ordinarily possess."

On that same day, Wilkeson sent to his editor some War Department documents before the president had seen them, notably the aforementioned report on the visit to Frémont. When the editors of the *Times* and the *Herald* read about the report—in the *Tribune*—they demanded equal treatment in the leaking of official documents. The *Herald* added that Wilkeson ought to be arrested as a common thief. However, because *Herald* managing editor Hudson and *Times* editor in chief Raymond constituted the "executive committee" of the Associated Press, they soon were able to announce the following:

> Arrangements have been completed between Heads of Departments in Washington and the representatives of the New-York press by which . . . all *official* documents, of whatever kind, emanating from the Departments, be delivered to the general agent of the Associated Press in Washington—and to him alone—for prompt and simultaneous transmission. [5]

The *Herald*'s Washington answer to Wilkeson was Henry Wikoff, a man of fascinating, but decidedly mixed, background, who at one time or another had been a U.S. diplomat, a representative of the British Foreign Office, a theatrical manager, and the convicted kidnapper of a wealthy spinster with whom he had a premarital disagreement. (He forced her, at gunpoint, to sign a marriage contract and spent fifteen months in jail as a result.)

Despite the November "agreement" on official documents, Wikoff scored a huge beat in December by obtaining an advance copy of the president's annual message to Congress, portions of which slipped by the censor and were published in the *Herald* before anyone in Congress had seen them. This sparked an intense investigation by a congressional committee—not to study the weakness in the censor's office but, rather, to demand that Wikoff reveal his source. He declined, was cited for contempt of Congress, and put in jail, but not for very long. Within days, the committee had swallowed the rather improbable story that the White House gardener had spotted the message on the president's desk, memorized large portions of the text, and passed them along to Wikoff.

At least, such was the sworn testimony given by the gardener himself. The common rumor, however, as reported in the *World*: "Friends of the *Herald* openly boasted that the Chevalier Wikoff obtained it through the medium of the highest lady in the land." Some years later, the Washington correspondent of the Boston *Journal* affirmed that the source of the information indeed had been the first lady, socially isolated by the snobs of Washington and flattered by Wikoff's warm attentions. The president, it seems, was successful in urging the Republican leadership to let the matter lie. [6]

Not to be outdone, Wilkeson obtained an advance copy of the annual report of the secretary of war. When the president read—in the *Tribune*—that Cameron was going to advocate the arming of freed slaves, he directed that portion of the as yet unsubmitted report to be rewritten—and told Cameron to get ready for his new assignment as ambassador to Russia. William Howard Russell's soon-to-be nemesis Edwin M. Stanton was nominated as his replacement. With his patron thus banished, Wilkeson's influence in Washington quickly evaporated, although he made an effort to maintain his "information agency" job. He sent samples of his work to the incoming secretary, but to no apparent effect. By late spring, Wilkeson had been reassigned to cover the Army of the Potomac.

Just after the turn of the new year, Wikoff had been joined in the *Herald*'s Washington bureau by another man with an unusual background: Malcolm Ives, a defrocked Jesuit and former professor of biblical literature who had turned to journalism when the church frowned on his lack of celibate fortitude. Ives had been writing editorials in the home office but was sent to Washington to pick up where Wikoff had been forced to step aside.

On January 10, Ives was among the first to hear the rumor that Stanton was about to replace Cameron. He rushed to tell Stanton—an old acquaintance—who assured him (as Ives wrote to Bennett) that "if he *did* receive the appointment, he would show that he was no middle measures man, but should throw overboard the rest of the press and cling to the Herald alone." [7] One hour later, Stanton was summoned to the White House to be given the official invitation by the president.

Stanton indeed was helpful, personally taking Ives to meet General McClellan. This quickly led to an amazing interview, during which McClellan pledged his absolute loyalty to the *Herald*. "Mr. Bennett has stood by me," he reportedly said, "in the hour of the bitterest anxiety of my whole life. . . . He and he alone, has upheld me, cheered me and encouraged me, when every other newspaper heaped upon me calumny and abuse, at the very time that I was saving them from the horrors of an invasion." [8]

Off and on during the next three weeks, Ives passed more tantalizing material on to New York: he had been invited to visit McClellan "*Every* day"; had been allowed a private peek at War Department correspondence; had been shown a list of pending movements; and had made arrangements for a signal to be sent from McClellan's headquarters to Bennett when an action was about to commence.

The resident *Herald* chief Washington correspondent, Simon P. Hanscom, became concerned about Ives's activities—whether to protect his employer or promote himself is open to question. On January 28 he stopped by the War Department to suggest that Mr. Ives, while admittedly a *Herald* employee, worked only in the New York office and was in Washington on private business. Any attempts he might make to get news, Hanscom reportedly said, "were unauthorized, obtrusive and in opposition to orders." [9] Someone told Ives, and Ives complained to Bennett, who—disenchanted with Hanscom for many reasons—fired his chief Washington correspondent and appointed Ives the successor.

That assignment lasted about two days. On the first day Ives wrote to Bennett that he had conquered the Navy Department: Assistant Secretary Gustavas Fox promised "to have *everything* given to the *Herald*—as far as he dares exclusively." The next day, as reported in a *Rebellion Record* entry for February 9, Doctor Ives, "a correspondent of the New York Herald," was arrested and sent to Ft. McHenry "on the charge of being a spy, and for violating the rules and regulations of the War Department. According to the [arrest] order of Secretary Stanton, Ives introduced himself into the chambers of the Department, when private consultations were being held, and demanded news for publication." [10] Actually, a rather drunk Dr. Ives had threatened to withhold favorable treatment in the *Herald* unless he was thenceforth given special access to inside information, and demanded an immediate audience with Stanton. In print, the *Herald* doubted that Ives was a spy, but disavowed any official connection with his actions (although the paper continued to pay his salary until he was released from confinement in May).

On February 3, 1862, Congress authorized the president to take possession of the telegraph and railroad lines in the United States, whenever, in his judgment, the public safety required it. Congress expressed the hope that all telegraph and railroad companies would cooperate, but warned that "any attempt to resist the unrestrained use by Government of such property, when too powerful to be suppressed by ordinary means, shall be punished by death, as a military offense." Congress did recognize that some companies might, by these seizures, suffer financial hardship, and created a special commission to assess and determine any damages that might be due. [11]

The president's concern for public safety was quickly affirmed. Stanton was sworn in on February 25, 1862, and the Act of February 3 was implemented the same day. All unauthorized telegraphic communications concerning military operations were forbidden; newspapers that published unauthorized military information, however obtained, and by whatever medium received, were to be cut off from the telegraph and forbidden to ship their product by railroad. [12] Stanton also assumed responsibility for censorship and assigned E. S. Sanford, head of the

American Telegraph Company, as military supervisor of telegrams, with the rank of colonel.

The chiefs of police of the major cities of the North were given notice that "all newspaper editors and publishers have been forbidden to publish any intelligence received by telegraph or otherwise respecting military operations by U.S. forces," and were directed, "Please see this night that this order is observed. If violated by any paper issued tomorrow, seize the whole edition and give notice to this department that arrests may be ordered." In Chicago, the presses were stopped at 3:00 A.M. while police read every word in the papers. The New York *World* was appalled: "The thing is incredible. . . . is it possible that this free government is thus prepared to adopt the first necessity of a military despotism. This is the people's war. . . . There must be freedom of information, and freedom of speech." The New York *Tribune* warned of "fearful" consequences. [13]

The orders to police were rescinded the next day, but the concept remained in force. On March 16, John Russell Young, newly installed as editor of Forney's Washington *Chronicle*, was arrested for publishing a "forbidden" item. The arrest was, at best, a tactical error: Forney, a Democrat who supported the administration and a personal friend of the president, had just been elected secretary of the U.S. Senate. The offending item was a notice that a particular division had passed through Alexandria on the way South. The offending editor apologized: the material had been put in the paper after he had gone to bed. The order was suspended.

A week later, the Post Office Department was persuaded to issue corollary instructions for the guidance of Federal postmasters:

> The Secretary of War now regulates the transmission of information by telegraph, affecting the conduct of the war, in order to prevent the communication of such information to the rebels. It is also thought necessary by the Secretary to put restrictions on the publication of facts of this character, however derived, and the aid of this department is requested for this purpose. You will, therefore, notify publishers not to publish any fact which has been excluded from the telegraph, and that a disregard of this order will subject the paper to be excluded from the mails. [14]

The postmaster general did not suggest how the publishers might know, with any reasonable certainty, that a "fact" had been "excluded." Chicago *Tribune* Washington correspondent Horace White (who doubled as clerk of the Senate Committee on Military Affairs) went to the Post Office Department for clarification; none was forthcoming. First Assistant Postmaster John A. Kasson told him that "the order had been issued in conformity with a wish of the Secretary of War, and he presumed that the language adopted was such as Mr. Stanton desired." In a note to his editor the next day, White added, "Kasson don't know what the order means—that is he *presumes* it means so & so, but he admits that the language is vague and mischievous, & moreover the whole thing is illegal. Stanton is a kind of Mephistopheles & the only good thing about him is that he hates McClellan profoundly." [15]

In truth, Stanton's relationship with McClellan had quickly deteriorated, perhaps because McClellan, who saw himself more as savior than warrior, thought *he* was in charge. Evidence of the change was not long in coming: speaking at a convention of railroad executives in February, Stanton paid a compliment to General Grant and did not even mention former railroad executive McClellan. However, a friend of McClellan's gladly briefed an absent Associated Press man on the speech, with this published result: "Secretary Stanton paid a high compliment to the young and gallant friend at his side, Major General McClellan, in whom he had the utmost confidence, and the result of whose military schemes, gigantic and well-matured, were now exhibited to a rejoicing country."

Stanton was not amused with this "impudent forgery." He complained that "agents of the A.P. and a gang around the federal capital appeared to be organized for the purpose of magnifying their idol." [16]

Joseph Medill, a proprietor of the Chicago *Tribune*, sent a note of welcome to Stanton—and a warning. "You will encounter rottenness and rascality from top to bottom," he wrote, "you will discover scores of lukewarm, half secession officers in command who cannot bear to strike a vigorous blow. . . . three fourths of all the 'West Pointers' in the army." Chicago *Tribune* Washington correspondent White offered a public echo of that private communication a week or so later: the "essentially aristocratic" West Pointers were too cautious, were "intensely pro-slavery," and did not have their heart in the war. [17]

This common belief among the Radicals was frequently rehearsed by the philosophically similar *Tribunes*. Issues of abolition aside, they held that the war was off to a sluggish start because the West Pointers were reluctant warriors, loath to engage in serious battle with their friends and former classmates at the military academy. The West Pointers could be expected only to go through the motions, all the while hoping for a timely political compromise. As Charles Mackay, writing from New York for the London *Times*, noted, "The innuendo is daily made that the West Pointers on both sides love each other too well to fight very desperately, and that some fine morning before anyone suspects the manoeuver they will unite their armies, and make an end of the Republic." [18]

The *Tribunes* favored the amateur generals, the "selfless patriots" who answered their nation's call because they wanted to, not because it was expected of them. The fact that many were ambitious politicians who either bought or bribed their way to general's stars seemed not to matter; as long as they stood foursquare for abolition, their motives were pure, and therefore holy.

Some newspapers in the South had equal doubts about the willingness of Confederate West Pointers to take on *their* friends and classmates, although the Mobile *Evening News* suggested that such concerns, when directed against rebels, were out of place:

> It was no idle or unmeaning boast of President Davis that he had the pick and choice of the officers of the old army. Notwithstanding the frequent flings at West Pointers, we may yet find it a cause of congratulation that we had at the head of our government one who was educated at West-Point himself, but who, by his service in the army and in the War Department, was so thoroughly acquainted with the military talent of all the United States officers. [19]

The paper claimed sixty-four West Point general officers for the South, and "but forty-one" for the United States, as of September 1862. For the record, for the war as a whole, 217 of the Union's 583 general officers had graduated from West Point and another 11 once had been students there (39 percent); of the Confederacy's 425 general officers, 146 were West Point graduates and 10 once had attended (37 percent). [20]

The Northern Radicals also suspected the motives of Secretary of State Seward, who favored compromise over combat. In October, Seward broadened the censor's scope to include the civil as well as the military operations of the government, and immediately was charged with using censorship to curtail criticism of anyone in the government (himself) or in the army (McClellan) who might be willing to settle for less than the total annihilation of slavery.

The House Committee on the Judiciary called in some journalists for comment. Sam Wilkeson affirmed that he had been restrained from sending anything "damaging to the character of the administration, or any individual member of the cabinet, or . . . the reputation of the officers charged with the prosecution of the war, and particularly those of the regular army." [21] Benjamin Perley Poore, Washington correspondent of the Boston *Journal*, was asked:

> Q: Suppose you had received information from a reliable quarter which clearly indicated the impolicy of trusting a command to General McClellan or any other officer in the army, would you have tried to transmit it by telegraph?

A: I would not have tried, because I understood that it was the request of the army that it should not be embarrassed by any remarks of the telegraph. [22]

The committee found enough evidence to make a point: dispatches that had been killed by the censor for no apparent reason, but that seemed to be supportive of the Radicals or critical of the West Pointers. The censorship, however, merely may have been erratic: the *Tribune* was denied permission to send dispatches that were allowed to the *World* and the *Herald*, but, then, the *World* was not allowed to confirm a story that already had appeared in the *Herald*. The underlying issue more likely was incompetence, not politics. This was one congressional hearing on media issues that enjoyed great support from the newspapers—even such a thoroughly Democratic paper as the Chicago *Times* accused Seward of "a most odious tyranny." [23]

McClellan, the West Pointer at the head of the army, was the Radical's favorite villain. At almost the moment that Stanton had been selected for his post, McClellan was refusing to share his plans with members of the cabinet, which reinforced the feeling among some in the cabinet that he did not *have* any plans. To be sure, McClellan's immediate concern, when he took command in July, had been the building of an army, and in this no one doubted his success. There indeed now was an Army of the Potomac, some 100,000 strong, equipped, trained, and with exceptional morale. However, it was an army that continued to face the routine of the camps and not an enemy in the field, while McClellan and his wife endured the rigors of Washington's social life. At some point, Stanton's patience ended. "This army has got to fight or run away," he snapped, "and while men are striving nobly in the West, the champagne and oyster suppers on the Potomac must be stopped." [24]

The *Herald* asserted on February 25, 1862, that McClellan was being cursed by the Radicals for his refusal to "sacrifice the chivalry of the nation upon the altar of their Negro mania." The Radical press certainly held that opinion, although not exactly in those terms. A *Tribune* editorial of March 12, 1862, questioned the "delays and procrastinations" and suggested that the general, or some in his company, might be "more anxious for the preservation of Slavery than for the exemplary crushing out of the rebellion."

On March 13, the *World*'s Stedman had an interview with Brig. Gen. Fitz-John Porter. As Stedman reported to his editor, "McClellan's wish has been, from the *first*, (*so F. J. P. was allowed to tell me*), to send 75,000 men by transports to the region between the York, Rappahannock, and James Rivers—and take Richmond." F. J. P. asserted that McClellan had been "continually thwarted and opposed" by the cabinet and anti-McClellan factions in the army—but that he will prevail. "The soldiers in the camp idolize McClellan," Stedman added, "and . . . are enraged at the attacks made upon him." The reporter also noted that "The rank and file have stopped buying the *Tribune*, so the army newsmen tell me." [25]

On March 14, McClellan finally stepped up to the plate:

> Soldiers of the Army of the Potomac:
>
> For a long time I have kept you inactive, but not without a purpose. You were to be disciplined, armed, and instructed. . . . I have held you back that you might give the death-blow to the rebellion that has distracted our once happy country. The patience you have shown, and your confidence in your General, are worth a dozen victories. . . . The period of inaction has passed. I will bring you now face to face with the rebels, and only pray that God may defend the right. In whatever direction you may move, however strange my actions may appear to you, ever bear in mind that my fate is linked with yours, and that all I do is to bring you, where I know you wish to be—on the decisive battle-field. It is my business to place you there. I am to watch over you as a parent over his children; and you know that your General loves you from the depths of his heart. It shall be my care, as it has ever been, to gain success with the least possible loss; but I know that, if it is necessary, you will willingly follow me to our graves, for our righteous cause. . . . [26]

At almost the same moment, the general was to be hoist a bit on his own petard. A frequently stated reason for his hesitancy had been the apparent strength of the Confederates, entrenched at nearby Manassas. Then, without warning or notice, the Confederates withdrew, leaving the field to a throng of curious newsmen who wandered through the abandoned fortifications and were amazed to find them to be fortifications in name only. Menacing batteries pointed toward the Federal lines turned out to be fakes, so-called Quaker guns made of painted logs. New York *Tribune* correspondent, Bayard Taylor, wrote:

> Utterly dispirited, ashamed and humiliated I return from this visit to the Rebel stronghold. . . . For seven months we have waited, organized a powerful army, until its drill and equipment should be so complete that we might safely advance against the "Gibraltar" of re-

bellion. . . . And now . . . we see that our enemies, like the Chinese, have frightened us by the sound of gongs and the wearing of devil's masks. [27]

Taylor was called before the Committee on the Conduct of the War. "Could you see any reason," he was asked, "why one hundred thousand men should not have captured the whole [enemy] force three months ago?" He responded, "Not the slightest." [28] Oliver Wendell Holmes, a Harvard professor of medicine by trade but a poet and essayist by inclination, could not resist a comment, offered through the *Atlantic Monthly*:

It was as if General McClellan had thrust his sword into a gigantic enemy, and, beholding him suddenly collapse, had discovered to himself and the world that he had merely punctured an enormously swollen bladder. There are instances of a similar character in old romances, where great armies are kept at bay by the arts of necromancers, who build airy towers and battlements, and muster warriors of terrible aspect, and thus feign a defence of seeming impregnability, until some bolder champion of the besiegers dashes forward to try an encounter with the foremost foeman, and find him melt away in the death-grapple. . . .

"The whole business," he concluded, "though connected with the destinies of a nation, takes inevitably a tinge of the ludicrous. [29]

12 / Command and Control

Guards will be placed along Chambers Creek, and no officer or
soldier will be permitted to pass to the rear, and no citizen to
the front of that line, without special authority. Commanders of Army
Corps and Divisions will see that their camps are cleared of all
unauthorized hangers-on, and any one attempting to evade this order
will be compelled to work on the intrenchments and batteries,
or in constructing roads. The Provost-Marshal of the army will
report to these headquarters any officer of whatever rank who may
neglect to enforce this order, or connive at its violation.
—By order of Major General Halleck, May 13, 1862 [1]

THROUGH MOST OF THE HISTORY of the United States, "freedom of the press" has meant that a newspaper had the right to print
whatever material came into its hands—a concept battered but not destroyed during the Civil War. The courts ultimately upheld the right to
publish, but the courts have never verified a corollary right for reporters to
gather that material. As Richardson wrote to his managing editor, "Until
it is clearly settled that an accredited Journalist, in the legitimate exercise
of his calling, has just as much *right* in the army as the Commander himself, and is there on just as legitimate a mission, he *will* be considered by a
large majority of Regular Army officers as an 'unauthorized hanger on,'
and treated accordingly." In truth, many professional military leaders, if
allowed to make the rules, generally would prefer the alleged World War
II press policy of Adm. Ernest J. King: "Don't tell them anything. When
it's over, tell them who won." [2]

Attempts at censorship were frustrating to reporters and generals alike—and editors continued to hold the position that the imposition of "official" censorship relieved them of any responsibility to police the copy. And, while one might think that as the war went on, experience and common sense would diminish the number and quality of journalistic indiscretions, such was not the case. This, from the New York *Tribune* of January 13, 1862: "In view of the anticipated early opening of the campaign by General Buell's army, the subjoined exhibition of the number of regiments composing it, their agglomeration into divisions, their present position, . . . &c., will doubtlessly be welcome."

Welcome to whom? Or this, from another *Tribune* correspondent, published the next day: "I presume I shall violate no confidence if I state on common rumor and belief that the expedition will rendezvous at Hatteras inlet, and that Pamlico and Albemarle Sounds will be the immediate field of operations. . . ."

Reporters frequently would argue that the enemy already knew, or could know, everything that a reporter might discover; camps were teeming with spies; the only group deprived of information was the public. In this, they were frequently wrong. A report sent to a newspaper by telegraph and returned by rail, in print—then to be traded as a by-product of the casual contact of soldiers across the lines—might often beat any communication a spy might try to smuggle through.

Secretary Stanton made a special effort to tighten censorship not only in Washington, but also in the field. However, with no firm or consistent guidelines, the field censors were free to alter or suppress dispatches at will. As Professor James Randall noted in a cautionary tale at the time the nation was entering World War I, "The struggle to set up rules of censorship was important. But the rules had to be written and learned while the fighting went on, as almost everything else concerning modern warfare had to be learned by an army in which few regular officers had actually commanded more than companies. . . ." Or, in the words of the author of *Bohemian Brigade*, "The administration blundered, early and often; but no wonder it was bewildered." [3]

For a brief time, Gen. Ulysses S. Grant's censor at Cairo was Captain Rawlins, the adjutant, a lawyer by training and a sensible man by inclination. However, the press of other duties led Rawlins to confer the role on a volunteer officer, Col. John Riggin, who apparently took this responsibility as if all eternity depended on his judgment and he would pass *nothing*, no matter how trivial, if it were in fact, a *fact*. However, Colonel Riggin delighted in passing along to the public—and therefore, to the possible confusion of the enemy—anything he deemed to be rumor, gossip, or wild speculation. Unfortunately, Colonel Riggin was not of the general's inner circle, and simply did not know where planning ended and wild speculation began. Thus, the secret mission to capture Fort Henry, February 1862, became celebrated as an "extra" edition of the Chicago *Times* before Colonel Riggin knew anything about it.

At times—for example, the Battle of Chancellorsville in May 1863—newsmen created codes or ciphers to evade the censor's eye. Warned that General Hooker would at some point block newspaper dispatches (but not, presumably, "personal" communications), a New York *Tribune* special with the curiously appropriate name of Josiah Sypher proposed the following to his editor: "draft" meant movement; "note," a battle; "interest," stood for victory; "send copy to Philadelphia Press" indicated the army was crossing the Rappahannock below Fredericksburg, and "send copy to Lancaster Express," meant the crossing was above. [4]

New York *Times* reporter L. L. Crounse devised his own code: "Will send you twelve pages tonight" meant "Hooker will fight today." "I must have another reporter," meant "Hooker will fight tomorrow." If he wrote, "Swinton's horse stolen long ago," his editor could print "Battle nearly through. Enemy giving way everywhere. We will win great victory." [5] Most newsmen evaded the censor by simply carrying their stories of Hooker's defeat to the home office.

As a practical matter and for much of the war, reporters could avoid telegraphic censorship through the simple expedients of mail, messenger, or personal delivery. As Southern reporter Peter Alexander noted, "Our passport system is a perfect humbug. On leaving any of our cities for a train of cars, you find an ignorant, illiterate boy with a musket in hand stationed at the doors of the cars, who asks you if you have a passport; on answering 'yes,' you are at once admitted, without the document being demanded for inspection. In my whole journey from Corinth to this place [Atlanta], I have not once shown my passports, and if I had, I doubt if the ignorant boys and men detailed for this service would have been able to read them." [6]

As a practical matter—for the army—the most effective form of censorship was simply to keep newsmen away from the camps. Effective, but not simple. Perhaps the first serious effort (this, for the Confederates) was precipitated by publication of William C. Shepherdson's December 30, 1861, report in the Richmond *Dispatch*:

> To-day our whole army is engaged in building log houses for winter quarters, or in moving to sites already selected. Several brigades will remain where they now are, near the fortifications in Centreville, and the remainder will fall back a mile or two upon Bull Run. Gen. Kirby Smith's brigade is at "Camp Wigfall," to the right of the Orange and Alexandria road, near the Run. Near by, the whole of Van Dorn's division are making themselves comfortable in their little

cottages which rise rapidly day by day, under the diligent hands of the soldiers. A few brigades are scattered down by Occoquan, where wood and water is plenty, the farthest being by Davis's Ford. The artillery, with the exception of Walton's battalion, has already been located between Cub Run and Stone Ridge. The cavalry has fallen back a little and they are now building stables and houses near Centreville. Gen. Stuart will remain in the advance. It is probable that Gen. Johnston will occupy the Lewis house, on the battle field, and Gen. Beauregard Weir's, his old headquarters. . . . In case of an attack by the Yankees, it will take about two hours to get the main strength of the army across Bull Run.

That reads more like the report of a spy than a newsman. A furious Gen. Joseph Johnston complained to Confederate secretary of war Judah P. Benjamin, who turned the problem back to Johnston, which, he suggested, "arises from your own too lenient tolerance of the presence of newspaper reporters within your lines." Johnston responded by banning all reporters. Shepherdson, a surgeon by trade, offered his medical services to the navy and for a time confined his newspapering to a few letters from the fleet, such as it was. Counterpart actions by the Federals were soon to follow, although, as already noted, Stanton's prohibition against newsmen on McClellan's peninsula operation had dwindled to include only William Howard Russell and, perhaps unintentionally, the English artist Frank Vizetelly.

However, the next major military—and media—conflict was to erupt in the West, just two days before Russell boarded the ship that was to take him home. To the North, it was the Battle of Pittsburg Landing, on the Tennessee River. The South called it the Battle of Shiloh:

Pittsburg, via Fort Henry, April 9, 3:20 A.M.—One of the greatest and bloodiest battles of modern days has just closed, resulting in the complete rout of the enemy, who attacked us at daybreak Sunday morning. The battle lasted without intermission during the entire day and was again renewed on Monday morning, and continued undecided until 4 o'clock in the afternoon, when the enemy commenced their retreat, and are still flying toward Corinth, pursued by a large force of our cavalry. The slaughter on both sides is immense. [7]

Thus began the first bulletin, sent off by the *Herald*'s Frank Chapman, who, in keeping with his well-deserved reputation for skating close to the edge, had obtained use of the government-controlled telegraph line by claiming to be a member of General Grant's staff.

The bulletin was reasonably accurate, although it failed to mention that the Union forces had been caught by surprise and that the Federal victory was a near thing. The follow-on coverage in the North was erratic: on one day, the Philadelphia *Inquirer* reported that Corinth had fallen; a day later the *Inquirer* identified Corinth as the "next objective." One newspaper reported casualty figures—killed, wounded and missing—on the order of 18,000 to 20,000 for the Federals, and up to 40,000 for the rebels (out of an entire force of only 44,000). The official tally logs the number of buried dead at: Federal, 1,754, Confederate, 1,728. Total Federal casualties were about 13,000, Confederate about 10,000.

The initial coverage also focused on minutiae, not substance. The St. Louis *Democrat* published a macabre story of hastily buried corpses being uncovered by the rains and rotting away in full view. In contrast, Charles Coffin's piece in the Boston *Journal* treated the subject of "graves" with a heart-warming story about a grieving widow and a faithful dog. Mrs. Pfeiff had come all the way from Illinois to find her husband's body, that she might take him home to rest. Because of the haste with which many had been buried (the *Democrat*'s tale was distasteful, but not inaccurate), few of the graves were marked. After two days of aimless, useless searching, Mrs. Pfeiff found the family dog, who had followed her husband to the war and now refused to leave his grave.

Franc Wilkie's story for the *Times* gave perhaps the first hint that the Federals may have been caught off guard: it reported that the wife of Col. William Hull had been visiting him in camp when the Confederates attacked. "Were you surprised?" Wilkie asked. "Well," she replied, "you can perhaps judge as well as I can as to that. We were in our tent and not prepared to receive company." [8] Off guard? Conjugal visits in a war zone?

Writing on April 9, the correspondent of the Cincinnati *Gazette* tried to put everything in perspective; his account burst over the Federal forces at Pittsburg Landing like a bombshell:

Fresh from the field of the great battle, with its pounding and roaring of artillery, and its keener-voiced rattle of musketry still sounding in my wearied ears; with all its visions and horror still seeming seared upon my eye-balls, while scenes of panic-stricken rout and brilliant charges, and obstinate defenses, and succor, and intoxicating success are burned alike confusedly and indelibly upon the brain, I essay to write what I know of the battle of Pittsburg Landing. [9]

This was a comprehensive and blistering report of some nineteen thousand words, written by twenty-six-year-old Whitelaw Reid. He told of troops so unprepared they were bayoneted, sleeping, as the rebels overran the camps. Where were the pickets? Why were there no defensive positions, weeks after the troops had been deployed on the bluffs, and after clear warning signals that enemy forces were operating in the vicinity?

It was a damning indictment, although in some particulars quite wrong. Union patrols had triggered the fighting when they ran into Confederate skirmishers; the only Federal soldier who may have been caught in bed was on the sick list. Reid had relied too much on the testimony of terrified soldiers who had abandoned the fighting to seek safety in the rear, and his anger led him into error. However, his report—reprinted by both the *Tribune* and the *Herald*—had a significant impact on public understanding of the battle. The *Herald* called it "the only detailed account given to the public, all the other statements being a mere compilation of bits and scraps, without beginning and without end." [10]

Nearly three weeks later, Henry Villard would write:

In the camps, as in the newspapers, you find it difficult to winnow the truth from the bushel of falsehood. Here are the ordinary obstacles to learning the facts about a battle—the jealousies, the cliques, the inordinate ambitions, the untrust-worthiness of eyes and ears during periods of great excitement. . . . Every journalist who has spent the last two weeks in riding from camp to camp in the fathomless mud to question witnesses, verify assertions, and sift the truth out of contradictions . . . has concluded that the deepest of all wells in which the truth was ever sought is the Battle of Pittsburg Landing. [11]

Grant's official report was brief and offered but the faintest illumination. As the New York *Tribune* pointed out, "All that the people really know . . . they have learned from newspaper correspondents, who are quite commonly regarded and treated as barely tolerated (sometimes as intolerable) nuisances in the camps." Nuisances, indeed, were some: "As we passed through the woods," wrote an Illinois colonel in his diary, ". . . a man on a gray horse and wearing citizen clothes was trying to hide behind a large tree from the Rebels in sight beyond the field. He claimed to be the correspondent of the N.Y. *Herald*, but I made him get out of the way of my men." [12]

Gen. Henry Halleck, dissatisfied with the actions of his subordinate, General Grant, shifted his own headquarters from St. Louis to Pittsburg Landing and soon shifted his enmity from Grant to the newsmen, whom he regarded as an irritating inconvenience.

Meanwhile, back East, the McClellan controversies continued apace. The Associated Press reported that a proposed congressional resolution against McClellan was abandoned, "it being but too evident that it could command only a few votes," while readers of the *Tribune* were told the opposite: "it was withdrawn . . . after a debate which showed a unanimous purpose to pass it." The New York *World* asserted that "The *Tribune* and its ten million adherents are howling against the General," while the New York *Times* offered that anyone "praised by the *Herald*, abused by the *Tribune*, has a claim upon the public sympathy that no man can disregard." [13]

McClellan's forces were now gathered on the Yorktown Peninsula for the first serious effort to push on to Richmond—and the War Department demonstrated that it was serious about censorship. As L. L. Crounse of the *Times* later remembered, "Arriving at Fortress Monroe I found that, in consequence of some indiscretions of overzealous correspondents, the most severe as well as absurd regulations had been prescribed with reference to their government." Censorship "extended to the mails . . . and no letter for publication, nor even private letter to the editor, could pass through the Post-Office without the approving initials of a young aide-de-camp on General Wool's staff." [14]

The Boston *Journal*, the New York *Journal of Commerce*, and the New York *Sunday Mercury* published a few hints about McClellan's plans; the editors were threatened with arrest. Military Supervisor of Telegraphs Sanford was directed "to stop all telegraphic communications to the Philadelphia *Inquirer*, until satisfactory proof is furnished to this department that the recent publication respecting operations by the army at Yorktown were duly authorized." [15] Sanford went to the peninsula for a firsthand look and found that, indeed, the report had been authorized by General Wool, the department commander.

Journalists with McClellan's army convinced Sanford that the censorship was too harsh. Accordingly, on April 12 (with Stanton's approval) Sanford abolished the local censorship and created, instead, a parole. This placed each correspondent on his honor to serve, in effect, as his own censor, to be guided by a long list of forbidden topics (such as: do not reveal the location of various headquarters or camps, the size and composition of the forces, any plan of operations). The guidelines were not illogical, but if taken literally and in the aggregate, would prevent publishing any information about any individual or activity until the entire campaign had been completed.

Or, as Crounse noted, Sanford's parole was "more precise and rigorous in its requirements than any ever administered to an enemy. . . ." The New York *Times* complained that it required reporters to be "paroled as if they were traitors," but Crounse affirmed that ". . . all the correspondents eagerly swallowed it, and the magic initials of *"E. E. S., Military Supervisor of Army Intelligence* obtained them free ingress and egress to the military lines for several months. . . . The document covered two printed pages of letter-paper, and many guards, terrified at its length, readily passed all who presented it rather than read it." [16]

One major indiscretion slipped through during the transition from censorship to parole. On April 26, 1862, *Harper's Weekly* published a drawing of McClellan's Yorktown headquarters, a graphic Federal counterpart to Shepherdson's verbal description of the rebel camp at Manassas and sufficiently accurate that it could have been used by Confederate artillery in bombarding the place. The New York *Times* of May 3, in fact, claimed that the Yorktown camp indeed had been shelled two days after that issue of *Harper's* had reached the army. Stanton, justifiably infuriated, blocked further publication of *Harper's*, a prohibition that lasted about as long as it took Fletcher Harper to travel to Washington to remind Stanton of the overwhelming and unabashed support being given by his paper to the war effort and, not incidentally, to the Lincoln administration.

On May 9, on no discernable evidence of success, a schizophrenic Congress passed a resolution in *support* of McClellan, commending his "high military qualities which secure important results with but little sacrifice of human life." [17] The resolution had been suggested by Forney, and, beyond the obvious pat on the back, it helped McClellan keep his job. Lincoln had just returned from an unsatisfactory visit to the general, fully intending to remove him. He decided to wait.

In the next day's *Herald*, George Alfred Townsend offered this warm description of a McClellan visit with the troops: "There was a large welcome in every heart for that stout little figure and blue soldier's overcoat. . . . He came, and listened, and spoke—that was all—and the mass of blind, purposeless movement unravelled itself and there was a plan and a battle." [18] There was to be, in truth, a series of battles on the 1862 peninsula road to Richmond, few of which would be recorded as Federal victories.

Activity near Shiloh had become a waiting game, with the Confederates at Corinth, Mississippi, some twenty-three miles from Pittsburg Landing, and the Federals moving forward at an average rate of advance of less than a mile a day. General Halleck, determined not to be caught unprepared, ordered the troops to dig themselves in every night. The press contingent had grown, from perhaps seven on the eve of the battle to more than fifty, and Halleck's impatience had grown apace.

Colburn of the New York *World* applied for what he assumed would be a routine renewal of an expired pass. Provost Marshal Maj. John Key denied the request, on the irrelevant grounds that some correspondents had been paid to write favorably of certain officers. Colburn, steaming, reported this insult to his fellow specials, who demanded the name or names of the offending scribes. At first, Major Key denied having made the statement, but finally admitted to the charge but could give no names.

Several of the Pennsylvania volunteer officers indeed had been courting attention from the Philadelphia *Press*. Charles Coffin of the Boston *Journal* asserted, however, that the issue at hand had little to do with Pennsylvania volunteers, but, rather, with a handful of jealous regular officers who were not getting enough credit in the press. However, volunteer or regular seems not to have made much difference when it came to "courting attention." William Bickham of the Cincinnati *Commercial* had tarred all newly made officers with the same brush: ". . . ex-butcher boys, country pedagogues, and counter-jumpers, elevated into positions of small trust" and irritated with reports that did not put their magnificent contributions in the proper perspective. "No complaint," he wrote with reasonable accuracy, "was ever made about reporters who flattered commanders." [19]

General Halleck did not seem to care, one way or the other, and issued Special Field Order 54 on May 13, 1862, which barred "unauthorized hangers-on" from his camps, under penalty of hard labor. The putative "hangers-on," the members of the press corps assembled, appointed Whitelaw Reid to turn their outrage into words, and then presented the subsequent memorial to the general:

> The undersigned, loyal citizens and accredited representatives of loyal journals, respectfully represent that they came here in compliance with the order of Secretary Stanton, authorizing journalists to accompany the army—some of them bearing passes issued by his authority, and have remained here several weeks, for the sole and exclusive purpose of recording the approaching battle.
>
> They are now informed that Field Order No. 54 requires them to leave the army lines.
>
> While they will not attempt to remain unless they can do so openly, and with the permission of Major General Halleck, there are many newspaper letter-writers attached to the camps in fictitious capacities, who, notwithstanding whatever precautions may be tak-

en, will succeed in evading Field Order No. 54, and remaining with the army, while the duly accredited and responsible representatives of the press are excluded, in manifest injustice to themselves and the journals which they represent.

While desirous of avoiding everything injurious to the army, or any portion of it, they represent that their exclusion, just on the eve of the event which they came here especially to record, will be unjust to the loyal public journals and to the country which looks to them for information; and respectfully ask whether . . . there are any conditions on which they will be permitted to remain. [20]

General Halleck responded that their loyalty was not at issue, but, rather, in order to ensure the exclusion of enemy spies from the camps, he was required to exclude all civilians, no exception. "I have no objections to what you may write," he declaimed. "I care nothing about what the newspapers publish." [21] The general said that he would place a bulletin board down at the landing—by this point, seventeen miles to the rear—on which would be posted the latest official dispatches. He also offered to listen to any scheme the reporters might devise that would meet his needs while permitting their continued presence with the army. They took his suggestion at face value and, a short time later, offered the following:

Resolved: That we will all present to General Halleck satisfactory proofs of our loyalty, give him our whereabouts in the army, that he may know where to find us at all times, and give the exact parole of honor which the Secretary of War has announced will be required of journalists as a condition precedent to their passing within the army lines, under his order, which is now in force in all the other military departments of the United States. [22]

General Halleck read the document and announced, "It will not do at all." [23] He repeated that he cared nothing for proofs of loyalty, and turned his back—whereupon Franc Wilkie lost his temper, damned the general and his staff and kicked over a chair. Wilkie was arrested and placed in the guardhouse for a couple of hours. When released, he discovered that his saddlebags had been rifled. He lost his temper again, was taken away by an armed escort and set on the road toward Pittsburg Landing. Wilkie vented his frustration a few days later in the Times, but, surprisingly, his target was not General Halleck, but, rather, the correspondents who had precipitated Special Order 54:

Almost every third man you meet is the "Reporter of the Something Diurnal." Half of them are individuals who board with some officer, and whose letters invariably inform the world that the gallant Colonel of the regiment pre-eminently distinguished himself in the late fight that his men fought a half day's hand-to-hand fight with the enemy, and finally fell back in splendid order some two hours after the——Regiment on the right and the——Battery on the left had disgracefully run away without firing a single shot. . . .

It is the writers of this class who are constantly giving the world information as to our strength and our position. . . . They do not hesitate to advise Gen. Halleck, condemn Gen. McClellan, and criticise the operations of the profoundest minds engaged in working out the tremendous problem now submitted to the National Government. They are particularly severe on West Pointers, and are ardent admirers of men in proportion as their early education unfits them for the vast and intricate responsibilities of Generalship. Invariably the officer who is most free with his table, bottle, horses and information is (to them) the greatest soldier. With them a small skirmish is ever a tremendous battle, in which one Federal drives a thousand, and two Federals ten thousand Confederates—a battle proper is a theme upon which they lavish more superlatives, hyperbole, exaggerations and nonsense than they would upon the crash of a dozen worlds butting against each other in space.

For such reasons as these and a thousand additional ones, the profession has been brought into disrepute—a disrepute which has fallen alike on those who deserve it, and those who do not. [24]

Other newsmen were quick to exercise the power of the press, with Halleck the target. Colburn of the *World*, who laid claim to having given Halleck his widely popular nickname of "Old Brains," was especially aggrieved:

Doesn't want us to publish the truth? We'll see. He may be able to control *some* of the truth, but not all. You wait. I regret that I ever tried to humanize this prig. As far as the *World* is now concerned, "Old Brains" is about to become a fussy, irritated old maid, a silly school girl . . . and, how about, vacillating coquette? [25]

Not all of the reporters accepted the expulsion order. Those ambitious enough to make the effort adopted one or another stratagem; some were legal, as with one correspondent who had signed on as a voluntary hospital assistant for the battle, and elected to continue in that "assignment." Some were patently otherwise. Villard took to wearing an army uniform and staying out of the way. Another reporter borrowed the complete kit of a sick member of Halleck's bodyguard and "joined" the unit.

As he reported in the Chicago *Tribune*: "Gen. Halleck little knew when he rode down the line, and glanced at his well appointed bodyguard that one of those 'd———d newspaper correspondents' looked him right in the eye, from under one of the infernally ugly looking trooper hats." [26]

Meanwhile, Halleck continued his cautious forward movement. "He built four lines of breastworks, each nearly ten miles long, so that if driven from one he could fall back to another," wrote Charles Coffin of the Boston *Journal*. "He dragged his heavy siege-guns through the mud from the Landing—planted them behind sodded earthworks, erected bomb-proof magazines, issued his final orders to his army of an hundred thousand men, opened fire with his heavy guns, threw forward his skirmishers, and found—a deserted town!" [27]

While Halleck so carefully prepared for a pitched battle, the Confederates, through another bit of legerdemain, managed to slip away unchallenged. First, General Beauregard did the sensible thing and, on May 24, banished all correspondents from *his* army. Then, he began withdrawing his troops, while empty railroad cars were noisily shuttled back and forth—to the frequent cheering of an enthusiastic rear-guard—to create the impression that reinforcements were arriving. On May 29, a somewhat crestfallen Halleck rode into the abandoned village; the rebel defenses about which he had been so concerned amounted to little more than a single line, not even as formidable as those his own forces constructed every time they moved forward into a new position.

By banning all "unauthorized hangers-on" in an ostensible move to keep spies out of the Federal camps, Halleck had lost the chance to get valuable intelligence from fugitive slaves or other friendly locals. Another Federal general had been hoist on his own petard, and another Federal army had, in effect, been hoodwinked by a set of Quaker guns.

13 / The Summer of '62

Fierce and desperate battle between two hundred thousand
men has raged since daylight, yet night closes in on an uncertain field.
It is the greatest fight since Waterloo, all over the field contested
with an obstinacy equal even to Waterloo. . . . But what can be foretold
of the future of a fight in which from five in the morning till
seven at night the best troops of the continent have
fought without decisive result?

—New York *Tribune*, dateline Battlefield of Antietam,
September 17, 1862 [1]

MCCLELLAN STUMBLED ALONG through Virginia, headed toward Richmond. A bird's-eye view of his target, as described in a Memphis paper on May 22, would have shown ". . . groups of excited men at every corner; dense crowds before the bulletin boards of the newspaper offices; long lines of army wagons rattling over the clamourous pavements; here and there, an officer in a smart, fresh uniform, in strange juxtaposition and contrast with a knot of pallid, ragged soldiers whom the bright sun had tempted to stroll out of the hated hospital; couriers, covered with the dust of the road, on broken down horses in feeble gallop towards the War Department." [2]

Richmond may have been McClellan's only goal but the Confederates were not the only enemy. On May 27, he wrote to Stanton to complain about newspapers that "frequently published letters from their correspondents with this army, giving important information concerning our movements, positions of troops, &c., in positive violation of your orders." A few days later, he offered a specific example: ". . . my order of the 25th May, directing the order of march from the Chickahominy and the disposition to be made of trains and baggage, is published in full in the Baltimore American of the 2d instant. If any statement could afford more important information to the enemy I am unable to perceive it." [3]

Important information, indeed. "Upon advancing beyond the Chickahominy," he had directed, "the troops will be prepared to go into battle at a moment's notice, and will be entirely unencumbered, with the exception of ambulances. All vehicles will be left on the eastern side of the Chickahominy, and carefully packed. The men will leave their knapsacks, packed, with the wagons, and will carry three day's rations. . . ." Little wonder that the Cincinnati Commercial voiced a complaint of its own against "the persistent impertinence of some members of our now unpopular profession." [4]

"Upon advancing beyond the Chickahominy," McClellan's troops met the Army of Northern Virginia, then commanded by Gen. Joseph E. Johnston, for the Battle of Seven Pines/Fair Oaks (May 31–June 1, 1862). Largely due to confusion among the rebel commanders—they had been given oral, not written orders—McClellan won a tactical victory, and Johnston, wounded in the engagement, was replaced by Gen. Robert E. Lee.

Richmond papers covered the battle as best they could; the Dispatch erroneously credited Maj. Gen. James Longstreet with success, when his misunderstanding of orders in fact had been responsible for much of the confusion, and denigrated the more useful contribution of recent North Carolina resident Maj. Gen. D. H. Hill. A soldier from North Carolina complained to the editor of the Wilmington Journal that, although North Carolina and Georgia had furnished fully one-half of the forces engaged, "North Carolina and Georgia have found no place in the Richmond papers." The editor agreed: the Richmond papers were "Virginia all over." [5]

The Enquirer rose to the defense of the Richmond press, noting that the army policy of excluding reporters had shifted sources to acquaintances and interested parties within the army. Further, urgent requests lodged with each unit for speedy casualty lists often went unheeded, as the responsible adjutants felt that their first responsibility was to their hometown papers "where they would be seen and read by those most interested." As the hometown papers nearest the action were those in Richmond, those would logically have the news first. The Enquirer also chastised the soldiers themselves for being "tardy or neglectful" in supplying the press with information; soldiers who felt "aggrieved" by the lack of publicity should contact the editors. [6]

A week after Seven Pines, troops in the Shenandoah Valley clashed in the Battle of Cross Keys. George Smalley of the New York Tribune called it a Federal victory; Charles Henry Webb of the New York Times put it straight:

The correspondents of some papers claim it as a victory. . . . These gentlemen, whose feelings and sympathies so influence them that they cannot record faithfully, will have a long account to settle with history some day. . . . Our Generals incline to estimate the enemy's loss as much greater [than ours], and stories are told of three or four hundred of their dead being counted in one pile. Chasing these stories up, I can only find the man who has been told by another man that someone else told him that, at a certain spot in an uncertain field, that number of dead was guessed at. . . . Will not truth and common sense satisfy the popular craving, or is it always necessary to pander to the appetite that demands a victory in all cases, an assurance that the enemy lost at least one more than we? [7]

As part of their more personal and continuing journalistic barrage, both the New York *Tribune* and the Philadelphia *Inquirer* accused McClellan of mistreatment of his own wounded soldiers, which prompted an inquiry from Secretary Stanton:

Very urgent complaints are being made from various quarters respecting the protection afforded to the rebel General Lee's property, called the White House, instead of using it as a hospital for the care of wounded soldiers. It is represented that they have even to purchase a glass of water for thirsty, wounded and suffering soldiers. [8]

McClellan's response was made within hours: the house in question was being "protected" because it had been "the house where [General] Washington had passed the first portion of his married life." It was small, he noted, could accommodate no more than thirty wounded soldiers if put to that purpose, and spring water was everywhere freely available, in plenty. McClellan's chief quartermaster added his opinion that "The author of this report to the contrary must be a simpleton or a malicious knave." [9]

Stanton acknowledged the "explanation which will enable me to correct this misrepresentation. Neither you nor I can hope to correct all such stories, but so far as it is in my power, I shall labor to do so." [10]

He must have been distracted. A week later, McClellan was hit by another missive, forwarded in the secretary's name, from Surgeon General William Hammond: "It has been represented to me by responsible gentlemen, that the White House and the inclosed grounds are admirably adapted for hospital purposes," he noted, adding that the sick were being deprived of good water and asking that the property be "turned over to the medical authorities." [11]

McClellan asked his own chief medical officer, Col. Charles Tripler, for his opinion. Dr. Tripler estimated the house could, at best, shelter two dozen patients, although there would be no room for attending nurses. He suggested that, in any event, any such use was irrelevant: "We now have one hundred and seventy hospital-tents" pitched on the surrounding plantation, he noted, with full administrative and commissary support.

Dr. Tripler also noted a curious anomaly. Sixty-five of the tents had plank floors; there had not been sufficient lumber to floor the rest. "The delay in receiving this, however, has developed an interesting and important fact: the mortality in the floored tents has been very sensibly greater than in those without floors. . . . In relation to the relative advantages of hospital-tents and buildings for hospital purposes, I think that, among those at all familiar with the subject, there is but one opinion—that the tents are decidedly the best." [12] Dr. Tripler did not know—indeed, it was not until the 1865 discoveries of Louis Pasteur that anyone knew—about the nature of bacteria, which would so easily multiply in the cracks between, and the warm dark places under, the floorboards.

McClellan's exasperation with newspaper-inspired meddling from Washington was clearly shown in his message of June 22, in which he gave Stanton a summary of Dr. Tripler's comments. "Those who have originated the false statements concerning this house, yard, and spring," he added, "are, in fact, as stated in my dispatch of the seventh instant, enemies of this army and of the cause in which it is fighting. They have imposed upon the Surgeon-General, and cause him to make official representations which, on examination, prove to be unfounded in truth. . . . They have unnecessarily occupied the attention of the Secretary of War, and have interrupted the Commander and the Medical Director of this army in the midst of the most arduous duties." [13]

This report may have allowed Stanton to shift his attention to other topics, but did nothing to change the attitude of at least one of the offending newsmen. The *Inquirer*'s Painter told the Joint Committee on the Conduct of the War, not quite three weeks later, that McClellan so scrupulously protected the property of Virginians that his own troops at times could not even take a drink from the well and, on one occasion, wounded men had been forced to lay in a "pigpen" while a decent wooden-floored building nearby was reserved for "rebel privates." [14]

However, by the time of that testimony, McClellan's push toward Richmond had come to naught—or, rather, had come almost to disaster in the series of actions known as the Seven Days' Campaign (25 June–1 July). They were fought in somewhat of a journalistic vacuum because access to a telegraph was almost impossible, even when the line was working, and it was fully out of commission for about two days when the rebels recaptured Lee's white house and cut the wire. Absent any real news, rumors began flying of fierce battles fought, bloody battles lost.

On Saturday, June 28, 1862, some of McClellan's officers managed to get messages through to friends in Philadelphia that they were "all right." Why would they *not* be all right, unless something was amiss? The Philadelphia *Press* made inquiry of the War Department. The War Department had no information.

In the meantime, Baltimore *American* editor Charles C. Fulton had left the battlefield at noon that day, elated with what he presumed would be a victory. He drafted his report as soon as he reached home and, as a courtesy, sent a summary to the War Department. This resulted in an urgent summons to Washington, where Fulton found himself briefing both the secretary of war and the president. Fulton then returned to Baltimore to smooth out his text, and, like any enterprising author, offered his story to the Associated Press:

> I am writing for the *American* a detailed account of events . . . before Richmond and on the Peninsula, during the last four days, including facts obtained from Washington, having been sent for by special train to communicate with the President.
>
> If you desire it, and will give due credit, I will send it to you. It will make four or five thousand words.
>
> *We have the grandest military triumph over the enemy, and Richmond must fall.* [15]

Two hours later, Fulton sent another telegram to the Associated Press. He had been denied permission to telegraph the story, he wrote, and thus was forced to withdraw his offer. The query and cancellation messages were published side-by-side in various New York papers the next morning—and Fulton was arrested.

His fellow journalists were puzzled: Fulton was a loyal patriot; his account of the fighting, published in the *American* of June 30, reflected the same (unfortunately, inaccurate) flavor of victory as his query. The New York *World* represented the opinion of journalists everywhere: this was the "most egregious not to say the most despotic blunder" of Secretary of War Stanton. [16] A U.S. senator demanded that the president state the reason for the arrest. Fulton spent two days in jail and was released, without comment or further sanction. He had been arrested, it appears, because he had mentioned communications with "the President" and, to the War Department, this was viewed as an outrageous breach of confidence.

The end of the Seven Days' Campaign saw McClellan's troops fighting their way to safety at Harrison's Landing on the banks of the James River, where they could be covered by the guns of the navy. McClellan had asked Washington for reinforcements, but none were forthcoming.

The *Herald* reported that, despite the bloody defeat, "Not a breath of complaint escapes officers or men of General McClellan, but the curses [are] loud and deep . . . against the real authors of this withdrawal," which the *Herald* reminded its readers were "the unprincipled and incarnate abolitionists, who by some means appear to have obtained control of army movements." [17]

Surprisingly, the *Tribune*'s reports of the withdrawal were not that much different from those of the *Herald*. This could have been another opportunity to blast McClellan; instead, one *Tribune* correspondent called the retreat to the James a "masterly movement"; another compared McClellan to a chess player sacrificing a pawn to set up checkmate. [18] Sam Wilkeson, who had been with McClellan since May, took aim at Washington, and was brutal:

> The refusal [of the Administration] to give this army ample re-enforcement on Friday last, came within a hair's breadth of ruining the nation. . . . I don't care about the questions—which legislators, soldiers, and politicians have debated—of this General's fitness to command. The York and James River Peninsula were not the place for that discussion. . . . When loyal New York regiments, lifted from their feet by the fire of Rebel brigades, cry out of their wounds and death for help; when the choicest of New-England and Michigan and Pennsylvania troops, outnumbered . . . by whole divisions of the enemy, beg for re-enforcements, I say that the blackest crime that power can commit is to stalk upon the field of peril and say, "Soldiers, I have no faith in your commander! Let your martyrdom proceed." [19]

The *Tribune* disavowed his opinion and disagreed with his position—but to its credit, published the letter. However, Wilkeson, physically and emotionally exhausted, went on—or was sent on—home leave. The Chicago *Times*, reprinting the letter on July 8, surmised that it "must have been admitted" to the *Tribune* by mistake. "It is, however, all the more valuable coming from the source that it does."

Also a bit of a surprise, a commendation from the Southern point of view was published by the Cologne (Virginia) *Gazette*:

> I must award to Gen. McClellan my fullest recognition. There are few, if any, generals in the Union army who can rival him. Left in the most desperate straits by his companion in arms, McDowell; victimized by the Secretary of War, Stanton, at Washington; offered up as a sacrifice to destiny by political jealousy; cut off from his basis of retreat, he selected a new line of safety of which no one had even

dreamed. He defended every foot of ground with courage and talent, and his last stand at Malvern Hill, as well as his system of defence and his strategic combinations, displayed high military ability. Yet his troops were too greatly demoralized by their seven days' fighting, and lost their stamina, while several of his generals could not comprehend the ideas of their commander, and sustained him but poorly, or not at all. At Harrison's Landing, where the James River forms a curve, he collected his shattered array under the guns of the Federal fleet. But, on our side, we had no longer an army to molest him. [20]

It is not hard to understand why this particular bit of Southern comment was reprinted in the New York *Herald*.

The Chicago *Times* had McClellan outnumbered to a degree not reflected on the battlefield: 200,000 rebels were on his front, the paper reported, McClellan needed at least 75,000 more men, and the administration's failure to support him was part of an "outrageous plot." On July 9, the paper even asked if McClellan's army was to be "annihilated in order to gratify the revenge, the malice, or the envy of Edwin M. Stanton."

Sometime later, it became apparent that, far from being hopelessly outnumbered, McClellan's army had been slightly larger than that of the enemy. However, the news reports reflected McClellan's own bitter arrogance. In a telegram to Secretary Stanton in the middle of the Seven Days' Campaign, believing that the enemy forces so greatly exceeded his own and frustrated because he was getting no reinforcements, McClellan made no attempt to shade his anger. "I have seen too many dead and wounded comrades," he wrote, "to feel otherwise than that the Government has not sustained this army. If you do not do so now the game is lost. If I save this army now, I tell you plainly that I owe no thanks to you or to any other person in Washington. You have done your best to sacrifice this army." [21]

Stanton's reaction? There was none, because he never saw that accusatory paragraph. Colonel Sanford, Military Supervisor of Telegraphs, thought it was too inflammatory and exercised his power as censor.

The Seven Days' Campaign marked the debut of Gen. Robert E. Lee as commander of the Army of Northern Virginia. To that point, he had done little to excite positive newspaper comment. In fact, to that point, one of the nicer things said about him had been, "Poor Lee! Rosecrans has fooled him again," after the Confederates had failed to bag the Federals in the western Virginia mountains. Lee took the jibes in stride, telling his wife, "I am sorry . . . that the movements of our armies cannot keep pace with the expectations of the editors of the papers. I know they can arrange things satisfactory to themselves on paper. I wish they could do so in the field." [22]

Now, the tide had shifted and the press swung around. "No Captain that ever lived," said the Richmond *Dispatch*, "could have planned or executed a better plan." The Richmond *Whig* went one better: Lee "amazed and confounded his detractors by the brilliancy of his genius, the fertility of his resource, his energy and daring. He has established his reputation forever." [23]

Edward Pollard of the Richmond *Examiner*, however, was reserving judgment. "The vulgar and unintelligent mind worships success," he wrote, adding:

> The extraordinary and happy train of victories in Virginia seems to have had no other significance or interest to a number of grovelling minds in the South, than as a contribution to the personal fame of General Lee, who by no fault of his own (for no one had more modesty, more Christian dignity of behavior, and a purer conversation), was followed by toadies, flatterers, and newspaper sneaks in epaulets, who made him ridiculous by their servile obeisances and excess of praise. [24]

During the Seven Days' campaign, Lee also demonstrated a solid grasp of press relations and realities. First, knowing that McClellan read the Richmond papers, he arranged for them to publish false reports that Confederate troops were being withdrawn and sent to reinforce Stonewall Jackson in the Shenandoah Valley when, in fact, Jackson was being pulled down to Richmond. (McClellan may have read the papers, but he still believed that his forces were outnumbered.) Also, Lee managed to impose some degree of censorship by keeping his plans to himself. When the Federals finally had been pushed back some thirty miles from the gates of the city, some Richmond editors protested Lee's continued silence. The general's response was a letter to the secretary of war, in which he complained that a recent item in the Richmond *Dispatch* had given the precise location of three of his divisions—an item that too easily could have been seen by the Federals. He asked the secretary to take "whatever steps necessary." Secretary Randolph instructed his staff to "Send copies of this letter to all the papers in the city, and express the hope that no steps may be necessary to stop such publications." [25]

Edward Pollard replied, "to assure you that in the future as in the past, the *Examiner* will be studious to observe that rule of reticence, which we agree with you is required by the interests of the public safety." Edward Pollard, who freely and frequently criticized the leaders of the Confederacy, had a selective interpretation of "the rule of reticence." [26]

Following the rebel success in withdrawing from Corinth at the end of May, Beauregard fell ill. He was replaced by Braxton Bragg, who was earning a reputation as the most disliked general officer in the Confederacy—as noted in the Atlanta *Confederacy*—"owing to his rigid and almost tyrannical system of discipline." [27]

Discipline was Bragg's personal god, and his form of worship was not necessarily illogical. Bragg executed deserters. (In this, he was supported by the Richmond *Dispatch*: "there is little pride and no honor in the deserter, and the fear of disgrace will not deter him from absconding. The penalty of death will. An example or two would have a fine effect.") [28] It was widely reported that Bragg had a soldier executed for shooting at a chicken. That was true; the soldier in question *had* been executed, and for shooting at a chicken—but because his undisciplined shot killed another soldier. Bragg also banned alcohol from his units, which perhaps had as much to do with his lack of popularity among the troops and newsmen as anything else.

Bragg bore unfriendly remarks in silence, until he saw a copy of the Montgomery *Daily Advertiser*, dated July 29, with an article by Wallace Screws. This not only presented full and precise details of the movements of the Army of the Mississippi, but also took a personal shot, proclaiming that General Bragg "uniformly sets at defiance the laws of his country for the appointment and promotion of officers and usurps all the powers of judge, jury and executioner in the treatment of his men."

Bragg then took a shot of his own, in the form of a note handed to Screws by the Inspector General:

You have committed a gross violation of all known rules in armies—not to declare to the enemy the movements of troops.

It is well ascertained that the enemy receive your papers and others regularly and by that means are kept constantly advised of our operations. As long as you confined yourself to personal abuse and detraction, though false and malignant, General Bragg, the target of your vehemence, chose to avoid any petty disputes and stayed above the fray. But when you assail our cause and expose our plans to the enemy, it becomes his duty to interfere; and you may rest assured he will do it. [29]

Screws was surprised at the strong language, and asked cautiously, "Am I under arrest?" Well, not exactly; the inspector general preferred the word *detained*; Screws was free to communicate with his employer, but not to file any news copy. Screws sent a copy of the note to *Daily Advertiser* editor Samuel G. Reid, and editor Reid assayed an editorial response in the form of an open letter to General Bragg:

> Allow me to say the arrest of our correspondent, on the pretense of giving information to the enemy, can only be regarded by all free-thinking men as another exhibition of that petty tyranny and vindictiveness for which you have gained an unenviable notoriety. No one doubts the correctness of the rule of the army not to give information to the enemy, but all will question its application in this case. The necessary inference from your words is that Wallace Screws is a spy, and that the people in the heart of the South, for whose information he was writing, are enemies of the country.
>
> The offense of our correspondent, if offense it may be called, in repeating the vague and uncertain reports about the movements of your troops, is not so grave an offense as that previously committed by yourself in authorizing the publication of a dispatch that your army was on the move. Here is a dispatch which appeared in our columns, under date of July 24, presumably by order of Gen. Bragg:
>
> "There has been unusual activity at Tupelo within the last few days. The grand army under command of Gen. Bragg, is on the move, and the loyal people of Memphis may soon have occasion to rejoice. One or more divisions will pass through here in a day or two, *en route* east."
>
> I was not in the office at night when this dispatch came, or we should not have published it. Everybody I met in the street was surprised that such a piece of information should be given an opportunity to go to the enemy. [30]

The editor added his doubts about "the statement that our papers are received regularly by the enemy. . . . The enemy has much more direct and certain means of getting information than by means of Southern newspapers." Well, perhaps. His editorial was reprinted in the New York *Tribune* on September 1.

In any event, Bragg retreated, and the reporter was released after a nominal arrest of ten days; the editor compromised and wished the general "all success in his movements against the enemy." And the general issued a general order:

August 20, 1862: No person not properly connected with this army will be permitted to accompany it—whenever found within the lines, they will be arrested and confined. [31]

It is probably only a coincidence, but just the day before, Henry Wager Halleck—newly promoted to the post of general in chief of the Union army and headquartered in Washington—had ordered all Federal commanders to "immediately remove from your army all newspaper reporters." [32]

As already noted, many journalists had easily adapted to Halleck's post-Shiloh crackdown and found refuge—or at least, accommodation—of one sort or another. Most saw that, whatever the rules and however enforced, their best chance for remaining in the field was to get close to the enforcer. This did not necessarily mean acting, in the stern phrase of the New York *Tribune* of May 26, 1862, as "the parasites and toadies of Commanding Generals," but that approach would not hurt. Charles Bickham of the Cincinnati *Commercial* aligned his fortunes with those of Maj. Gen. William S. Rosecrans:

There can be no mistake that in coolness, readiness, and fertility of resource, celerity of thought and decision, and comprehensive grasp of mind in the midst of the most trying situations of peril, personal and military, Gen. Rosecrans . . . proved himself perfectly equal to the tremendous responsibility which devolved upon him. You rarely found more practical skill, profound strategy and executive faculty with a mind which grasps general principles, and eagerly inquires into, and handles remote details, embodied in one character, and yet Gen. Rosecrans has demonstrated that he combines all. [33]

Bickham tagged Rosecrans with the nom de guerre, "Old Rosey," and expanded his reportage a few months later, publishing a memoir: *Rosecrans's Campaign with the Fourteenth Army Corps or the Army of the Cumberland: A Narrative of Personal Observations*, by "W. D. B." (A dollar a copy in paper, twenty-five cents extra for cloth.) When Rosecrans was relieved in October 1863, Bickham had become so thoroughly identified with the general that his own "army" career came to an end.

New York *Tribune* correspondent George Washburn Smalley—Yale 1854, Harvard Law School 1855, and Wilkeson's replacement as senior field correspondent—found his refuge with Maj. Gen. John Pope. Smalley was delighted with the "very good-natured" and abolitionist-minded general, although, as Smalley told his editors, Pope "will have facts his own way." The general, he wrote, "personally corrects!" his dispatches. At least once, Pope, "rather worried by the *Times* and *World*'s attacks," asked

Smalley to forward "for editorial use" some points the general felt should be made. [34]

Pope showed Smalley Halleck's August 19 directive banning reporters, but assured him that "This is not an official interview. I imagine you needn't go until you get the order." Smalley, with remarkably poor judgment, sent a message to the *Tribune* Washington bureau with that good news, which provoked a quick missive from Halleck to Pope: "I think your staff is decidedly leaky," he wrote. "The substance of my telegrams to you is immediately telegraphed back here to the press. . . . Clean out such characters from your headquarters." Pope complied on August 22, although one correspondent, more tenacious than the rest, was to be arrested nine times by the provost marshal before conceding defeat. [35]

The *Tribune* told Smalley to "Keep as near the army as possible and lose no opportunity of getting news at any expense of trouble or money." [36] Smalley regrouped his staff, stationing two men at Alexandria to question officers coming in from the field, one man at Manassas Junction, and another at Fredericksburg.

As a result of Halleck's order, the Federal defeat at Second Manassas, August 26–28, was underreported to the nation at large—but was no secret in the streets of Washington, where the invasion fears of 1861 were revived. Adams Sherman Hill, who earlier had taken over Wilkeson's *Tribune* post at the seat of government, assured the home office that "In the absence of instructions, I take my duty to be, being accredited near the Gov't., I stay while it stays and skedaddle when it skedaddles." [37]

A lexicographic sidebar: Hill used the word *skeddaddle*, which had become common currency, but had not previously been in common usage. The London *Times* noted its increasingly frequent appearance, and a letter to the editor endeavored an explanation. "Skeddaddle," the writer noted, was "excellent Scotch. . . .the Americans only misapply the word, which means, in Dumfries, 'to spill'—milkmaids, for example, saying, you are 'skedaddling' all that milk."

The *London Spectator* took exception: "The *Times* . . . [is] wrong, for the word is neither new nor in any way misapplied. The word is very fair Greek, the root being that of 'skedannumi,' to disperse, to 'retire tumultuously,' and it was probably set afloat by some professor of Harvard."

The Louisville *Journal* elaborated: the Greek version of *skeddaddle* "occurs in Homer, Hesiod, Aeschylus, Sophocles, Herodotus, Thucydides, and Xenophon, and it was used to express in Greek the very idea that we undertake, in using it, to express in English." The *Journal's* examples were specific: Homer's "Iliad," 19:171, has it *skedason laon*, for scattering, dispersing; in the "Odyssey," *skedasis* describes the *scattering* of Penelope's suitors when Ulysses returns home. In a more poetic vein, in Prometheus, Aeschylus applies *skeda* to making "the sun disperse the hoar frost of the morn." [38]

Peremptory "expulsion" from an army while it faced an enemy in the field carried, for at least three Northern correspondents, the penalty of temporary capture. The experience of the *Inquirer*'s Painter was perhaps the most interesting, and easily the most frustrating. Picked up by a group of J. E. B. Stuart's cavalry, he was treated with courtesy and pretty much allowed the run of the camp, as a consequence of which he learned that the troopers had been ordered to launch a raid into Maryland, crossing the Potomac at Point of Rocks about thirty-five miles upriver from Washington.

Painter found his horse, slipped away, and set out for Washington to tell the War Department. The War Department was not interested: everyone knew that the rebels were about to attack Washington, and appropriate defensive preparations were under way. Painter tried logic: Stuart's fifteen hundred men were hardly a threat to the capital, but could wreak havoc in the Maryland countryside. The War Department was not interested.

Painter sent a reporter to Point of Rocks, who watched as rebel troops crossed the river on September 5. Painter took this information to the War Department on the following day, but with no confirmation from any other source, the department remained skeptical. It was to be another eighteen hours before any Federal efforts were made to catch up with Stuart, and by then, the War Department was forced to admit that much more than a cavalry raid was under way. Painter had known only of Stuart's orders, but between September 5 and 7, Lee moved his entire army across the river and occupied Frederick, Maryland. The immediate capture of Washington had not been in his plan.

The Richmond *Dispatch* suggested an alternative motive:

The road to Pennsylvania lies invitingly open. There are no regular soldiers on the route, and it would be a task of little difficulty to disperse the rabble of militia that might be brought to oppose them.

The country is enormously rich. It abounds in fat cattle, cereals, horses, and mules. Our troops would live on the very fat of the land. They would find an opportunity, moreover, to teach the Dutch farmers and graziers, who have been clamorous for this war, what invasion really means. . . .We hope the troops will turn the whole country into a desert. . . . [39]

On September 8, General Lee called on the citizens of Maryland to help to throw off the "foreign yoke," that they may once again enjoy the inalienable rights of freemen and restore the independence and sovereignty of their state:

> The people of the Confederate States have long watched with the deepest sympathy the wrongs and outrages that have been inflicted upon the citizens of a commonwealth, allied to the States of the South by the strongest social, political, and commercial tiers, and reduced to the condition of a conquered province. . . . Believing that the people of Maryland possess a spirit too lofty to submit to such a government, the people of the South have long wished to aid you in throwing off this foreign yoke. . . . In obedience to this wish our army has come among you, and is prepared to assist you with the power of arms in regaining the rights of which you have been so unjustly despoiled." [40]

Lee's explanation was backed by a specific invitation, issued by the colonel who took "command" of Frederick: "I am authorized immediately to muster in, for the war, companies and regiments. . . . Come all who wish to strike for their liberties and homes. Let each man provide himself with a stout pair of shoes, a good blanket, and a tin cup—Jackson's men have no baggage. . . . Officers are in Frederick to receive recruits, and all companies formed will be armed as soon as mustered in. *Rise at once!*" [41]

The citizens of Maryland stood back, and watched.

At exactly the same time, but perhaps without coordination, General Bragg had launched an invasion of the equally rich and peaceful state of Kentucky. He, too, invited the citizens to rise up in support—not once, but many times, and somewhat more in the manner of Beauregard than Lee: "Kentuckians, the first great blow has been struck for your freedom," he proclaimed on September 5, 1862. "The manacles will soon fall from your limbs, when we know you will arise and strike for your freedom, your women, and your altars." A week later, he wrote: "We come to guarantee to all the sanctity of your homes and altars, to punish with a rod of iron the despoilers of your peace, and to avenge the cowardly insults upon your women." Bragg then called on the women themselves to do battle:

"Women of Kentucky, your persecutions and heroic bearing have reached our ear. Banish henceforth forever from your minds the fear of loathsome prisons or insulting visitations. Let your enthusiasm have full rein. Buckle on the armor of your kindred, your husbands, sons, and brothers, and scoff with shame him who would prove recreant in his duty to you, his country, and his God." [42-1]

By the end of the month, Bragg had been joined by his close friend, editor John Forsyth of the Mobile *Register*, who, given the rank of colonel, had agreed to help out with this literary warfare. Forsyth set aside chivalric defense of women and altars in favor of a more practical political and economic persuasion:

> By the invasion of our territories by land and from sea, we have been
> unwillingly forced into a war for self-defense, and to vindicate a great
> principle, once dear to all Americans, to wit, that no people can be
> rightly governed except by their own consent. . . . It is from the East
> that have come the germs of this bloody and most unnatural strife . . .
> it is from the East that will come the tax-gatherer to collect from you
> the mighty debt which is being amassed mountain high for the pur-
> pose of ruining your best customers and natural friends. [42-2]

The citizens of Kentucky acted like their countrymen in Maryland, and stayed out of the way. But, along the way, Bragg's forces endured several resounding defeats, ending with the Battle of Perryville on October 8, 1862. Along the way, Forsyth, who had taken the propaganda assignment with the understanding that he also would be able to cover the campaign for four major newspapers (so much for the banning of newsmen), turned his energies to reporting.

He may have hoped to enhance the reputation of his friend and patron; he succeeded in reigniting press criticism against Bragg. The Columbus *Sun* scoffed: "All the silly efforts upon the part of a certain class of newspaper correspondents and 'small editors' to manufacture a great man out of General Bragg have failed. His late campaign in Kentucky speaks for itself . . . in language which all cannot fail to understand." [43] The Richmond *Examiner* complained:

> Of genius, military or civil, [Bragg] has none. Even in judgment and
> sagacity, for large affairs he is notoriously deficient. As commander-
> in-chief, he is worse than inexperienced, for he has grown old and
> hardened in a subaltern position of a regular army. With an iron
> heart and iron hand and a wooden head, his failure in a position
> where the highest intellectual facilities were demanded was predes-
> tined. [44]

After the Seven Days' Campaign, McClellan hunkered down at Harrison's Landing. He had, essentially, been stripped of any meaningful authority, although his supporters continued to champion his cause: "Little George," noted the Philadelphia Press, exhibited a modesty most becoming to a true leader; "the victories he won" were "ornaments" enough. [45] Which victories were those, we might wonder?

On August 3, Halleck ordered McClellan to move his forces in support of Pope. The move did not begin until August 15, and, once under way—according to the Tribune—was too timid to be of any assistance to Pope, whose forces were defeated two weeks later. When Pope was relieved of command on September 5, he was replaced, over the objections of Secretary Stanton, by the once-again ascendant McClellan.

Herald Washington bureau chief Whitely warned, in a letter to Bennett on September 9, that the abolitionists in Washington "mean revolution, anarchy and secession. These men are mad. They openly threaten to depose the President if it can be accomplished." Whitely suggested that such talk might soon "drive the army and the people" to declare "McClellan military dictator. The idea is becoming familiar to people here." The Herald openly played on that theme two days later, when it called on McClellan to become a kind of American Cromwell and "insist upon the modification and reconstruction of the Cabinet, in order to have it purged of the radical taint . . . [and] demand indemnity for the past and security for the future [since he was now] master of the situation." [46]

The "dictator" theme was not exclusive to some quarters in Washington. Maj. John Key (who had helped precipitate the correspondents' "rebellion" at Shiloh), was now McClellan's judge advocate. On September 16, Key confided to Tribune correspondent Nathaniel Paige that McClellan's officers had lost faith in the administration and were ready to march on Washington to install a military dictatorship. Key claimed to have argued against the move, but suggested that his success was perhaps only temporary.

Paige, however, was not Key's only confidant, and within a week, President Lincoln had been informed that Key had told a fellow officer that the object of the "game" is "that neither army shall get much advantage of the other; that both shall be kept in the field till they are exhausted, when we will make a compromise and save slavery." Summoned before the president, Key had no acceptable rebuttal. Thereupon, the president wrote, "In my view, it is wholly inadmissible for any gentleman holding a military commission from the United States to utter such sentiments. . . . let Major John J. Key be forthwith dismissed from the military service of the United States." [47]

McClellan dichotomies were back in fashion. In the edition of September 11, 1862, the Boston *Journal*'s man in Washington, Benjamin Poore, reported that McClellan was the most "beloved and honored" commander since George Washington. On the other hand, the next day's Cincinnati *Commercial* reported Whitelaw Reid's glimpse of the man behind the curtain, carefully nurturing the "beloved commander" image. Reid cited one incident: the army was on the move, and the route of march had been arranged to pass by McClellan's headquarters. Most of the troops showed the proper enthusiasm as they spotted the general—except one unit, which marched in "moody silence" until challenged by McClellan.

"What regiment is this?"

"The Third Vermont."

"*And a gallant regiment it is*," exclaimed the young general, "with an enthusiasm apparently as natural as if it were the very regiment over whose services he felt the proudest." The troopers' noisily positive reaction was predictable and McClellan's hold on that unit's affections, secure.

Another example of McClellan's unique genius: he created a visible method by which distinguished units might be given public honor, in perpetuity:

> It is ordered that there shall be inscribed upon the colors or guidons of all regiments and batteries in the service of the United States, the names of the battles in which they have borne a meritorious part. The names will also be placed on the Army Register at the head of the list of the officers of each regiment.
>
> It is expected that troops so distinguished will regard their colors as representing the honor of their corps—to be lost only with their lives; and that those not yet entitled to such a distinction will not rest satisfied until they have won it by their discipline and courage. . . . [48]

Then, having created the honor, the general spread it as widely as possible—too widely, perhaps. Following the Battle of Williamsburg, May 5, 1862, McClellan appeared to give credit for the victory to each of a series of participating regiments. He told the Fifth Wisconsin: "Through you we won the day, and 'Williamsburg' shall be inscribed upon your banner." He told the Seventh Maine: "You and your comrades arrested the progress of the advancing enemy, and turned the tide of victory in our favor. . . . In recognition of your merit, you shall hereafter bear the inscription 'Williamsburg' on your colors." And, he told the Thirty-third New

York: "The other troops engaged elsewhere fought well and did their whole duty too; but you won the day, and to you and your comrades belongs the credit of victory of Williamsburg." They too would merit the inscription, "Williamsburg," on the regimental flag. [49]

Maj. Gen. George Brinton McClellan entering Frederick, en route to the Battle of Antietam—heedless, apparently, to his horse's trampling of the adoring crowds.

Now, however, Lee was in Maryland and McClellan was in pursuit—
a pursuit, he hoped, which could be conducted without the encumbrance
of newsmen. However, the standing War Department order that banned
unauthorized hangers-on had not allowed for command indifference and
journalistic ingenuity. Some of the specials had been with the army so
long that they had become more or less invisible and, not having left during any of the "expulsions," did not have to find a way to get back in. Richardson, urgently shifted from his post in Cincinnati, obtained access
through the sentries with an old but undated pass signed by General
Burnside. At one point, Richardson and several other correspondents
found themselves seated at breakfast with General Marcy and several
others of McClellan's staff. Marcy said he should not order them out, but
was a good deal curious to know how they got in. Richardson slyly suggested that this was a military secret. None of the officers seemed to care.

Smalley wrangled an "assignment" as a volunteer aide-de-camp to
General Sedgwick. "I had met General Sedgwick before," he wrote in his
postwar memoir, "and when I had to consider how I was to get leave to go
with the troops I went to General Sedgwick and told him my difficulty.
'Come along with me,' he said. That was all the appointment I had. It
would not have been possible in a European army, but in the armies of
the Union many things were possible. And it was quite sufficient to take
me outside of Mr. Stanton's order about correspondents. I was not a correspondent; I was one of General Sedgwick's aids." He was given an immediate assignment: indefinite leave on special duty. [50]

Smalley, wearing a new blue uniform, attached himself to Hooker's
entourage on the eve of the Battle of Antietam. "I rode with the staff," he
wrote, "not one of whom I knew. Nobody took the trouble to ask who I
was or why I was there. For aught they knew I might have been a Rebel
spy." [51] The day of the battle (September 17, 1862) he found himself
pressed into direct service by General Hooker:

Early in the morning he had scattered his staff to the winds, and was
riding alone, on the firing line. Looking about him for an officer, he
saw me and said, "Who are you?" I told him. "Will you take an order for me?" "Certainly." There was a regiment which seemed wavering, and had fallen a little back. "Tell the colonel of that
regiment to take his men to the front and keep them there." I gave
the order. Again the question:

"Who are you?"

"The order is General Hooker's."

"It must come to me from a staff officer or from my brigade
commander."

"Very good. I will report to General Hooker that you decline to obey."

"Oh, for God's sake don't do that! The Rebels are too many for us but I had rather face them than Hooker."

And on went his regiment. I returned to Hooker and reported. "Yes," said he, "I see, but don't let the next man talk so much;" and I was sent off again. [52]

Smalley spent the day on such special missions, he and his horse both being nicked several times by enemy fire. His coolness under fire prompted Hooker later to say: "In all the experience I have had of war, I never saw the most experienced and veteran solider exhibit more tranquil fortitude and unshaken valor than was exhibited by that young man." [53]

Later in the day, with McClellan hesitant and unwilling to commit his reserves, the outcome of the battle was very much in doubt. Hooker had been taken out of action by a painful wound in the foot, and Lt. James H. Wilson, one of McClellan's staff officers—having noted what was clearly a cordial relationship between the reporter and the general—asked Smalley to urge Hooker to assume command of the army. "Most of us think that this battle is only half fought and half won," he said. "There is still time to finish it. But McClellan will do no more." Smalley argued that this was, essentially, a mutiny. Wilson responded, "I know that as well as you do." [54]

Smalley declined to play an active role but agreed, at the least, to check on the general's condition. In so doing, he offered Hooker his candid opinion that ". . . it was no longer a field of battle; that McClellan was resting on his arms; that he would not use his reserves; and that there was every prospect that Lee would escape with his beaten army across the Potomac." Smalley conveyed the suggestion that Hooker was needed back on the field. The general, in obvious pain, said, "You need not go on. You must see that I cannot move." [55]

Smalley reproduced his conversation with Wilson in an 1894 magazine piece, the accuracy of which was quickly challenged by that officer (who had advanced from second lieutenant to major general in four years of war). Wilson acknowledged the conversation, but denied the specific quotes and the mutinous intention; he only wanted Smalley to persuade Hooker back into action. Smalley's 1912 *memoir* presents a truncated but not essentially different version of the incident. [56]

That night, in a farmhouse crowded with wounded, three *Tribune* correspondents shared a borrowed candle, compared notes, and passed bits of copy to Smalley, who organized the framework for the report. At midnight, his pockets stuffed with the collated notes, Smalley set out for the telegraph office at Frederick, Maryland, which he found to be closed; he napped on the doorstep until the operator arrived for work at seven. The operator was uncertain about sending press copy; his responsibility was to the government, and he might not have any spare time. He agreed, how-ever, to send Smalley's material while he could, and Smalley drafted a brief summary, which he handed to the operator, sheet by sheet.

Thereupon followed another example of a newsman providing news to the president in advance of—or in the absence of—official reports. To that point, the most significant word that had reached Washington was a brief and frustrating note from McClellan: "We are in the midst of the most terrible battle of the war—perhaps of history. . . ." [57]

Smalley assumed that *his* message was being sent as it had been ad-dressed, to the *Tribune* in New York. However, the telegraph relay station in Baltimore routed it to the War Department instead, and by noon it was in front of an anxious commander in chief. Smalley's lead was hardly re-assuring:

Fierce and desperate battle between two hundred thousand men has raged since daylight, yet night closes in on an uncertain field. It is the greatest fight since Waterloo, all over the field contested with an obstinacy equal even to Waterloo. . . .

Early in the afternoon, the War Department began relaying the dis-patch, one page at a time, to the *Tribune* bureau in Washington. To save time, bureau chief Hill asked the telegraph company to have the Baltimore office resend the original copy to New York. The Baltimore office did not get the request, or ignored it, or was busy with other material, and did nothing. The greatest fight since Waterloo—and the bloodiest day in U.S. history—was in journalistic limbo. Eventually, Hill realized that something was amiss and sent his copy of the dispatch directly to New York.

In the meantime, Smalley did not know if his report had been seen by anyone, anywhere. He tried to hire a locomotive to take him to Baltimore but was told that he did not have the proper authority. Late in the day, he found a spot on a military train, reaching Baltimore just before the Wash-ington-to-New York night express was due to pass through. He had ten minutes to make a choice: try to send a full report—as yet largely unwrit-ten—by telegraph, or catch the train. The telegraph operator would not guarantee use of the line. Smalley took the train. By the time he reached the *Tribune* office in New York early the next morning, he had fleshed out his preliminary dispatch to fill more than five full columns in the extra edition, which was on the streets by eight o'clock that morning.

It was a remarkable piece. Smalley identified what were perhaps the two major factors that forestalled a Union victory: Burnside's indecision and McClellan's mismanagement. "Burnside hesitated for hours in front

of the bridge which should have been carried at once by a *coup de main*,"
he wrote, thus soon becoming "outnumbered, flanked. . . . His position is
no longer one of attack; he defends himself with unfaltering firmness, but
he sends to McClellan for help." [58]

Now it was McClellan's turn to be hesitant:

> Burnside's messenger rides up. His message is: "I want troops and
> guns. If you do not send them, I cannot hold my position half an
> hour." McClellan's only answer for the moment is a glance at the
> western sky. Then he turns and speaks very slowly: "Tell Gen. Burn-
> side this is the battle of the war. He must hold his ground till dark at
> any cost. I will send him Miller's battery. I can do nothing more. I
> have no infantry." [59]

"No infantry," but, as Smalley pointed out, fifteen thousand fresh
troops, "impatient to share in this fight," were held in reserve. All day.

The military result may have been stalemate, but it was clear that the
Tribune had won the journalistic Battle of Antietam: Smalley's piece was
reprinted in almost fourteen hundred newspapers. The dispatch was lauded by a *Tribune* competitor, the New York *Evening Post*, as "a truly admirable
account, which ranks for clearness, animation, and apparent accuracy with
the best battle pieces in literature, and far excels anything written by
Crimean Russell." Lincoln's personal secretary John Hay told *Tribune* bureau chief Hill that it was far better than any official report written since
the beginning of the war. After the war, Albert Richardson called it the best
piece of battle reporting of the war and Henry Villard agreed, adding "The
quickness and range of comprehension, fulness of correct information, and
expeditious working up for publication . . . were truly remarkable." [60]

The *Herald* had been thoroughly scooped—nothing original appeared
in the *Herald* until two full days later, although no one seems to know
why, because the paper, as usual, had arranged to have a well-organized
team of reporters on the battlefield. The New York *Times* (which had to
run Smalley's piece because it had none of its own) had fallen victim to
poor field communications, and afterwards instituted a policy of ensuring
that each correspondent was given written, not oral, orders. The Philadelphia *Inquirer* missed out entirely—Uriah Painter was in Ohio on what
the Boston *Journal* facetiously called a "Union mission." He was getting
married. [61]

Some Northern papers were hostage to their own editorial policies.
The *World*, for example, saw a great victory, "beyond a shadow of suspicion" because of "the heroic gallantry of our men and officers, and the
splendid management of Gen. McClellan." The Southern point of view

also was varied. To the Richmond *Enquirer*, the battle was "one of the most complete victories that has yet immortalized the confederate [*sic*] arms." The *Enquirer*'s report noted force levels about twice the actual numbers of 35,000 for the Confederates, and 87,000 for the Federals. The Charleston *Courier*'s dispatch (dateline: Sharpsburg) started out nearer the mark, but soon drifted away: "Last night, we were inclined to believe it was a drawn battle . . . but to-day the real facts are coming to light, and we feel that we have indeed, achieved another victory." However, P. W. Alexander had it right in his report to the Savannah *Republican*: "The prospect is, we shall have to return to Virginia." [62]

Some Southern coverage of Antietam, lifted from four different newspapers, flows together like bits of a novel. The narrative begins in the Mobile *Daily Advertiser and Register* as Lee's army moves through Northern Virginia; the correspondent had never seen such picturesque and bewitching scenery:

the deep blue mountains running in parallel lines, the quiet valleys, the clear rocky streams, the white farm houses and immense barns, wheat stacks and hayricks, the great cattle grazing on the hillsides, the long dusty column of the Confederate army threading their way across the valleys and through the gaps in the mountains, and the clusters of simple country people who have gathered along the road side or in front of their houses to witness the passing spectacle. [63]

The Charleston *Daily Courier* describes the welcome given to the troops as they pass through Leesburg:

The doorways and curbstones are like living bouquets of beauty. Everything that wears crinoline or a pretty face is out, and such shouts and wavings of handkerchief and hurrahs by the overjoyed gender never emanated from human lips. "What regiment is that?" "Sixth Georgia, Ewell's division." "Hurrah for you! Hurrah! Kill all the Yankees!" screamed a bevy of girls. "Hurrah for the gals! Coming back to marry the whole town." shout the Confederates. "Got any tobacco?" says another. "Got any shoes? Gives us a slice of bacon and bread. Hopp, hi hi!" and then the whole crowd break out into a series of yells and screeches that only require the addition of an Indian war dance to complete the scene. I never heard such tumult or saw such enthusiasm in my life. [64]

An army correspondent for the Memphis *Daily Appeal* reported quite a different reception in Maryland, where they found all stores closed, and an almost complete refusal to take any money but specie. And the women—God bless their pretty faces— didn't seem to appreciate the self-sacrificing devotion of the boys, and with few exceptions took particular care, by a contemptuous elevation of their tiny proboscis, to show their contempt of "you dirty rebels." [65]

A Maryland farmer, watching the troops cross the Potomac from Virginia, told the special from the Charleston *Daily Courier:* "Wall, I declare. I've been to shows and circuses and theaters and all them things but I never seen such a sight'n all my life. Why, you've got soldiers enough to whip all creation." [66]

But creation was not whipped at Antietam, nor the Yankees, and a few days later, as the same troops were retracing their march through the same Virginia countryside, the change in the tone was remarkable:

The columns wound their way over the hills and along the valleys, like some huge, indistinct monster. The trees and overhanging cliffs and the majestic Blue Ridge loomed up in dim but enlarged and fantastic proportions, and made one feel as if he were in some strange and weird land of grotesque forms, visited only in the hour of dreams. [67]

McClellan once again proved to be his own worst enemy. Instead of pursuing the greatly outnumbered and seriously damaged Confederate forces, he sat down to write complaining letters: *his* forces had been fighting for six months and were tired; *he* lacked supplies and equipment. The *Tribune* looked into McClellan's complaints and came up with a different story: the troops themselves—according to interviews—were disappointed that they were not sent immediately after the fleeing rebels. As for shortages, the *Tribune* obtained assurances from the supply department that any and all of McClellan's requisitions had promptly been filled and army correspondent "J. R. S." (probably Josiah Rinehart Sypher) puzzled over the contrast: the defeated, barefoot, and coatless rebels who could move as fast and far as they had to, while the reasonably well-supplied and reasonably victorious Union army had to wait around for more supplies. [68]

General Halleck made inquiries of his own. McClellan had complained of a shortage of horses and that the supply department had been sending him, on average, no more than 150 per week. He seems to have misplaced a decimal point: supply department records documented an average delivery of 1,459 horses, each week, for six weeks, which were in addition to some 3,000 mules assigned to the Army of the Potomac. All orders for clothing and shoes had been filled, Quartermaster General Meigs affirmed, and if more were needed, they easily could have been delivered even if the army had gone after the retreating Confederates.

On October 1, Halleck "urged" McClellan "to cross the river at once and give battle to the enemy." On October 6, McClellan was "peremptorily ordered to cross the Potomac and give battle to the enemy. . . ." Three weeks later, Halleck noted in a report to Secretary Stanton, the Army of the Potomac had not yet moved. [69]

McClellan was relieved of army command, once and for all time, a week after that.

14 / A Matter of Color

Will they carry [the liberated slaves] home to Yankee land
and provide for them, or teach them habits of thrift and industry?
Or will they turn them loose here to fight their way in the unequal
contest with white men? Or will they send them back to Africa to
return to their original barbarism and heathenism,
and raise children for the slave market?
—Richmond *Enquirer*, November 9, 1860

WHILE THE LINCOLN ADMINISTRATION avowed that eman-
cipation of the slave and the abolition of slavery were not the goals of the
war, it was commonly held that the status of blacks was indeed the reason, and that issues of states' rights and property rights grew out of, and
were not superior to, the moral issue of slavery. The Southern states
formed the Confederacy precisely because they believed that the election
of Abraham Lincoln was the harbinger of forced abolition.

As Confederate vice president Alexander Stephens explained on
March 21, 1861: the "proper status of the Negro in our form of civilization," was "the immediate cause of the late rupture and present revolution." Addressing a large crowd in Savannah, Georgia (and as quoted in
the Savannah *Republican*), Stephens acknowledged that arguments about
slavery were neither new nor unique to Lincoln and the Republicans:
"Jefferson . . . had anticipated this, as the 'rock upon which the old
Union would split.'" Jefferson, he said, and most of the "leading states-
men at the time of the formation of the old Constitution" believed that
slavery was "wrong in principle, socially, morally and politically." They believed that slavery was evil, he said, but did not know what to do about it;

they assumed that time would correct the problem, and slavery would pass away. "Those ideas, however, were fundamentally wrong."

They rested upon the assumption of the equality of the races. . . . Our new government is founded upon exactly the opposite ideas; its foundations are laid, its cornerstone rests, upon the great truth that the Negro is not equal to the white man; that slavery—subordination to the superior race—is his natural and normal condition. This our new government, is the first in the history of the world based upon this great physical, philosophical, and moral truth. [1]

The government soon had a rebel version of God on their side. A Pastoral Letter from the bishops of the Protestant Episcopal Church in the Confederate states, November 22, 1862, affirmed that black slavery was part of God's plan:

The time has come when the Church should press more urgently than she has hitherto done upon her laity the solemn fact that the slaves of the South are not merely so much property, but are a sacred trust committed to us as a people, to be prepared for the work which God may have for them to do in the future. While under this tutelage, he freely gives us their labor, but expects us to give back to them that religious and moral instruction which is to elevate them in the scale of being. [2]

Thus, we might presume that the Confederacy was formed to protect the blacks. Why was the war being fought? The Memphis *Appeal* knew with a certainty "that the true animus of the Lincoln war upon the South is a desire to exterminate the institution of slavery":

The radical portion of the abolition press echo these infamous sentiments with the most scrupulous faithfulness. Chief among them we notice the New York *Times*, whose editor . . . comes to the sage and deliberate conclusion that "there is one thing, and only one, at the bottom of the fight—and that is the Negro." He thinks that both sections are attempting to deceive the country in the alleged excuses for their conduct—the South erring in the pretense of fighting for independence, and the North fighting for the re-establishment of the Government. [3]

Northern newspapers had widely varied views on slavery as an institution, and on blacks as individuals. The position of the abolitionist was always clear: slavery was wrong, blacks were human beings, no compromise, and there was no doubt about the purpose of the war: "It is war to the utter annihilation of slavery. The day of honeyed words has passed. The day of bloody deeds has come. And let those who do the fighting get the pay." [4]

Some Northern papers, less committed but nonetheless supportive, saw opposition to slavery as an easy issue, compared with other public issues of the day—the tariff, credit, the price of land, public works, immigration policy, and the exploitation of labor. Some papers took the Jeffersonian view: slavery was an unpleasant anachronism; it would disappear in time but in the meantime, it provided a reasonable accommodation to the needs of an inferior group of beings.

Then came the Democratic papers, which, as noted in chapter 2, saw reconciliation with the South as the only route back to political power. Whatever a Democratic editor may have felt about slavery as an individual, all knew that compromise was impossible as long as "abolition" was the issue. Allegiance to the Constitution, yes. Abolition, no.

Historian Bernard Weisberger wrote that the Democratic editors committed a tactical as well as moral mistake, by blaming the "infernal nigger" for the nation's problems and by echoing the "same Paleolithic States' rights and proslavery arguments which had cozened the South out of the Union." They made it easy for Republicans to win elections, he added, "with the charges that all Democrats were tools of Richmond when some Democratic spellbinders insisted on sounding like Richmond. Racism was not altogether unpopular in the North, but it had only a limited pay-off at the ballot box." [5]

In truth, overt prejudice against blacks was more virulent in some Northern communities, which feared being overrun by liberated slaves, than in the South, where blacks and whites had lived together, amicably or not, for centuries. "Our nation is wild with Negrophobia," wrote the editor of the Baltimore *American:*

This country will never reach the prosperity of which it is capable until the white people receive some small share of public attention. At present Sambo has the best of the corn crib and the meat house, and is made a lion of besides. We are in favor of feeding him well and treating him well, but are opposed to all Lions and especially to African lions. We are in favor of removing Sambo from the Senate and the House of Representatives and keeping him in the corn field and the kitchen. That is his "manifest destiny," and it is there only that he can *shine* to advantage. [6]

Racism often was the filter through which different correspondents described the same event, and the filter worked both ways. Federal troops moving through Mississippi, the New York *Tribune* reported, were guilty of wanton vandalism, making "complete havoc of everything in the shape of provisions, portable wares of value, and even furniture. . . . It is but justice to the troops to add that these outrages are perpetrated principally by stragglers, who belong to the same category with the 'vultures' that rifle the dead on the field of battle." [7] It might have been honest, as well as "justice to the troops," to mention that the stragglers were black Federal soldiers. Franc Wilkie of the New York *Times*, revealing his own racism, offered a different picture of the same event:

> Nothing came amiss to these rejoicing Africans; they went around the streets displaying aggregate miles of double-rowed ivory, and bending under an enormous load of French mirrors, boots, shoes, pieces of calico, wash-stands and bowls, hoop skirts, bags of tobacco, parasols, umbrellas, and fifty other articles equally incongruous. I noticed among the crowd several pretty but poorly-dressed white girls, who were delightfully familiar with the soldiers, and who were about equally active in toting off plunder and chewing tobacco. [8]

Some newspapers applied a political/racial litmus test to senior officers, evaluating their effectiveness insofar as their policies were in congruence with those of the editors. The Democratic Chicago *Times* asserted that, in the eyes of the Radical press, an "abolition General" could "do no wrong, commit no blunders, make no mistakes, moral, social, or political" and when he lost battles, it was only through the "treachery, cowardice or ignorance" of his subordinates. Even the despised West Pointer could find redemption with the Republicans if he would "repent, partake of the sacraments of orthodox abolitionism, put on the white robes of the 'loyal' elect, take a harp in his hands to chant the praises of the redeemed nigger and the abolition God. . . ." [9]

Here's a brief case study on Maj. Gen. Don Carlos Buell, vilified by the Radicals and lauded by the Democrats. Henry Villard—who had worked both sides of that political equation but whose sentiments were Republican—reported that Buell was consistently discourteous to reporters, "as hostile as Sherman but not so redeemingly human." Charles Coffin of the Boston *Journal* noted that "every secessionist" held Buell in high regard. The Missouri *Democrat* reported that Buell was so overly cautious that he had threatened to arrest Grant for capturing Nashville ahead of plan. For the New York *Tribune*, Junius Browne cited his "inglorious, disastrous career" and the "disgust and contempt" he aroused in others; he was "Utterly unfit for his position." The Chicago *Tribune* declared that "Buell is a failure—a contemptible failure." For the Cincinnati *Commercial*, Joe McCullagh wondered how long "an army of lions was to be commanded by a jackass." Another *Commercial* reporter complained that Buell had less "love for the Union" than for slavery, and was too concerned with guarding rebel property than in chasing after Gen. Braxton Bragg following Bragg's defeat at the Battle of Perryville. Whitelaw Reid, for the Cincinnati *Gazette*, wrote that questions were being asked by Buell's own men, "Major General and privates alike. Why were all those blunders committed at Perryville? Why, if it was meant to pursue Bragg in earnest at all did it take a week to march from Perryville to Danville—ten miles?" [10]

Charles Mackay, writing for the London *Times* at this same time, asserted that Buell—after McClellan "the next most important Federal officer in command of an army in the field"—was accused by the Radicals "of having stated at the commencement of his military career that he did not know who was right or wrong in the struggle—the North or the South, and to have acted throughout the war on the lazy principle of poco-curantism [nonchalant indifference]." [11]

Buell, like McClellan, was a hero in the *Herald*. One day, the *Herald* predicted, the nation would "call these two men blessed." His disfavor in the Radical press, the *Herald* said, grew out of his refusal "to make the Negro question superior to the question of the Union." The Cincinnati *Enquirer* charged that the Republicans were out to destroy him with pens "tipped with gall." In a series of reports, the Chicago *Times* praised Buell's cautious tactics as grand strategy, and charged that his newspaper critics were enjoying the delights of Louisville, "playing euchre or poker and drinking whiskey" rather than getting out in the field. The real issue with Buell, according to that reporter, was that Buell was "not prosecuting any anti-slavery crusade. . . ." As for the Battle of Perryville, this *Times* said: "Never in the history of this war has the dissipation of an army been so complete. As an army, Bragg's force has ceased to exist. In front of Buell's advance the country is filled with a fugitive mob—nothing more; no organization; no concert of action; no plan of campaign; nothing but complete rout and demoralization." [12]

Sometimes, you can't tell the players without a program.

In the weeks immediately following the surrender of Fort Sumter, Federal forces moved to reinforce outposts still open to reinforcement. On May 20, 1861, the London *News* reported:

> The mood of the slaves becomes a very interesting inquiry. Thus far, the most certain fact is, that wherever any Federal force has appeared, slaves have deserted to them at every opportunity. Hitherto,

they have all been returned [but] after the first collision in the field there will be an end of returning [deserting slaves]; and the fugitives will be too useful as guides and aids to be slighted.

On May 24, and not associated with any "immediate collision" in the field, three escaped slaves presented themselves to Maj. Gen. Benjamin F. Butler, newly arrived as commander of Federal forces at Fortress Monroe, Virginia. Under a flag of truce, an agent for their owner came over and requested their return, citing the Fugitive Slave Act. Butler replied, that, as the citizens of Virginia had just voted, the day before, to approve the ordinance of secession, he was "under no obligations to a foreign country, which Virginia now claims to be. . . . I shall hold these Negroes as contraband of war, since they were engaged in the construction of your battery and are claimed as your property." [13]

Thereupon, what began as a trickle became a flood. By May 27, entire families were crossing into his camps—"amounting, as I am informed, to what would in good times be of the value of $60,000," he told General Scott. "I have . . . determined to employ, as I can do very profitably, the able-bodied persons in the party, issuing proper food for the support of all, and charging against the services the expense of care and sustenance of the non-laborers. . . ." [14]

Butler sought guidance from the War Department: "As a political question and a question of humanity, can I receive the services of a father and a mother and not take the children? Of the humanitarian aspect I have no doubt; of the political one I have no right to judge." Secretary Cameron gave a properly legal response: do not let anyone under your command interfere with relations between slaves and their owners, unless you happen to be in a state that is in rebellion—in which case, "refrain from surrendering to alleged masters any persons who come within your lines." The question of wages, expenses, and final disposition of the people was reserved "for future determination." [15]

The future came quickly. By the end of July, Butler was host to "900 Negroes, 300 of whom are able-bodied men, 30 of who are men substantially past hard labor, 175 women, 225 children under the age of 10 years, and 170 between 10 and 18 years, and many more coming in." Not all were escaped slaves; many fell under the heading of "abandoned property," as a consequence of the shifting military situation. "The questions which this state of facts presents are very embarrassing," Butler told Secretary Cameron. "First, what shall be done with them? And, Second, What is their state and condition? Upon these questions I desire the instructions of the Department." [16]

Congress answered in part with the first Confiscation Act, August 6, which affirmed that any master who had caused his slave to be "employed in hostility to the United States" lost the right of ownership. On the "more difficult question . . . in respect to persons escaping from the service of loyal masters," Cameron advised, "it seems quite clear that the substantial rights of loyal masters are still best protected by receiving such fugitives, as well as fugitives from disloyal masters, into the service of the United States and employing them under such organizations and in such occupations as circumstances may suggest or require." [17]

It became common, in many, but not all, areas under Federal control, to accept and employ fugitive slaves "as laborers on the fortifications and military works, paid as day-laborers in the service of the Government." [18] The pay scale for contrabands at Fort Monroe was set at eight dollars a month for men, four dollars a month for women. In the West, General Sherman freely employed escaped slaves, but set up an escrow for their wages until the courts might determine if they were now slave or free; Grant extended their services beyond manual labor, to also include duty as teamsters, cooks, hospital attendants, and nurses, especially if a soldier could thereby be freed for more direct military service.

Gen. Henry Halleck sailed a different course. On November 20, 1861, he issued General Order 3, the first of what became a series of directives—including the "unauthorized hangers-on" of Pittsburg Landing—that were intended to keep fugitive slaves away from his army and out of his hair:

1. It has been represented that important information respecting the numbers and condition of our forces is conveyed to the enemy by means of fugitive slaves who are admitted within our lines. In order to remedy this evil, it is directed that no such persons be hereafter permitted to enter the lines of any camp, or of any forces on the march, and that any now within such lines be immediately excluded therefrom.
2. The General Commanding wishes to impress upon all officers in command of posts and troops in the field the importance of preventing unauthorized persons of every description from entering and leaving our lines, and of observing the greatest precaution in the employment of agents and clerks in confidential positions. [19]

When Halleck learned that a general officer in his command had directed another officer to surrender a fugitive to a man who claimed him to be "the property of his father-in-law," he provided this amplification: hands-off meant hands-off:

This [action] is contrary to the intent of General Orders No. 3. The object of those orders is to prevent any person in the army from acting in the capacity of Negro-catcher or Negro-stealer. The relation between the slave and his master is not a matter to be determined by military officers [but] must be decided by the civil authorities. One object in keeping fugitive slaves out of our camps is to keep clear of all such questions. . . . [20]

Halleck assured his commanders that General Order 3 did not apply to "the authorized private servants of officers, nor to Negroes employed by proper authority in camps," but only to "fugitive slaves" and did not prevent anyone from "the exercise of all proper offices of humanity in giving them food and clothing outside, where such offices are necessary to prevent suffering." [21]

Everyone, however, knew what he meant. General Order 3 was racism wrapped in an official cloak. "Halleck," said the Chicago *Times*, "intended to preserve the government for the benefit of the white race, whose ancestors framed it." [22]

The Democratic newspapers had a field day with the former field hands and kitchen help, now in government employ. The Ohio *Statesman* snickered, "Two slaves who run away from their masters in Virginia, are set to work at once by Gen. Butler, and made to keep at it, much to their annoyance. One of them having been put to it rather strong, said, 'Golly, Massa Butler, dis nigger never had to work so hard before; guess dis chile will secede once moah.'" The *Herald* assured its readers that the fugitives were looking for "the blessed land of Canaan" with "little work, [and] plenty of hog and hominy." They were "happy, careless, good-for-nothing" with a "chronic antipathy to labor," although they did not mind running errands and catching shellfish to sell to the soldiers. [23] "Their Elysium had come," wrote *Herald* correspondent George Alfred Townsend:

> There was no more work. They slept and danced and grinned, and these three actions made up the sum of their existence. . . . Such soulless, lost, degraded men and women did nowhere else exist. The divinity they never had; the human they had forgotten; they did no great wrongs—thieving, quarreling, deceiving—but they failed to do any rights. . . . [24]

In the spring of 1862, a group of missionaries and schoolteachers moved in to run the cotton plantations along the South Carolina coast, paying the former slaves for their labor, with a bit of schooling and religion thrown in for good measure. One *Herald* correspondent was appalled: such mischievous interference with accustomed good order and discipline would "create Negro insurrection, and result in the indiscriminate slaughter of the white race, of every age and sex, in every section of the South." [25]

Another *Herald* reporter suggested that the Negroes were incapable of learning anything, but that the missionaries might have "a good deal of fun" in trying. On the other hand, the *Tribune* speculated that the slave, any slave, already trained in useful skills of agriculture and crafts, would have a better chance of surviving in a free labor market than his master. [26]

The presence of a large number of former slaves at Fortress Monroe, combined with the gullibility of a naïve correspondent, led the Philadelphia *Press* to report that "two hundred and seventy two contrabands" were lured out to a waiting ship offshore, ostensibly to do labor in her hold but "on no condition, were these men allowed to return" ashore. The ship then "skipped" out to sea under cover of darkness and headed for "Cuba or the West Indies," her human cargo to be sold back into slavery, being worth, "in Cuba, from one thousand two hundred dollars to one thousand five hundred dollars each." The reporter did admit that, "owing to the embargo recently placed upon naval officers, who 'say their mouths are sealed,' we are not able to present the facts of the case well authenticated." [27]

The New York *Times* branded this tale "a ridiculous invention, well calculated to do mischief," and Col. C. B. Wilder, the man responsible for coordinating all "contraband" activities at Fortress Monroe, sent a letter to the *Times* endorsing that opinion. "It seems incredible," he wrote, "that any well-informed correspondent could be so far imposed upon as to give publicity to a statement so devoid of all elements of probability, and so evidently the offspring of malice and wickedness." [28]

The great number of fugitives at Fortress Monroe also inspired comment in the Richmond *Dispatch*, July 18, 1862:

> It appears from statements in the Northern newspapers that McClellan proposes to employ Negroes to perform the hard labor on his fortifications, with a view to save his troops from the perils of sunstroke. This is the sort of freedom the deluded slaves enjoy when they get in to the clutches of the abolitionists. They are worked to death, in order to save the lives of a proportionate number of miserable Yankees, not one half of whom can lay as much claim to respectability as the blackest cornfield Negro in Virginia. We hope our authorities, in negotiating for an exchange of prisoners, will make the invaders account for at least a portion of the "contrabands" they have stolen, though in making up their relative value it should appear that one nigger was equal to two Yankees.

As the London *News* had predicted, "the fugitives will be too useful as guides and aids to be slighted." Someone coined the term, *intelligent contraband*, to identify former slaves who gave "useful" topographic and military information to the Federal army; they became an asset in the Republican press and a joke in the Democratic. The New York *Tribune* cited a domestic in West Virginia who warned a visiting reporter not to talk so freely about military matters; her master was a "secesh." The *Tribune* lauded a slave in Missouri who warned a Federal scouting party of an ambush, just ahead, and another, in South Carolina, was credited with drawing a map in the sand, "with perfect distinctness . . . [showing] the location of forces, giving their names and strength, and marking the points of approach." Sam Wilkeson chided Federal authorities for not trusting the runaways, who could give vital "intelligence upon which our columns could safely march." [29] Wilkeson also gave the *Tribune*'s readers the "verbatim" musings of a slave named Tom:

> *You have got to have us, Mr. W. Our climate will kill your troops. . . . The South is a wilderness. You are ignorant of it, and can he ambushed every day. And . . . if with half a million men you overrun it, it would take a million men to occupy it. . . .* You white men of the North will go into Slavery, unless you take us black men of the South out of Slavery; and, Mr. W., you have not a great deal of time left in which to decide what you will do. [30]

The Cincinnati *Enquirer* scoffed at field hands who spoke about military operations "as glibly as so many 'Patent-office Reports'" and the *Missouri Republican* affirmed that the Negro whose "imagination stretched the most" was favored in the Republican press. [31]

If abolition of slavery was to be an outcome of the war, emancipation of those already enslaved was a first step, a step taken prematurely by several senior Federal officers—to the president's distress and, in one case, to the embarrassment of the *Herald*. That paper had become the champion of the great Pathfinder, John C. Frémont, while he was the Union commander in Missouri in 1861. Frémont—even though a Republican—was "just the man for the job, busy night and day preparing for a vigorous campaign." [32]

However, Frémont, went well beyond the *Herald*'s territory when, in August 1861, he put the following codicils into a declaration of martial law: any civilian caught in rebellion would be shot, and their property confiscated—including slaves. The *Herald*, trapped between warm support of Frémont and bitter opposition to abolition, called Frémont's move "very unfortunate." [33] The president, then trying to keep a delicate balance between the Union and the slaveholding border states, called it a mistake and took bold corrective action: the order was modified to con-

form with the Act of August 6, thus applying only to slaves directly employed in support of the rebels.

The *Tribune* was delighted with Frémont and upset with the president: "Mr. Lincoln and his advisers may not yet be aware of the fact; but
there is war in Missouri. A desperate, unscrupulous, bloodthirsty foe is
over-running the State. . . . Gen. Frémont's policy was *simply a matter of
military necessity. . . .*" [34]

On May 9, 1862, Maj. Gen. David Hunter issued a proclamation
freeing the slaves in South Carolina, Georgia, and Florida, the three-state
area under his "authority" although not necessarily under his control; it
was canceled by the president ten days later. The *Herald* applauded the
cancellation and offered the opinion that the government had been "losing money" on Hunter. [35]

Hunter also raised a regiment of black troops, creating another controversy. The War Department refused to sanction his action, but the
pressure to accept Negroes into the Federal armed forces was increasing—in large part, from the blacks themselves. In the same edition (May
20, 1861) in which the paper reported that escaped slaves were coming
across Federal lines, the London *News* noted:

In the free States the people of color are eager to help on the loyal
side. They have for many weeks past formed themselves into companies, and got themselves drilled and armed—refused at present a
place in the loyal forces, but resolved to be ready for the call, which
they believe will come. The authorities of Pennsylvania have refused a passage through their State to companies of free Negroes
from New England and New York; but the Black volunteers extend
their organization week by week.

Free blacks in New Orleans also formed a regiment, and offered their
services to the Confederacy. However, at this early stage of the war, there
was no interest—North or South—in accepting the service of blacks as
soldiers; enlistments were going well, it was not yet much of a war, and
besides, for both sides, it was a white man's war—a "civilized" war. When
General Hunter began assembling his regiment, the Chicago *Times* was
more than appalled at this "invitation to a carnival of barbarities—a solic-
itation that Negroes [should] apply the torch to the homes and dip their
knives in the heart's blood of white men—a bugle call rousing the baser
passions of the black race to surfeit themselves in the ravishment of the
white mothers and daughters of the South." [36]

General Hunter's action also prompted a debate in the House of Representatives, the substance of which was reported by Whitelaw Reid, by

this time assigned as the Washington correspondent for the Cincinnati *Gazette*:

> Charles A. Wickliffe [Whig., Ky.] . . . charged officers of the Government and of the army with having undertaken, without law, against order, and in violation of every principle of humanity, to assume the power of enlisting slaves to serve against their masters. . . . Robert Mallory [Dem., Ky.] made the usual Kentucky speech against arming the Blacks. He ridiculed the idea of making them soldiers; said a single cannon shot would put ten thousand of them to flight; and closed by declaring that arming them was barbarous, inhuman and contrary to the practice of all civilized nations, and that it was most as bad as putting the tomahawk into the hands of the savage. This stirred up Thaddeus Stevens [Rep., Vt.], who inquired, how does it come that they are so dangerous to their masters, when a single cannon shot will put ten thousand to flight? Or how is it that they have not courage enough to make soldiers when you call them as savage and dangerous as Indians? But the gentleman was mistaken in his fact. Common history, he repeated, proved them false. It had been the general practice of civilized nations to employ slaves for military purposes, whenever and wherever needed.
>
> Owen Lovejoy [Rep., Ill.] here begged leave to interrupt, and read from a common school history about Jackson's arming slaves in the War of 1812 and his promise to give freedom to all who served. He then read Jackson's General Order, thanking the Negroes for their gallant success, saying that he had not been unaware of their good qualities as soldiers, but that they had far surpassed his highest expectations and reassuring them of emancipation as a reward for their conduct. Lovejoy concluded his demonstration . . . by reference to another history, showing that one-fourth of the men who helped with [Commodore Oliver Hazard] Perry's victory on the lakes were Negroes. The effect of all this was sensational. Men who had been denouncing Hunter couldn't have been more astonished if one of Hunter's own bombshells from Port Royal had been dropped among them. [37]

On July 17, 1862, Congress broadened the 1861 Confiscation Act to apply to all slaves who came within Union lines, repealed the provisions of a 1792 law barring blacks from service in the militia, and authorized the enlistment of free blacks and freedmen. On August 4, a delegation from Indiana met with the president to offer two regiments of black soldiers. The president declined the offer. "To arm the Negroes," he said, "would turn 50,000 bayonets from the loyal Border States against us that were for us." Six weeks later he said to someone else: "if we were to arm [the Negroes], I fear that in a few weeks the arms would be in the hands of the rebels." [38]

A writer for the New York *Times* warned, "I am quite sure there is not one man in ten but would feel himself degraded as a volunteer if Negro equality is to be the order in the field of battle. . . . I take the liberty of warning the abettors of fraternizing with the blacks, that one Negro regiment, in the present temper of things, put on equality with those who have the past year fought and suffered, will withdraw an amount of life and energy in our army equal to disbanding ten of the best regiments we can now raise." [39]

It is a peculiar artifact of the history of this time that, amid violent arguments for and against allowing blacks to serve in the army, no one paid much attention to the fact that they already were serving, in large numbers, in the navy. Blacks had been employed in the maritime trades from time immemorial, in proportion about equal to their representation in the population at large, and they, and white seamen as well, drifted in and out of naval service depending on the availability of jobs. The war, of course, opened plenty of opportunities. The U.S. Navy was the only integrated service, with blacks serving in all enlisted rates and ratings and living cheek by jowl with white sailors until 1912, when the administration of Woodrow Wilson began to impose segregation on the Federal government.

On August 20, President Lincoln's attention was directed to another matter of transcendent importance. Horace Greeley, impatient with the slow pace of government and the apparent indifference of the president to the plight of escaping slaves, addressed an open letter under the heading, "The Prayer of Twenty Millions." He expressed the disappointment and pain felt by "all who desire an unqualified supression of the rebellions now desolating our country. . . .We think you are unduly influenced," Greeley charged, "by the councils, the representations, the menaces, of certain fossil politicians hailing from the Border Slave States" who wanted him to forget that the "inciting cause" of the rebellion was slavery:

> We complain that the Confiscation act which you approved is habitually disregarded by your Generals, and that no word of rebuke for them from you has yet reached the public ear. Frémont's Proclamation and Hunter's Order favoring Emancipation were promptly annulled by you; while Halleck's Number Three, forbidding fugitives from slavery to rebels to come within his lines—an order as unmili-

tary as inhuman, and which received the hearty approbation of every traitor in America—with scores of like tendency, have never provoked even your remonstrance. . . . We ask you to render it due obedience by publicly requiring all your subordinates to recognize and obey it. . . . I entreat you to render a hearty and unequivocal obedience to the law of the land. [40]

In his public response, the president did not rise to the bait: "I have just read yours of the nineteenth, addressed to myself through the New York *Tribune*," he wrote:

If there be in it any statements or assumptions of fact which I may know to be erroneous, I do not now and here controvert them. If there be in it any inferences which I may believe to be falsely drawn, I do not now and here argue against them. If there be perceptible in it an impatient and dictatorial tone, I waive it in deference to an old friend whose heart I have always supposed to be right. . . .

If I could save the Union without freeing *any* slave, I would do it; and if I could save it by freeing *all* the slaves, I would do it; and if I could do it by freeing some and leaving others alone, I would also do that. What I do about slavery and the colored race, I do because it helps to save the Union; and what I forbear, I forbear because I do *not* believe it would help to save the Union. . . . I have here stated my purpose according to my view of *official* duty, and I intend no modification of my oft-expressed *personal* wish that all men, everywhere, could be free. [41]

Greeley more or less threw up his hands in surrender. He told an associate, "Lincoln added insult to injury by answering my 'Prayer of Twenty Millions,' which asked only for the honest enforcement of an existing law, as if it had been a demand for the abolition of slavery; thus adroitly using me to feel the public pulse, and making me appear as an officious meddler in affairs that properly belong to the government. No, I can't trust your 'honest Old Abe,' He is too smart for me." [42]

Greeley's "Prayer" had been prompted by a private report from Sam Wilkeson that Secretary of State Seward—whom Greeley did not trust—had blocked some sort of antislavery move on the part of the president. Unbeknownst to Greeley, the president had drafted a proclamation calling for full emancipation of all slaves in the rebellious states, which he presented to the cabinet on July 22. Seward did object, but more along the lines that any public release at that time, considering the recent military setbacks on the peninsula, would be perceived as a move of despera-

tion. Thus, the proclamation was postponed, to await the appropriate battlefield victory. It arrived as Antietam, September 17.

The document, delivered to the press on September 22, proclaimed
that, as of January 1, 1863,

> all persons held as slaves within any State, or any designated part of
> a State, the people whereof shall then be in rebellion against the
> United States shall be then, thenceforward and forever free, and
> the executive government of the United States, including the mili-
> tary and naval authority thereof, will recognize and maintain the
> freedom of such persons, and will do not act or acts to repress such
> persons, or any of them, in any efforts they may make for their actu-
> al freedom. . . . [43]

The *Tribune* was jubilant: "It is the beginning of the end of the rebellion, is the beginning of the new life of the nation. . . . GOD BLESS
ABRAHAM LINCOLN." The Wooster (Ohio) *Wayne County Democrat*
called it "The Death-Blow of the Nation," and published letters from
serving soldiers, which the editor intimated were representative of many:
"I did not enlist to free the infernal niggers," said one. Another wrote, "If
the President makes this a war to carry out his Emancipation Proclamation and it gets to be so understood by the army he will have to get a new
set of soldiers." A third gave this prediction: "Those men of the South
who have had no reason to fight, now have a reason to protect their
slaves; and they say that we may kill them all but we can never whip
them. They further say that if we succeed in whipping them they will
teach their children to fight us." [44]

The Chicago *Times* reported that streams of blacks had been spotted
at Memphis, ready to move to the North. At the beginning of November,
a *Herald* reporter at Nashville warned that freed blacks were drifting
North "in sufficient numbers to alarm the working people and the taxpay-
ers." The Chicago *Tribune* scoffed: Blacks did "not wish to remove to the
cold and frigid North. This climate is more genial, and here [the South] is
their home. Only give them a fair remuneration for their labor, and strike
off their shackles, and the good people of Illinois need not trouble themselves at the prospect of Negro immigration."[45]

Editors in the South warned of the most dire consequences. The
Richmond *Examiner* branded the Emancipation Proclamation as a call for
the insurrection of four million slaves and a "reign of hell on earth." To
the Richmond *Whig*, "It is a dash of the pen to destroy four thousand millions of our property, and is as much as a bid for the slaves to rise in insurrection, with the assistance of aid from the whole military and naval

power of the United States." [46] Charles Mackay, writing for the London *Times*, expanded on that theme:

> Mr. Lincoln proposes to enact that every slave in a rebel State shall be for ever after free, and he promises that neither he, nor his army, nor his navy will do anything to repress any efforts which the Negroes in such rebel states may make for the recovery of their freedom. This means, of course, that Mr. Lincoln will, on the 1st of next January, do his best to excite a servile war in the States which he cannot occupy with his army. He will run up the river in his gunboats; he will seek out the places which are left but slightly guarded, and where the women and children have been trusted to the fidelity of coloured domestics. He will appeal to the black blood of the African; he will whisper the pleasures of spoil and the gratification of yet fiercer instincts; and when the blood begins to flow and shrieks come piercing through the darkness, Mr. Lincoln will wait till the rising flames tell that all is consummated, and then he will rub his hands and think that revenge is sweet. [47]

Interesting to note: another correspondent for the London *Times*, writing just a month later, reported that "not one of those prophecies which we have all believed and been deluded by in England with regard to the weak spot of slavery festering at the heart of the South has found one tittle of realization. Women and children without one adult white male have constantly lived in the voiceless solitudes of the South surrounded by Negroes; in no instance known to me has anything but the greatest loyalty and affection been evinced." [48]

Toward the end of 1862, the first regiments of black soldiers were mustered into militia service in South Carolina, Missouri, and New Orleans (where free blacks who first had offered their services to the rebels signed on to fight for the Union). Several bills concerning enlistment of black soldiers in the army were pending in Congress; the topic was not altogether popular. One Democratic paper in Ohio sounded more like a Southern sheet, but echoed the sentiments of many:

> The Abolition hero and legislator, Gen. Jim Lane, of Kansas, has introduced into Congress a bill authorizing the President to raise two hundred thousand Negro soldiers, to be armed and equipped in the manner of white soldiers. The bill will probably pass. This announcement will startle the people of the country who desire that the war shall be conducted in accordance with the rules of civilized

warfare. Savages are to be let loose, to ravish, burn and destroy. The conflict is to be degenerated into a wholesale butchery on both sides. [49]

The bills came up for debate in the House at the end of January 1863. The Democrats hoped, through one or another parliamentary maneuver, to stall the process until the current session of Congress expired on March 4. Whitelaw Reid once again recorded the proceedings for the Cincinnati *Gazette*. Among the more interesting arguments in favor:

Owen Lovejoy [Rep., Ill] "Would I arm Negroes? Ay, sir, not only would I arm Negroes, but I would arm mules and make them shooting machines to kill rebels if I could."

William Dunn [Rep., In.] "The gentleman asks how we can exchange them if taken prisoners and speaks as if offering to exchange a black man for a white one would be a great outrage on the white population. I tell the gentleman that a black man who fights for my country, is *better than any white man who fights against her*! . . . If the gentleman's own son was fighting in this war, would he rather having him shot by a white traitor than saved by a loyal black soldier?"

William D. Kelley [Rep., Pa.] "Is the life of the Negro more sacred than that of the white man? Why should not American Africans encounter the power of the enemy or suffer the malaria of the swamps? Why should your son and my brother and our friends die, that the Negro may live? The Negro is not one whit better than ourselves; he is our equal in right in that great forum where *absolute* justice prevails, before God our common father. The Negro is not better than we; the Negro should share the dangers and sufferings of this war." [50]

After six days of protracted debate, the Negro Regiment Bill passed by a vote of 83 to 55. It authorized the enlistment of any number of blacks, but not exceeding 300,000, to be paid at the same rate as white soldiers and to be officered by white men. Slaves of loyal masters in the border states should not be enlisted, and recruiting of black in such states would be subject to the consent of the governors thereof. The War Department immediately authorized the enlistment of black soldiers in Massachusetts. However, the black population in Massachusetts was too small to support the call, and recruiting was conducted all over the North.

Black enlistments were inhibited by Confederate warnings—indeed, by an Act of the Confederate congress in May, which held that captured officers of black regiments were subject to execution, and the soldiers themselves, were to be executed or sold into slavery. [51] With one major exception—the alleged massacre at Fort Pillow, Tennessee, in April 1864—and a few scattered incidents, the threat was greater than the reality. However, the threat served the purpose, and influenced many prospective enlistees. Even so, 200,000 blacks had been brought into the army by the end of the war. Some 29,000 served in the navy—about 25 percent of the total enlisted force.

Fort Pillow has long been a controversial topic. When only 58 blacks out of 262 assigned to the Federal garrison survived an attack by troops commanded by Maj. Gen. Nathan Bedford Forrest, the event was branded in the North as an atrocity and in the South as just a lot of fierce fighting. It was probably a bit of both. There were reports that black soldiers had been killed after surrendering; there is evidence that some were. There was one certainly unintended consequence for the South: Ever after, Federal black troops went into battle yelling "Revenge Fort Pillow" and fought with additional fury, both to "revenge" and to avoid being captured. [52]

15 / The Press Reports a Battle: Fredericksburg, I

Although we are not yet fully informed of the present positions of the
enemy, there seems to be good ground to claim that
General Burnside has succeeded
in outgeneralling and outwitting them. His decoys to make them
believe that we were about to cross our main force at Port Conway,
seem to have succeeded admirably. . . .
—New York *Times*, dateline December 11, 1862

MCCLELLAN WAS REPLACED as commander of the Army of
the Potomac by his good friend and former Illinois Central associate, Maj.
Gen. Ambrose Burnside. Burnside was surprised. He already had been offered the assignment twice before, and twice had refused. Once again, he
asked to be excused and for the same reason: he did not feel himself to be
qualified for high command, and again suggested that McClellan continue in the post. However, the president wanted a change. McClellan was
sent into a sort of exile at Trenton, New Jersey, where he awaited his next
brush with destiny, the Democratic nomination for the presidency in
1864.

The *Herald* predicted that many high-ranking officers would resign
unless McClellan was restored. The New York *Times* assured its readers
that "there will be no resignations on account of the removal of Gen. Mc-
Clellan." The *Times* was the more accurate, but the *Herald* had the right
flavor. McClellan's popularity with the troops remained the stuff of leg-
end, and on the day of his grand, ceremonial farewell—as reported in the
Herald on November 12—men were weeping, running forward to touch
his horse, crying out "Fetch him back, Fetch him back!" *Tribune* reporter

Richardson had a slightly different view of the affair: he was physically assaulted by three drunken staff officers, retaliating for the *Tribune*'s anti-McClellan stance. In his postwar memoir, Richardson noted that McClellan apologized for this "cowardly and shameful act," and had the offenders placed under arrest. "The officers," he wrote, "were soon heartily ashamed." [1]

This marked the beginning of Ambrose Burnside's brief but spectacular ride as force commander—brief, as in fewer than ninety days, and spectacular, as in being marked forever as the commander of what is usu-

Maj. Gen Ambrose Burnside assuming command of the Army of the Potomac.

ally thought of as the dumbest and bloodiest Federal defeat of the war. In a study of *journalistic* history, however, Fredericksburg is perhaps the one battle that had everything. It was covered on-scene by specials from Northern, Southern, and international newspapers, there were soldier-correspondents on both sides, and artists for at least four illustrated papers. It was a battle viewed by some correspondents as if they were spectators at an athletic competition, high in the press box, watching the action below while other reporters were down on the field with the players. It was a battle reported with color, flair, and style, the copy written under the pressure of competition and fear, most of it late at night by flickering candlelight. It was a battle where the censors tried to block the news, and some Northern editors tried to suppress the news, but the news got through—and that is part of the story.

Ambrose Burnside got the job as commander of the Army of the Potomac not so much for his military skills—he had a mixed record to this point—but because Lincoln hoped, perhaps, that McClellan's army would rally around the eminently likable Burnside. *Harper's Weekly* played cheerleader: "it is a source of unmixed satisfaction to know that the Army of the Potomac is led by a man like Burnside, a soldier who to the greatest military skill unites dash, energy, and the prestige of success, and a man of the most exalted character and the noblest heart. The country unites in the cry, 'God speed Burnside!'" [2]

Many newspapermen liked Burnside, and said as much in public and private correspondence. Richardson found him "very obliging and approachable," with "moral courage, and perfect integrity." Henry Villard noted "a prepossessing *bonhomie* that made one feel at home with him at once. Indeed, he wore his genial, frank, honest, sincere nature on his sleeve." However, Villard added, "there was nothing in his exterior or in his conversation that indicated intellectual eminence or executive ability of a high order." William Swinton of the New York *Times* observed that, "Measured in the order of pure intellect, Burnside has no claims to first rank," and William Howard Russell, who had left the country but not the war, predicted that "unless he be taken in hand either by a man of determination and settled purpose, or be directed by some superior intellect, he will tumble into a quagmire of strategy, and be extinguished. . . . " Richardson, in a private letter to his editor, offered the equally prophetic comment, "I am very sure of one thing: Whenever he gets a positive order to Go, he will Go if it breaks his neck." [3]

Burnside's position as commander of the Army of the Potomac was awkward. "He has to lead into action," wrote Russell's London *Times* replacement Francis Lawley, "an army disgusted with the removal of its recent and favored leader." [4] Also, it was an army of which more than two-thirds of the corps and division commanders had seniority of service and experience. Of his three principal commanders: Maj. Gen. Edwin Sumner was commissioned five years before Burnside was born, Maj. Gen. Joseph Hooker had graduated from West Point ten years before Burnside, and Maj. Gen. William Franklin five years before. Burnside, class of 1847, had spent five years in the army with but one minor prewar combat experience, against the Apaches. (While McClellan was only one year senior to Burnside, he had seen extensive service in Mexico and had been out of the army for only four years before the war began.)

Of the three, General Hooker must be considered a special case: he had expected to get the job himself, and was going to prove difficult. Burnside, "who disliked very few people," according to modern biographer William Marvel, "was one of many who disliked Joe Hooker very much. He found him arrogant, devious and dangerously selfish." [5]

Such feelings were shared by many in the media. On first meeting Hooker, Henry Villard was impressed; the general was "fully six feet high, finely proportioned, with a soldierly, erect carriage . . . he looked, indeed, like the ideal soldier. . . ." That image held for but a few minutes, until Hooker began berating almost everyone in the army. "His language was so severe," Villard later wrote, "and, at the same time, so infused with self-assertion as to give rise immediately to a fear on my part that he might be inclined to make use of me for his glorification and for the detraction of others." Hooker confided to another *Tribune* special, Charles A. Page, that "McClellan knows that I am a better general than he ever dared hope to be," and told a *Herald* reporter that Burnside was a "fool." [6]

Hooker was by this time almost universally known as "Fighting Joe." The reason is not that which appears in some standard references (*Encyclopedia Britannica*: "because of his vigorous leadership in the field") but, rather, was the result of a typesetter's error. In June, during the Seven Days' Campaign, a last-minute addition to an Associated Press dispatch was headed "Fighting—Joe Hooker." Rather than tacking a few lines about Hooker at the end of the previous copy about "Fighting"—as intended by the author—more than one typographer set it as a new item under the head, "Fighting Joe Hooker." [7] Hooker did not like the tag because he thought it made him seem impetuous. He was.

Burnside was under pressure from the administration, from newspapers urging immediate attack (the *Tribune* once again directing the war), and from the army itself. "If we don't take Richmond by spring," one officer remarked, "the Confederacy is a fixed fact." [8]

By the time Burnside had assumed command, McClellan had shifted into Virginia, where the army was facing enemy forces along a general line between Warrenton and Culpeper. Burnside met with Halleck and the president to propose a bold move: quietly disengage from that contact, make an end run east and then south and cross the Rappahannock at Fredericksburg. The enemy would be caught off guard, and Burnside—supported by a new Potomac River depot at nearby Aquia Creek—would be on the way to Richmond.

Halleck was skeptical, but the president, having given Burnside the charge to charge ahead, approved, but with the same caveat that he had offered McDowell before Bull Run a year and a half earlier: the plan would only work "if you move very rapidly." [9]

Burnside took that guidance to heart. He moved 120,000 troops and the Union share of what Villard called "the greatest assemblage of artillery in any battle of the Civil War" from Warrenton to Falmouth, across the river from Fredericksburg, in what may have been record time. The first units arrived on November 18, having covered forty miles in two and a half days—as reported in the *Tribune*, to the "mute astonishment" of "officers wont to believe that a great command cannot move more than six miles a day." [10]

Burnside rode in a day later. However—and this is the biggest "however" of Burnside's career—the pontoon bridges he needed to cross the four-hundred-foot-wide river had not yet left Washington and would not begin to arrive for another week. When the War Department ordered the pontoons, the request was not flagged as "urgent" and no delivery date was specified. When officials sought information about the status of the movement, they never advised the movers that the operation for which the pontoons were needed already was under way.

In perhaps the biggest *irony* of Burnside's career: he would not have needed the pontoon bridges if he had not previously been responsible for the destruction of all the fixed bridges that crossed the river at Fredericksburg. As part of a "blocking" force protecting Washington while McClellan was floundering around on the peninsula, Burnside's Ninth Corps occupied Fredericksburg from mid-May until the end of August. On May 14, he even had been visited by the president, who "rode through the streets of Fredericksburg . . . greeted by the troops and many of the citizens with the utmost enthusiasm." [11]

However, on August 31, following Pope's defeat at Second Bull Run, Burnside evacuated the city and burned railroad buildings, a machine shop and foundry, a quantity of army stores, and three temporary bridges that had been built by the Union army to replace bridges destroyed by the rebels in May. [12]

Burnside's disengagement and end run had been carried off so well that his arrival at Falmouth was indeed a surprise for the rebels, and, had the pontoon bridges been waiting, Burnside may well have been half way to Richmond before they could react. However, General Lee managed to get two divisions to Fredericksburg the day after Burnside arrived, and joined them himself the next day.

Confederate sharpshooters began sniping at the Federals across the river, which prompted a threat of retaliation from the commander of a Union division: he would bombard the town unless it surrendered, immediately. With General Lee looking over his shoulder, Mayor Frank Slaughter arranged a tepid compromise: the sniping would cease until the Federals did something to provoke a resumption. Lee suggested that the town be evacuated, and residents began filtering out into the countryside. Many took the daily train to Richmond.

A few Northern correspondents had followed Burnside to Falmouth. Others, who had gone home expecting that the army would follow the practice of 1861 and go into winter quarters, made hasty efforts to catch up. The *Herald* managed to get nine men on scene, the New York *Times* seven, *Tribune* four, and Philadelphia *Inquirer* four. The Boston *Journal* and Cincinnati *Commercial* had one man each. Artists represented the New York *Illustrated News*, *Harper's Weekly*, and *Frank Leslie's Illustrated Weekly*.

Fredericksburg was to be one of the few battles directly covered by the Richmond papers, with at least the *Enquirer* and *Dispatch* on scene and Capt. John Esten Cooke, a staff officer with General Stuart, acting as soldier-correspondent for the *Whig*. Also viewing things from the Southern side were London *Illustrated Times* illustrator Frank Vizetelly and Francis Lawley of the London *Times*.

On November 21, Lawley sketched a verbal portrait of General Lee that became a cornerstone of Lee iconography:

> General Lee is, I believe, between 50 and 60 years of age [he was in fact 55], but wears his years well, and strikes you as the incarnation of health and endurance, as he rears his erect soldierlike form from his seat by the fireside to greet courteously the stranger. . . . His manner is calm and stately, his presence impressive and imposing, his dark brown eyes remarkably direct and honest . . . the confidence and sympathy which he inspires are irresistible. A child thrown among a knot of strangers would be inevitably drawn to General Lee in the company, and would run to claim his protection. [13]

The press raised some questions: why Fredericksburg? The Memphis *Appeal* called this "the very worst and most difficult route" to Richmond and suggested that this must be a ruse, a feint to cover attack from some other quarter. Why wait for pontoons? The Philadelphia *Inquirer* reported that the river was fordable "in many places." In this, however, the reporter showed a certain military innocence. Here, "fordable" meant that horses, and perhaps walking infantry—*tall* walking infantry—might cross, but not the artillery and heavy supply wagons. Burnside indeed had considered sending some cavalry across, but was warned that, should the river flood— a common event at that time of year—the troopers would be isolated. [14]

Burnside sat down to ponder his options. There were not many and, despite the increasingly frigid weather, going into winter quarters was not among them; McClellan had been savaged when he did so the year before, rather than push on to Richmond. At a meeting on November 25, Lincoln assured Burnside that he would be "patient." Nice sentiment, but not very practical. Burnside pondered. In a letter published in the New York *Times* on November 27, William Swinton confessed a foreboding of disaster. [15]

On November 30, Lee welcomed the arrival of Stonewall Jackson and the rest of the Army of Northern Virginia. Lawley predicted "that Nemesis awaits General Burnside's army. . . ." [16]

Burnside decided to make the river crossing not at Fredericksburg, but a dozen miles downstream, and his engineers began preparing the ground. When the Confederates divined his intention, Lee shifted Jackson's corps to cover that position, whereupon Burnside changed his mind, and decided to cross the river right into the town, instead. General Sumner suggested an alternative crossing, a mile to the east, and Burnside elected to make both. In the meantime, to hold Jackson's attention on the now-abandoned crossing downstream, Burnside arranged for three hundred empty wagons to be shuttled back and forth, and set a regiment of Maine woodsmen to laying down a corduroy road through the woods to the river's edge.

At the same time, rebel troops were seen working on their own positions in the hills behind Fredericksburg. The Federals seem not to have paid much attention, and, according to "WHIT" of the New York *Times*, many speculated that this, too, was a feint, "in order to conceal their movement toward Richmond." [17]

On December 9, Burnside issued orders "to throw five bridges across the river" during the night of December 10–11, three into Fredericksburg and two at the nearby downstream position. When some of the division commanders expressed concern, or confusion, about the overall plan, Burnside called a meeting. About this, *Harper's Weekly* reported:

A council of war was held . . . it is understood that Generals Sumner, Franklin, Hooker, and all the corps commanders who had been invited were decidedly opposed to a movement across the river and up the slope. IT IS RUMOURED THAT BURNSIDE THEN SAID THAT HE WAS ORDERED TO CROSS THE RIVER AND AT-TACK THE BATTERIES IN FRONT, AND THAT HE WOULD DO IT, NO MATTER WHAT THE COST. [18]

Burnside may or may not have made such a bold statement, and the December 27 date of publication—almost two weeks after the disaster that soon followed—strongly suggests post facto elaboration. The official record shows that all of the commanders except Hooker gave grudging support to his plan.

Murat Halstead, editor of the Cincinnati *Commercial*, arrived in Falmouth at just that time, and found a colonel of his acquaintance "writing a few lines giving direction as to the disposition of his effects if he should be killed in the impending conflict." While the army had not gone into winter quarters, the colonel's brigade had occupied much of the previous three weeks—with little else to do—getting ready, just in case. They were bunking in large and solid log huts; the colonel himself "had a neat and spacious brick chimney, in which a cheerful fire crackled, and the walls of his tent were slender pines; the roof composed of his shelter tent." [19-1]

The editor was invited to join a group of officers ostensibly celebrating some promotions. Celebrating? "They all felt that it was the last night before battle," he reported, "and in all probability the last of some of them on earth."

A savory article of whiskey punch was freely circulated [which] seemed to cheer but not to inebriate. Many patriotic songs were sung with a fervor and melody most affecting and beautiful. I will never forget one, "The Hills of Old New England," (the officers were, without exception, New Englanders), or "E Pluribus Unum," those not singing, shouting "Never, never," at the words of the song that the nation would fall if the banner of stars were trailed in the dust. There was a solemn, touching charm about the singing of a song, the leading words of which were: "Unfurl the glorious banner." [19-2]

Halstead noted that another song, "McClellan is our leader, so march along," was an army favorite, "given with great gusto, followed by a toast, 'The health of Little Mac.'"

At three o'clock on the frigid winter morning of Thursday, December 11, with a thin coating of ice over much of the river and a heavy blanket of fog covering everything else, Burnside's engineers began laying down the pontoon bridges at Fredericksburg. Alerted by the sounds of hammering, the Confederates were ready when, at about six o'clock, pale daylight and the progress of the effort brought the bridge-builders near enough to be seen through the fog. A brigade of rebel infantrymen, most working from well-prepared rifle pits and protected positions in the cellars of buildings along the waterfront, took a quick and heavy toll. The engineers pulled back.

Union infantry moved up and directed fire into the town, but shooting through the fog was not very productive. When the engineers went back to work, so did the enemy. A few pieces of field artillery were wheeled up to the river's bank, but, also shooting blindly into the fog, accomplished little.

Sometime before noon, the fog lifted and exposed the entire bridge-building effort to rebel fire; thereupon Burnside launched the heaviest artillery barrage of the war. The New York *Times* reported that "143 guns opened on the devoted city of Fredericksburg, and up to the latest moment the firing continued without interruption. Its destruction appears certain. . . ." The Cincinnati *Commercial* waxed poetic: ". . . the crack of the shells and the undercurrent of echoes shivering in incessant waves against the hill-sides, made up an appalling concert. It seems as if there was a vast flight of malignant monsters, the surly whir of whose invisible and awful wings convulsed all the air." The Boston *Journal* was more literal: "The earth shook beneath the terrific explosions of the shells. . . . Sixty solid shot and shells a minute were thrown, and the bombardment was kept up till nine thousand were fired." [20]

Captain Cooke's report in the Richmond *Whig* quoted a philosophical General Lee: "It is delightful to them to destroy innocent people, without being hurt themselves. *It just suits them.*" That sentiment was echoed in the Richmond *Enquirer*: "No notice was given of an intention to shell. . . . Truly, the Yankees are waging a war of extermination." [21]

Extermination, or barbarity. In his *Southern History of the War*, assembled as the war went on and published in book form in 1866, the Richmond *Examiner*'s Edward Pollard overlooked the reason for the bombardment and, instead, indicted the Yankees for forcing innocents from their homes:

Little children with blue feet trod painfully the frozen ground. . . .
Hundreds of ladies wandered homeless over the frozen highway,
with bare feet and thin clothing, knowing not where to find a place
of refuge. Delicately nurtured girls, with slender forms, upon which
no rain had ever beat, which no wind had ever visited too roughly,
walked hurriedly, with unsteady feet, upon the road, seeking only
some place where they could shelter themselves. [22]

However many shells were hurled, and no matter how awesome (or heart-wrenching) the scene, the bombardment did not have the intended effect. When the engineers returned to bridge-building, the sniper fire was as heavy as before.

What happened next was well reported by many correspondents, but not in sufficient detail to satisfy Maj. Thomas H. Hunt, commander 7th Michigan Volunteers. Noting "many accounts in our various Northern journals," which gave credit for the first crossing of the river to somebody else, Major Hunt set the record straight for the Detroit *Free Press*:

Troops of the Seventh Michigan charge upslope into the city of Fredericksburg.

Not having the good fortune to belong to one of those regions which have gained their reputation by corresponding with the papers, and never having written a line for publication myself, it is with the greatest reluctance that I make the attempt, but a sense of duty, in justice to our noble little regiment, and to our State, which all justly feel proud of, compelled me in this case to offer a few facts. [23]

His unit had been sent to the riverbank to cover the bridge-building efforts and, when the bombardment failed to stop the Confederate sharpshooters, Burnside called for volunteers from the infantry to cross the river in small boats and storm the rebel positions. Some of the engineers were expected to act as oarsmen. However, Major Hunt wrote, "we were told that the officers of the engineer corps could by no means induce their men to undertake the job," so the men of the 7th Michigan, "at a given signal . . . rushed to the boats, carried them to the water, jumped into them and pushed elegantly out into the stream, amidst a shower of bullets from the enemy which killed and wounded several of our men . . . the regiment charged gallantly up the ascent, taking possession of the rifle-pits and buildings, also taking thirty-five prisoners. . . . It was said by the many thousands who witnessed this feat that it was the most gallant of the war, and I feel that our State should have the credit due her." Major Hunt charitably added that the Nineteenth and Twentieth Regiments of Massachusetts Volunteers "came to our support as soon as they possibly could."

The bridge-building was completed about four thirty in the afternoon, and the latest Federal occupation of Fredericksburg began. There was no significant opposition, and the town proper, perhaps fifteen blocks along the river and five blocks deep, was quickly overwhelmed by some forty thousand of the invading troops and a few of the reporters. "ES" of the New York *Times* described what they found: most of the houses had been damaged to some degree, although only about twenty had been set on fire. [24]

Sunset approached, and the rebels took to lobbing an occasional artillery shell over the Union forces; the Cincinnati *Commercial* described the scene:

The horizon was hazy as on a day of Indian summer. The sun, sinking in a sky of royal purple, looked like a big drop of arterial blood. . . . As the [enemy's] shells burst in mid air, they formed little smoke-balloons, that quickly expanded and faded as they grew. As the air darkened, the red flashes of the guns gave a new effect—the roar of each report being preceded by a fierce dart of flame, and the explosion of each shell was announced by a dash of fire on the clouds, like a Mars of the first magnitude, created and extinguished in an instant. And, towering between us and the western sky, which was still showing its faded scarlet lining, was the huge somber pillar of grimy smoke that marked the burning of Fredericksburg. [25]

An official press release noted "Skirmishing, no general fighting, seven hundred prisoners taken." [26] Swinton now seemed satisfied that all was well:

Although we are not yet fully informed of the present positions of the enemy, there seems to be good ground to claim that General Burnside has succeeded in outgeneralling and outwitting them. His decoys to make them believe that we were about to cross our main force at Port Conway, seem to have succeeded admirably. . . . Completely deceived by these feints, the main rebel force, including Jackson's command, seems to have been, two or three days ago, transferred twenty or twenty-five miles down the river. [27]

New York *Times* reporter "J" affirmed that "It is the general impression that the enemy have proceeded in the direction of Richmond, leaving a small rearguard to dispute our advance." [28] A few days later—before more timely news had reached New York—the *Times* commented, editorially (and prophetically), on "The Non-Defense of the Rappahannock by Lee."

Much astonishment has been expressed in some quarters that Lee did not interpose a more serious resistance to Burnside's crossing of the Rappahannock. Save the covert efforts of a few hundred sharpshooters, and the occasional firing of a few batteries, he kept his great army absolutely idle during the twenty-four hours occupied in the construction of the bridges and the passage of our troops. It cannot be said that he was taken by surprise, or in anywise deceived by stratagem. . . . Lee belongs to that class of military men who believe rivers to be a bad military line. He prefers the fortified ridges of hills in the rear. These he will dispute with a tenacity of which he made no show near the banks of the stream. [29]

Murat Halstead explored the topic for the *Commercial*: "On Friday morning [December 12] those of us not fully posted, and not conversant with all the mysteries of "strategy," expected a battle. But the morning passed quietly. . . . The enemy's batteries were ominously silent. If the rebel general had any particular objections to the presence of our troops in the town, why did he not open upon them from his batteries?"

Burnside's pontoons were connected to make a bridge across the four-hundred-foot-wide
Rappahannock. Confederate sharpshooters largely kept the bridge-builders at bay, even
after the city was taken under heavy artillery fire.

He posed that question to a number of "military gentlemen," and got a wide range of answers. "One said: 'The enemy have not ammunition to spare.' Another: 'Oh! A bombardment don't amount to anything anyhow.' Another: 'They don't care about bombing us, it is an inconsequential sort of business. We threw four thousand shells yesterday, and it amounted to nothing.'" One officer surmised that "General Lee will have a big thing on us about the bombardment. . . . He is playing for the sympathies of Europe." Another "thought that the enemy were skeddadling"—an idea shared, at that moment, by many.

"But I think," Halstead wrote, "that a private soldier came closer to the mark than anyone else. He said, with the usual expletives: 'They want us to get in. Getting out won't be quite so smart and easy. You'll see if it will.'" [30]

Any plans for a smooth advance *through* the town having been frustrated by the delay in getting *into* the town, the troops settled in for another day. It was not going to be a good day, for the soldiers or the town. Halstead reported that even while troops were still crossing into Fredericksburg, "Some adventurers were straggling back, bearing boxes of [stolen] tobacco, which was as eagerly sought by our men as if it had been gold, or something more precious even than fine gold." [31]

In a censored letter of December 14, published the next day, "ES" of the New York *Times* offered a hint of more serious problems: "In spite of prompt and general efforts to guard the houses from intrusion and pillage by the establishment of guards, a good many residences have suffered more or less spoliation. Household articles, such as cooking utensils and crockery, pickles, sweetmeats and flitches of bacon, were observed among the troops, as I passed through the different streets. . . . Considering all the terrible circumstances of provocation, the preservation of the town from total destruction, and its wholesale pillage by the army, are in the highest degree creditable to the Union troops, and to their discipline." [32]

A few days later, however, when uncensored reports got through (and when Southern reporters could get back into the town), most newspapers told an unvarnished story of uncontrolled looting and destruction of private property.

Cincinnati *Commercial*: "The furniture and movable property of whatever kind which the bombs had spared, the soldiers speedily 'possessed.' Some of them took intense satisfaction in lugging mattresses before their bivouac-fires to sleep upon, and showed their taste for handsome bound books, and articles of ladies' wearing apparel. The streets were full of soldiers lounging and smoking about their fires, or wrapped in their blankets and sleeping, their muskets stacked, in numbers that indicated the immense mass of troops that occupied the place." [33]

New York *Tribune*: "The old mansion of Douglas Gordon—perhaps the wealthiest citizen in the vicinity—is now used as the headquarters of General Howard, but before he occupied it, every room had been torn with shot, and then all the elegant furniture and works of art broken and smashed by the soldiers. . . . When I entered it early this morning, before its occupation by Gen. Howard, I found the soldiers of his fine division diverting themselves with the rich dresses found in the wardrobes; some had on bonnets . . . and were surveying themselves before mirrors, which, an hour or two afterwards, were pitched out the window and smashed to pieces upon the pavement. . . ." [34]

Richmond *Enquirer*: "The wanton destruction of property in town can neither be imagined nor described . . . clothing has been stolen from every house, the furniture recklessly destroyed or thrown into the streets, beds ripped open, pictures disfigured and destroyed, pianos ruthlessly robbed of the keys." [35]

Looting by Federal soldiers was well-reported in some papers; however, the editor of the New York *Illustrated News* declined to publish this sketch. It would be bad for Union morale.

(By suggesting that all of the damage had been wrought by the Federals, the *Enquirer* was a bit disingenuous. An earlier edition of the paper had reported looting by the Confederate troops who occupied the town after the residents fled.)

> London *Times*: "Everywhere the houses have been plundered from cellar to garret; all smaller articles of furniture carried off, all larger ones wantonly smashed. Not a drawer or chest but was forced open and ransacked. The streets were sprinkled with the remains of costly furniture dragged out of the houses in the direction of the pontoons stretched across the river." [36]

The *Times* correspondent added that the mayor's wife had returned from temporary shelter in the countryside, to find her house ransacked and gutted. When a Federal officer offered a few words of apology, she replied, pointing to half a dozen dead Federals lying within sight of her house. "I am repaid for all I have suffered by the sight of these."

Friday's Richmond *Examiner* reported that "The General conclusions from what we learn up to the hour of writing are, that the enemy had effected a passage of the Rappahannock, probably in considerable force; that the action of yesterday was without any important fruits or prefatory to a more important action now pending; and that today will witness a large and important, but, perhaps indecisive battle on the disputed lines of Fredericksburg. As confirmatory of this prospect, *an order was received last night at the Medical Purveyor's office, for all the ambulances and stretchers that could possibly be sent from this city. These are the gloomy indications of the work to-day.*" The Richmond *Dispatch* echoed the forebodings of some on the Union side, that "so far from having secured any advantage by the passage of the river, [the Federals] have placed themselves in exactly the position our commanding general wishes them." [37]

Darkness settled over the second night of this occupation of Fredericksburg. The London *Times* correspondent reported that Confederate pickets "could hear the earnest and impassioned speeches of Federal orators rousing the spirit of their troops, and making vehement appeals to the sanctity of the 'old flag.'" One of the rebels told him, "There must be a want of grit among the Yankees, otherwise they wouldn't want all this talking to." Lawley's pro-Southern sentiments stood revealed when he next compared the "spirit of the two armies—the Confederates, so calm, so resolute, so satisfied with their generals, so suffering, yet rejoicing to suffer, as long as hardship is the price of liberty; the Federals, lashed into the field by the thong of golden bounties, and in the field lashed against the enemy by the invective and appeals of able spokesmen. . . ." [38]

The scene was described by the Richmond *Enquirer:*

The campfires now gleam on every hill and hillside, and along the horizon flare up in broad sheets of pale light that indicate the presence of the "ample forces." Our men joke and laugh around their camp fires as they prepare rations for the morrow in careless confidence, for they know we have the men and the generals equal to the coming trial. Everybody expects the great battle will take place within the next twenty-four hours. Long trains of wagons are wending rearward, laden with baggage, hospital tents are being pitched, and ambulances ranged in convenient position, and the decks generally cleared for action. [39]

A myth was building, the myth of the "Lost Cause" wherein the gallant cavaliers, the "chivalry," eventually—*improbably*—were bested in a series of contests with the Yankee hordes, but never really *defeated*. Myth-making is helped by powerful classical symbols, and there was one at hand the night of December 12: The aurora borealis, a rare sight in that latitude and never before seen by many of the men camped along the hillsides, flashed in the Northern skies. Note the *Enquirer's* misunderstanding that "broad sheets of pale light" were reflections of the enemy campfires.

Lawley understood the aurora, and no doubt explained it to his companions, and reported that this phenomenon, "which overspread the heavens, and darted blood-red tongues of flames swiftly from the meridian down to the horizon, was accepted by the Confederates as the cross outlined on the sky was accepted by Constantine—an earnest of assured victory." [40]

16 / The Press Reports a Battle: Fredericksburg, II

Such a sight has rarely been seen by man. It is doubtful whether any living pen could do justice to its horrors; but it is certain that it would be easy to write more than any ordinary reader would care to read.
—London *Times*, January 23, 1863

THE ATTACK WAS TO BEGIN at first light, a little past six o'clock on Saturday, December 13. William Franklin, on the plain east of town, would seek to turn the enemy's right. Edwin Sumner's men, already in Fredericksburg proper, would probe the enemy strength behind the town, and then, if necessary, storm the position, according to the Cincinnati *Commercial*, "in heavy forces." [1]

Another morning fog impeded visibility, but Franklin's troops began crossing the river to assemble on the plain, without opposition. Halstead wrote, "At nine o'clock there had been little firing, and guesses were freely offered that the enemy had skedaddled again . . . that Burnside had been detained by wooden guns; that there never had been any rebel force in or about Fredericksburg of any consequence. . . ." [2]

At about nine thirty, Franklin's men began moving forward, and from a vantage point high on a hill above the town, the man from the Richmond *Enquirer* was watching:

Now the morning fog has lifted, revealing the dark and heavy columns of the enemy. . . . Whole fields are gleaming with bayonets. They continue to pour out upon the plain in a stream that seems to come from an inexhaustible fountain. The meadows are black with them, tens of thousands in solid numbers. We can only vaguely conjecture at this distance the number. Old soldiers think there are sixty thousand. Where are our men?

The enemy, now formed in three heavy columns, advances to attack our right; on they go at double quick toward the woods, making the earth shake under their tread with colors flying and arms glistening in the sunlight. Where are our men? [3]

The question was soon answered: "A long sheet of flame from the skirts of the woods at the foot of the hills, a cloud of smoke, a roar and rattle of musketry tell of their whereabouts."

Once started, the fighting was brisk. George Meade's division advanced for a distance, but was driven back. David Birney's division played through to the front, also to be beaten back. The enemy's right was not being "turned" or moved in any direction, whereupon Burnside tried to shift the focus, to take some of the pressure off Franklin. He ordered the first assault on the enemy positions on Marye's Hill, behind the town.

It was not until this moment that the Federals discovered that the enemy was in a virtually impregnable position. Riflemen lay, waiting, in a series of freshly dug pits and behind a stone wall that ran along a sunken—theretofore unseen—road. Perhaps three hundred pieces of artillery were arrayed in the heights beyond.

What followed was described in Swinton's postbattle dispatch to the *Times*:

> They were literally mowed down. The bursting shells make great gaps in their ranks; but these are presently filled by the "closing up" of the line. For fifteen immortal minutes at least they remain under this fiery surge. Onward they press, though their ranks grow fearfully thin. They have passed over a greater part of the interval and have almost reached the base of the hill, when brigade after brigade of rebels rise up on the crest and pour in fresh volleys of musketry at short range. . . . Flesh and blood could not endure it. They fell back shattered and broken, amid shouts and yells from the enemy. [4]

It was the first of six assaults, each more futile than the last. Federal artillery assayed a covering barrage; the euphemism "friendly fire" had not yet been invented, but according to Halstead, "at least half the shells" fell into the Federal ranks, "killing more of our men than the enemy." [5] The error was soon noticed, and corrected.

"It became perfectly apparent to all observers," the Cincinnati editor wrote, that the fortunes of the day on our side were desperate. It was manifestly absolutely impossible for our columns of unsupported infantry to carry the terrible heights.

Our only hope then, was in Franklin. It might be possible that he would do something grand on the left, break the enemy's line, turn his position, and come sweeping across the crest, from which the murderous artillery "volleyed and thundered." But it was drearily evident that Franklin's progress was slow. We could hear the grumbling of his guns, and see, in the distance, the battle-cloud that swelled from the combat, but alas, that cloud did not advance by perceptible degrees." [6]

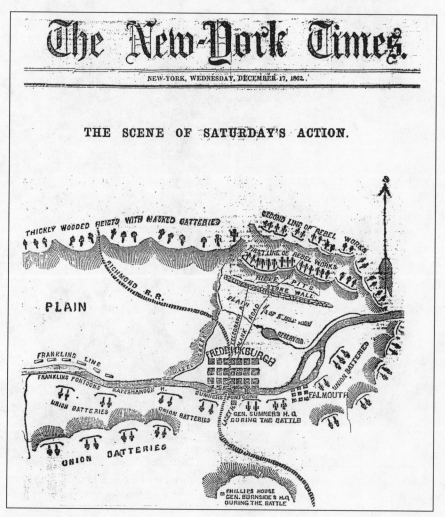

Map of Fredricksburg.

Thomas Nast sketched the most comprehensive panorama of the war. In the background, Federal forces move against the Confederate right at Fredericksburg; in the right foreground, fresh troops held in reserve await orders—all the while watching the surgeons at work on the left.

Swinton, standing near General Sumner, heard the same story. "Where is Franklin? . . . Everything depends on Franklin's coming up on the flank." Franklin, "plainly observable by the line of smoke and fire a couple of miles to our left below . . . was making no nearer." Burnside sent an officer to urge Franklin forward; the officer returned with the message that Franklin's forces were "fully engaged" [7] (although as it turned out, he had five divisions in reserve, which were never brought into play).

And the assaults on Marye's Heights continued.

A sunken road and a wall of stone
And Cobb's grim line of grey
Lay still at the base of Marye's Hill
On the morn of a winter's day.

And crowning the frowning crest above
Sleep Alexander's guns,
While gleaming fair in the sunlit air
The Rappahannock runs.

On the plains below, the blue lines glow,
And the bugle rings out clear,
As with bated breath they march to death
And a soldier's honored bier.

For the slumbering guns awake to life
And the screaming shell and ball
From the front and flanks crash through the ranks
And leave them where they fall.

"The Angel of Marye's Heights" written by Confederate infantryman Walter A. Clark, went on to tell the story of a rebel solider who took food and water to the Federal wounded, where they lay. He had a lot to do: by nightfall, more than twelve thousand Union soldiers were killed, wounded, or missing.

A large number of Federal troops—wounded or otherwise—were trapped on the battlefield. As Col. R. B. Potter, Fifty-First Regiment, New York Volunteers, wrote to a newspaper friend:

We had to lie perfectly flat, as the enemy could depress their artillery sufficiently to rake every thing eighteen inches above the surface of the ground, and to raise a head or hand was sure to bring a pop from a concealed sharp-shooter. [We lay] thus for near thirty hours, with nothing to eat or drink, not daring to move or speak in a loud tone, and not allowed to sleep. . . . [8]

Artist Frank Vizetelly of the *Illustrated London News* brought a more realistic—and less dramatic—look to the war. Here, the Confederate defenders at Marye's Heights.

The wounded were covered by a blessed blanket of unseasonably warm weather. "A kind Providence cared for the wounded," Halstead wrote. "The air was as mild in the night, as if the month were June, and the wind came balmy from the South. If the night had been cold, hundreds of wounded, faint with the loss of blood, would have perished." [9]

Lawley presented the view from the rebel lines:

Such a scene . . . would baffle any mortal pen to describe. In addition to the agonized cries for water, and to the groans of tortured and dying men, may be heard voices, constantly growing fainter and fainter, shouting out names and numbers of their regiments in hope that some of their comrades may be within hearing, or that a party from their regiment may have been sent out to fetch in its wounded men. "Fourteenth Massachusetts!" "One Hundred and Fourth Pennsylvania!" "Forty-seventh North Carolina!" Such are some of the shouts which ring through the night air. . . . [10]

Those wounded who could be reached had been moved, he wrote, ". . . into the narrow limits of the town. . . . Hardly a house or shed but was converted into a hospital; the churches and municipal buildings were crowded to bursting with dying and mangled men. Shutters and boards were laid down in gardens and yards, and upon them layer after layer of wounded men was stretched." Of those who were even less fortunate: "Their bodies, which lie in dense masses, as thick as autumn leaves, within 40 yards of the muzzles of the Confederate guns, are best evidence of their bravery as well as to the desperate plight of their bitterly-deceived commanders." [11]

The editor of the *Commercial* noted with regret that "Two of the young officers . . . whose rich voices swelled the song of 'the glorious banner'" were among the dead, "one shot through the head, and the other through the heart, while upholding the regimental flag, the color-sergeant being shot down early in the action." [12] Halstead's assessment was tentative, but brutal:

> The extent of the disaster is not yet fully known. It is known that we gained nothing—that all we lost was thrown away. We did not take a battery or silence a gun. We did not reach the crest of the heights held by the enemy in a single place. But so determined was Gen. Burnside to carry out his program, that he ordered a renewal of the attack on Sunday morning, and determined to rush a column of fifteen thousand men upon the rebel batteries. The orders to this effect were actually given, and the divisions to make the assault assigned their places, when the vehement protest and expostulation of General Sumner, who declared his troops unfit for the enterprise, prevailed, and the madness that would have decimated the army was quieted. [13]

Lawley, noting the large number of European mercenaries in the Federal army, offered a particularly ethnocentric comment:

> It is not likely that the full details of this battle will be generally known in the North for weeks and weeks; but if, after the failure of this last and feeblest of all the Federal attempts to reach Richmond . . . the Irish and Germans are again tempted to embark on so hopeless a venture, then it is the conclusion irresistible that, in addition to all the shackles of despotism which they are alleged to have left behind them in Europe, they have left also that most valuable attribute of humanity, which is called common sense. [14]

Henry Villard followed the initial assault as far as the first ridge outside of town, then lay on the ground to observe; by the middle of the afternoon he had seen enough. He contacted his assistants, talked with senior officers, assembled some notes, took a short nap and, at about three o'clock in the morning, mounted his horse and set out for Aquia Creek, where he hoped to catch a ride up the river to Washington. It became a journey through hell, six hours to cover twelve miles along a muddy and trackless route, but Villard was stopped when he reached the Aquia Creek depot, where he was told that he could go no farther: the quartermaster was under orders to halt anyone headed north without a special permit from Burnside himself.

Frustrated by the bureaucracy and spurred on by a desire to beat the competition—part of which arrived at the depot at just that moment in the form of William Coffin of the Boston *Journal*—Villard scouted around and found a pair of fishermen who agreed to row him out into the middle of the Potomac. There, he hailed a passing steamer; the captain shouted back that he was not authorized to carry passengers. Villard grabbed a dangling rope and clambered aboard, telling his boatmen to clear off quickly, and mollified the captain's "wrathy" anger by the payment of fifty dollars for the forty-mile passage to Washington.

He reached the *Tribune* office about nine thirty that evening, where Sam Wilkeson—back on duty in his old job as Bureau Chief—teamed him with a shorthander. They fleshed out a story that Wilkeson knew would never get past the censor, so he hired a messenger to carry the dispatch aboard the night train to New York.

Villard, exhausted, but satisfied, then went to Willard's Hotel for dinner. He was buttonholed by the chairman of the Senate Military Affairs committee. What was the story? What was happening at Fredericksburg? "Senator," Villard replied with a touch of Teutonic majesty, "you know whatever news I have belongs to my paper, but, for the sake of the cause, I will tell you in strict confidence that Burnside is defeated. . . . " [15] Shortly thereafter, he was summoned to the White House to repeat his story for the president.

Lincoln was gracious, "very much obliged to you for coming, for we are very anxious and have heard very little." Villard urged that Burnside be ordered to pull back across the river. Lincoln was noncommittal: "I hope it is not so bad as all that." [16]

But Lincoln had already heard a similar report from another source, sufficiently alarming to cause him to ask General Halleck to order Burnside to withdraw. Halleck declined, with the argument that the general in the field was the best judge of "existing conditions." Villard need not have worried: Burnside's team had already convinced him that further attempts against Marye's Heights would be futile, although they had to dissuade him from one final, grand gesture: leading his old division in the van, to inspire the rest of the force.

Villard's copy had put the *Tribune* editors in a quandary. Here, they had a report of a great—an improbably great—disaster, possibly due to the culpable incompetence of a commander for whose appointment they were in part responsible. There was no corroboration from any source, official or otherwise. Greeley elected caution, and the *Tribune* issued a greatly watered-down version, and that, only in one limited edition of the morning run of December 15.

Meanwhile, back in Fredericksburg (as the London *Times* noted):

Prophecies that the Yankees had had enough of it, and would get back across the river as best they could, were more abundant, and when the morning of the 15th broke and still the Federals failed to advance, it became incontestable that the Federal army was in a perilous strait, with a deep river and three pontoon bridges behind, and with a victorious and elated enemy and 300 pieces of artillery in front. [17]

The wounded still on the field, by agreement, at last were carried off that afternoon. That night, Burnside, with tears running down into his namesake whiskers, ordered the abandonment of Fredericksburg. "A more favorable night for their purpose cannot be conceived," Lawley wrote.

On the afternoon of Monday the wind began to rise, and by 7 in the evening it blew a hurricane from the south, so that all sound from the Federal army was carried away to the north in a direction contrary to the position occupied by the Confederates. At the same time there fell a deluge of rain. Great credit is certainly due to the Federal Generals for passing nearly 100,000 men and all their cannon in one night across three pontoon bridges without accident or confusion. . . . when the morning of the 16th dawned great was the surprise of General Lee and of the Confederates to find that not one Yankee, save those who lay stiff and stark and a few wounded men in Fredericksburg, too badly injured to bear transportation across the river, remained on the southern side of the Rappahannock. [18]

A few wounded men . . . along with some deserters and, in Lawley's words, a scattering of drunks "too over-powered by the liquor they had stolen to leave with their army." [19]

To this point, newspaper readers in the North had seen only sketchy details of the battle. Some reports—news and official—had been delayed when Confederate cavalry cut the telegraph line to Washington. Those reports that did get through were heavily censored; it was little wonder that the *Tribune* so easily discounted Villard's report.

The New York *Times* collected a series of fragments in the edition of December 15:

11:00 a.m., December 13: The great battle, so long anticipated between the two contending armies, is now progressing. . . . At this writing, no results are known.

10:00 p.m., December 13: Along the whole line the battle has been fierce all day, with great loss to both sides. To-night each army holds its first position, with the exception of a slight advance on our left.

11:00 p.m., December 13: The troops advanced to their work at ten minutes before 12 o'clock at a brisk run, the enemy's guns opening upon them at a very rapid fire. When within musket range at the base of the ridge, our troops were met by a terrible fire from the rebel infantry, who were posted behind a stone wall and some houses on the right of the line. . . .

11:30 a.m., December 14: During last night and this forenoon the rebels have considerably extended their works and strengthened their position. Large bodies of troops are now to be seen where but few were to be seen yesterday.

Our dead which were killed yesterday, while charging in front of the enemy's works, still remain where they fell. When attempting their removal last night, the rebels would open fire with infantry, but the wounded have all been removed from the field, and all the dead obtained are now being buried.

The events of the last two days have increased the enthusiasm of the whole army toward its Commander, and strengthened confidence in the Generals leading the Grand Divisions.

December 14, dateline Washington: It is thought here that about 40,000 of our troops were engaged in yesterday's battle. From information received early this morning, preparations were making all night for a conflict to-day, Gen. Burnside remaining on the field, giving orders, looking to the position and condition of his forces.

Additional surgeons, and everything which the necessities of the wounded require, have been dispatched from Washington to the battle-ground.

It is proper to caution the public against hastily crediting the many unsupported rumors concerning yesterday's battle. Some of them here prevalent have no other basis than surmise, and are mere inventions in the absence of facts. Rebel sympathizers are responsible for not a few of these fictions.

Gentlemen in high public positions repeat the assertion, as coming from Gen. Burnside, that *he has men enough, and, therefore, desires no further reinforcements.* [20]

So . . . a great battle had been fought, the ground fiercely contested, but the wounded were properly being cared for, the troops had faith in their commander, the situation was under control, and "rumors" to the contrary were rebel propaganda. The newspapers of December 16 told of desultory skirmishing, and published a few optimistic dispatches that had been written before the battle but were delayed in transmission, adding to the public confusion. It was a confusion greatly aggravated by Burnside's announcement later that evening:

> The Army of the Potomac was withdrawn to this side of the Rappahannock River, because I felt fully convinced that the position in front could not be carried, and it was a military necessity either to attack the enemy or retire. A repulse would have been disastrous to us under the existing circumstances.
>
> The army was withdrawn at night without the knowledge of the enemy, and without loss, either of property or men. [21]

Withdrawn? "Why," queried an editorial in the December 17 New York *Times*, "should he bring back his entire army to this side of the Rappahannock, when the successful crossing of that river, four days before, had been held up as one of the greatest achievements of the war?" [22]

The *Times* had the answer, just arrived and published elsewhere in the paper, in the form of a brutally frank dispatch from Swinton written at midnight, December 13:

> The nation will stand aghast at the terrible price which has been paid for its life when the realities of the battle-field of Fredericksburg are spread before it. . . . the result thus far leaves us with a loss of from ten to fifteen thousand men, and absolutely nothing gained. Along the whole line the rebels hold their own. Again and again we have hurled forward our masses on their position. At each time the hammer was broken on the anvil!
>
> I have no heart, in the mood which the events of today have inspired, to write other than a bald record of facts. [23]

What "thoughts and feelings" passed through Burnside's mind? "No illusions," Swinton wrote, "could make *him* believe that a victory had been achieved. . . . In spite of all the glosses of official telegrams which you may receive, it seems here to-night that we have suffered a defeat. . . . Saturday, the 13th day of December, must be accounted a black day in the calendar of the Republic." [24]

To the editors of the *Times*, "the brightness of Thursday darkens into the carnage and gore of Saturday, and to-day we behold our great army, its banners dropping and dripping with blood, encamped on the spot from which, less than a brief week ago, it started out on its work of conquest. It is discouraging, and none but a fool would attempt to conceal it." [25]

The editor of the Philadelphia *Press* most certainly had not seen that edition of the *Times*—or any credible report—when he wrote, the same day, "We are gratified beyond measure in being able to assure the country, that the wild rumors of defeat and disaster are without foundation, and

that it [the army] is still anxious and ready to move against the enemy."
The editor had been instructed by his boss, John Forney, "Don't treat Fredericksburg as a disaster." Under the circumstances—presumably known
to Forney—that was not a useful instruction. [26]

Lawley entered Fredericksburg with the returning rebel forces—to be met
with the sight of

> Death, nothing but death everywhere. . .great masses of bodies
> tossed out of the churches as the *sufferers* expired; layers of corpses
> stretched out in the balconies of houses as though taking a siesta. In
> one yard a surgeon's block for operating was still standing, and,
> more appalling to look at even than the bodies of the dead, piles of
> arms and legs, amputated as soon as their owners had been carried
> off the field, were heaped in a corner. There were said to be houses
> literally crammed with the dead, but into them, horrified and aghast
> at what I saw, I could not look. . . . [27]

The *Southern Illustrated News*, which had neither artist nor correspondent on scene, relied on second- and third-hand reports and demonstrated one reason that the newspaper eventually would fail: inaccuracy.
The *News* confused the dates, and ascribed what had been the aimless
looting of Friday to a revenge for Saturday's horrors:

> Persons in Fredericksburg at the time, who have since come away,
> assert that the scene of Saturday night were terrific beyond description. The Yankees had become completely demoralized by their defeat. Their officers were utterly unable to restrain them—they
> pillaged every house that had been left. The whole army seemed to
> be a drunken mob. This frightful scene continued until Monday
> night, when, under cover of the darkness, Burnside withdrew his
> whole force to the Northern bank of the Rappahannock. . . . [28]

As usual, casualty estimates varied widely and were influenced by the
loyalty of the estimator. The Knoxville *Register* set the Federal forces engaged at 200,000 men, the Confederates at 20,000 (the actual numbers of
troops engaged were closer to 106,000 and 72,000) and claimed 19,000
Federal casualties, 1,800 for the Confederates. The London *Times* reported
1,493 dead at Marye's Heights, 800 more with Franklin's divisions, with as
many as 21,000 wounded. The *Southern Illustrated News* put the Yankee
loss in killed, wounded, and prisoners, at about 18,000 men with corresponding rebel losses in killed, wounded, and missing, at more than 2,000.

Coverage was often more graphic than in our own day. Here, the Federal dead of Fredricksburg, being buried under flag of truce.

The estimates of the Cincinnati *Commercial* were reasonably accurate, setting total Federal dead and wounded at between 10,000 and 12,000. Burnside's official report cited 1,152 killed, "about" 9,000 wounded, with 700 taken prisoner (and quickly exchanged for a like number of Confederates). Lee reported "about" 1,800 Confederates killed and wounded. Actual totals were 12,653 for the Federals, 5,309 for the Confederates.

The newspaper postmortems were reasonably similar. The Cincinnati *Commercial* offered sad comment: "No troops in the world would have won a victory if placed in the position ours were. Few armies, however renowned, would have stood as well as ours did. It can hardly be in human nature for man to show more valor, or generals to manifest less judgment, than were perceptible on our side that day." The New York *Times* gave credit to the rebels: "They did well to let us so easily into Fredericksburg, firing but half a dozen guns when they could have brought a hundred to bear upon us. The city itself was the veriest trap that ever was laid—and we have walked into it." The Richmond *Enquirer* offered a compliment of sorts to the Federals: "The enemy fought well. Our forces did better. . . ." [29]

The London *Times* challenged "the most deeply read student of military history" to find "any precedent in which battle has ever been delivered under circumstances more unfavorable to the assailing party, or upon ground from which any great master of the art of war would more naturally have recalled, had initiative remained within his own option." [30]

The *Enquirer* agreed: "The Yankees had assayed a task which no army ever marshaled, or that ever will be organized, could have accomplished. . . ."[31]

The *World*, *Herald*, and *Express* played politics: Stanton and Halleck were guilty of mismanagement for ordering Burnside to attack Fredericksburg "without regard to military expedience or foresight." [32]

The New York *Times* looked elsewhere for the villain "who is responsible for the delaying of the pontoon bridges ten days beyond the time promised Gen. Burnside, thus enabling the rebels to render their position impregnable. . . ." [33]

To the New York *Tribune*, the disaster resulted from "a combination of adverse influences" and, despite some miscalculations, the editors decided, no one individually was to blame. [34]

Burnside himself settled the argument: "For the failure of the attack I am responsible," he wrote to Halleck, "as the extreme gallantry, courage and endurance shown by them [the troops] was never exceeded, and would have carried the points had it been possible. . . . The fact that I decided to move from Warrenton on to this line rather against the opinion of the President, Secretary of War, and yourself, and that you left the whole movement in my hands, without giving me orders, makes me the only one responsible." [35]

A. D. Richardson, who had not been present at the battle but arrived at Falmouth a few days later, asked Burnside if "Franklin's slowness was responsible for the slaughter?" The general replied, "No. I understand perfectly well that when the general commanding an army meets with disaster, he alone is responsible, and I will not attempt to shift that responsibility to any one else." [36]

The editors of the New York *Times* suggested that some responsibility, indeed, should be laid elsewhere—on the "people at home":

It is due in part to their own premature urging that Gen. Burnside was forced to enter upon a winter campaign. No greater injustice could be done Gen. Burnside than to measure his ability and skill as a commander by the result of Saturday's engagement. . . . So long as the opinion of any impatient and inexperienced public is taken as a basis upon which to found military operations, just so long will misfortunes and blunders attend the conduct of the war. [37]

Harper's Weekly was not so sanguine:

We are indulging in no hyperbole when we say that these events are rapidly filling the hearts of the loyal North with sickness, disgust, and despair. . . . The people have shown a patience, during the past year, quite unexampled in history. They have borne, silently and grimly, imbecility, treachery, failure, privation, loss of friends and means, almost every suffering which can afflict a brave people. But they can not be expected to suffer that such massacres as this at Fredericksburg shall be repeated. Matters are rapidly ripening for a military dictatorship. [38]

Meanwhile, Henry Villard ran into a different sort of "impatience" when he presented his expense account to his bureau chief in Washington, Sam Wilkeson, for payment. When Wilkeson, who had been drinking, saw the claim for fifty dollars paid to a freighter captain, he exploded in a rage. Villard denounced his "insolence." Wilkeson hit Villard, whereupon Villard knocked him down. Several times. Later, Wilkeson, under pressure from his editor, apologized. A few months later, he left the *Tribune* and went to work for the *Times*. He claimed to be dissatisfied with Greeley's efforts to broker a peace settlement. [39]

17 / The Other War

Come with sword or musket in your hand, prepared to share with us our
fate, in sunshine and storm, in prosperity and adversity, in plenty and
scarcity and I will welcome you as brother and associate.
But come as you now do expecting me to ally the honor and reputation
of my country and my fellow soldiers with you, as the representative of
the press, which you yourself say make no slight difference
between truth and falsehood, and my answer is, Never!

—Major General W. T. Sherman to *Herald* reporter T. W. Knox,
April 7, 1863 [1]

IN THE FALL OF 1861, following his visit with General Frémont in
St. Louis, Secretary of War Cameron stopped in Kentucky to meet with
Brig. Gen. William Tecumseh Sherman. The general had just succeeded
to command of the Department of the Cumberland, replacing "hero of
Fort Sumter" Robert Anderson, who had fallen ill, and was outnumbered
and threatened by attack from three separate rebel armies.

To this point, not including his four years at West Point (class of
1840), Sherman's military experience largely had consisted of thirteen
generally boring years of garrison duty, service as the (civilian) comman-
dant of a new military school in Louisiana, and an unsettling assignment
as a brigade commander at Bull Run. There, Sherman's troops were badly
mauled and he placed much of the blame on what he saw as his own failure as a leader: "I am absolutely disgraced," he wrote to his wife on August 3. [2] Now, he seemed overwhelmed by the responsibility of trying to
hold the entire state of Kentucky with units of an untrained home guard.
He sent anxious letters to fellow generals, the War Department, even the
president. A few weeks before the secretary's visit, Florus Plympton of the

Cincinnati *Commercial* presented himself to the general, armed with a sheaf of letters of introduction, including one from his editor and another from Sherman's brother-in-law, and asked for an interview. Sherman not only turned down the request—he summarily ordered the correspondent to take the next train back where he came from. Plympton protested: "But General! The people are anxious. I'm only after the truth." Sherman blew up. "We don't want the truth told about things here—that's what we *don't* want! Truth, eh? No sir! We don't want the enemy any better informed than he is." He added, "Make no mistake about that train," and then, a few moments later, blurted out, "See that house? They will feed you—say I sent you—but don't miss that train!" [3]

Cameron's visit, made partly in response to Sherman's barrage of letters, gave the general an opportunity to explain his situation first hand, and, hopefully, get relief in the form of fresh supplies and perhaps some regular soldiers. However, just as the meeting was about to begin, Sherman noticed some strangers in the group, and was reluctant to continue until the secretary affirmed that "They are all my friends, all members of my family and you may speak your mind freely." Cameron did not mention that two of them were journalists—Sam Wilkeson and a reporter for Forney's Philadelphia *Press*.

Reassured, Sherman held back nothing. His present force of some 18,000 men was woefully inadequate; he could not hold the territory with fewer than 60,000 men, and useful offensive operations would require 200,000. "Great God!," Cameron is reported to have exclaimed, "Where are the men to come from?" [4] Two weeks later, Wilkeson's "report" appeared in the *Tribune*, and Sherman, whether in direct reaction or simple recognition of the fact that he was not, at that moment, up to the job, asked to be relieved. On November 9, he was transferred to St. Louis to await further assignment.

After they left the meeting in Louisville, Cameron had told Wilkeson that he thought Sherman was crazy (or words to that effect) to expect the level of support he was seeking. Wilkeson described the meeting to Villard (who at this point in his career had left the *Herald* and was with the Cincinnati *Commercial*). Villard, the German immigrant whose grasp of the English language was improving but was still handicapped by less than four years of experience, passed the comment on to *Commercial* editor Murat Halstead, who was already at odds with Sherman over the Plympton incident. [5] The vernacular became a clinical diagnosis in the *Commercial*, December 11, 1861:

> The painful intelligence reaches us, in such form that we are not at liberty to discredit it, that Gen. William T. Sherman, late Commander of the Department of the Cumberland, is *insane*. It appears that he was at times when commanding in Kentucky, stark mad. . . .

The harsh criticisms that have been lavished on this gentleman, provoked by his strange conduct, will now give way to feelings of deepest sympathy for him in this great calamity. It seems providential that the country has not to mourn the loss of an army through the loss of mind of a general into whose hands was committed the vast responsibility of the command of Kentucky.

This insult was widely reprinted, although *Frank Leslie's Illustrated Newspaper* boiled it down to the essence: "Personal. General Sherman, who lately commanded in Kentucky, is said to be insane. It is charitable to think so." [6] Halstead, however, soon was persuaded by one of Sherman's relatives that the charge was not true and printed a correction on December 13. No one seems to have noticed.

As for the truth about Sherman's mental condition, many observers, not only Secretary Cameron, saw him as troubled, nervous, obsessed, and, at times, a bit deranged. Historians have offered different opinions, but it is probable that he suffered at the least from clinical depression. This is not a permanent condition, and usually works itself out over a period of several months. In fact, Sherman enjoyed the timely support of a pair of sympathetic commanders: Henry Halleck, at St. Louis, who initially assigned Sherman to less arduous duties, allowing him to recover his spirit, and Ulysses Grant, who then helped him find his true measure.

Sherman harbored an already well-developed antipathy toward the press, dating back to his days as a bank manager and community leader in San Francisco from 1853 to 1857. At one point, he became embroiled in a dispute with a scurrilous newspaper editor, who, at about the same time, murdered a fellow editor for revealing in print that he was a convicted felon. This event triggered a series of vigilante activities in San Francisco, the whole unseemly affair leaving Sherman with the beginnings of a life-long bitterness toward the newspapering profession, which he made no attempt to soften or conceal. A grand irony: one of the few newspapermen with whom Sherman was comfortable was Henry Villard.

In the year that followed the *Commercial*'s "revelation," Sherman had redeemed himself at Shiloh and was, as a result, promoted to major general and assigned to command the District of Memphis. However, just six months into that job, the insanity charge would be resurrected by some in the press, and Sherman would call for the first court-martial of a newsman in U.S. history.

By December 1862, the Federals controlled the Mississippi River with the sole exception of that portion flowing by the Confederate stronghold of Vicksburg. One of the Union's political generals, John A. McClernand, a former Democratic congressman from Lincoln's home district in Illinois, had, in essence, recruited his own army to attempt the capture of Vicksburg, and the president agreed to let him try.

Lincoln may have had misgivings about McClernand's military acumen, but had no doubts about his political clout. General Grant wished to avoid testing either, and therefore met with Sherman to plan a coordinated attack on Vicksburg. They would use elements of McClernand's "army" before that general could arrive. Sherman loaded his transports at Memphis and, hoping to forestall interference from pestiferous newsmen, included the following guidance in General Order 8, December 18, 1862:

I. The expedition now fitting out is purely of a military character, and the interests involved are of too important a character to be mixed up with personal and private business. No citizen, male or female, will be allowed to accompany it unless employed as part of a crew or as servants to the transports. . . .

V. Should any citizen accompany the expedition below Helena, in violation of these orders, any colonel of a regiment or captain of a battery will conscript him into the service of the United States for the unexpired term of his command. If he show a refractory spirit, unfitting him for a soldier, the commanding officer present will turn him over to the captain of the boat as a deck-hand, and compel him to work in that capacity, without wages, until the boat returns to Memphis.

VI. Any person whatever, whether in the service of the United States, or transports, found making reports for publication, which might reach the enemy, giving them information, aid, and comfort, will be arrested, and treated as spies. [7]

To ensure wide dissemination, Sherman published the order in the next day's Memphis papers. Nonetheless, perhaps a dozen journalists decided to take their chances and stay with the expedition, although some later complained that the order had reached them only after the transports had already gotten under way from Memphis.

When Sherman learned that correspondents were indeed lodged on the transports, he called for a census of all embarked personnel and ordered that any reporter thus uncovered should be sent to the front lines under arrest to "pass powder." As the Chicago *Times* reported, this order "was more honored in the breach than in its observance." The reporters managed to skate along the edge without falling in, and, according to the *Times*, "not one of them . . . suffered any great physical inconvenience from the petty prejudice" of General Sherman. [8]

Sherman's troops were to land at Chickasaw Bayou on the Yazoo River, about six miles upstream of Vicksburg, and assault Vicksburg from the rear. The landing went off on schedule, but before they could get into the city, the troops had to get past the Chickasaw Bluffs. The weather was abominable, the rebels were dug in and waiting, and Grant's effort to attack along another axis, which would have diverted the enemy, had been derailed by a Confederate raid on his supply line. By the time Sherman called retreat on December 29, the Federals had lost 208 killed, 1,005 wounded, and 563 missing out of a force of 31,000 men. The Confederate losses were 63 killed, 134 wounded, and 10 missing, from a force of 14,000.

Some of the newsmen, not knowing that the plan called for a coordinated attack, assumed that Sherman alone had rushed into action hoping to capture Vicksburg before McClernand arrived. Others knew of the plan, but were incensed with the execution. Sherman, obsessed with intruding newsmen, ordered the army's postal agent to search through the outgoing mailbags for any suspiciously heavy letters; call it, censorship by other means. The New York *Times* called it an outrage:

Had the commanding general, W. T. Sherman, and his Staff spent half the time and enterprise in the legitimate operations of their present undertaking than they have in bullying correspondents, overhauling mailbags and prying into private correspondence, the country would not now have the shame of knowing that we have lately experienced one of the greatest and most disgraceful defeats of the war. [9]

On January 4, McClernand arrived to assume command. Sherman reported for duty, thanked his troops for their "zeal, alacrity, and courage," and offered a testy observation:

A new commander is now here to lead you. He is chosen by the President of the United States, who is charged by the Constitution to maintain and defend it, and he has the undoubted right to select his own agents. I know that all good officers and soldiers will give him the same hearty support given me. There are honors enough in reserve for all, and work enough, too. [10]

In the meantime, the battle between Sherman and the correspondents took on new and disquieting dimensions. The postal agent did indeed discover some news dispatches in the mail, addressed not openly to newspapers, but to blind mail drops in Memphis and Cairo—clear evidence of intentional deception. One of the letters had been written by Tom Knox of the *Herald*. It was a relatively tame report of the operation—tame, that is, when compared with his next dispatch, which he hand-carried to Cairo for safe mailing and to which he added this prefatory comment:

> On Tuesday morning last, I mailed to the *Herald* a full account of the operations of the right wing of the Thirteenth Army Corps. . . . That letter . . . [was taken] from the mail and turned over to General Sherman. . . . If General Sherman has obtained from it any facts that may aid him in making up his official report, he is welcome. . . . Had they [Sherman's staff] all acted as earnestly and persistently against the rebels as against the representatives of the Press, there is little doubt that Vicksburg ere this were in Union hands. [11]

Just as Knox was about to put this report in the mail, he was handed back his original letter, which had been "released" from captivity and sent to find him in Cairo. He mailed both to the *Herald*, which wove both together in publishing the story of Chickasaw Bayou. The original dispatch had lauded the contributions of Generals Frank Blair and Frederick Steele. The added text took on General Sherman:

> General Sherman was so exceedingly erratic that the discussion of a twelve month ago with respect to his sanity was revived with great earnestness. . . . Gen. Sherman has persistently refused to allow a hospital boat to go above, although their detention is daily fatal to many lives. The only known reason for his refusal is his fear that knowledge of his mismanagement will reach the Northern press. . . . Insanity and inefficiency have brought their result: let us have them no more. With another brain than that of General Sherman's, we will drop this disappointment at our reverse, and feel certain of victory in the future. [12-1]

When copies of this January 18 edition of the *Herald* reached Sherman's headquarters on the 24th, the general went into the mid-nineteenth-century version of "orbit" and had not come down when Grant arrived five days later to assume overall command. Sherman asked Grant for his opinion. Grant—whose attitude toward the press had long been laissez-faire—suggested that Sherman do nothing. However, he said, if Sherman insisted on making an example, he would support his decision.

Sherman insisted. When Knox returned from Cairo, he was hauled in for questioning by General Sherman. Was Knox married? Why was he not in the army? Did he see General Order 8? Then, while a staff officer read the dispatch aloud, Sherman demanded the source for every statement.

Next, he confronted Knox with a collection of battle plans and reports and offered a rebuttal, point by point, of the *Herald*'s dispatch.

Knox thereby learned that much of his report had been in error, and promised to make corrections. However, with more courage than sense, he noted that his ability to get accurate information in the first place had been hampered by Sherman's policy against correspondents.

The general's wrath was next directed at one of his own commanders, Frank Blair, who had allowed Knox aboard his headquarters boat in patent violation of General Order 8. Sherman sent Blair a list of twenty-two items gleaned from his interrogation of Knox, and demanded to know if he had been the source for any or all. In reply, Blair acknowledged that he indeed had shared his official report and some other information with the reporter. However, it became clear that there was little congruence between what Blair provided and what was published, so he was off the hook.

Blair didn't much care one way or the other because, in addition to his present employment as a major general of volunteers, he had just completed his second term as a member of Congress, was the brother of Lincoln's postmaster general, and the son of the political kingmaker who lived across the street from the White House in the residence still known today by the family name. "I confess myself greatly mortified and annoyed," General Blair wrote to Sherman, "in being called on to answer such interrogations under such circumstances. . . . I hope to receive no more letters of the same character from you and shall not answer them if I do." [12-2]

Sherman asked the naval commander, Admiral Porter, for his opinion "generally whether I acted the part of an intelligent officer or an insane fool." Porter responded with the gentle suggestion, "As . . . you have no political aspirations, you can well afford to pass without notice what is said by the press. . . ." [13]

Sherman could not take the hint, and had Knox brought in for another interview, during which the reporter managed to top his previous blunder. When asked for his "motive" in writing the story, he replied, "Of course, General Sherman, I had no feeling against you personally, but you are regarded the enemy of our set, and we must in self-defense write you down." [14]

Sherman sent Blair a sort-of thank-you note, promising no more interrogatories. "I could hardly believe that a white man could be so false as this fellow Knox," he added, ". . . and am glad that your letter enables me to put the fellow where he really belongs, as a spy and an infamous dog." The day would come, he predicted, when "every officer will demand the execution of this class of spies, and without hesitation I declare that if I am forced to look to the New York *Herald* for my lord and master instead of the constituted authorities of the United States my military career is at an end." [15]

On February 1, Knox gave Sherman a properly penitent letter. He apologized for his errors, affirmed that he was now "fully convinced of your prompt, efficient and judicious management of the troops under your control," and offered to correct any offending statements. It was too late. In a note to Admiral Porter a few days later, Sherman vowed: "I am going to have the correspondent of the New York *Herald* tried by a court martial as a spy, not that I want the fellow shot, but because I want to establish the principle that such people cannot attend our armies, in violation of orders, and defy us, publishing their garbled statements and defaming officers who are doing their best." In a private letter to Mrs. Sherman a week earlier, however, he had not been so benign: "I . . . shall try him, and if possible execute him as a spy." [16]

There were three charges against Knox: that he had violated General Order 57 by providing the enemy, directly or indirectly, with information about army strength; that by accompanying the transports he had willfully disobeyed Sherman's General Order 8 (which required he be charged as a spy), and that he had violated the War Department order of August 26, 1861, by submitting letters for publication without approval. The court—consisting of a brigadier general, four colonels, and two majors—was in session from February 6 to February 18. The principal witness for the prosecution was General Sherman.

The defense successfully argued that Knox could not have given information to the enemy, since his dispatch was not written until four days after the action and not published for another two weeks; the defense further pointed out that the order of August 26 had been modified by Sanford's "parole" of April 1862, which permitted publication of the names of units engaged after an action had been completed.

As for boarding the transport without authority, the defense noted that the correspondent had in his possession a valid pass issued by General Grant only two days before Sherman's general order. Nonetheless, it was on this charge, and this charge only, that Knox was found guilty—a guilt, however, assessed without "criminality." He was sentenced to banishment from the Army of the Tennessee, not to return under threat of imprisonment.

Sherman had been prepared to take action against eight other correspondents; he dropped the charges, but not the subject. The day of the verdict, he vented his frustration in a letter to his brother, Sen. John Sherman, in which he expressed disdain for those who "will not fight, but who follow our army and pick up news for sale, and who are more used to bolster up idle and worthless officers than to notice the hard-working and meritorious whose modesty is equal to their courage. . . . The press has now killed McClellan, Buell, Fitz-John Porter, Sumner, Franklin, and Burnside. Add my name and I am not ashamed of the association. If the press can govern the country, let them fight the battles." [17]

Sherman told Grant's confidant John Rawlins that supporting the cause of freedom of the press "has lost us millions of money, thousands of lives, and will continue to defeat us to the end of time, unless some remedy be devised." He petitioned Grant for review of the court's verdict and referral to "the Commander-in-Chief." [18]

Grant took no action, but the matter did indeed come to the attention of the commander in chief by an unusual route and with an unexpected result. As they had in earlier disputes over issues of freedom and constraint, journalists came together in support of Knox. In Washington, John Forney launched a signature drive on a petition asking President Lincoln to reinstate Knox. On March 20, 1863, an appropriate delegation called at the White House to present the petition: Richardson of the *Tribune*, a man from the New York *Times*, and a congressman from Colorado (where Knox last made a home). The president said that he was willing to intervene, but only if General Grant agreed.

The delegation reminded the president of the close personal relationship between Grant and Sherman, and suggested that the probability of General Grant overturning an order initiated by his subordinate was remote. After a moment's thought, the president replied, "I should be glad to serve you or Mr. Knox, or any other loyal journalist. But, just at present, our generals in the field are more important to the country than any of the rest of us—or *all* the rest of us. It is my fixed determination to do nothing whatever which can possibly embarrass any one of them. Therefore, I will do cheerfully what I have said, but it is all I can do." [19]

Thereupon the president moved to a writing desk, took pen and paper to hand, and executed the following:

Whom it may concern:

Whereas, it appears to my satisfaction that Thomas W. Knox, a correspondent of the New York *Herald*, has been, by the sentence of a court-martial, excluded from the military department under command of Major-General Grant, and also that General Thayer, president of the court-martial, which rendered the sentence, and Major-General McClernand, in command of a corps of the department, and many other respectable persons, are of the opinion that Mr. Knox's offense was technical, rather than wilfully wrong, and that the sentence should be revoked; Now, therefore, said sentence is hereby so far revoked as to allow Mr. Knox to return to General Grant's head-quarters, and to remain if General Grant shall give his express assent, and to again leave the department, if General Grant shall refuse such assent.

A. Lincoln [20]

The memo was sent to Knox; Knox approached Grant, who, displeased with the reporter's aspersions against "one of the ablest soldiers and purest men in the country," would do nothing "unless General Sherman first gives his assent to your remaining." Knox sent an ambiguous note to Sherman, neither an apology nor a pleading. "Without referring in detail to past occurrences," he wrote, "permit me to express my regret at the want of harmony between portions of the Army and the Press, and the hope that there may be better feeling in the future" [21]

Sherman responded, "notwithstanding the President's endorsement," he could not accept Knox back into his lines, and turned the reporter back on himself:

After having enunciated to me that fact that newspaper correspondents were a fraternity bound together by a common interest that must write down all who stood in their way, and that you had to supply the public demand for news, true if possible but false if your interest demanded it, I cannot be party to a tacit acknowledgment of the principle.

Come with sword or musket in your hand, prepared to share with us our fate, in sunshine and storm, in prosperity and adversity, in plenty and scarcity and I will welcome you as brother and associate. But come as you now do expecting me to ally the honor and reputation of my country and my fellow soldiers with you, as the representative of the press, which you yourself say make no slight difference between truth and falsehood, and my answer is, Never! [22]

The *Herald* article submitted by Knox, for all its fire, was not the most critical report of Sherman's leadership at Chickasaw Bayou. On the same date, the following was published in the Missouri *Democrat:*.

We have met the enemy and they are not ours, but, on the contrary, quite the reverse. . . . But the matter is too grave to treat lightly. A stupid blunder, and an ignoble attempt to forestall another general's laurels, have brought shame and calamity to our country, desolation and woe to more than two thousand households, and peril to the cause of liberty and free government. . . . the causes will be found in the mismanagement, incompetence, and probable insanity of the commanding general, and the intemperance, negligence, and general inefficiency of nearly the whole of the line and field-officers of his command. [23]

There were examples. Embarkation of the transports was a scene of "unparalleled" confusion: "batteries were on one boat, and caissons belonging to them on another; and the horses and artillerymen on still another. . . ." There was an explanation: ". . . on the day previous the army had been paid off for the first time in several months, and men and officers were nearly all lively with drink." Drinking continued as the boats moved down the river, as "nearly every soldier had managed to obtain a canteen of whiskey, enough to keep him drunk for two days . . . and for that space of time such a scene of riot and filthiness was scarce ever witnessed. . . . Among the officers, affairs were but little better. . . . A large proportion of the officers were drinking the entire trip, and their behavior was unbecoming in the extreme." [24]

On the subject of purloined mail, the *Democrat* went the *Times* and the *Herald* one better: Sherman was guilty of the "heinous crime, punishable by imprisonment in the penitentiary, of violating the seals and perusing the contents. . . . The outrage is inexcusable in any aspect. . . . the violation of the sanctity of a private seal admits of no palliation." [25]

So, why did Sherman pick on Knox? The *Democrat* correspondent was anonymous, known only as "D" (then and now). Knox was easily identified: his name was on the intercepted letter, and he had made no secret of his personal opinion that Sherman was "making an ass of himself." The mysterious "D" largely charged Sherman with criminal negligence and malfeasance. The well-known Knox aggressively picked at the scab on the "insanity" wound. [26]

After the Knox court-martial had ended, reporters for the Democratic papers, especially the *Missouri Republican* and the Chicago *Times*, weighed in with fresh complaints: the army was suffering from exceptionally high levels of disease and the medical services were incompetent. Even the New York *Times* took a shot: Franc Wilkie wrote that officers were living in all the best homes in the neighborhood while the sick were left to die "in narrow boats and dirty huts, lately used by Negroes." He estimated that almost two-thirds of the daily death toll of one hundred could be laid to "the culpability and negligence of those in command." Sickness was a problem, but it was more from the malevolence of nature than the negligence of man. An investigation by the Western Sanitary Commission found that the major problem was exaggeration in the newspapers, not sickness in the camps. [27]

Knox may have been the first journalist tried by court-martial, but he was not the only one. A month later, General Hooker ordered court-martial for another *Herald* reporter, Edwin F. DeNyse, who had written of "unmistakable preparations now being made for the speedy movement of the army." [28] He was found guilty of a security violation and sentenced to six months at hard labor. Hooker commuted that to banishment from the army, with orders never to return.

Benjamin F. Taylor of the Chicago *Journal* avoided a Sherman court-martial in May 1864 by quickly heading for home. He had said in one of his letters, "our lines now extend from Nashville to Huntsville." An anonymous correspondent wrote on May 11, "It is reported that General Sherman, upon reading this item, wrote an order to his Provost Marshal-General, directing the immediate arrest of a spy, one Benjamin F. Taylor, his trial by drum-head court-martial, and execution." The reporter added a pleading in defense of journalists: "as the news of all engagements must drift to the rear sooner or later, it seems plausible that a trustworthy correspondent can send it with less injury to the service than when borne by demoralized stragglers, or by wounded men, whose observations can hardly go beyond their brigades." General Sherman observed to his wife, at about this time, "Had I tolerated a corps of newspaper men how could I have made that march a success?" [29]

The last Civil War journalist to be tried by court-martial was Bradley Sillick Osbon, a reporter connected first with the *World* and then with the *Herald*, although by the time of the trial he had started his own New York–based naval news syndicate. His troubles began in late October 1864, when the War Department was preparing to mount an expedition against the port of Wilmington, North Carolina. Osbon offered his clients "a full & accurate epitome of the grand movement against Wilmington" to include a list of ships, their armament, a description of the enemy's harbor defenses, and an abstract of the official battle plan. "I will supply this in *advance*," he wrote, "so that upon receipt of the telegram announcing the attack, you can publish, thereby being in advance of the New York papers." [30]

A number of clients signed on. This might have been scored as a commendable initiative *if* everyone had waited for "the telegram." Several did not, and published the story far enough in advance for it to be copied into the Richmond newspapers on December 22, two days before the attack was launched. Thus alerted, General Lee was able to arrange for timely reinforcement by a full division of troops, and the expedition was a failure, although the military ineptitude of the commander of the Federal ground forces, General Butler, was a contributing factor. Butler was removed from command, and on the first day of the new year, B. S. Osbon was arrested at his office in New York and taken to Washington.

On January 24, Osbon was brought before Gen. Abner Doubleday and "commanded" to plead guilty. He declined, and would have been brought to trial at once, but fell ill and was kept in prison for another two months. Then, when his health was reasonably restored, he was taken back to New York for trial by a military court led by former *Tribune* Washington bureau chief, Brig. Gen. Fitz-Henry Warren. On June 5, more than five months after his arrest (and almost two months after the Confederate surrender at Appomattox), he was found to be "not guilty." He was not released, however, until the middle of July.

The case of Osbon merits a brief sidebar. Before the war, he had been a professional sailor and maritime mercenary. Through most of the war, he was in active Federal naval service, participating in twenty-seven engagements and being wounded seven times, while at the same time working as a newspaper correspondent. In fact, Osbon had been one of the first specials to go off to the war, with a dual assignment as signal officer on a ship that attempted to rescue the garrison at Fort Sumter and as reporter for the New York *World*. It was on this mission that he unwittingly set the stage for his over-long 1865 incarceration and trial by incurring the wrath of a navy captain who would soon be appointed assistant secretary of the navy.

Gustavas V. Fox was commanding officer of the rescue effort and of the ship that carried Major Anderson and his men from Charleston to New York. Captain Fox knew that Osbon was a reporter, but neither of *them* knew—no one knew—whether Anderson would be treated as a hero or as a traitor. Afraid that his career might be tainted by public criticism either for the failed rescue effort or for his association with Anderson, Fox asked Osbon to keep his name out of any newspaper copy. Osbon complied. Then, when all were welcomed as heroes, a petulant Fox complained that he had been treated unfairly because Osbon failed to credit him as commander of the expedition. Osbon responded by publishing the reason; Fox never forgave him this mild humiliation, and apparently took his revenge by engineering Osbon's court-martial. [31]

18 / Transitions, 1863

Stonewall Jackson is dead. While we are only too glad to be rid, in any
way, of so terrible a foe, our sense of relief is not unmingled with
emotions of sorrow and sympathy at the death of so brave a man.
Every man who possesses the slightest particle of magnanimity must
admire the qualities for which Stonewall Jackson was celebrated—his
heroism, his bravery, his sublime devotion, his purity of character. He is
not the first instance of a good man devoting himself to a bad cause. . . .
—Washington *Daily Morning Chronicle*, May 13, 1863

TOWARD THE END OF JANUARY 1863, Ambrose Burnside
made plans once again to assault Fredericksburg, this time from the rear.
This time, the weather proved to be the more formidable (but less fatal)
enemy, and, after fighting wind, rain, and mud, Burnside canceled the operation. His replacement by Gen. "Fighting Joe" Hooker was announced
two days later. Burnside continued to serve—with mixed results—until
the end of the war, when he managed to gain victories of a different sort:
he was three times elected governor of Rhode Island and was a member of
the U.S. Senate until his death in 1881.

Hooker assumed command under perhaps the most unusual endorsement ever handed a general by his commander in chief:

I have placed you at the head of the Army of the Potomac. Of
course I have done this upon what appear to me to be sufficient reasons, and yet I think it best for you to know that there are some
things in regard to which I am not quite satisfied with you. I believe
you to be a brave and skillful soldier, which, of course, I like. I also

believe you do not mix politics with your profession, in which you are right. You have confidence in yourself, which is a valuable, if not an indispensable, quality. You are ambitious, which, within reasonable grounds, does good rather than harm; but I think that during General Burnside's command of the army you took counsel of your ambition, and thwarted him as much as you could, in which you did a great wrong to the country and to a most meritorious and honorable brother officer. I have heard, in such a way as to believe it, of your recently saying that both the Army and the Government needed a dictator. Of course, it was not for this, but in spite of it, that I have given you the command. Only those generals who gain success can set up dictators. What I ask of you is military success, and I will risk the dictatorship. [1]

The source for the "dictator" charge was New York *Times* editor Henry Raymond, passing along a comment that Hooker had made to Swinton. The general, true to form, had denounced Burnside as "incompetent," but extended his judgment also to the "imbecile" president and government at Washington. In Hooker's estimation, "Nothing would go right," as Swinton relayed the comment to Raymond, "until we had a dictator and the sooner the better." [2]

Lincoln acknowledged the insult: "Hooker does talk badly; but the trouble is, he is stronger with the country today than any other man." When Raymond suggested that Hooker surely would not retain public support if his true character were revealed, the president said, "The country would not believe it; they would say it is all a lie." [3]

What was Hooker's reaction to the letter? Sacramento *Union* correspondent Noah Brooks later wrote that Hooker told him, "This is just such a letter as a father might write to his son. It is a beautiful letter, and, although I think he was harder on me than I deserved, I will say that I love the man who wrote it." [4]

Hooker was to have a five-month tryout as commander of the Army of the Potomac; a correspondent for the New York *Times* predicted that "the new General will do one of two things, and that right speedily—destroy the rebel army, or our own." Hooker's tour was marked with mixed and generally unsatisfactory results, but along the way he found an amazingly simple way to impose some discipline on the press corps. Plagued with newspaper leaks, he complained to Secretary of War Stanton, who gave the problem back to Hooker, just as Confederate secretary Benjamin had done with Joseph Johnston fifteen months earlier. "You will have to protect yourself by rigid measure against the reporters in your army," Stanton wrote, " and the Department will support you in any measure you are pleased to take on the subject. . . ." [5]

Burnside's "mud-march": his final attempt to take Fredricksburg was foiled by a less fatal enemy—the weather.

Whereupon, on April 30, 1863, Hooker issued General Order 48. Decrying "the frequent transmission of false intelligence, and the betrayal of the movements of the army to the enemy, by the publications of injudicious correspondents of an anonymous character," he ordered that all published letters include the name of the author. In an amplifying message to the Associated Press, he reiterated the generally accepted ground rules (do not give the location of units; do not publish official reports without permission), and added:

> After any fight the reporters can open their fire as loudly as they please, but avoid, unless it is a general battle, giving the designation of forces engaged. Require all reporter's signatures to their published letters. These rules being observed, every facility possible will be given to reporters and newspapers in this army, including the license to abuse or criticize me to their heart's content. [6]

Signatures on all published letters? Indeed, "by" lines were now required by general order. Pen names and anonymity, now banished, or the offending journalist would in turn be banished from the army. This certainly ran counter to normal (although not exclusive) newspaper practice. As Sam Wilkeson had said, "The anonymous greatly favors freedom and boldness in newspaper correspondence." Unfettered freedom, of course, was at the heart of the issue.

Reaction among the correspondents was mixed. Lynde W. Buckingham of the *Herald* complained, "It is discouraging for correspondents to have their names paraded before the public as authors of carefully written letters; for sometimes the letters are written on horseback or in woods, and often with the shells screaming to us to 'hurry up!'" Thomas M. Newbould of the New York *Tribune* declined the honor: "I do not desire the ostentation." He preferred to be identified simply as "N." Nonetheless, the *Tribune* thenceforth tagged his dispatches with his full name. [7]

However, many, if not most, of the specials welcomed the opportunity to be given public credit. George Alfred Townsend added a pungent thought: a byline made a reporter "exert extraordinary means to achieve success." [8]

During the week following the publication of General Order 48, and while the newsmen were absorbing its impact, the general himself was being soundly defeated by Robert E. Lee at the battle of Chancellorsville (May 1–4, 1863). Lee then started moving North, poised for an invasion of Pennsylvania, and Hooker's army nipped away with not much more effect than a terrier worrying a bull.

The New York *Tribune*'s Josiah Sypher offered an account that was highly critical of Hooker's progress, or lack thereof. Hooker ordered him arrested, but Sypher headed for New York. There were suggestions that Hooker was drinking too much; Navy Secretary Gideon Welles confided to his *Diary* that "No explanation has ever been made of the sudden paralysis which befell the army at that time. It was then reported, by those who should have known, that it was liquor." [9]

The *Tribune* heard about the drinking, and that Hooker had lost the confidence of his men, and sent George Smalley back to the army more as a confidential agent than a reporter. By his own account, Smalley found a demoralized force, but wrote that "not one witness could testify to having seen General Hooker the worse for whiskey." Smalley suggested that a blow to the head, from a falling porch beam in an action on May 3, might have been the cause of Hooker's apparent indecisiveness. However, according to the testimony of others, Smalley found Hooker to be "the mere wreck of what he was last fall . . . played out by wine and women." Smalley asked senior officers, "off the record," who they would prefer to see in command? The consensus was "Meade." [10]

When he returned to New York, Smalley asked managing editor Sidney Gay for guidance in writing his "report." Gay said, "Write an editorial, keep to generalities, and forget most of what you have told me." [11] In the event, nothing about his mission or his findings ever appeared in print in the *Tribune*. But an item in the May 18 New York *World* revealed that "confidential agents from New York" had been sent South on a scouting expedition:

> One of them, a prominent *Tribune* man, spent a couple of days with the army and went away much astonished. It is stated that, after a long interview with the general commanding one of the corps, he asked: "In case Hooker is relieved, who is the proper man to command the army?" The general answered emphatically, "George B. McClellan."

On June 9, Hooker's force engaged in one spectacular but inconclusive confrontation: the largest cavalry action ever fought on the North American continent, at Brandy Station, Virginia. It was spectacular in that the Union forces (including some artillery and infantry) numbered 11,000; it was inconclusive in that the Confederates did not lose the ground, but the Federals gained important knowledge of Lee's movements. The Federal cavalry also gained some respect; up to that point, the Southern born-to-the-horse cavaliers were assumed to have the edge over the "city-bred" Yankees.

J. E. B. Stuart had been caught by surprise, but the telegraphic censor at Richmond deleted any mention of "surprise" from a report filed by Peter W. Alexander for the Mobile *Register*. In a later dispatch, the irritated correspondent suggested,

To be consistent, the Government should establish a censorship over the mailbags, over the railway trains, and over the minds and tongues of men; for there was scarcely a letter sent from the army the day after the battle that did not admit the surprise, nor was there an individual, white or black, who left here by railroad who had not heard of it and who would not speak of it. [12]

Hooker continued to be harassed by irresponsible newspaper reports. He sent a confidential memorandum to all editors on June 18 asking for them to exercise discretion in arranging their reports. The same day, the *Herald* published in exact detail the location of each of Hooker's corps and cavalry units. Hooker complained to Halleck; Halleck offered what seems to have become the universal guidance governing military-media relations:

I appreciate as fully as yourself the injury resulting from newspaper publication of the movements, numbers, and position of our troops, but I see no way of preventing it as long as reporters are permitted in our camps. I expelled them from our lines in Mississippi. Every general must decide for himself what persons he will permit in his camps. [13]

Hooker responded by banishing one reporter, a *Tribune* man. Perhaps he did not know the identity of the offending reporter from the *Herald*.

Maj. Gen. George Gordon Meade was appointed commander of the Army of the Potomac on June 28, about five weeks after George Smalley told the editors at the *Tribune* that "senior officers" would prefer Meade over other candidates. Was this a coincidence? Unknown. It is known that Hooker, wrapped in a dispute with Halleck, had voluntarily asked to be relieved, but the choice of successor was up to the president.

During this same period, another professional newspaperman was sent to investigate rumors of intemperance by another Union general. This mission was triggered, in part, by two notes sent by Murat Halstead (Cincinnati *Commercial*) to Secretary of the Treasury (and former Ohio governor) Salmon P. Chase. In the first, dated February 19, 1863, and written in the aftermath of the Chickasaw Bayou debacle, editor Halstead forwarded a letter from one of his correspondents:

There never was a more thoroughly disgusted, disheartened, demoralized army than this is, and all because it is under such men as Grant and Sherman. Disease is decimating its ranks, and while hundreds of poor fellows are dying from smallpox and every other conceivable malady, the medical department is afflicted with delirium tremens. In Memphis smallpox patients are made to walk through the streets from camps to hospitals, while drunken doctors ride from bar rooms in government ambulances. How is it that Grant, who was behind at Fort Henry, drunk at Donelson, surprised and whipped at Shiloh, and driven back from Oxford, Miss., is still in command? [14]

Halstead added a personal note: "Governor Chase, these things are true. Our noble army of the Mississippi [sic] is being wasted by the foolish, drunken, stupid Grant. He can't organize or control or fight an army. . . . There is not among the whole list of retired major generals a man who is not Grant's superior." [15]

The editor followed up six weeks later with an even more violent charge: Grant was a "poor drunken imbecile" who would fail, "miserably, hopelessly, eternally. . . . Anybody would be an improvement on Grant!" [16] There had been other press complaints directed against General Grant, sufficient now to cause the secretary of war to dispatch his new special assistant, Charles A. Dana, formerly managing editor of the New York *Tribune*, as a confidential observer.

Dana arrived at Grant's headquarters during the first week in April, ostensibly to look into the pay service of the Western armies; for the following three months, he filed daily reports with the War Department covering actions, activities, and the deportment of certain senior officers. Grant may have been apprehensive, at first, at having a company spy planted in his camp, but Dana quickly recognized Grant's special genius and suggested as much to his management. Grant, who hated writing reports, quickly realized that if Dana was keeping the department posted on most of the daily detail, he did not have to.

Grant had returned to the army with a reputation as a problem drinker. The reputation may or may not have been deserved—historians are of mixed mind on this—and there is enough evidence from Grant's friends and supporters, let alone his enemies, to support a charge that he may have gotten drunk a few times in the first half of the war. This may have contributed to the establishment of one of the war's closest relationships between a senior commander and a special correspondent.

Sylvanus Cadwallader of the Chicago *Times* arrived at Grant's headquarters in August 1862. He quickly demonstrated that he was a "straight-shooter," even if working for a strongly opposition newspaper, and Grant just as quickly demonstrated his respect for straight-shooting reporters. The *Times* had published a piece highly critical of looting by Federal troops. Grant asked him for the name of the author. Cadwallader said it was his. Grant said, "I simply want to say to you that if you always stick as close to the truth as you have here, we shall have no quarrel. The troops did behave shamefully." [17] The two men hit it off, and for the rest of the war, Cadwallader had such a special relationship with Grant that the *Herald* would eventually hire the correspondent away from the *Times* in order to guarantee access to the general.

The story is told—it was told, indeed, by Cadwallader himself in a memoir written after Grant's death but not published until 1955—that some of that reporter's success with Grant grew out of a few incidents in May and June of 1863. At least once, Cadwallader may have rescued a drunken General Grant from a runaway horse and twice locked him in a room, away from public scrutiny, until he sobered up. Cadwallader's account, clearly self-serving, is viewed as suspect by some historians, but letters and reports by Grant's close friend and adjutant John Rawlins, and Dana himself, support some aspects of Cadwallader's account in general, if not in specific. [18]

Whatever the truth of Grant's alleged missteps, at just this time, Franc Wilkie contributed a "portrait" to the New York *Times* that easily was the equal of that of Lee written by Lawley for the London *Times* six months earlier, and just as solidly created—for then, and yet today—what became the public image of the man:

> Almost at any time one can see a small but compactly-built man of about forty-five years of age walking through the camps. He moves with his shoulders thrown a little forward of the perpendicular, his left hand in the pocket of his pantaloons, an unlighted cigar in his mouth, his eyes thrown straight forward, which, from the haze of abstraction that veils them, and a countenance drawn into furrows of thought, would seem to indicate that he is intensely preoccupied. The soldiers observe him coming, and, rising to their feet, gather on each side of the way to see him pass—they do not salute him, they only watch him curiously, with a certain sort of familiar reverence. His abstract air is not so great, while he thus moves along, as to prevent his seeing everything without apparently looking at it; you will see this in the fact, that however dense the crowd in which you stand, if you are an acquaintance, his eye will for an instant rest on yours with a glance of recollection, and with it a grave nod of recognition. A plain blue suit, without scarf, sword, or trappings of any sort, save the double-starred shoulder strap—an indifferently good "Kossuth" hat, with the top battered in close to his head; full beard, of a cross between "light" and "*sandy*;" a square cut face, whose lines and contour indicate extreme endurance and determination, complete the external appearance of this small man, as one sees him passing along, turning and chewing restlessly the end of his unlighted cigar. . . .

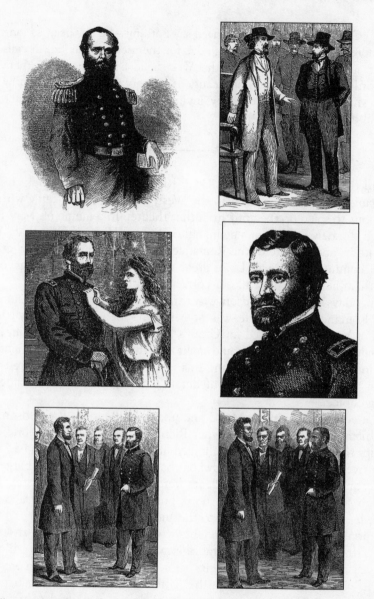

The illustrated weeklies had a lot of trouble with General Grant. Early in the war, Grant wore his beard long, but soon cut it back; some artists in New York, unaware of this ton-sorial shift, stuck with a source-photo of a long-bearded Grant. The matter was compli-cated by the fact that some artists were also using a photo of a man named William Grant who bore a resemblance to, but certainly was not, Ulysses S. Both men posed for a photo portrait at a studio in Cairo, Illinois, at about the same time. The confusion was understandable—at first. However, *Harper's* used the bogus Grant throughout the war.

Note the almost-twin illustrations at the bottom, of Grant receiving his commission as lieutenant general. On the left, as it appeared in *Harper's*; on the right, a visibly re-touched version that appeared in Charles Coffin's history, *Redeeming the Republic*, pub-lished in 1889 by Harper & Brothers.

Of Gen. Grant's ability I need say nothing—he has been so long before the public that all can judge for themselves. The South calls his successes "luck"; we in the West believe that he owes them mostly to the possession of a cautious military judgment, assisted by good advisers, and backed by invincible perseverance, endurance and determination. [19]

Toward the end of April, Albert Dean Richardson was sent back to duty as *Tribune* chief correspondent in the West; the assignment came with instructions to spice up the copy from that theater. In a memo on May 1, he assured the new *Tribune* managing editor, Sidney Howard Gay, that "Your suggestions about more of the Romance & picturesqueness of war, & less of the common place will be of great service to me. I will endeavor to have them acted upon by all our correspondents." [20]

Two days later, Richardson was thrown, almost fatally, into some of that "Romance & etc." He was at Milliken's Bend on the Mississippi, north of Vicksburg, headed for Grant's headquarters at Grand Gulf, fifty-five miles downstream. He could make it a three-day journey by land, or do it in eight hours by boat. Land was safer; the river route required running a seven-mile stretch of Confederate batteries. Richardson made the wrong choice.

Late on the evening of May 3 and under a full moon, Richardson, fellow *Tribune* special Junius Browne, Richard Colburn of the *World*, and perhaps thirty other passengers climbed aboard a barge about to be towed down river. By 1:30 A.M., the towboat had been destroyed, the barge was ablaze, and the three correspondents were floundering in the water. They tried to swim to the Louisiana shore, but were quickly hauled aboard a Confederate rowboat and taken to the Vicksburg city jail. [21]

Initially, the three correspondents were reported to have been killed. When that news reached General Sherman, he said, "That's good! We'll have dispatches now from hell before breakfast." The irrepressible Browne would later respond that the "gifted general" had been geographically confused: "The army correspondents do not usually date their dispatches from his headquarters." [22]

Colburn was released almost at once; the two *Tribune* men were shifted to Richmond to become residents first of Libby Prison, then Castle Thunder, and finally the prisoner of war camp at Salisbury, North Carolina. President Lincoln tried to intervene, on the grounds that they were noncombatants. All efforts were rebuffed by the Confederate commissioner of exchange Robert Ould. The commissioner was implacable: as he told his counterpart U.S. commissioner, "The *Tribune* did more than any other agency to bring on the war. It is useless for you to ask for the exchange of its correspondents. They are just the men we want, and just the men we are going to hold." They would not be released, he averred, because "they are the worst and most obnoxious of all non-combatants. . . ." Ould tried to make a case that the association with the *Tribune* really was not the main issue, anyway: it was the fact that the North was holding as noncombatants "delicate and noble-souled women who are languishing in your prisons." (This was in reference to some women who were being held as Confederate spies.) "Richardson and Browne will be released just as soon as you agree to discharge non-combatants." [23]

In January 1864, the Confederate secretary of war ordered that Richardson and Browne stand as hostages for "Citizen-Prisoners now in the North." This was not for any designated prisoners, one for one, as usual in the holding of hostages—but for *all* of them. [24] Thus, Richardson and Browne *may* have been held hostage not only to the policies of the *Tribune*, but also to Federal reluctance to enter into a general agreement to exchange noncombatants. For reasons more related to international than national politics, the Federal government was leery of doing anything that might give formal recognition to the Confederacy. However, the fact that correspondents for no other newspaper were held as long or under such conditions as Richardson and Browne suggests that Confederate authorities were being disingenuous.

At one point, Richardson was incensed to learn that a captured Confederate journalist—"Edward A. Pollard, a malignant Rebel, and an editor of the Richmond *Examiner*, most virulent of the southern papers"—was paroled "to the city of Brooklyn." Pollard had been captured aboard a blockade runner headed for England; his story, to make arrangements for publication of his next book. Some detractors suggested that he merely was trying to escape an enlarged Confederate draft. [25]

The news of Pollard's parole, Richardson wrote, "cut us like a knife. We, after nearly two years of captivity, in that foul, vermin-infested prison, among all its atrocities—he, at large, among the comforts and luxuries of one of the pleasantest cities in the world!" Richardson made a point of fingering "Mr. Welles, Secretary of the Navy" as the "person who set Pollard at liberty." While the circumstances of their captivity were quite different, it was captivity nonetheless, and Richardson did not know that Pollard had been offered in trade, nor did he know that General Grant had ordered that Pollard would be held until Richardson was released or exchanged. [26]

In December 1864, Richardson and Browne parlayed assignment to the camp hospital, with some freedom of movement, into an escape from the camp and almost a month of hide-and-seek across the winter mountains of North Carolina and Tennessee. Each created a memoir of their wartime and prison experiences: Richardson's *The Secret Service, The Field, The Dungeon, and The Escape* and Browne's *Four Years in Secessia*. Richardson's is by far the more readable.

On the same day that the *Tribune* correspondents reached safety in Knoxville, Commissioner Ould, a bit out of touch with current events, had sent a note to the captive Pollard: "I am compelled by a sense of duty to decline the exchange," he wrote. "I have already refused to exchange Richardson for half a dozen different named parties. . . ." [27] One might wonder what role Pollard's open antagonism to the Davis administration had played in this decision.

If the major Union "casualty" of Chancellorsville was the removal of General Hooker as commander of the Army of the Potomac, the South lost the man widely regarded as its best combat commander, Thomas J. Jackson, a.k.a "Stonewall." Jackson was celebrated on both sides by a nation that needed heroes, even if among the enemy. Following the Battle of Cross Keys in June 1862, an admiring Charles Henry Webb of the New York *Times* had written:

> One thing is certain, Jackson is equally eminent as a strategist and tactician. He handles his army like a whip, making it crack in out of the way corners where you scarcely thought the lash would reach. This retreat of his, if retreat it can be called, has been conducted with marvelous skill., He has not much mercy on his men, but he gets extraordinary marches out of them on very short commons. [28]

Six months later, and a few days after he had created his verbal portrait of Lee for the London *Times*, Francis Lawley met Jackson: "We had been taught to expect a morose, reserved, distant reception," he wrote in his letter of November 21, 1862; "we found the most genial, courteous, and forthcoming of companions. A bright, piercing, blue eye, a slightly aquiline nose, a thin, tall sinewy frame . . . a most undemonstrative, reticent man, doubtless, in all that regards his vocation of a soldier. . . ." Lawley acknowledged the common image of Jackson as frequently "wrapt in prayer," and echoed Webb's laudatory comment:

> Throughout this war it has been the practice of General Jackson to throw himself, disregarding his own inferiority of numbers, upon large bodies of his enemy, and the day is ordinarily half-won by the suddenness and desperation of the attack. His usual policy then is to retire, upon which the correspondents of the Northern journals,

who upon the day of General Jackson's onslaught have been half-frightened out of their lives, announce with their usual fanfares a great Federal victory, and joy and exultation are universal. In a few days, however, when the Federals have reached some spot where it suits General Jackson to attack them, he pounces upon them again, and frequently the very fame of his second approach drives his opponents to a precipitate retreat without fighting, if the ground admits of such a possibility. The upshot of nearly a year and a half of General Jackson's conduct of the war, frequently at the head of no more than a handful of men, is that no permanent foothold has been gained by the Federals in the Valley, and that, at will, General Jackson has run his opponents, sometimes including at once two or three Federal Generals of rank, out of the Valley. [29]

The January 1863 issue of the *Southern Literary Messenger* offered: "But place him on the battlefield—let the cannon begin to thunder, the small arms to rattle, and the sabers to flash in the sunlight—and the quiet farmer, the awkward, calculating pedagogue, becomes a hero . . . full of fire and energy, quick as lightning and terrible as the thunderbolt. . . . He is the idol of the people, and is the object of greater enthusiasm than any other military chieftain of our day. . . . No man possess[es] a kinder heart or larger humanity . . . ."

Jackson died on May 10, 1863. He had been hit, twice, by the accidental shots of fellow rebels, lost his left arm, and succumbed to pneumonia a week later. He was thirty-nine years old.

Every man who possesses the slightest particle of magnanimity must admire the qualities for which Stonewall Jackson was celebrated— his heroism, his bravery, his sublime devotion, his purity of character. He is not the first instance of a good man devoting himself to a bad cause. . . . [30]

That, from John Forney's Washington *Chronicle*, in an epitaph of sorts. Some who were closer to Jackson saw him in a different light: merciless, unbending, unforgiving, a general who took discipline beyond anything Braxton Bragg had ever attempted. Jackson is reported to have executed summarily—within twenty minutes of the offense—a soldier who entered a civilian house against orders, and "used insulting language to the women of the family." [31]

Robert L. Dabney, who for a time had been Jackson's chief of staff, wrote, "the character of his thinking was illustrated by the declaration which he made upon assuming this command, that it was the true policy of the South to take no prisoners in this war. He affirmed that this would be in the end truest humanity, because it would shorten the contest, and prove economical of the blood of both parties." Dabney reported that when a Confederate officer expressed regret that so many Union cavalrymen had been killed in an unsuccessful attack, Jackson asked, "Why do you say you saw those Federal soldiers fall with regret?" The officer explained that their bravery merited a better fate. "No," said Jackson coldly, "shoot them all: I do not wish them to be brave." Confederate diarist Mary Chesnut affirmed as his view that "There cannot be a Christian soldier. Kill or be killed, that is their trade, or they are a failure. Stonewall was a fanatic." [32]

Brig. Gen. Alexander Lawton told Mrs. Chesnut that Jackson "had no sympathy with human infirmity. . . . He classed all who were weak and weary, who fainted by the wayside, as men wanting in patriotism. . . .[he] did not value human life where he had an object to accomplish. . . . there was much fudge in the talk of his soldier's love for him. . . . They feared him and obeyed him to the death. Faith they had in him, stronger than death. . . . I doubt if he had their love." [33]

General Lawton may have been mistaken on that last point, but he was on the mark when he added, "And now that they begin to see a few more years of Stonewall Jackson would have freed us from the yoke of the hateful Yankees, they deify him." [34]

That deification came swiftly. A biographical sketch published soon after his death asserted that Jackson "laid down his life for his men." The pneumonia that killed Jackson had been contracted, the author said on no known evidence, because the general had placed his own cape over a sleeping officer the night before Chancellorsville. A genuine eulogy in the Lynchburg *Virginian* claimed that Jackson "was just as kind, as gentle and as tender, as he was stern and inexorable in his requirements when duty and the interests of his country demanded, and as he was lion-like in battle." [35]

The *Southern Illustrated News* predicted, "The literature of the future will be rich with the inspiration of his career. Poets will sing of him, and romanticists will weave his deeds into the warp and woof of fiction." [36]

The cold-blooded killer become romantic hero. Next Chapter.

19 / The Poet as Historian, I

Just a few words here in regard to "Barbara Frietchie,"
a touching poem which sprang full-armed from the loyal brain
of Mr. Whittier. An old woman, by that now immortal name,
did live in Frederick in those days, but she was eighty-four years old and
bed-ridden; she never saw General Jackson,
and General Jackson never saw her.

—"Stonewall Jackson in Maryland," *Century Magazine*,
June 1886 [1]

NEWSPAPERMEN AND THEIR ACCOUNTS, alike, have largely turned to dust; the historian has taken to the field, along with the novelist and movie-maker, to shape our impressions of the war. And yet, we all grew up with impressions of the war, formed before we could read, shaped from the cradle by the songs and poems that became a part of our cultural heritage. Some of the songs have become so familiar that we may have forgotten their origins in the war. "Tenting on the Old Camp Ground" is not a camping-out song.

Poetry was common staple of the nineteenth-century press. Most of it was not very good, although some of the writers had better-than-average talent: some had established reputations before the war, some scribbled their verse during the war, some wrote poetic footnotes after the war. Some of the finest poetry of the day—of any day—was written by such newspapermen as William Cullen Bryant (editor of the New York *Sun*), Henry Timrod (who covered the battle of Shiloh for the Charleston *Mercury* and became known as "the poet laureate of the Confederacy"), and Walt Whitman (former editor of the Brooklyn *Eagle*). Their efforts, while transcendent, were not directly connected with Civil War journalism.

But two Civil War poems merit review, two poems that have become more a part of history than history itself: "Barbara Frietchie," here, and "Sheridan's Ride," explored in chapter 21.

Barbara Frietchie.

On August 24, 1863, *Atlantic* magazine editor James Thomas Fields sent a note to the newspaperman-poet John Greenleaf Whittier: "Barbara is most welcome, and I will find room for it in the October number, most certainly. . . .You were right in thinking I should like it, for so I do, as I like few things in this world. . . . Inclosed is a check for fifty dollars, but Barbara's weight should be in gold." [2]

"Barbara" is one of the best-known of all Civil War poems. Indeed, according to Whittier biographer Whitman Bennet, it may be "the greatest modern short ballad in the English language" (although twentieth-century critic Edmund Wilson called it "poetic claptrap.") [3]

Up from the meadows rich with corn,
Clear in the cool September morn,

The clustered spires of Frederick stand
Green-walled by the hills of Maryland.

Round about them orchards sweep,
Apple and peach tree fruited deep,

Fair as the garden of the Lord
To the eyes of the famished rebel horde,

On that pleasant morn of the early fall
When Lee marched over the mountain wall,

Over the mountains winding down,
Horse and foot, into Frederick town.

Forty flags with their silver stars,
Forty flags with their crimson bars,

Flapped in the morning wind: the sun
Of noon looked down, and saw not one.

Up rose old Barbara Frietchie then,
Bowed with her fourscore years and ten;

Bravest of all in Frederick town,
She took up the flag the men hauled down;

In her attic window the staff she set,
To show that one heart was loyal yet.

Up the street came the rebel tread.
Stonewall Jackson riding ahead.

Under his slouched hat left and right
He glanced: the old flag met his sight.

"Halt!"—the dust-brown ranks stood fast;
"Fire!"—out blazed the rifle-blast.

It shivered the window, pane and sash;
It rent the banner with seam and gash.

Quick, as it fell, from the broken staff
Dame Barbara snatched the silken scarf;

She leaned far out on the window-sill,
And shook it forth with a royal will.

"Shoot, if you must, this old gray head,
But spare your country's flag," she said.

A shade of sadness, a blush of shame,
Over the face of the leader came;

The nobler nature within him stirred
To life and that woman's deed and word:

"Who touches a hair of yon gray head
Dies like a dog! March on!" he said.

The poem, likewise, marched on—through nine more verses, two of
which honored the memory of Stonewall Jackson:

Barbara Frietchie's work is o'er,
And the Rebel rides on his raids no more.

Honor to here! And let a tear
Fall, for her sake, on Stonewall's bier.

The poem was inspired by a story of doubtful accuracy, complaint
about which was destined to haunt Whittier ever after; a storm of protest
arose almost from the moment of publication in the October *Atlantic*.
Residents of the town, relatives of Dame Barbara, companions of General
Jackson, all questioned the truth of the tale, and the questions continued

for more than a quarter of a century. In a letter published in the Baltimore *Sun* on August 27, 1874, Frietchie's nephew Valerius Ebert said that his aunt had been confined to her bed and could hardly have been snatching flags in and out of attic windows. For a lecture on October 23, 1884, Frederick native (and Confederate general officer) Bradley T. Johnson drew up a map, showing Jackson's route through the town and the location of Dame Frietchie's house, some three hundred yards off that path. "I had known Barbara Frietchie all my life," he said. "I knew where she lived as well as I knew the town clock." [4]

Whittier remained steadfast in defending the "truth" of the poem. Francis F. Browne, assembling a collection of Civil War poetry in 1885, asked the poet for a comment. Whittier responded, "Of the substantial truth of the heroism of Barbara Frietchie I can have no doubt. . . . Barbara Frietchie was the boldest and most outspoken Unionist in Frederick, and manifested it to the Rebel army in an unmistakable manner." [5]

The controversy was reignited in the summer of 1886 with the publication of the poetry collection (*Bugles and Echoes*) and, especially, Henry Kyd Douglas's reminiscence, "Stonewall Jackson in Maryland," in the June issue of the *Century* magazine's "Battle and Leaders" series:

Just a few words here in regard to "Barbara Frietchie," a touching poem which sprang full-armed from the loyal brain of Mr. Whittier. An old woman, by that now immortal name, did live in Frederick in those days, but she was eighty-four years old and bed-ridden; she never saw General Jackson, and General Jackson never saw her. I was with him every minute of the time he was in that city,—he was there only twice,—and nothing like the scene so graphically described by the poet ever happened. The story will perhaps live, as Mr. Whittier has boasted, until it gets beyond the reach of correction.

Whittier again rose to the defense, in a letter dated June 10 and published in the September issue of the *Century*. Stung by criticism, the gentle Quaker denied any propensity for "boasting," and affirmed: "The story was no invention of mine. It came to me from sources which I regarded as entirely reliable; it had been published in newspapers, and had gained public credence in Washington and Maryland before my poem was written. I had no reason to doubt its accuracy then, and I am still constrained to believe that it had foundation in fact. If I thought otherwise, I should not hesitate to express it. . . . " When Douglas's article was reprinted in the book version of *Battles and Leaders*, the paragraph was softened. The assertion that the poem "sprang full-blown" was deleted, and the "boasted" sentence was replaced with "Mr. Whittier must have been misinformed as to the incident." [6]

Whittier's "entirely reliable" source was a lady novelist, Mrs. Emma
D. E. N. Southworth, who had passed him a tale then making the rounds
in Washington. In truth, *she* gave him the story "full-blown," wanting
only the poet's touch:

> When Lee's army occupied Frederick, the only Union flag displayed
> in the city was held from an attic window by Mrs. Barbara Frietchie,
> a widow lady, aged ninety-seven years. . . . When . . . the advance
> of Lee's army, led by the formidable rebel general "Stonewall" Jack-
> son, entered Frederick, every Union flag was lowered, and the hal-
> liards [*sic*] cut; every store and dwellinghouse was closed; the
> inhabitants had retreated indoors; the streets were deserted. . . . But
> Mrs. Barbara Frietchie, taking one of the Union flags, went up to
> the top of her house, opened a garret window, and held it forth. The
> rebel army marched up the street, saw the flag; the order was given,
> "Halt! Fire!" and a volley was discharged. . . . The flagstaff was part-
> ly broken, so that the flag drooped; the old lady drew it in, broke off
> the fragment, and, taking the stump with the flag still attached in
> her hand, stretched herself out as far as she could, held the stars
> and stripes at arm's length, waving over the rebels, and cried out in
> a voice of indignation and sorrow: "Fire at this old head, then, boys;
> it is not more venerable than your flag." They fired no more; they
> passed in silence and with downcast looks; and she secured the flag
> in its place, where it waved unmolested during the whole of the
> rebel occupation of the city. [7]

The "heroic old lady," Mrs. Southworth concluded, "died a few days
after; some thought she died of joy at the presence of the Union army,
and some that she died of excitement and fatigue. . . . " Mrs. Southworth
was easily the most popular American romance novelist of her day, with
at least sixty titles to her credit; she could now add coauthorship of one
of the best-known American poems. As Whitter acknowledged in a note
to Mrs. Southworth, September 8, 1863: "I heartily thank thee for thy
kind letter and its inclosed message. It ought to have fallen into better
hands, but I have just written a little ballad of 'Barbara Frietchie,' which
will appear in the next 'Atlantic.' If it is good for anything thee deserve all
the credit of it." [8]

Responding to the rancorous exchanges of that summer of 1886, the
Philadelphia *Times* assigned George O. Seilheimer to assemble an investi-
gative report. He wrote that Barbara's niece and adopted daughter, Mrs.
Handschue, affirmed that Mrs. Frietchie waved no flags at Jackson's
men—but asserted that she *did* wave a flag, six days later, when Burnside's
troops marched through the town. Barbara's grand niece, Mrs. Abbott
told that story:

Aunt . . . and cousin Harriett . . . were on the front porch, and aunt was leaning on the cane she always carried. When the troops marched along aunt waved her hand, and cheer after cheer when up from the men as they saw her. Some even ran into the yard. "God bless you, old lady," "Let me take you by the hand," "May you live long, you dear old soul," cried one after the other, as they rushed into the yard. . . . cousin Harriett Yoner said, "Aunt ought to have a flag to wave." The flag was hidden in the family Bible, and cousin Harriet got it and gave it to aunt. Then she waved the flag to the men and they cheered her as they went by . . . [9]

Mrs. Abbott did not explain Dame Barbara's timely release from the "confinement" noted in 1874 by nephew Ebert. More to the point, however, Seilheimer identified "Mrs. Mary S. Quantrell, another Frederick woman" as the defiantly patriotic flag-waver, but stated that "Jackson took no notice . . . and as Mrs. Quantrell was not fortunate enough to find a poet to celebrate her deed she never became famous." [10]

In another letter to the editor of the *Century*, two years later—still protesting—Whittier wrote that he "also received letters from several other responsible persons wholly or partially confirming the story, among whom was the late Dorothea L. Dix." [11] However, while pleading his case, Whittier acknowledged the controversy in a head-note to accompany later editions of the poem:

This poem, was written in strict conformity to the account of the incident as I had it from respectable and trustworthy sources. It has since been the subject of a good deal of conflicting testimony, and the story was probably incorrect in some of its details. It is admitted that Barbara Frietchie was no myth . . . that when the Confederates halted before her house, and entered her dooryard, she denounced them in vigorous language, shook her cane in their faces, and drove them out; and when General Burnside's troops followed close upon Jackson's, she waved her flag and cheered them. It is stated that Mary Quantrell, a brave and loyal lady in another part of the city, did wave her flag in sight of the Confederates. It is possible that there has been a blending of the two incidents. [12]

Or, perhaps, the blending of several *other* incidents. There seem to have been at least two bona fide flag events in or about Frederick at about the same time, witnessed and certified, the first of which comes in three slightly different versions. One is set forth in Charles Osborne's 1992 biography of Jubal Early. His brigade was marching through the mostly deserted streets of Frederick—had they expected the Marylanders to flock to the cause, they were quickly disabused—when they came upon two little girls, perhaps ten and six. The elder was waving a small flag, and repeating the phrase, "Hurrah for the stars and stripes." The soldiers were amused, except for one man of unknown provenance who made a move to take away the flag. Early called him a fool, and told him to leave the girl alone: "she could do no harm with her 'candy flag.'" [13]

A second version of the same incident, adding detail, was told in Lenoir Chambers's 1958 biography of Stonewall Jackson. The eldest girl, aged "eleven or twelve," was saying, "Hurrah for the Stars and Stripes! Down with the Stars and Bars!" to the amusement of the marching soldiers. "A one-legged man who had followed the army on horseback—General Early thought he had been drinking—said something of an uncomplimentary nature about the girls, and Early shooed him away." [14]

In his 1899 memoir *I Rode with Stonewall* (not published until 1940), Henry Kyd Douglas offered a third version of the young-girl flag-waving tale:

In Middletown two very pretty girls with ribbons of red, white and blue in their hair and small Union flags in their hands, came out of their house as we passed, ran to the curb-stone, and laughingly waved their colors defiantly in the face of the General. He bowed and lifted his cap and with a quiet smile, said to his staff, "We evidently have no friends in this town." The young girls, abashed, turned away and lowered their tiny battle flags. That is about the way he would have treated Barbara Frietchie! [15]

Douglas also suggested that, had Whittier realized that Dame Frietchie's sentiments were actually on the other side, "his fervent desire to make her immortal would have cooled off more quickly and he would not have been so anxious for that poem to live." [16] However, Douglas is the only person to suggest that the allegedly rebellious Barbara was a rebel.

The last Frederick flag-waver was reported by Early's biographer: in the western part of the city, a woman, who Early described as "coarse and dirty," popped out of an alley with an equally dirty U.S. flag. A passing member of Hays's Louisiana brigade made comment, "dom'd old dirty rag," whereupon the woman popped back out of sight. [17]

After about four days in town, the Confederate army marched out of Frederick and headed toward destiny at Antietam Creek. The men were singing and the the band was playing—another irony in a war filled with ironies—"The Girl I Left Behind Me." [18]

Several of Whittier's biographers have tried to separate the controversy from significance. "Imaginative art is seldom anchored in precise fact," wrote John A. Pollard in 1949. George Rice Carpenter in 1903 stated that "whether the supposed incident actually occurred or not is of no importance." "Of no importance" of course, except, perhaps, to a historian attempting to assemble a biography of Stonewall Jackson. [19]

And it is in the context of "Jackson," then already a man turned into myth, that the poem had so much resonance. This is myth of a different sort: let us raise the devil to the pantheon; let us show that even the most vigorous champion of the Confederacy may yet, deep down, have some regrets. Well, at the time the poem was written, Stonewall Jackson had been dead for several months. It is far easier to glorify heroic enemies, dead, than enemies alive and deadly.

Barbara Frietchie, aged ninety-six, died three months after the event. She is buried in the Mt. Olivet cemetery in Frederick. Despite the long-since settled facts of the case, such is the lingering power of the poet that the Barbara Frietchie house in Frederick (where the name is spelled *Fritchie*) is today treated as a national monument; Winston Churchill, it is said, once stood in the front yard and recited, line for line, the poem. It is not even the original house, but a 1927 re-creation containing some of the parts of the original, which had been destroyed by flood in 1868. For all his troubles, Whittier had been given a cane made from a salvaged timber.

Mary S. Quantrell, whomever she may have been and wherever she may have lived, is long forgotten. The flag from the Bible, a thirty-four-star model, was small, of silk, and is preserved only in an old photograph. The poem survives; the couplet:

> "Who touches a hair on yon gray head
> Dies like a dog! Ride on!" he said.

remains among the best in the language. Even if it is lousy history.

20 / Watershed

Oh, you dead, who at Gettysburg have baptized with your blood the
second birth of freedom in America, how you are to be envied!
I rise from a grave whose wet clay I have passionately kissed and I look
up and see Christ spanning this battlefield with his feet
and reaching fraternal and loving up to heaven. His right hand opens
the gates of Paradise—with his left, he sweetly beckons to these
mutilated, bloody, swollen forms to ascend.
—Samuel Wilkeson, New York *Times*, July 6, 1863

IN THE MIDDLE OF JUNE 1863, the Confederate army led by Robert E. Lee was still moving northward, intentions unknown but reasonably predictable, preceded by a wave of panic among civilians desperate to get out of the way—and newsmen desperate to get near the story. At Harrisburg, Pennsylvania, directly on the presumed line of march, the state capitol had been completely denuded of every thing of value, from the portraits of the governors to the books in the library, all packed in freight cars and made ready for instant departure, while representatives of at least twenty out-of-town newspapers tripped over each other trying to chase down "reliable sources." They were not very effective. The New York *Times* took all of the reports issued from Harrisburg on one day, facetiously added the numbers of "positively" confirmed rebel units on the march, and came up with "a total strength of the enemy of not less than five hundred thousand men." Lee's actual strength was about 89,000. [1]

When Maj. Gen. George Gordon Meade took command of the Army of the Potomac on June 28, 1863, the *Herald* acknowledged the change, but could not let go of a favorite theme:

Many liked General Hooker and had faith in him; most believe in the ability of General Meade to fill his place. It may come inopportunely, but I must say that General McClellan is the man the rank and file of the army want at their head. They cannot get over worshiping him and clamoring for him. [2]

By the time that item appeared in the July 2 *Herald*, Meade was two-thirds of the way through the watershed battle of the war: Gettysburg. On the same day that Meade replaced Hooker, Lee had been diverted from his objective—which indeed had been Harrisburg—when he learned that the Army of the Potomac was advancing from the east.

By the time the battle had ended, so, too, was finished the Confederate invasion of the North, although this fact was not immediately apparent to newspaper readers in the South. Southern reporting was delayed by geography and weather—the Potomac was flooded and temporarily impassable—and for several days the only information available in Richmond came from Yankee newspapers. Their glowing reports of "victory" were disbelieved, especially when a telegram came in from a station agent at Martinsburg with the "news" that an all-but-annihilated Federal army was retreating toward Baltimore, with General Lee in hot pursuit. The Savannah *Republican* called it "The Best News of the War," with Meade's army surrounded by "one of the most brilliant movements on record." [3] It was to be at least a week before accurate reports began to reach the Southern newspapers.

Northern reporting was hampered by problems with the telegraph: the line had been cut in numerous places by Stuart's men just before the action began. Uriah Painter, Philadelphia *Inquirer*, had to ride to Baltimore to file a story of the first day's fighting. While passing through Hanover on his way to the battlefield, Aaron Homer Byington of the New York *Tribune* learned of the breaks in the line, rounded up a local telegrapher, a battery, some wire, and a railroad handcar, and took a team out to repair the gaps. The telegraph operator was persuaded to grant Byington and a reporter for the Philadelphia *Press* (who had helped with the repairs) a two-day monopoly on the wire.

Byington headed for Gettysburg, sixteen miles away, gathered information, rode back to Hanover, and filed a dispatch on the first two days' fighting. Byington's message, signed with his name, reached the War Department in Washington, which, to that point, had heard nothing of the battle. The president, then hovering over the telegrapher's desk, asked, "Who is Byington?" No one knew. They sent a message to Hanover: "Dispatch about a battle received. Who are you?" Byington replied, offering Secretary of the Navy Gideon Welles as a reference. Roused out of his bed at midnight, the secretary acknowledged his acquaintance with the fellow former Connecticut journalist. The War Department sent another message to Byington, asking that he turn the line over to official traffic, but gave him assurance that his own copy could be sent during breaks in transmission. [4]

Meanwhile, the other Northern journalists were scurrying around, looking for some way to file their copy. Frank Chapman arrived in Baltimore early on the morning of July 4, ahead of any others, persuaded the local manager of a telegraph office to open early, and started sending his copy to the *Herald*. Just as he was about to leave the office to get more information, T. C. Grey of the *Tribune* rode up with his own copy, whereupon Chapman pulled out his pocket Bible to the page beginning, "In the beginning. . . ." He told the manager, "just keep your men busy sending this until I get back." He kept the office tied up all day, alternating scripture with Chapman. [5]

Frustrated, other journalists headed for the home office by horse, boat, and train. Coffin traveled all the way to Boston, sending paragraphs by telegram at each major stop along the way and delivering the bulk of his copy on arrival. Reid traveled to Cincinnati by way of Philadelphia—a roundabout route, but the only one with an open rail connection. Reid's report added one bit of color: after the fighting had ended, "A band came marching in over the hillside; on the evening air its notes floated out—significant melody—'Hail to the Chief.' 'Ah! General Meade,' said W[ilkeson], 'you're in very great danger of being President of the United States.'" [6]

The most memorable bit of reporting to come out of Gettysburg was that of Sam Wilkeson himself, then working for the New York *Times*. It was written as he sat by the body of his nineteen-year-old son, wounded in the leg and left to die, unattended, in a barn:

Who can write the history of a battle whose eyes are immovably fastened upon a central figure of transcendingly absorbing interest—the dead body of an oldest born son, crushed by a shell in a position where a battery should never have been sent, and abandoned to death in a building where surgeons dared not to stay?

The battle of Gettysburg! . . .

Oh, you dead, who at Gettysburg have baptized with your blood the second birth of freedom in America, how you are to be envied! I rise from a grave whose wet clay I have passionately kissed and I look up and see Christ spanning this battlefield with his feet and reaching fraternal and loving up to heaven. His right hand opens the gates of Paradise—with his left, he sweetly beckons to these mutilated, bloody, swollen forms to ascend. [7]

July was a good month for the Union. The day after the shooting ended at Gettysburg, General Grant accepted the formal surrender of the Confederate citadel at Vicksburg. It was not a good month for the city of New York, however, which erupted in riots in which almost a hundred people may have been killed, either by the rioters or by police and soldiers putting down the riot. Estimates vary, but most evidence does not support contemporary newspaper reports of "a thousand" dead. The riots were ostensibly in protest over the first drawing for the draft, but most of the violence was directed against blacks and newspaper offices. The *Tribune* was attacked several times and broken into at least once. Both the *Tribune* and the *Times*, located across the street from each other, turned themselves into arsenals—the up-to-date *Times* acquired a pair of Gatling guns, placed in full view of the street, one of which was manned for a time by editor Henry Raymond himself. The staff of the theoretically pacifist *Tribune* knew so little about firearms that the ammunition they procured would not fit their rifles; however, a brave show at all the windows served the purpose.

The Union record for the rest of the year was mixed. Bragg scored a Confederate victory over Rosecrans at Chickamauga at the end of September, but Grant and the Union won at Chattanooga two months later. There, Hooker redeemed some of his lost luster by taking his forces to the top of Lookout Mountain. Quartermaster General Meigs called it "Hooker's battle . . . above the clouds"; a phrase that caught the public fancy. Grant later wrote that "The battle of Lookout Mountain is one of the romances of the war. There was no such battle, and no action even worthy to be called a battle on Lookout Mountain. It is all poetry." [8]

Cadwallader agreed with Grant, calling it "a long, protracted, magnificent skirmish from 8:00 A.M. till dark." Well after dark, actually; a reporter for the Cincinnati *Gazette*, watching from the city far below, captured some of the magic:

That night, in front of General Thomas's headquarters in Chattanooga, I stood watching the combat going on, away up there upon that mighty wall of limestone; and the long line of fires which marked the course of our entrenchments; the shouts of the combatants yelling defiance at each other; the fierce jets of flame from the muzzles of a thousand muskets; the spluttering sound of the discharges, muffled by distance; the great brow of the mountain looming dark and awful through the night; the single signal light upon the extreme crest, which, waving to and fro, revealed to the rebel leader on Mission Ridge, the take of disaster and woe—all these days together formed one of the scene in that wonderful three day's drama, which will linger forever in my memory, haunting even my dreams. The battle that night upon Lookout Mountain! Seen from

Chattanooga, it was the realization of olden traditions; and super-natural armies contended in the air! [9]

The censor at first refused to let Cadwallader file his own dispatch for the Chicago *Times*. Cadwallader appealed to Grant, who without even reading the copy, wrote an authorization on the back of the manuscript.

Three days before the battle at Chattanooga began, and about five months after the Battle of Gettysburg, the government dedicated a cemetery in honor of the fallen. There is a myth that Lincoln scribbled the Gettysburg Address on the back of an envelope en route to the ceremonies and that, once delivered, the world did in fact take "little note" of his remarks. It has been known for some time that the first part of this myth is wrong—the address went through several drafts, copies of which abound and none of which are on envelopes—but many accept without question such reports as that in Philip Knightley's 1975 study of war correspondents, *The First Casualty*:

> No correspondent attending the dedication of a national cemetery at Gettysburg took any notice of President Lincoln beginning, "Four score and seven years ago. . . ." At the best, they reported, as did the Cincinnati *Commercial*, "The President rises slowly, draws from his pocket a paper, and when the commotion subsides, in a sharp, unmusical treble voice, reads the brief and pithy remarks," and, at the worst, ended their accounts of the event with the single sentence "The President also spoke." [10]

At the best, Knightley offers interesting anecdotes about war correspondents and a reasonable set of notes to aid the serious researcher; at the worst, this London-based Australian writer continues the European bias displayed in the report of the London *Times*, published December 4, 1863:

> The inauguration of the cemetery at Gettysburg was an imposing ceremony, only rendered somewhat flat by the nature of Mr. Everett's lecture, and ludicrous by some of the luckless sallies of that poor President Lincoln. . . . The Hon. Edward Everett is a lady's orator . . . on all occasions where words are wanted—not thoughts—where feelings are to be tickled—not roused— nothing can be more refreshing or pleasing than to hear and see Mr. Everett. Here, however, mere rhetoric was out of place, and whatever effect the lecture may have had on the feminine part of the audience, which mustered

rather strong on the spot, there is no doubt that it reads tame beyond belief, and is such a performance as would scarcely win the
prize for composition over the common run of under-graduates.

Knightley also displays a lack of diligence in researching his subject.
It would not have been too difficult to discover that the press of the day
not only mentioned the president's remarks, but also in large measure saluted their merit. Even the London *Times*, the day before the above-
quoted paragraphs, began a somewhat foreshortened (by about a quarter)
version of the address with—yes—"Four score and seven years ago." The
New York *Times* printed the text, in full, on the front page.

Frank Leslie's Illustrated News reported:

The ceremonies began with a prayer the Rev. Dr. Stockton, Chaplain of the House of Representatives. The Hon. Edward Everett
then delivered his address, one of those classic, eloquent orations
which have no equal in this country. Recalling the honors paid by
Athens to her fallen brave, he spoke of the occasion which called
them together, of the importance to all of the great battle, and what
that victory effected. After glancing at the early history of the war,
he gave an elaborate and highly-wrought account of the battle.

At the close President Lincoln addressed the assembly:

"Fourscore and seven years ago our fathers brought forth upon
this continent a new nation, conceived in liberty and dedicated to
the proposition that all men are created equal. . . ." [11]

Leslie's account continued with the balance of the president's remarks,
although not verbatim, as the reporter seems to have experienced some
difficulty reading his notes: "The world will little know and nothing
remember of what we see here, but we cannot forget what these brave
men did here" and "We Imbibe increased devotion for that cause for
which they gave here the last full measure of devotion; we might here resolve that they shall not have died in vain; that the nation shall, under
God, have a new birth of freedom, and that the Government of the
people, for the people, and for all people, shall not perish from earth." [12]

Harper's Weekly reproduced little, but fully recognized the value of
Lincoln's spare prose:

The President and the Cabinet were there, with famous soldiers and
civilians. The oration by Mr. Everett was smooth and cold. Delivered, doubtless, with his accustomed graces, it yet wanted one stir-
ring thought, one vivid picture, one thrilling appeal.

The few words of the President were from the heart to the
heart. They can not be read, even, without kindling emotion. "The

world will little note nor long remember what we say here, but it can never forget what they did here." It was as simple and felicitous and earnest a word as was ever spoken. [13]

The winter of 1863–64 brought a watershed of a different sort: the *Herald* floated a trial "Grant for President" balloon, noting the "affection of the soldiers everywhere for General Grant" and their "determination that the next President be a military man" [14], and Congress reinstituted the rank of lieutenant general, with Grant appointed to the post. Halleck continued as the administrative head of the army, but Grant was now running the show.

General Grant arrived in Washington on March 7 to take up his new duties, and by March 26 had established his headquarters in the field, at Culpeper, Virginia. At almost the same moment, Secretary of War Stanton once again began curtailing media access to the army, refusing to issue new passes even to reporters—such as the *Herald*'s Frank Chapman —who had long been with the army but temporarily had left the camps for a bit of rest and relaxation. The *Herald*, thus left without a senior correspondent in the field, devised a clever solution: hire Sylvanus Cadwallader as the *Herald*'s chief correspondent. Grant's favorite reporter had no trouble arranging access for himself and the rest of the *Herald*'s team.

The New York *Tribune* had a similar problem, as the newspaper's entire Army of the Potomac staff was in Washington on the day Stanton's order was made public. Sam Wilkeson, who had left the *Times* and now was back in his old job as the *Tribune*'s Washington bureau chief, challenged his men to find a way to get back to the army. Two of them rode the sixty miles to Grant's headquarters and simply slipped through the picket lines. The New York *Times* asked Grant's congressman, Elihu B. Washburne, for a hand; he escorted William Swinton to the headquarters and introduced the correspondent to Grant, who had not before met this eastern theater veteran, as an "historian."

In the normal course of affairs, a military commander upset with an offending correspondent would simply banish him from camp, and the correspondent, or his editor—in *their* normal course of affairs, would respond in kind, but not kindly, in print.

However, on one unusual occasion, the prescribed punishment was public humiliation and the response of the newspapermen was . . . silence—a silence with, perhaps, profound consequence. In late May 1864, General Meade still commanded the Army of the Potomac and was headed, steadily, toward Richmond. Grant, as general in chief, generally exercised supervisory, but not tactical, control. At one point, however, during the Wilderness campaign, the Philadelphia *Inquirer* reported the (unsubstantiated) charge that:

> History will record, but newspapers cannot that on one eventful night during the present campaign Grant's presence saved the army, and the nation too: not that General Meade was on the point of committing a blunder unwittingly, but his devotion to his country made him loth to risk her last army on what he deemed a chance. Grant assumed the responsibility, and we are still on to Richmond. [15]

One of Grant's staff officers would note, after the war, that "Meade was possessed of an excitable temper which under irritating circumstances became almost ungovernable," and the accusation of timidity in the face of uncertain odds was, most certainly, "irritating." Meade demanded to know the identity of the reporter—it was Edward Crapsey, soon hauled forward and standing before the general. The general demanded to know the source of the allegation. The reporter said it was "the talk of the camp." [16]

Meade's immediate reaction might be imagined; his next move was to order Crapsey to be drummed out of the army, while the band played "Rogue's March" and the correspondent was set backward on a mule and decorated with placards, front and back, proclaiming him to be a "Libeler of the Press." In a letter to his wife that evening, Meade boasted that the event was "much to the delight of the whole army, for the race of the newspaper correspondents is universally despised by the soldiers." [17]

When Crapsey reached Washington, a group of his friends, journalists all, incensed, vowed to treat Meade as a nonperson. His name would be deleted from any published general order; he would not be mentioned in any dispatch unless in connection with a defeat; and all military success was to be credited to General Grant. As coconspirator Whitelaw Reid explained to his editor (in a letter that he submitted for publication, but that his editor wisely elected to file away instead):

> Major Gen. Meade may have the physical courage which bulls & bull dogs have; but he is as leprous with moral cowardice as the brute that kicks a helpless cripple on the street, or beats his wife at home. [18]

The press indeed pretty much ignored Meade for at least six months, except in the most negative of connotations. "Historian" William Swinton, unwittingly, gave them a golden opportunity when was banished from the Army of the Potomac—according to his employer, the New York *Times*, for upsetting General Meade with allegedly inaccurate reporting.

Major-Gen. Meade accuses Mr. Swinton of having "forwarded for publication *incorrect statements* respecting the operations of the troops." What these statements were,—in what respect they were incorrect—or what means were afforded of correcting them, we are not informed. Gen. Meade must have a very vague idea of the duties of a correspondent, and of the difficulties which attend their performance, if he requires perfect and exact accuracy in regard to all the details of army operations, as the condition of remaining within his lines. He has not always found it easy to be thus exact in his own official reports, even after he had taken some weeks to compile and prepare them. . . . Judging from Gen. Meade's previous action in similar cases, Mr. Swinton is quite as likely to have been excluded for being too accurate as for any other offence. [19]

The editor took the typographic equivalent of a deep breath, and added: "If [Mr. Swinton] had been a little more disposed to pander to the personal vanity and the uneasy jealousy of Officers, he might have had a longer career as a correspondent, but it would scarcely have been more honorable to himself or more serviceable to the country." [20]

In truth, Swinton's letters contained some errors; however, he was banished not for the alleged sin of "inaccurate reporting" but as the culmination of a series of relatively more serious offenses. On May 6, he was caught eavesdropping on a meeting between Generals Grant and Meade, and at the end of the month he was challenged, in essence, for bribing a telegraph operator to gain access to confidential documents.

In truth—Swinton's expulsion was recommended by *Burnside*, *Grant* issued the order on July 1, and *Meade* merely forwarded it to the provost marshal. However, in large part because of the journalist's vendetta, it was Meade who took the hit.

An 1878 letter to the editor of the Philadelphia *Weekly Times*, signed by a writer identified only as "W" but who may have been Sam Wilkeson, said, "I have always thought and often said . . . that Crapsey's punishment made General Grant President of the United States." Professor J. Cutler Andrews, in his otherwise impeccable *The North Reports the Civil War*, agreed, in suggesting that "It is just possible that Meade's ill-treatment of Crapsey and the repercussions that followed cost the Philadelphia general the Presidency of the United States." [21]

Well . . . a nice thought, but un unlikely outcome. Meade, born in Spain of American parents, did not quite qualify for the office, as the "natural born citizen" clause of the Constitution is generally understood.

21 / The Poet as Historian, II

Up from the south at break of day,
Bringing to Winchester fresh dismay,
The affrighted air with a shudder bore,
Like a herald in haste to the chieftain's door,
The terrible grumble, and rumble, and roar,
Telling the battle was on once more,
And Sheridan twenty miles away.

—Thomas Buchanan Read, "Sheridan's Ride" [1]

By THE SUMMER OF 1864, the North had become war weary, and opposition press and politicians were pressing hard for a settlement with the South. This being the year of a presidential election, the Democrats had nominated General McClellan on a "peace" platform (which he disavowed), the insubordinate now raised up to challenge the commander in chief. General Frémont threatened to run as the candidate for a splinter party, but changed his mind.

Then, within a five-week period in August and September, Adm. David Farragut's victory at Mobile Bay, Sherman's capture of Atlanta, and Gen. Philip Sheridan's defeat of the Confederates at Winchester, reinvigorated the flagging spirits of Northern voters. However, one final event stood above all and gave the nudge to put many into the Lincoln camp. Just over two weeks before the election, Sheridan turned a burgeoning defeat into total victory with a classic display of leadership, and twelve days later, painter-poet James Buchanan Read turned some enthusiastic newspaper coverage into something close to myth, in a poem widely distributed—and published on election day in the New York *Tribune*.

Sheridan's Ride.

Historians call the action the Battle of Cedar Creek; Read called his
poem, "Sheridan's Ride."

Up from the south at break of day,
Bringing to Winchester fresh dismay,
The affrighted air with a shudder bore,
Like a herald in haste to the chieftain's door,
The terrible grumble, and rumble, and roar,
Telling the battle was on once more,
    And Sheridan twenty miles away.

And wider still those billows of war
Thundered along the horizon's bar;
And louder yet into Winchester rolled
The roar of that red sea uncontrolled;
Making the blood of the listener cold,
As he thought of the stake in that fiery fray,
    And Sheridan twenty miles away.

But there is a road from Winchester town,
A good broad highway leading down:
And there, through the flush of the morning light,
A steed as black as the steeds of night
Was seen to pass, as with eagle flight,
As if he knew the terrible need:
He stretched away with his utmost speed:
Hills rose and fell; but his heart was gay,
    With Sheridan fifteen miles away.

Still sprang from those swift hoofs, thundering south,
The dust, like smoke from the cannon's mouth,
Or the trail of a comet, sweeping faster and faster,
Foreboding to traitors the doom of disaster.
The heart of the steed and the heart of the master
Were beating like prisoners assaulting their walls,
Impatient to be where the battle-field calls;
Every nerve of the charger was strained to full play,
    With Sheridan only ten miles away.

Under his spurning feet the road
Like an arrowy Alpine river flowed,
And the landscape sped away behind
Like an ocean flying before the wind;
And the steed, like a bark fed with furnace ire,
Swept on, with his wild eye full of fire.
But lo! he is nearing his heart's desire;
He is snuffing the smoke of the roaring fray,
    With Sheridan only five miles away.

The first that the general saw were the groups
Of stragglers, and then the retreating troops:
What was done? what to do? a glance told him both.
Then striking his spurs, with a terrible oath,
He dashed down the line, 'mid a storm of huzzahs,
And the wave of retreat checked its course there, because
The sight of the master compelled it to pause.
With foam and with dust the black charger was gray;
By the flash of his eye and the red nostril's play,
He seemed to the whole great army to say,
"I have brought you Sheridan all the way
    From Winchester town, to save the day."

Hurrah! hurrah! for Sheridan!
Hurrah! hurrah! for horse and man!
And when their statues are placed on high,
Under the dome of the Union sky,
The American soldier's Temple of Fame,
There with the glorious general's name,
Be it said, in letters both bold and bright:—
"Here is the steed that saved the day
By carrying Sheridan into the fight,
    From Winchester—twenty miles away!

A bit of background. Sheridan became commander of the newly established Middle Military Division on August 7, 1864. Secretary of War Stanton had objected to the assignment: he believed that Sheridan, at thirty-three, was "too young" for such an important command. Considering the relative youth of so many other senior officers, we might surmise that Stanton was reacting more to stature than chronology. Sheridan, was less than five and a half feet tall, weighed less than 120 pounds, and had a somewhat disproportioned body—barrel chested, broad shouldered, and short legged. Abraham Lincoln described him as "a brown, chunky little chap, with a long body, short legs, not enough neck to hang him, and such long arms that if his ankles itch he can scratch them without stooping." General Grant saw him as "big enough for the purpose." [2]

About a month before the Cedar Creek action, Sheridan's forces hit and, in his own words, "completely defeated" Confederate forces under General Early at the northern end of the Shenandoah Valley (September 19, 1864). Sheridan called it the Battle of the (creek named) Opequon. The Confederates, looking to the nearest municipality, called it the Battle of Winchester; actually, it was the third battle of that name, but the first to be a Yankee victory. This time, the Confederates won the battle of names.

"We have sent them whirling through Winchester," Sheridan reported by dispatch, "and we are after them tomorrow." [3]

Jerome Bonaparte Stillson, correspondent for the New York World, was one of only two specials close at hand, but his effort to file a story was blocked by the censors—out of "petty spite," according to his editors, because the World was supporting McClellan. Stillson, a twenty-three-year-old with modest experience and, to this point, no demonstrated skill or ambition, put his nose to the ground, interviewed Federal troops and rebel prisoners alike, assembled his notes and headed to New York, by horse and train, to deliver his material in person. His seven-column story put the third Battle of Winchester in the history books (with, perhaps, a bit too much of typical nineteenth-century over writing):

Here is no cowardly fear of what is in a soberer time called death. This tremendous work and excitement of fighting has crushed out *all* fear. Every eye looks forward from these ranks, looks with a hope and an expectation of something in the achievement of which, the accident of death is held as nothing. [4]

Sheridan was coming around to Sherman's views about newspapermen, and had just savaged one correspondent for some mild inaccuracies in a New York Times account of an earlier action. As recounted in an unsigned article in Macmillan's Magazine for August 1904, Times reporter George F. Williams was confronted by Sheridan with the charge, "So, you have been making fun of me in your damned newspaper!" When Williams demurred, Sheridan yelled, "You are ordered to leave my department within twenty-four hours."

Williams reminded the general that his department covered most of the northeastern United States. "Even if I go back to New York, I shall be within the lines of your command."

"Oh, go to the devil if you like. I don't care where you go."

"All right, general, but I am afraid I shall not be out of your department even with his Satanic Majesty!" [5]

That makes a good story, although it smacks a bit of the writer getting back in print rather than in person. However, by virtue of this expulsion, Williams became the first special to reach Washington after the capture of Winchester and was invited—at 2:00 A.M.—to brief the president at the White House. Lincoln, in appreciation, gave Williams what amounted to a presidential press pass, good anywhere, any time, and invited him to return for a visit the next time he was in town.

Williams, "being very young . . . supposed the President's invitation was merely a compliment." A month later, he was back in Washington and the president's secretary John Hay accosted him: "Mr. Lincoln saw you on the Avenue today. He is surprised that you have not come to see him." Williams quickly went to the White House, where Lincoln explained his interest: "I am always seeking information, and you newspaper men are so often behind the scenes at the front I am frequently able to get ideas from you which no one else can give." Lincoln asked Williams for his opinion of Sheridan, and was given a complimentary report, to which he offered the comment. "General grant does seem able to pick out the right man for the right place at the right time. He is like that trap hammer I saw the other day . . . always certain in his movements, and always the same." [6]

Winslow Homer's "Sharpshooter," perhaps the most widely reproduced Civil War illustration.

Francis C. Long of the *Herald* was riding along as Sheridan's forces pursued the retreating Confederates. When the chase was broken off, well down in the Shenandoah Valley, he headed for the nearest telegraph station—which was at Harper's Ferry, more than one hundred miles as the horse rides—to file his copy. A competitor, T. C. Grey of the *Tribune*, was already at the station, with only scanty information "furnished," as the journalistic cliché went, "by an intelligent contraband." However, spotting the *Herald* man, Grey determined to hold an exclusive for the *Tribune* and monopolized the line, first, with what little he had, and then—much to the amusement of the telegrapher and the disgust of Long—flourished his pocket Bible and turned Chapman's Gettysburg trick back on the *Herald* with a threat of the "Genesis" ploy. Long gave up the fight, borrowed a fresh horse, and rode another seventeen miles to the next telegraph station, Frederick, Maryland.

Southern reports of the loss at Winchester gave credit to the Federal cavalry and largely laid blame on the Southern cavalry. The Petersburg *Daily Express*, September 23, 1864, noted the "splendid condition" of Sheridan's troopers; Early's cavalry was pronounced "utterly worthless" in the October 4 Mobile *Register*. Another account, written by a special from Raleigh and reprinted in the Richmond *Whig*, not only alluded to a "disgraceful stampede" of a group of cavalrymen, but also reported that they had dashed through the streets of Winchester shouting, "The Yankees are coming," and triggered an even greater rush out of town. "Officers who have seen much that is exciting about battlefields," the reporter wrote, "tell me they never witnessed anything that will begin to compare with the stampede at Winchester." [7]

However, Jubal Early was a Virginian, and by and large the Virginia papers were supportive. The Lynchburg *Republican* tagged the Confederate retreat with the euphemistic "retrograde movement." The Richmond *Dispatch* bragged that "with the exception of the loss of ground, all the advantage of the battle remained on our side." To which, the Charleston *Daily Courier*, not in thrall, replied, "A slight exception verily . . . " [8]

Readers of the *Whig* came to the defense of Brig. Gen. John Imboden, another Virginian, who had been commander of Early's cavalry. One letter writer complained that "Imboden's men" would never have behaved in the manner described, and a colonel who had been with Imboden's brigade during the action claimed that Brig. Gen. John McCausland's cavalrymen, not his, had been at fault, and anyway, all of them had sensibly retreated in the face of "superior numbers" and that if anyone "ran away," it was the infantry. [9]

Peter Alexander, writing for the Savannah *Republican*, charged that "officers of high position—yes, of very high position—have, to use an honest English word, been drunk—too drunk to command themselves, much less an army, a division, a brigade, or a regiment." Alexander had not, himself, been present at the battle and did not cite his source.[10]

In rebuttal, the Richmond *Examiner* published a letter from a "well-informed" cavalry officer: "It won't do to look for scape-goats in the shape of John Barleycorn and 'a valley which is running with apple-brandy.' I tell you, dear sir, *there is nothing running in this valley like our cavalry; the valley is now our valley of humiliation.*" This writer charged that "There was more brandy, and more drinking, and more good living in this valley in the glorious times of Jackson than there is now," but that Jackson was successful because he had cavalry worthy of the name. [11]

Sheridan's "tomorrow" stretched into a month-long push into the valley, during which his troops were put to executing a policy that earned him the title "Chief of the Barn Burners" in the Richmond *Dispatch.* "I passed one plantation," a correspondent wrote, "on which not a house was left, the cattle lay dead in the field, and even the shocks of corn as they stood in the field were burned." [12]

Harper's Weekly noted that "The order to transform the Valley into a barren waste, with nothing which should tempt the enemy to return, was carried out with unsparing severity." [13] The score included 2,000 barns filled with wheat, hay, and farming implements; more than 70 mills filled with flour and wheat; 4,000 head of stock taken, and 3,000 sheep butchered and parceled out to the troops. Sheridan offered no apology, cited the earlier horrors of Confederate raids, bushwhackers, and the burning of Chambersburg, Pennsylvania, at the end of July, and suggested that Early's force plundered "more horses and cattle" in Maryland than the Federals took in the valley. The Federals also destroyed at least one news-paper office—the Harrisonburg *Rockingham Register.*

Some years later, responding to criticism that Sheridan's action had been inhumane, Gen. Wesley Merritt wrote: "There is little doubt, however, that enough was left in country for the subsistence of the people, for this, besides being contemplated by orders, resulted of necessity from the fact that, while the work was done hurriedly, the citizens had ample time to secrete supplies, and did so." Judging from that brief sample, it seems well that General Merritt had not sought a career as a journalist. [14]

On October 15, with all quiet on the valley front, Sheridan went to Washington for a conference. He was back in Winchester late on the 18th, where he bedded down for the night. Confederate reinforcements spent that same night sneaking down along mountain trails—so steep, at times, that the troops controlled their descent by holding on to the bushes, and with such stealth that they had left everything behind which might clink or clank and give away their approach. They attacked the sleeping Federals at dawn, quickly taking out 300 of the 340 pickets, in an attack coordinated with the remnants of the otherwise "completely defeated" forces of Early. Within a matter of minutes, the Federal lines had crumbled, leaving behind sixteen hundred prisoners, twenty pieces of artillery, and uncounted quantities of supplies. As distraught Federal soldiers hustled back toward Winchester and safety, many Confederates were distracted by the abundance of riches upon which they had stumbled and abandoned the pursuit to pick through stores of food and clothing. They also allowed themselves to be amused by thousands of absentee ballots, scattered around camp, which had been shipped to the troops in anticipation of the forthcoming election.

That respite was not apparent to the scattering Federals, and the day would have stood forever as a disaster, but for the "ride." In the simplest telling: Sheridan was alerted to the attack, moved to the front, and rallied the troops. Some newspapers—which bitterly opposed Lincoln's reelection—discounted the early reports of victory: "Intelligent readers," cautioned the Boston *Courier*, "will doubtless analyze for themselves the series of ante-election victories which may now be expected by telegraph." [15]

However, the majority of Northern newspaper coverage—from which poet Read took his text—was an exciting tale of certain defeat turned to victory. The best report was by young Mr. J. B. Stillson, appearing in—again, of all unlikely places—the virulently anti-Lincoln, pro-McClellan New York *World*:

At 10 o'clock, just as the last retreat alluded to was about completed, and as the army was getting into its new position, a faint hurrah from the rear, along the pike, announced his coming. He rode his famous black horse, and asked questions as he rode, of those along the line.

"Where is the Nineteenth corps?" he inquired of a mounted officer near one of the batteries in rear of the cavalry.

"On the right, general, in those woods," was the reply.

Riding on still farther, he said to another whom he recognized, "Now, all I want by God, is to get those men up in the rear and whip these rascals back."

One of his staff officers, coming out to meet him, announced that the situation of the army was "awful."

"Pshaw!" said Sheridan, "it's nothing of the sort. It's all right, or we'll fix it right!"

The general rode on with his staff and escort, which soon became in the distance a mass of dust and gleaming hoofs. Galloping past the batteries to the extreme left of the line held by the cavalry, he rode to the front, took off his hat and waved it, while a cheer went up from the ranks not less hearty and enthusiastic than that which greeted him after the battle of Winchester. Generals rode out to meet him, officers waved their swords, men threw up their hats in an extremity of glee. General Custer, discovering Sheridan at the moment he arrived, rode up to him, threw his arms around his neck, and kissed him on the cheek. Waiting for no other parley than simply to exchange greeting, and to say, "This retreat must be stopped, by God," Sheridan broke loose, and began galloping down the lines, along the whole front of the army. Everywhere the enthusiasm caused by his appearance was the same. It increased at last until that part of the army in line of battle became a new being, having twice its previous will to fight, and until that part of the army in rear, hearing of it, became partially ashamed of secession, and came back. [16]

The army, indeed, was rallied, although most accounts suggest that the retreat had already been halted and that it only was left to Sheridan to organize a counterattack. In that, there was some delay—Sheridan was spooked by reports that Confederate reinforcements were about to strike at Winchester, in his rear. An organized counterattack finally began about four o'clock. Early was driven back, the lost ground and equipment were recovered, and Sheridan was a hero.

Stillson's account electrified the nation and was widely reprinted. For some reason, the New York *Times* was limited for almost a week to printing official dispatches, but the editors nonetheless recognized the merits of the tale:

Gen. Sheridan, the gallant hero of the Shenandoah Valley, gives to the country, by virtue of his own brilliant genius, and the indomitable valor of his army, another substantial victory, more important, so far as the trophies of battle are concerned, than any he has yet won. . . . He is deserving of the praise that is given him. The way in which he "wrested victory from the jaws of defeat"; the way in which he repulsed assault; the way in which he assaulted; the style of victory he won; the number of famous victories he has achieved in one short month—all mark him worthy of the remarkable eulogium of the Lieutenant-General in styling him "one of the ablest of Generals." Napoleon used to do such things as Sheridan has been doing during the past four weeks. [17]

A dispatch written by *Times* correspondent E. A. Paul on the 20th, "delayed for several days in transmission," was published on the 27th. Paul added telling detail of the rebel assault, under cover of fog "so dense that one man could not see another at a distance of ten feet." Of the central event, he wrote: "The hour of 10 o'clock had arrived, when all of a sudden—no man present will ever forget the moment—cheers were heard from the rear!" Paul himself may not have been one of those who were "present," but he knew how to insert himself into a story. "Talk of popular favorites," he added, "Sheridan was the most popular man in the world at that moment; his presence inspired confidence more than what he said."

The poem that celebrated the event sprang forth quickly, but not spontaneously, from Read's facile brain. He was at home in Cincinnati the first day of November, talking with popular actor James Murdoch, in town for a patriotic poetry-reading fund-raiser that night. Read's brother-in-law came by, waving the latest issue of *Harper's Weekly*. "Buck," he said, "there's a poem in that picture." Murdoch wondered if Buck could put something together for that night's performance. [18]

The poem, exaggerated, but not altogether inaccurate, has so colored all subsequent comment that much of the truth remains buried under myth. Here's some of the myth: From *Frank Leslie's Illustrated Newspaper*, November 12, 1864: "The news of the disaster to his forces reached him at Winchester, from which point he immediately set forth to reach his army." From *The Civil War Album*, published 128 years later: "Sheridan was in Winchester, nearly 20 miles away, but upon hearing the distant gunfire he galloped off toward the battlefield." From the 1996 CD-ROM version of Compton's Interactive Encyclopedia, "At that time Sheridan was returning from a conference in Washington, D.C. Reaching Winchester, 20 miles (32 kilometers) away, he learned of the turn of events. Speedily he rode forward and reorganized the Union troops."

"Immediately set forth," "galloped off," "speedily he rode forward," and consistent references to "20 miles" are myth, not reality. Even a serious history of Civil War journalism (*Bohemian Brigade*) fuzzes the story by omitting some details:

Sheridan was still abed when an aide knocked to report distant artillery fire. The General must have slept with the windows closed. It was probably Grover, he said, making a reconnaissance. He dozed a few minutes longer, then reluctantly got up and climbed into his clothes. A knock again. "The firing is still going on, sir."

"Does it sound like a battle?" The aide said no. Sheridan buttoned his tunic. Grover, banging away to find out what Early was up to. . . . "Order the horses saddled." [19]

In his autobiography, written long enough after the event to be credible, Sheridan told much the same story as that given above, but portrayed himself as not quite so purposeful. That first interruption came at six o'clock; Sheridan did indeed surmise, "It's all right; Grover has gone out this morning to make a reconnaissance, and he is merely feeling the enemy." However, now "restless," he did get up and get dressed. A little later, the picket officer did come back and report that the firing, "which could be distinctly heard from his line on the heights outside Winchester, was still going on. I asked him if it sounded like a battle, and as he again said that it did not, I still inferred that the cannonading was caused by Grover's division banging away at the enemy simply to find out what he was up to." [20]

Sheridan went downstairs and ordered that "breakfast be hurried up." *Then* he "ordered the horses to be saddled and in readiness." Readiness, that is, for a ride that started "between half-past 8 and 9." Something close to three hours after he was first awakened. So much for "immediately" galloping off. [21]

As he rode toward the front, the sound of firing continued, steadily growing. Sheridan reported:

Just as we made the crest of the rise beyond the stream [Mill Creek] there burst upon our view the appalling spectacle of a panic-stricken army—hundreds of slightly wounded men, throngs of others unhurt but utterly demoralized, and baggage-wagons by the score, all pressing to the rear in hopeless confusion, telling only too plainly that a disaster had occurred at the front. On accosting some of the fugitives, they assured me that the army was broken up, in full retreat, and that all was lost; all this with a manner true to that peculiar indifference that takes possession of panic-stricken men. [22]

At that moment, Sheridan realized that he must get to the front as quickly as possible and rally the troops in person; he rode on ahead, then, accompanied by two aides and twenty troopers. Thus, the distance covered by "the ride" was about twelve miles from Mill Creek to the front lines, over a route crowded in places with vehicles and wounded men and demoralized men. The elapsed time was between one and two hours.

It was not, however, the *ride* that turned the day, but the *arrival*, a dynamic display of direct and classic leadership. "I already knew," Sheridan wrote in his autobiography, "that even in the ordinary condition of mind enthusiasm is a potent element with soldiers, but what I saw that day convinced me that if it can be excited from a state of despondency its power is almost irresistible." As reported by one sergeant in a letter home, the general was direct and to the point: "Turn boys, turn, we're going back. Come on back, boys—Give 'em Hell, Goddamn 'em. We'll make coffee out of Cedar Creek tonight." It is well that Mrs. Sheridan did not hear this exhortation; it has been reported that she took great offense to the rather benign phrase in the poem, that Sheridan uttered "a mighty oath." Oaths were not an acceptable part of Mrs. Sheridan's upright frame of reference. In his autobiography, Sheridan tried to smooth it out: "I said nothing except to remark, as I rode among those on the road: 'If I had been with you this morning this disaster would not have happened. We must face the other way; we will go back and recover our camps.'" [23]

Sheridan, who understood the reality of the battlefield, confided to Gen. George Crook, "Crook, I am going to get much more credit for this than I deserve, for, had I been here in the morning, the same thing would have taken place." [24] President Lincoln—who understood the value of good manners—sent a thank-you note on October 22. General Sheridan sent General Custer—who understood the value of flamboyance—to Washington, for a ceremonial presentation of captured flags (and the men who captured them) to the secretary of war.

On the other side of the line, General Early addressed his defeated force on the 22nd. He said that he spoke, not "in anger [but] in kindness, though in sorrow. . . . I had hoped to have congratulated you," he said, "on the splendid victory you won on the morning of the 19th . . . but I have the mortification of announcing to you that, by your subsequent misconduct, all the benefits of that victory were lost. . . . " [25]

"Many of you," Early continued,

including some commissioned officers, yielding to a disgraceful propensity for plunder, deserted your colors to appropriate to yourselves the abandoned property of the enemy; and, subsequently, those who had previously remained at their posts, seeing their ranks thinned by the absence of the plunderers, when the enemy, late in the afternoon, with his shattered columns, made but a feeble effort to retrieve the fortunes of the day, yielded to a needless panic, and fled the field in confusion, thereby converting a splendid victory into a disaster. [26-1]

A case could be made, and is made in Thomas A. Lewis's 1988 *Guns of Cedar Creek*, that Early was looking for scapegoats, that any charge of "misconduct" might more properly be laid on his own vacillation, in his puzzling failure, first, to pursue the fleeing enemy and, later, to attack the still demoralized force. Lewis acknowledges some looting, but suggests that pillaging by active forces was minimal, with "citizens, teamsters" and other noncombatants being the principal actors. [26-2]

The Southern Press Association prepared an account of the action of the 19th, based on official dispatches, which was apparently suppressed in Richmond. On October 24, the Richmond *Whig* published a carefully guarded report. On October 29, the Richmond *Dispatch* was bold enough to accuse Early's men of taking time off for "plundering" despite specific orders otherwise. But the *Dispatch* echoed earlier complaints, and laid most of the blame on the failure of the cavalry—or, rather, of the "mounted infantry . . . for cavalry, properly so called, we have none. . . . We must have *cavalry*, real *cavalry*, to confront the Yankees if we do not wish to be beaten in every battle."

Peter Alexander's earlier charge of widespread high-level drunkenness now resurfaced, but was largely dismissed in the Virginia papers. On November 21, Alexander called for a congressional inquiry; the Confederate senate referred the matter to its military committee, and nothing happened. Alexander's angry reaction (published in the Savannah *Republican* two weeks later): "We pass laws against drunkenness in the army but never enforce them except against privates and officers of inferior grade. . . . I cannot recall an instance in which an officer has been tried under the act of Congress 'to punish drunkenness in the army.'" Alexander noted numerous offenses he had witnessed, including surgeons "so stupefied by liquor that they could not distinguish between a man's arm and the spoke of a wagonwheel, and who would just as soon have sawed off the one as the other." [27]

Artist James Taylor, by coincidence, had been standing on Sheridan's route to the front. "Now the big, black, white-fetlocked Rienzi, bearing the general, thunders by like a whirlwind," he later wrote. "[Sheridan] is braced well back in his saddle, his body forward bent and his feet in the hooded stirrups are on a line with the animal's breast, that being the only position in which his short legs could insure his seat on the rough Racker. Sheridan, whom I marked closely, wore a beard, a regulation cap with two silver stars. . . ." [28]

A beard—rather than, as more often, only a mustache—and a regulation cap, rather than his accustomed porkpie model. The poem is not the only artifact of the ride to slightly distort history: most of the published newspaper engravings show a clean-shaven and porkpied Sheridan.

Nor, to be accurate, is "Sheridan's Ride" the *only* poem; Herman Melville ventured forth with a victory ode. A look at one verse is enough to demonstrate why Melville's effort not well known:

House the horse in ermine—
For the foam-flake blew
White through the red October;
He thundered into view;
They cheered him in the looming,
Horseman and horse they knew.
The turn of the tide began.
The rally of bugles ran.
He swung his hat in the van;
The electric hoof-spark flew. [29]

As election day 1864 passed into history, it became apparent that Lincoln had won handily: 212 electoral votes to McClellan's 21 (the general taking only New Jersey, Delaware, and Kentucky). But in the tightest of races, Lincoln won Connecticut by fewer than 2,000 votes, and New York by only 6,749 votes of almost 750,000 cast. The *Herald* had given tepid support to McClellan—"rather a choice of evils than a choice of excellencies," [30] which may have influenced a number of voters, but Connecticut and New York were swamped with perhaps 200,000 copies of the *Tribune* and "Sheridan's Ride" just as the polls began to open.

The ride helped Sheridan win promotion to major general in the regular army (he already held that rank in the volunteers). The war continued for another six months. Sheridan was shifted to join the concentration of Union forces that were finally in a position to truly threaten Richmond, and was present in the final moments at Appomattox.

Sheridan is regarded by many historians as the most important Union cavalry commander and, overall, third in "rank" behind Grant and Sherman in contributing to the Federal victory. He capped his career by following Sherman into assignment as chief of staff of the U.S. Army in 1884, and died in 1888.

And what of the horse? "Sheridan's Ride" might more properly be named "Sheridan's Horse." "A steed as black as the steeds of night," possessed of a gay heart, swift and thundering hoofs, and a fire-filled wild eye. The horse was a five-year-old Morgan gelding named Rienzi, an 1862 gift of Capt. Archibald P. Campbell and the officers of the Second Michigan Cavalry. Rienzi (named after the Mississippi town in which Sheridan was then encamped) stood sixteen hands, about two inches higher at the shoulder than his new master. The general described Rienzi as "strongly built, with great powers of endurance . . . he could cover five miles an hour at his natural walking gait." While Captain Campbell had a great "affection" for the horse, Sheridan later noted, he thought him to be "untrustworthy" and "could not be persuaded to ride him." [31]

The horse certainly served General Sheridan with distinction, and, fittingly, poet Read had called for honor to both man and horse:

> Be it said, in letters both bold and bright:—
> "Here is the steed that saved the day
> By carrying Sheridan into the fight,
>   From Winchester—twenty miles away!"

And so it came to pass that the steed that saved the day—the most famous horse of his day, is remembered still. Not with a statue placed on high, but himself, in person, stuffed, his fiery eye replaced with glass. Rienzi—later called "Winchester" but without much enthusiasm—was donated to an army museum by the Sheridan family upon the horse's death in 1878. He is now an exhibit at the Smithsonian Museum of American History, Washington, D.C.; third floor, East Wing, Armed Forces Hall.

22 / Endgame

The walk was long, and the President halted a moment to rest.
"May de good Lord bless you, President Linkum!" said an old Negro,
removing his hat and bowing, with tears of joy rolling down his cheeks.
The President removed his own hat, and bowed in silence:
it was a bow which upset the forms, laws, customs, and ceremonies of
centuries of slavery. It was a death-shock to chivalry,
and a mortal wound to caste.

—Lincoln visits Richmond, April 4, 1865 [1]

THE FEDERAL ARMY continued to beat against the defenses of Richmond and nearby Petersburg. "If Richmond can be held till November," said the *Dispatch* in September, "it will be ours forever, for the North will never throw another army into the abyss where so many lie." At the end of November, with Richmond still in friendly hands, a correspondent for the Columbia *South Carolinian* assured his readers that the city was almost untouched by the war; the restaurants were "kept in a style of magnificent abundance," well-stocked with choice wines, venison, turtle, and other such delicacies, and women paraded along Main street, "attired with a richness and elegance, and in raiment that you will see nowhere else in the Confederacy." The writer failed to note that the prices in those restaurants were so high that few could afford them. [2]

A month later, the *Dispatch* assured its readers that the "struggling new nation" actually possessed a larger amount of territory free of enemy occupation that at the beginning of the previous year and that Confederate forces "were as numerous and formidable as they had been twelve months before." The editor of the Meridian (Mississippi) *Daily Clarion* declared that the Confederate cause was "brighter to-day, in reality, than in any period of our history." [3]

Good propaganda, bad history.

Desperate times bring desperate measures. By the middle of October, some Confederate leaders were seriously considering putting blacks in the army. Richmond correspondent Peter Alexander reported plans to organize blacks into segregated units under the command of white officers; he speculated that, while inferior to a white soldier, the Southern slave would perform better in combat than the Northern black, "and no doubt is entertained that Negroes will do to fight Negroes." General Lee, he wrote, was in favor, Bragg and Davis were opposed, and so was the Richmond press, with one exception. [4]

That one exception was the *Enquirer*, which wanted the government to draft as many as 250,000 slaves and give them freedom as a reward. A reader protested: "it is for the Southern white man to achieve his own independence, to secure himself in the possession of his slave, and to secure to the slave the possession of a good master." [5]

The *Examiner* scoffed. The editor claimed that the record of black regiments in the Union army demonstrated the uselessness of blacks as soldiers; the idea of freedom as a reward was a wrongheaded abolitionist idea, "for the Negro could not be better off than he was as a slave." President Davis proposed that the government purchase 40,000 slaves for employment in support roles, granting them freedom at the end of their service. The *Whig* reminded the president that "servitude is a divinely appointed condition for the highest good of the slave," and that, rather than being a "reward," freedom would be harmful. [6]

The Confederate house of representatives asserted that the army would never need to employ blacks as soldiers because "the valor, constancy and endurance" of the white army "will continue a sufficient guarantee of the rights of the States and the independence of the Confederate States." Despite the military realties not too many miles outside the city limits, one member assured his comrades that "no exigency now exists, nor is likely to occur, in the military affairs of the Confederate States, to justify the placing of Negro slaves in the army as soldiers in the field." Another representative said he was ashamed even to debate the question. "All nature cries out against it. The Negro race was ordained to slavery by the Almighty. . . . the Negro will not fight." [7]

On January 8, a general officer in Georgia wrote, "the proposition to make soldiers of our slaves is the most pernicious idea that has been suggested since the war began. . . .You cannot make soldiers of slaves, nor slaves of soldiers. . . . The day you make soldiers of them is the beginning of the end of the revolution. If slaves make good soldiers our whole theory of slavery is wrong." The *North Carolina Standard* warned against surrender to the abolitionists, accepting "the very doctrine which the war was commenced to put down." To the Charleston *Mercury*, this was tantamount to proclaiming equality among the lower classes, reducing poor whites "to the level of a nigger" where "His wife and daughter are to be hustled on the street by Black wenches, their equals. Swaggering buck niggers are to ogle and elbow them." A congressman from Mississippi bemoaned, "Victory itself would be robbed of its glory if shared with slaves." [8]

During the first week of February, Confederate vice president Alexander Stephens and assistant secretary of war John A. Campbell met with Lincoln and Secretary of State Seward at Hampton Roads. The Confederates were seeking a negotiated peace settlement, but Lincoln's demand for unconditional surrender ended the conference and General Grant's continued pounding against the trenches of Petersburg ended most resistance to the idea of putting blacks in the army. On February 18, Robert E. Lee formally urged the Confederate congress to authorize the enlistment of blacks:

> They possess all the physical qualifications, and their habits of obedience constitute a good foundation for discipline. . . . I think those who are employed should be freed. It would neither be just nor wise, in my opinion, to require them to serve as slaves. The best course to pursue, it seems to me, would be to call for such as are willing to come—willing to come, with the consent of their owners. An impressment or draft would not be likely to bring out the best class, and the use of coercion would make the measure distasteful to them and to their owners. [9]

A reader of the *Whig* wrote in protest, "It is not true that to make good soldiers of these people, we must either give or promise them freedom. . . . As well might one promise to free one's cook . . . with the expectation thereby securing good dinners." [10]

A group of Confederate soldiers, perhaps more directly concerned than most in this debate, told the editors of the *Whig* that, "if the public exigencies require that any number of our male slaves be enlisted in the military service in order to [maintain] our Government, we are willing to make concessions. . . ." [11]

Jefferson Davis tried to settle the question: "We are reduced to choosing whether the Negroes shall fight for or against us." On March 7, by a vote of 40 to 37, the house authorized Davis to accept the "loan" of slaves for employment as soldiers, "provided that nothing in the act should be construed to alter the relation between master and slave." The Senate said "no," with the members from Virginia having the deciding vote. [12]

The Virginia legislature passed a bill of its own authorizing the enlistment of blacks into the state militia, and convinced the senators to change their minds about the congressional bill. On March 13, President Davis signed the "Negro Soldier Law," and three days later, all the Richmond papers carried advertisements for black troops. According to *Examiner* editor Edward Pollard—who recently had been exchanged and was back in Richmond—"two fancy companies" were raised and paraded through Capitol Square as "decoys" to obtain more recruits. Charles Coffin of the Boston *Journal* estimated that perhaps fifty men had been enlisted. [13] None seem to have seen any combat service.

At this same time, Pollard, aroused by the political maneuvering for "peace," published an open letter to the citizens of Virginia in general, and the residents of Richmond in particular. "Shame upon the Congress that closed its doors that it might better consult of dishonorable things! Shame upon those leaders . . . who, while putting in newspapers some cheap words of patriotism . . . and go off and talk submission with their intimates in a corner!"

Do not these men, he asked, ever think of the retributions of history?

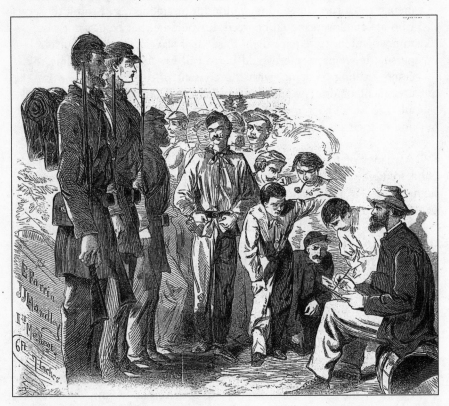

Winslow Homer self-portrait: the artist at work.

"Honor," they say, "is a mere rhetorical laurel." . . . "let us be done with this sentimental rubbish, and look to the care of our substantial interests." My friends, this is not rubbish. The glory of history is indifferent to events; it is simply honor. The name of Virginia in this war is historically and absolutely more important to us than any other element of the contest; and the coarse time-server who would sell an immortal title of honor as a trifling sentimentalism, and who has constantly in his mouth the phrase of "substantial interests," is the inglorious wretch who laughs at history and grovels in the calculations of the brute. . . . Honor such as this is not a piece of rhetoric or a figure of speech; it is something to be cherished under all circumstances, and to be preserved in all events. [14]

If his readers would resist to the end, then for the future and evermore each of them could proudly say, "I, too, was a Virginian, but not of those who sold the jewels of her history for the baubles and cheats of her conquerors." [15] Stand fast, agreed the *Dispatch* on March 27, and wait for the "inevitable" war between the United States and France. The *Sentinel* lamely asserted on April 1, "We are very hopeful of the campaign which is opening, and truest that we are to reap a large advantage from the operations evidently near at hand. . . . We have only to resolve that we never will surrender, and it will be impossible that we shall ever be taken."

And then, on Sunday, April 2, midway through the worship service at St. Paul's Episcopal Church, President Davis was handed a note from General Lee. His lines were broken; Richmond must be evacuated. The president quickly departed the service, and the government began a hurried attempt to remove itself, its records, and its money out of town, with but limited success. Before the next dawn, the sounds of explosions told of bridges falling down and half-built warships being turned to kindling.

And then the town itself fell afire. Lt. Gen. Richard Ewell, commanding the defense of Richmond, had ordered that the tobacco stores be burned, lest the Yankees profit from their conquest. The fires got out of hand, and the flames were carried on the spring wind, across the streets, up into the heart of the town—rushing with equal vengeance through stores, banks, and bawdy houses. In all, nine thousand buildings were destroyed. Within an hour the rich became bankrupt, the prostitutes, temporarily unemployed.

As day came full upon the city, the Confederate soldiers were gone, replaced first by cavalry in blue (black and white), then by infantry (black and white). There was no time for contemplation of victory or defeat; all hands were turned to quenching the flames. General Grant rode into town, but was soon headed west in pursuit of Lee's army.

Thirty-year-old Thomas Morris Chester, the only black special for a major daily newspaper, had been hired in August 1864 by John Russell Young, editor of Forney's Philadelphia *Press*. The move seemed improbable to many at the time because, to that point, the policies of the *Press* had been solidly Democratic. However, the paper made a marked shift to the support of the administration, and Chester may have been added as a symbolic gesture. Be that as it may, he was an experienced journalist and trained shorthander, and was the first correspondent to enter the city limits of Richmond.

Chester chose a symbolic gesture of his own, by writing his first dispatch from Richmond while seated at the desk of the speaker of the Confederate house of representatives, April 4, 1865: "Seated in the Speaker's chair, so long dedicated to treason, but in future to be consecrated to loyalty, I hasten to give a rapid sketch of the incidents which have occurred since my last dispatch." He was to be interrupted by an angry rebel officer, just paroled. As remembered by eyewitness Charles Carleton Coffin of the Boston *Journal*, the officer shouted:

"Come out of there, you black cuss!"

Mr. Chester raised his eyes, calmly surveyed the intruder, and went on with his writing.

"Get out of there or I'll knock your brains out!" the officer bellowed. Pouring out a torrent of oaths; and rushing up the steps to execute his threat, found himself tumbling over chairs and benches, knocked down by one well-planted blow between the eyes.

Mr. Chester sat down as if nothing had happened.

The rebel asked a nearby Federal officer for the loan of a sword, to "cut the fellow's heart out." That officer demurred, but with some amusement offered to clear a space for a fair fight. The rebel "left the hall in disgust. 'I thought I would exercise my rights as a belligerent,' said Mr. Chester." [16] Coffin may not have been fully forthcoming in his report; we may presume that the Confederate did not use such socially acceptable words as "black cuss" or "fellow."

There had been some gamesmanship among the Federal troops gathered on the outskirts of Richmond; the prize was at hand, to whom should go the honor? Chester wrote, "There may be others who may claim the distinction of being the first to enter the city, but as I was ahead of every part of the force but the cavalry, which of necessity must lead the advance, I know whereof I affirm when I announce that General Draper's brigade [of black soldiers] was the first organization to enter the city limits." [17] Somehow, most Northern papers failed to note this event and gave credit to other units—white units—as being first across the line.

Chester set the record straight in his letter of April 10, 1865, "Who first entered Richmond?"

> In this connection it is not inappropriate to do justice to the 1st Division of colored troops, under General Kautz, to which belongs the honor of being the first to enter Richmond. Quite an effort is being made to give that credit to Gen. Devin's division, but, whatever may be the merits of his troops, they cannot justly lay any claims to that distinction. The white soldiers, when orders for advancing were passed along the line, were posted nearer Richmond than the Negroes. But, with that prompt obedience to orders that has ever made the discipline of the blacks the pride of their officers, they soon passed over their own and the rebel works, [overtook the white units] and took the Osborne road directly for the city. When within a few miles of the city, I heard Gen. Kautz give the order to Gen. Draper to take the left-hand side of the road, that Devin's division might pass by. Gen. Draper obeyed the order implicitly, and, in order that he might not be in the way with his brigade, put it upon a double-quick, and never stopped until it entered the limits of the city. *The colored troops had orders not to pass through the city,* [and therefore halted just inside the city limits]. . . . When Devin's division came within the outskirts of the city, and marched by General Draper's brigade, who had stacked their arms, and whose drum corps was playing national airs, they were loudly cheered by the colored troops, and they failed to respond, either from exhaustion or a want of courtesy. To Gen. Draper belongs the credit of having the first organization enter the city, and none are better acquainted with this fact than the officers of the division who are claiming the undeserved honor. [18]

Chester also reported that the first Federal units to enter Petersburg were the 7th United States Colored troops, recruited in Maryland, and the 8th United States Colored Troops, recruited in Philadelphia. "It must be a source of great gratification," he wrote April 19, "to the friends of this element of Union strength to be assured that the first organizations to enter these strongholds of the rebellion, Richmond and Petersburg, were colored troops." [19]

At noon on April 3, as soon as news of Richmond's surrender had reached Washington, Whitelaw Reid of the Cincinnati *Gazette*, Lorenzo L. Crounse of the New York *Times*, and Charles A. Page of the New York *Tribune* walked aboard a government boat about to leave for Richmond. Secretary Stanton was once again refusing to issue passes in an effort to keep newsmen away from the news, but this trio talked their way aboard by showing old passes at the gangway and bought their passage with three twenty-dollar bills for the crew's "welfare fund." Charles A. Dana, now serving as an assistant secretary of war and understanding the ways of correspondents better than most, sent an emissary to the pier to ensure the purity of the passenger list; he arrived just as the ship was casting off and too late to have any impact.

In Richmond, reporters converged on the best hotel in town, which somehow had survived the fire. Coffin laid claim to being the first Northern guest to register at the Spottswood House. Reid laid claim to being the first arrival "direct from Washington or the North." Both were correct, but Reid's claim was not as honest. [20] George F. Williams—the New York *Times* "British tourist" of 1860—wondered if a trunk he had left behind when forced to leave town was still somewhere in the building. It was not.

Shortly after noon on April 4, Abraham Lincoln stepped ashore from a navy boat and, accompanied by his son Tad, Admiral Porter, a dozen armed sailors, and one correspondent (Charles Coffin), walked through the smoldering ruins to the Confederate version of the "White House." The president quickly was surrounded by a throng of blacks. Coffin wrote:

> They pressed around the President, ran ahead, and hovered upon the flanks and rear of the little company. Men, women and children joined the constantly increasing throng. They came from all the streets, running in breathless haste, shouting and hallooing, and dancing with delight. The men threw up their hats, the women waved their bonnets and handkerchiefs, clapped their hands, and shouted, "Glory to God! glory! glory! glory!"—rendering all the praise to God, who had given them freedom, after long years of weary waiting, and had permitted them thus unexpectedly to meet their great benefactor. . . . The walk was long, and the President halted a moment to rest. "May de good Lord bless you, President Linkum!" said an old Negro, removing his hat and bowing, with tears of joy rolling down his cheeks. The President removed his own hat, and bowed in silence: it was a bow which upset the forms, laws, customs, and ceremonies of centuries of slavery. It was a death-shock to chivalry, and a mortal wound to caste. [21]

President Lincoln walked through the door of the Confederate president's house, now turned into Yankee military headquarters, just forty hours after Jefferson Davis had walked out.

The only newspaper office in the city not destroyed by the fire was the *Whig*, which soon resumed publication "under new management" (although under the same ownership). The *Whig* blamed destruction of the city on the deliberate, wanton, and reckless torching of the tobacco warehouses, denounced subsequent pillaging by "a band of drunken Confederate stragglers," and praised Union soldiers for fighting the fires. [22] That was almost true; pillaging had been the sport of many. As one Northern reporter later described the scene:

> By the red, consuming light, poured past the straggling Confederate soldiers, dead to the acknowledgment of private rights, and sacking shop and home with curses and ribaldry; the suburban citizens and the menial Negroes adopted their examples; carrying off whatever came next to their hands, and with arms full of "swag," dropping it in the highway, lured by some dearer plunder. Negroes, with baskets of stolen champagne and rare jars of tamarinds, sought their dusky quarters to swill and carouse; and whites of the middle, and even of the higher class, lent themselves to theft, who, before this debased era, would have died before so surrendering their honor. [23]

The other newspapers of the Confederacy, such as remained in business, remained defiant. "Richmond and Petersburg have fallen," wrote the editor of the Columbia *South Carolinian*, "but they have gone down in a blaze of glory, and with a record unstained by one blot of shame. All that the enemy have gained has been purchased at a terrible price in blood, while our own army, although suffering severely, is still strong, intact, and ready for its future work." [24]

The newspapers of the Union were ecstatic, and even the New York *World* joined in the celebration: "The taking of Richmond was a greater event, and more fully justified exuberant rejoicing, than any previous achievement in the history of the war." The *Herald* took that to the next higher level: it was "one of the grandest triumphs that has crowned human efforts for centuries." [25]

The New York *Times* and the *Tribune* each spread a woodcut of an eagle across half the front page; the *Tribune* added an Irish drinking song, modified for the occasion, that began "Bad luck to the man who is sober to-night" and proposed good health to every official who had been connected with the military department of the government. Horace Greeley, however, could not resist pointing out that Richmond "might have been ours long ago." [26]

At the *Sun*, the staff poet was put on overtime:

> Richmond is ours ! Richmond is ours !
> Hark ! to the jubilant chorus !
> Up, through the lips that no longer repress It,
> Up, from the Heart of the People ! God bless it !
> Swelling with loyal emotion,
> Leapeth our joy, like an ocean !
> Richmond is ours ! Richmond is ours !
> Babylon falls, and her temples and towers
> Crumble to ashes before us !
>
> Glory to Grant ! Glory to Grant !
> Hark ! to the shout of our Nation !
> Up, from the Irish heart, up from the German
> Glory to Sheridan ! Glory to Sherman !

And so on. It was a long poem; you get the idea.

George Alfred Townsend, who had been in Europe for about a year and a half and now was working for the *World*, arrived in Richmond a few days after the surrender. On April 9, 1865, the twenty-five-year-old world traveler attended Sunday service at the spiritual home of Jefferson Davis and General Lee, St. Paul's Episcopal. The congregation that Sunday included Federal soldiers, some Confederate officers, and a coterie of Richmond ladies, of whom, Townsend wrote:

> Those who dressed the shabbiest had yet preserved some little article of jewelry: a finger-ring, a brooch, a bracelet, showing how the last thing in a woman to die is vanity. Poor, proud souls! Last Sunday many of them were heiresses; now many of them could not pay the expenses of their own funerals. [27]

The preacher selected the Forty-fourth and following Psalms; was this a pointed message to his audience, regular parishioners or the uninvited?

> Through thee will we push down our enemies; through thy name will we tread them under that rise up against us. . . .Though thou has sore broken us in the place of the dragons, and covered us with

the shadow of death . . . Yea for thy sake are we killed all the day long. . . . Arise for our help, and redeem us for thy mercies sake.

God is our refuge and strength, a very present help in trouble. . . . He maketh wars to cease unto the end of the earth; he breaketh the bow, and cutteth the spear in sunder; he burneth the chariot in the fire.

It was the Sunday before Easter, Townsend wrote, and the service included the prescribed readings for the day: Christ betrayed by Iscariot, deserted by his disciples, proclaiming that the Son of Man will return to Jerusalem, "sitting on the right hand of power, and coming in the clouds of heaven." The symbolism was not lost on the vanquished.

At the very hour of the Sunday service, Gen. Robert E. Lee was agreeing to meet later in the day with Lt. Gen. Ulysses S. Grant to discuss the terms of surrender for his army. The meeting began about two thirty; by four o'clock, it was finished. No correspondents witnessed the proceedings, but waiting outside were at the least Sylvanus Cadwallader for the *Herald* and Henry Wing for the *Tribune*. A Federal officer came out on the porch, doffed his hat, and swiped a handkerchief across his forehead three times. This prearranged signal sent the *Tribune*'s man on a quick ride to the nearest telegraph key. He had no details, but needed none: he beat the dreaded *Herald* with a simple dispatch: "Lee has surrendered." [28]

It was time for more celebration, but the darkest hour of the war, perhaps of the century, was near at hand. On April 11, President Abraham Lincoln stood on a White House balcony and addressed a happy crowd of celebrants. He promised, soon, to announce his plans for reconstruction. John Wilkes Booth, standing in the crowd below, was incensed. He told a companion, "That means nigger citizenship. Now, by God, I'll put him through. That is the last speech he will ever make." It was. [29]

There continued to be holdouts, both among Confederate newspapers and isolated units in the field. "The End Is Not In Sight," proclaimed the Augusta *Constitutionalist* on April 18. Victory and the "glorious independence of the South" was still possible; Confederate armies were strong and undaunted . . . but not, however, for long. Gen. Joseph Johnston agreed to surrender terms with General Sherman that same day; Lt. Gen. Richard Taylor, defending Mobile, surrendered May 4. President Andrew

Johnson declared that the rebellion had ended May 10. There were still a few pockets of armed resistance, but they were of little consequence.

The fugitive Jefferson Davis was accused of complicity in the assassination of Abraham Lincoln, and Federal authorities offered a reward of $100,000, in gold, to "any person or persons who will apprehend and deliver" the former president "to any of the military authorities of the United States." [30] Davis was, coincidentally, captured (by the "military authorities" themselves) on the same day that the president announced the end of hostilities, and his capture was the grand anticlimax of the war.

Davis, his wife Varina, and an attending guard force had been headed south, but were overtaken at their campsite, some fifty miles north of the Florida border, early in the morning of May 10. Davis was later to describe his capture in rather awkward terms:

I stepped out of my wife's tent and saw some horsemen, whom I immediately recognized as cavalry, deploying around the encampment. I turned back and told my wife these were not . . . marauders, but regular troopers. She implored me to leave her at once. I hesitated, from unwillingness to do so, and lost a few precious moments before yielding to her importunity. My horse and arms were near the road on which I expected to leave, and down which the cavalry approached; it was therefore impracticable to reach them. I was compelled to start in the opposite direction. [31]

Davis tried to throw on some sort of disguise; he grabbed what he thought was his raglan, "a water-proof, light overcoat, without sleeves," but which turned out to belong to his wife, instead, "so very like my own as to be mistaken for it." As he left the tent, Varina "thoughtfully" added a shawl to his costume. Thus, he moved off wearing a woman's overgarment and shawl, which, when confronted by a Yankee trooper, he threw off with a defiant refusal to surrender. The trooper pointed a carbine at the president; Varina ran up and threw her arms around her husband, thus ending any hope of escape or of surrender with dignity.

While the Chicago *Tribune* celebrated the capture of the epitome of human infamy, the *Herald* took a different tack, and unwittingly helped to change the course of history. The "Details of His Capture" began with this extended headline deck:

He Disguises Himself in His Wife's Clothing, and, Like His Accomplice Booth, Takes to the Woods. He is Pursued and Forced to a Stand. He shows Fight and Flourishes a Dagger in the Style of the Assassin of the President. His Wife Warns the Soldiers Not to "Provoke the President for He Might Hurt 'Em." He fails to Imitate Booth and Die in the Last Ditch. His Ignominious Surrender." [32]

The rumors that Davis had been dressed as a woman reached Washington before the newspaper accounts. Brig. Gen. James H. Wilson (the same officer with whom Smalley was to have the dispute over comments at Antietam) was in command of the capturing force but was not an eyewitness. He telegraphed Stanton, "The captors report that he hastily put on one of Mrs. Davis' dresses and started for the woods." Stanton ordered an officer to "procure the disguise worn by Davis at the time of his capture." The officer did, and, indexed as the "Shawl, waterproof and spurs worn by Jeff. Davis on the day of his capture," the "disguise" was locked in a box at the War Department. It remained in the box, unseen, until after the turn of the century. [33]

In the contemporary newspaper reports, where the myth could grow unhampered by the out-of-sight reality, the waterproof became a hoop-skirt. The shawl became a bonnet. The President became a laughing-stock. The event inspired cartoons, jokes, poems, and songs with titles such as "Jeff in Petticoats." The authors of The Confederate Image (1987) discovered at least thirty-two independently published prints of Jeff Davis in skirts, bearing such imaginative titles as The Belle of Richmond and Jeff's Last Shift. [34]

Frank Leslie's account was more imaginative than most, dressing Davis "in petticoats, morning dress and a woolen cloak, with a hood closely drawn over the head and a pail on her arm. . . ." The Herald predicted that Davis would be hanged—more for his alleged role in the assassination than in his treason, and proclaimed that "His life has been a cheat. His last free act was an effort to unsex himself and deceive the world." Davis biographer Robert McElroy wrote, "For the rest of his life Davis resented the thought that friend and enemy could believe him guilty of seeking safety by a method so 'unbecoming a soldier and a gentleman.'" [35]

However, the symbolically emasculated rebel president had become a target for ridicule, not revenge, and the ridicule probably saved his life. He was transformed from the devil incarnate into a pathetic joke, and four years of editorial demands for a public hanging no longer mattered.

Davis spent two years in prison, and was paroled under a $100,000 bond in 1867. The second signature affixed to his bail bond was that of Horace Greeley—an act of kindness that would come back to haunt the great abolitionist during his unsuccessful 1872 run for the presidency, against Grant.

There were also holdouts of a different sort. When the fighting had ended, Charles Coffin reported that the men and women of "one of the most aristocratic families" of Richmond "were exceedingly bitter and defiant.

They would never yield. They would fight through generations, and defeat the Yankees at last." [36]

A few months later, Edward Pollard asserted that "The Confederates have gone out of this war, with the proud, secret, deathless, *dangerous* consciousness that they are THE BETTER MEN. . . ." He urged the South to continue "to assert, in the forms of her thought, and in the style of her manners, her peculiar civilization, and to convince the North that, instead of subjugating an inferior country, she has obtained the alliance of a noble and cultivated people, and secured a bond of association with those she may be proud to call brethren!"

Yes, he admitted, the South had lost a war that had decided the restoration of the Union and the abolition of slavery, and he agreed that the South "must submit fairly and truthfully to *what the war has properly decided.*" But, he argued, with his sights on bigger game, "The war did not decide Negro equality; it did not decide Negro suffrage; it did not decide States Rights. . . . and these things the war did not decide, the Southern people will still cling to, and still assert them in their rights and views." He therefore rallied his readers to join him in pursuing "the true cause" of the rebellion: white supremacy. The goal was simply defined: allow the black to continue to work as a laborer, but keep him "in a condition where his *political* influence is as indifferent as when he was a slave." [37]

The shooting may have stopped, but it was going to be a long war.

23 / CODA

It is plain that journalist will henceforth and forever be an important and crowded profession in the United States. . . .

—James Parton, *North American Review*, April 1866 [1]

TOWARD THE END, the war had begun to outrun the news; battles were being fought and territory secured without the benefit of newspaper blessing. In this, the weekly illustrated press was most affected, as the constraints of time affected timeliness. Most Southern papers had long since been relying on news from the Northern press or from Southern newspapers being published in Yankee-held territory, which was about the same thing. John Forsyth's Mobile *Register* was almost alone in maintaining a staff of special correspondents, almost to the end.

The special correspondents scattered into various postwar assignments. Some continued to work as journalists: George Smalley went to Europe as bureau chief for the New York *Tribune*, then became American correspondent for the London *Times*; Thomas Knox became a foreign correspondent for the *Herald*. Wallace Screws's career survived Bragg's wrath; he was to move up and serve as editor of the Montgomery *Advertiser* for fifty years. Jerome Bonaparte Stillson, who had put the third battle of Winchester in the history books, worked for a time as managing editor of the *World*, but preferred the life of a correspondent; he shifted to the *Herald* in time to cover the Sioux uprising in 1876. He just missed being with George Armstrong Custer at the massacre at the Little Big Horn, but managed to get an exclusive interview with the victor, Chief Sitting Bull. William F. G. Shanks became, in turn, editor of *Harper's Weekly*, the

New York *Times*, and the New York *Tribune*. Franc Wilkie had stopped reporting from the field in 1863, when he was appointed an editorial writer for the Chicago *Times*, for which paper he later worked as European bureau chief. George Alfred Townsend became a feature writer, specializing in political observation and social satire. In 1896, he led the campaign to raise money for the War Correspondents' monument on South Mountain.

Albert Deane Richardson, while still employed by the *Tribune*, wrote three successful books (including a well-regarded biography of Ulysses S. Grant). However, he was shot and fatally wounded in November 1869 by the jealous ex-husband of his new fiancée. Richardson and the lady were married on his death bed.

Charles Dana became an owner, and editor in chief, of the New York *Sun*. His successor as managing editor of the New York *Tribune*, Sidney Gay, was discharged by Greeley in 1866. Gay became managing editor of the Chicago *Tribune*, and then shifted to writing books. His successor at the *Tribune* was John Russell Young, who held the job for three years; he then became a foreign correspondent for the *Herald*, served as minister to China from 1882 to 1885, and ended his working days as Librarian of Congress.

Whitelaw Reid became editor (and principle owner) of the *New York Tribune*, was the (unsuccessful) Republican candidate for vice president in the 1892 election, and served as U.S. ambassador to England from 1905 to 1912.

Some of the correspondents stopped working as newspapermen but stayed in the trade. William Swinton became professor of English at the University of California and a prolific author of grade-school textbooks. Adams Sherman Hill (who had been ready to "skedaddle" if the rebels moved on Washington) became head of the English Department at Harvard. Charles Carleton Coffin wrote eight books, gave more than two thousand lectures, and was elected to the Massachusetts assembly and senate.

Some left journalism for the world of business. Edmund Stedman—who had been so thrilled to ride "in the van" at Bull Run—quit working for the *World* when it changed management and policy in 1862 and became a stockbroker. Toward the end of the war, Henry Villard formed a small news service, but by 1868 he had broadened his interests. At one point, he acquired the New York *Evening Post*, but that was a financial, not a journalistic, move. He also became president of the Northern Pacific Railroad, and assembled the group of companies then known as the Edison General Electric Company, the forerunner of today's General Electric.

Sam Wilkeson became a public relations man for financier Jay Cooke, and was secretary of the Northern Pacific Railroad when Villard came in as president. Whatever may have been the lingering effect of their wartime dispute, Wilkeson remained in that post.

Sylvanus Cadwallader became a sheep rancher in Montana.

While newspapers had an undoubted impact on the war, so, too, had the war impacted newspapers. Coverage that before the war had been limited, and local, became broad and national. A population that largely had consisted of isolated groups, each knowing little of the rest of the nation, was brought together in the shared experience of the war—a war, brought to them in the newspapers. And, wheretofore the "newspaper" had been little more than a journal of literature and opinion, it now in fact was focused on the "news." As a contemporary observer noted, the emphasis had shifted from editorials (which "do not much influence the public mind, nor change many votes") to something much broader:

> The power and success of a newspaper depend wholly and absolutely on its success in getting and its skill in exhibiting the news. The word "newspaper" is the exact and complete description of the thing which the journalist aims to produce. The news is his work; editorials are his play. The news is the point of rivalry; it is that for which nineteen-twentieths of the people buy newspapers; it is that which determines the rank of every newspaper. . . .[2]

James Gordon Bennett would certainly agree; he was now the "king of the hill":

> Just as there is a "*Herald*'s headquarters" tent with every army, and a *Herald* bureau in Washington, so there shall be a *Herald* legation in all the chief cities from Melbourne to Spitzbergen. Using the Atlantic cable and the Russian telegraph, these correspondents, who have acquired experience, tact and vigor in the school of war, will send us every item of our intelligence throughout the world, so that we shall place before our readers in every morning's *Herald* a complete photograph of the world of the previous day. . . . What we have done is a guarantee of what we shall do. The United States, the City of New York and the New York *Herald* have a future compared to which the present is as nothing. [3]

In fact, the future of the *Herald* would not stand comparison with "the present." The paper would be run into the ground by a profligate James Gordon Bennett Jr., and in 1924, Whitelaw Reid's son and daughter-in-law, then running the *Tribune*, bought what remained of the *Herald* and began publishing as the New York *Herald Tribune*. Reid's grandson and namesake became editor in 1947, but by 1963, after some more mergers and failures, that newspaper almost disappeared. The *Herald Tribune* survives today as an international edition published in Paris. It is owned, in part, by the New York *Times*.

———————————

The war ended, and the postmortems began. Seemingly, anyone with an axe to grind or a view to propound rushed forth with a history or an apologia or a memoir. Many would be given additional airing in the amazingly successful "Battles and Leaders of the Civil War" series, published in the *Century* magazine between November 1884 and March 1888. The war was a generation past, passions had cooled, and the *Century's* announced goal was to celebrate "heroic events" that were now passing into "our common history, where motives will be weighed without malice, and valor praised without distinction of uniform. . . ." [4] The series was so popular that the circulation of the *Century* almost doubled within the first six months and, along with the four-volume hardcover version (which contained most of the articles, although not always in original text), "Battles and Leaders" earned the original publishers more than $1 million. Available today in facsimile edition, the book version is still earning money for someone.

However, a brief comment: a detailed analysis of the entire series, published in 1973 by Yale University history professor Rollin G. Osterweis, suggested that the war was being refought with a subtle Southern bias, and that the historic record was being "adjusted." One example: the first article of the series was on Bull Run, written by P. G .T. Beauregard. "That one army was fighting for Union," he noted, "and the other for disunion is a political expression; the actual fact on the battlefield, in the face of cannon and musket, was that the Federal troops came as invaders, and the Southern troops stood as defenders of their homes. Further than that we need not go. . . ." The corresponding Northern view was "Recollections of a Private," which presented a limited but critical appraisal of "bungling" by Federal generals. [5]

The pen, mightier indeed than the sword? Further than that, *we* need not go.

———————————

Debate on the proper role of the war correspondent would continue, without resolution, for years to come. In his postwar memoir, *Tribune* correspondent Junius Browne offered the ideal: the correspondent "is at his post to relate what he sees; to applaud valor and merit wherever found; to point out abuses and blunders that would not otherwise be reached, save through the endless duration of military investigations and courts-martial." [6] General Sherman, in closing his memoirs, offered a quite different opinion, grounded more in reality. Newspaper correspondents, he wrote, were the

> world's gossips . . . gradually drifting to the headquarters of some general, who finds it easier to make reputation at home than with his own corps or division. They are also tempted to prophesy events and state facts which, to an enemy, reveal a purpose in time to guard against it. Moreover, they are always bound to see the facts colored by the partisan or political character of their own patrons, and thus bring army officers into the political controversies of the day. [7]

Politics and personalities (and Sherman's petty jealousies) aside, there is no doubt that many newsmen—especially in the North—revealed secrets best left unwritten, and many editors passed along material best left unpublished. Some were in tune with the 1862 lament of the Cincinnati *Commercial* that "The people want news more than they want victories"; some were so vehemently opposed to the war that they *wanted* to interfere. As we have seen, such censorship as the Federal government tried to impose at the source of news was erratic and ineffective, and most attempts to control the content of newspapers ran up against the First Amendment guarantees that "the freedom of the press shall not be abridged." Efforts to control the activities of newsmen by withholding passes, ejecting them from camp, and threatening court-martial were likewise erratic—and often illogical. Little wonder that one correspondent, a bit more snobbish than most, suggested that "the class of correspondents in the field has been far below what it ought to be, for it has really required some sacrifice of self-respect for an honorable and just man to enter the field and submit to the imposed restrictions as well as reflections." [8]

It is interesting to note that President Lincoln was universally hospitable and courteous to journalists and that the press policy of General in Chief Grant had long been along Constitutional lines: no prior restraint. Grant trusted the gentlemen of the press to do the right thing, unless and until someone demonstrated otherwise. Then, as was the case with William Swinton, he took appropriate action.

The men at the top of the Confederate government were not so comfortable with newsmen—Jefferson Davis surrounded himself with a palace guard and rarely spoke with newsmen, or in public. It made little difference, because the newsmen of the South, almost without exception, willingly supported the cause and few efforts were needed to keep them in line.

Harper's Weekly was positively schizophrenic in its depiction of blacks. Most illustrations were blatantly racist caricatures, as in this detail of a plantation cook feeding some children. Yet the portrait below is in a very different style, showing Robert Smalls, a slave who stole a steamship from his owner and turned it over to Federal authorities. This realistic portrait foreshadows Small's postwar service in the House of Representatives. Schizophrenic? Both illustrations appeared on the same page of the June 14, 1862, issue.

During the years following the Civil War, the government slowly developed policies that led to the recognition of an official status for correspondents and to a better control of the flow of information. Slowly. The Spanish-American War of 1898 was a journalistic free-for-all, to the delight of the newspapers and the despair of the military. That war, however, was too brief, just over three months, for any of it to matter very much except perhaps to Lt. Col. Theodore Roosevelt, U.S. Volunteer Cavalry Reserve. American reporters trying to cover World War I were granted formal accreditation (after having posted bond to cover expenses), but largely were kept to the rear and given "such 'hand-picked' news touching military movements as the belligerent governments" saw fit to issue. [9] For World War II, journalists were given accreditation along with a protocol rank equivalent to that of a major; censorship was extended to cover not only the press dispatches, but also the personal letters of the troops.

As a major step forward, some professional journalists who had served during that war, either in the military or as accredited war correspondents, became the cadre for a new military specialty of "public affairs." In theory, the public affairs specialist is the journalist's friend at court, providing access and information on the one hand, while explaining the realities of the news business to senior officials, on the other. It actually works that way, most of the time.

The press policies of World War II continued through the Korean conflict. Some of the rules were markedly different—and somewhat bizarre—for Vietnam. Accreditation was required, yes, but anyone who wanted it could get it, including one seventeen-year-old girl who flew in to do a high school "honors" project. There was no formal censorship, either of the press or individuals.

The Gulf War was a free-for-all of a different sort. The resident population of western journalists in Saudi Arabia went from roughly zero to thousands, almost overnight, and every journalist wanted to be free to cover anything and everything. As a practical matter and to impose some order on chaos, the U.S. Department of Defense assigned most journalists to live with and report on specific units. (Units that declined the honor came too late to the realization that, because they were not much mentioned in news coverage, so too are they now largely missing from histories of the war.) There was no formal censorship, but all copy was subjected to a security review. This proved to be cumbersome and, just as fast-moving events at the end of the Civil War outran the ability of the newspapers to keep up, the fast-moving troops in the Gulf outran the procedures that had been arranged for reviewing and filing copy. At war's end, the media and the military tried to work out some mutually accept-able rules for future conflicts. They agreed on some general principles, and agreed to disagree on others—notably, the need for security review. The media said, you can trust us to understand the need for security; the military said, we trust you but have no idea what conditions might prevail in the next war.

The rush of technology has brought great changes to the nature of war, and to the nature of journalism, as well. Today, it is not only the war correspondent who can view a battle in real time, but also, via satellite and television, so may the audience back home—and any enemy able to download the signal. This poses a special burden for the information gate-keepers: what transmissions should be permitted, and when?

However, human nature seems not to have been much affected. Let two contemporary commentators have the final words, offered in television broadcasts on July 2, 1998. Reflecting on the aftermath of a discredited CNN accusation that U.S. troops had used nerve gas during the Vietnam War, a senior professional journalist said, "People who know better do very bad things in journalism," and a retired general officer charged that the "rush to glory for the sensational story is one of the greatest problems the press has today." [10]

The more things change, the more they remain the same. . . .

Notes and Sources

Chapter 2: State of the Art

1. Bernard A. Weisberger, *Reporters for the Union* (Boston: Little, Brown and Company, 1953), 14.
2. Ibid., 13.
3. Douglas Fermer, *James Gordon Bennett and the New York Herald* (New York: St. Martin's Press, 1986), 187.
4. William Harlan Hale, *Horace Greeley Voice of the People* (New York: Harper & Brothers, 1950), 66–67.
5. Weisberger, *Reporters*, 14.
6. Hale, *Greeley*, 252.
7. James E. Pollard, *The Presidents and the Press* (New York: Macmillan, 1947), 298.
8. Philadelphia *Morning Pennsylvanian*, February 6, 1861.
9. J. Cutler Andrews, *The North Reports the Civil War* (Pittsburgh: University of Pittsburgh Press, 1955), 34.
10. Albert D. Richardson, *The Secret Service, the Field. the Dungeon and the Escape* (Hartford: American Publishing Company, 1865), 18.
11. Andrews, *North Reports*, 61.
12. Richardson, *Secret Service*, 18.
13. Samuel Wilkeson to Sydney Howard Gay, August 6, 1862, quoted in Andrews, *North Reports*, 359.
14. *Preliminary Report on the Eighth Census* (Washington, 1862), 103; New York *Herald*, April 5, 1862.
15. Weisberger, *Reporters*, 253.
16. All Dickens quotations are from the 1844 edition, Charles Dickens, *Martin Chuzzlewit* (New York and London: White and Allen).

Chapter 3: Rehearsals

1. Weisberger, *Reporters*, 33; James Redpath, *The Roving Editor or. Talks with the Slaves in the Southern States* (New York: A. A. Burdick, 1859), 300.
2. New York *Tribune*, October 28, 1859.
3. Oliver Carlson, *The Man who Made News: James Gordon Bennett* (New York: Duell, Sloan and Pearce, 1942), 282.
4. New York *Tribune*, April 12, 1860.
5. New York *Tribune*, March 9, 1859.
6. Weisberger, *Reporters*, 62.
7. New York *Herald*, February 16, January 5, May 28, January 7, 1860.
8. Delivered June 16, 1858, at Springfield. Illinois.
9. Richmond *Enquirer* September 28, 1860.
10. Baltimore *American*, September 27, 1860.
11. Harrisburg *Telegraph*, November 7, 1860.
12. Ibid., November 12, 1860.
13. Quoted in the New York *World*, November 28, 1860.
14. Sandusky (Ohio) *Daily Commercial Register*, December 5, 1860.
15. Boston *Journal*, December 17, 1860.
16. Montgomery *Confederation*, December 7, 1860; Memphis *Daily Appeal*, December 10, 1860.
17. Donald E. Reynolds, *Editors Make War: Southern Newspapers in the Secession Crisis* (Nashville: Vanderbilt University Press, 1970), 157.
18. Richmond *Examiner*, quoted in the Richmond *Enquirer*, December 25, 1860.
19. Newark (New Jersey) *Daily Advertiser*, January 12, 1860.
20. Margaret Leech, *Reveille in Washington* (New York: Carroll & Graf, 1986), 15.
21. Moore, *Rebellion Record*, vol. 1, 43.
22. Muscatine (Iowa) *Daily Review*, November 13, 1860, in Howard Cecil Perkins, *Northern Editorials on Secession* (1942. Reprint, Gloucester, Massachusetts: Peter Smith, 1964), 1035.
23. Chicago *Times*, December 14, 1860, ibid., 1040.
24. Baltimore *American*, January 4, 1861.
25. Erie *Weekly Gazette*, April 4, 1861, Perkins *Northern Editorials*, 1049–1050.
26. Cutler, *North Reports*, 19.
27. Richardson, *Secret Service*, 122–123.
28. Ibid., 19.
29. Ibid., 41.
30. Ibid., 61–64.
31. New Orleans *Crescent*, February 28; March 26, 1861.

32. Weisberger, *Reporters*, 179–180.

33. J. Cutler Andrews, *The South Reports the Civil War* (Princeton: Princeton University Press, 1970), 49–50.

34. Martin Crawford, ed., *William Howard Russell's Civil War: Private Diary and Letters. 1861–1862* (Athens and London: University of Georgia Press, 1992), xxiv.

35. William Howard Russell, *My Diary. North and South* (London: Bradbury and Evans, 1863), vol. 1, 21.

36. Crawford, *Russell's Civil War*, 24.

37. Russell, *Diary*, vol. 1, 29, 37.

38. Ibid., 38.

39. Ibid., 39; Crawford, *Russell's Civil War*, 89.

40. Russell, *Diary*, vol. 1, 57.

41. Ibid.; vol. 1, 79.

42. London *Times*, Russell's letter of March 28, 1861.

43. Russell, *Diary*, vol. 2, 8; London *Times* letter of June 20, 1861.

44. Russell, *Diary*, vol. 2, 18.

45. London *Times*, letter of June 20, 1861.

46. Ibid.

47. Russell, *Diary*, vol. 2, 25.

48. London *Times*, letter of May 30, 1861.

49. Ibid., letter of May 28, 1861.

50. Russell, *Diary*, vol. 1, 214.

51. Ibid.

52. London *Times*, letter of April 19, 1861; *Harper's Weekly*, July 27, 1861.

53. Crawford, *Russell's Civil War*, 90.

54. Russell, *Diary*, vol. 1, 286.

55. Ibid., vol. 1, 339.

56. These quotes from the New York *Times* and New York *Tribune* were published in the August 3, 1861, edition of *Harper's Weekly*.

57. Russell, *Diary*, vol. 1, 142.

58. Ibid., vol. 2, 8; vol. 1, 170.

59. Ibid., vol. 1, 139.

Chapter 4: Sumter

1. Richmond *Enquirer*, October 26, 1860.

2. Buffalo *Commercial Advertiser*, March 8, 1861.

3. Bedford (Pennsylvania) *Gazette*, April 12, 1861.

4. New York *Herald*, April 9, 10, 11, 1861.

5. New York *Times*, April 15, 1861.

6. New York *Tribune*, April 15, 1861.

7. New York *Herald*, April 15, 1861.

8. New York *Times*, April 15, 1861.
9. Emmet Crozier, *Yankee Reporters*, (New York: Oxford University Press, 1956), 50.
10. New York *Tribune*, April 16, 1861.
11. Ibid.
12. New York *Evening Day Book*, April 17, 1861.
13. Richardson, *Secret Service*, 10, 110.
14. Richmond *Enquirer*, April 13, 1861; Vicksburg *Whig*, April 20, 1861.
15. Richardson, *Secret Service*, 117.
16. Louis M. Starr, *Bohemian Brigade, Civil War Newsmen in Action*, (Madison: University of Wisconsin Press, 1987; reprint of the 1954 edition), 37.
17. New York *Times*, April 28, 1861.
18. Virginia *Sentinel*, April 27, 1861.
19. Richmond *Whig*, April 28, 1861.
20. New Orleans *Picayune*, May 10, 1861.

Chapter 5: An Age of Innocence

1. Charleston *Mercury*, April 30, 1861.
2. Burlington (Vermont) *Daily Times*, May 14, 1861.
3. Mobile *Telegraph*, August 20, 1862.
4. Albany (Georgia) *Evening Journal*, May 10, 1861; Raleigh *Democratic Press*, May 8, 1861.
5. London *News*, May 20, 1861.
6. Richardson, *Secret Service*, 111.
7. All, quoted in Edward Pollard, *Southern History of the War* (New York: Fairfax Press, 1990; reprint of the 1866 edition, 2 vols. in 1), vol. 1, 76.
8. Raleigh *Standard*, April 24, 1861; Eufala (Alabama) *Express*, April 25, 1861; Milledgeville (Georgia) *Southern Recorder*, April 30, 1861.
9. New Orleans *Picayune*, May 3, 1861.
10. Richmond *Examiner*, May 25, 1861; Richmond *Enquirer*, May 25, 1861.
11. Pollard, *Southern History*, vol. 1, 81; Russell, *Diary*, vol. 1, 342.
12. New York *Tribune*, April 17, 1861.
13. Ibid., April 22, 1861.
14. Memphis *Appeal*, June 19, 1861.
15. Frank Moore, ed., *The Rebellion Record. A Diary of American Events, with Documents, Narratives, Illustrative Incidents, Poetry, etc.* (New York: Arno Press, 1977; reprint of 12 vols. issued 1861–1868), vol. 1, Documents, 339.
16. Baltimore *American*, June 18, 1861.

17. New York *Tribune*, June 25, 1861.
18. Philadelphia *Press*, July 18, 1861.
19. Leech, *Reveille*, 89, 85.
20. Charleston *Mercury*, May 31, 1861.
21. Ibid., July 11, 1861.
22. Moore, *Rebellion Record*, vol. 2, 14.
23. Richmond *Dispatch*, June 30, 1861.
24. New York *Tribune*, May 23, 1861; New York *Times*, May 25, 1861
25. *National Intelligencer*, June 13, 1861; Chicago *Tribune*, June 24, 1861.
26. Mobile *Register*, July 7, 1861; *Frank Leslie's Illustrated Weekly*, July 27, 1861.
27. Savannah *Republican*, June 4, 1861; *National Intelligencer*, June 13, 1861.
28. Cincinnati *Commercial*, June 20, 1861; Cincinnati *Enquirer*, July 3, 1861; Washington *Star*, July 8, 1861; Moore, *Rebellion Record*, vol. 2, Diary, 23.
29. Russell, *Diary*, vol. 2, 150.
30. New York York *Tribune*, July 13, 1861.
31. Charleston *Mercury*, July 13, 1861.

Chapter 6: A Battle Too Soon

1. Russell, *Diary*, vol. 2, 187.
2. Andrews, *North Reports*, 86.
3. Moore, *Rebellion Record*, vol. 2, Documents, 319, 320.
4. Ibid., vol. 2, Documents, 332.
5. New York *Tribune*, July 19, 1861.
6. Crozier, *Yankee Reporters*, 98.
7. New York *Times*, July 21, 1861.
8. London *Times*, August 6, 1861.
9. Ibid; a similar version is found in Russell's *Diary*, vol. 2, 218.
10. Starr, *Bohemian Brigade*, 46; Crozier, *Yankee Reporters*, 113.
11. New York *Tribune*, July 22, 1861.
12. New York *Times*, July 22, 1861.
13. London *Times*, August 6, 1861.
14. New York *World*, July 22, 1861; New York *Tribune*, July 23, 1861.
15. Philadelphia *Inquirer*, July 22, 1861; New York *World*, July 22, 1861.
16. London *Times*, August 6, 1861; July 31, 1861; Andrews, *North Reports*, 97.
17. Starr, *Bohemian Brigade*, 48.
18. Ibid., 49.
19. London *Times*, August 6, 1861.
20. New York *World*, July 23, 1861.

21. Savannah *Republican*, July 29, 1861.
22. Mobile *Register*, July 24, 1861; Memphis *Daily Appeal*, July 25, 1861.
23. New Orleans *True Delta*, July 23, 1861; New Orleans *Picayune*, July 23, 1861.
24. Charleston *Courier*, July 23, 1861.
25. New Orleans *Crescent*, July 23, 1861.
26. Richmond *Dispatch*, July 29, 1861.
27. Charleston *Mercury*, July 25, 1861; London *Times*, November 22, 1862; Mark Mayo Boatner, *The Civil War Dictionary* (New York: Vintage Books, 1991), 808.
28. Boston *Journal*, July 7, 1862.
29. London *Times*, August 6, 1861.
30. Moore, *Rebellion Record*, vol. 2, Documents, 80–81, 88–89, 109, 110.
31. Ibid., vol. 2, Documents, 109, 81.
32. Philadelphia *Press*, July 23, 1861.
33. Moore, *Rebellion Record*, vol. 2, Documents, 109.
34. *Harper's Weekly*, August 3, 1861.
35. Baltimore *American*, July 26, 1861.
36. Moore, *Rebellion Record*, vol. 2, Documents, 75.
37. Albany (New York) *Evening Journal*, July 27, 1861.
38. Hale, *Greeley*, 249.
39. Starr, *Bohemian Brigade*, 54.
40. Andrews, *North Reports*, 100.
41. New York *World*, July 23, 1861; Baltimore *American*, July 26, 1861.
42. Albany (New York) *Evening Journal*, July 27, 1861.
43. *Harper's Weekly*, August 3, 1861.
44. Moore, *Rebellion Record*, vol. 2, Documents, 116.
45. Baltimore *American*, July 26, 1861; New York *World*, July 23, 1861.
46. Moore, *Rebellion Record*, vol. 2, 55; *Star* comment, reported in the New York *Commercial Advertiser*, August 7, 1861.
47. Moore, *Rebellion Record*, vol. 3, Documents, 29.
48. Ibid., vol. 2, Diary, 72.
49. Ibid., vol. 2, Documents, 538.

Chapter 7: Bull Run Russell

1. Russell, *Diary*, vol. 2, 337.
2. Moore, *Rebellion Record*, vol. 2, 115.
3. Ibid., vol. 2, Documents, 62–63.
4. Ibid., vol. 2, Documents, 60.
5. Ibid., vol. 2, Poetry and Incidents, 29.
6. Ibid., vol. 2, Documents, 63.
7. Ibid.

8. Ibid., vol. 3, Rumors and Incidents, 13.
9. Russell, *Diary*, vol. 2, 296-297.
10. Ibid., vol. 2, 309.
11. Ibid., vol.2, 322.
12. Ibid., vol. 2, 337.
13. New York *Times*, November 11, 1861.
14. Russell, *Diary*, vol. 2, 401–402, 413.
15. Crawford, *Russell's Civil War*, xiv.
16. Russell, *Diary*, vol. 2, 433.
17. London *Times*, March 2, 1861.
18. Russell, *Diary*, vol. 2, 435–436.
19. Ibid.
20. Ibid., vol. 2, 437.
21. London *Times*, April 24, 1862.
22. Brayton Harris, "The Role of the Press in the Civil War," *Civil War* 15 (December 1988), 23.
23. Russell, *Diary*, vol. 2, 439.
24. Crawford, *Russell's Civil War*, 237.
25. Russell, *Diary*, vol. 2, 439–442.
26. New York *Times*, April 10, 1862.

Chapter 8: Sedition and Supression: North

1. Philadelphia *Press*, August 23, 1861.
2. New York *World*, September 13, 1861.
3. Moore, *Rebellion Record*, vol. 3, Diary, 36.
4. New Haven *Palladium*, August 26, 1861.
5. Moore, *Rebellion Record*, vol. 2, Documents, 490.
6. Buffalo *Courier*, August 24, 1861; New York *Herald*, August 21, 1861.
7. Moore, *Rebellion Record*, September 18, 1861; Richardson, *Secret Service*, 163.
8. St. Louis *Evening News*, September 23, 1861.
9. *Ohio Statesman*, September 26, 1861.
10. Starr, *Bohemian Brigade*, 63.
11. Andrews, *North Reports*, 130.
12. New York *Tribune*, October 8, 1861.
13. Ibid., November 7, 1861.
14. Moore, *Rebellion Record*, vol. 5, Documents, 2.
15. New Orleans *Delta*, June 8, 1862.
16. Moore, *Rebellion Record*, vol. 5, Documents, 136.
17. Ibid., Diary, 2.
18. New Orleans *Delta*, July 12, 1862.
19. New York *World*, August 29, 1864.

20. New York *Daily News*, October 6, 1864.
21. Moore, *Rebellion Record*, vol. 7, Diary, 5.

Chapter 9: Sedition and Supression: South

1. Alexandria (Louisiana) *Constitutional*, February 16, 1861.
2. Letter, February 18, 1862, to Virginia governor John Lechter; quoted in Reynolds, *Editors Make War*, 173.
3. Ibid., 206.
4. Richmond *Examiner*, March 3, 1863.
5. Mobile *Daily Tribune* as reprinted in the Richmond *Examiner*, June 9, 1863; Mobile *Daily Advertiser and Register*, November 19, 1864.
6. Andrews, *South Reports*, 515.
7. Ibid.
8. E. Merton Coulter, *The Confederate States of America. 1861–1865* (Baton Rouge: Louisiana State University Press, 1950), 503.
9. Knoxville *Whig*, January 19, 1861; Charleston *Mercury*, May 1, 1861.
10. Moore, *Rebellion Record*, vol. 1, Rumors and Incidents, 109.
11. Ibid., 26.
12. New York *Commercial*, August 3, 1861.
13. Knoxville *Whig*, September 7, 1861.
14. Moore, *Rebellion Record*, vol. 4, Diary, 2.
15. Richardson, *Secret Service*, 155.
16. Newbern (North Carolina) *Progress*, March 23, 1862.
17. Richardson, *Secret Service*, 265.
18. Reynolds, *Editors Make War*, 207.
19. Charleston *Mercury*, March 22, 1862.
20. Andrews, *South Reports*, 288.
21. Mark E. Neely Jr., Henry Holtzer, and Gabor S. Boritt, *The Confederate Image: Prints of the Lost Cause* (Chapel Hill and London: University of North Carolina Press, 1987), 23.
22. Ibid., 29.
23. *Southern Illustrated News*, July 25, 1863.

Chapter 10: Modus Scribendi

1. L. L. Crounse, "The Army Correspondent," *Harper's New Monthly Magazine* (October 1863), 627.
2. New York *Tribune*, June 29, 1864; letter, Samuel Wilkeson to Sidney Gay, July 5, 1862, quoted in Starr, *Bohemian Brigade*, 148; New York *Herald*, June 7, 1862; Charleston *Courier*, September 3, 1862.
3. Starr, *Bohemian Brigade*, 112–113.
4. Richmond *Dispatch*, March 14, 1862.

5. Andrews, *North Reports*, 70.
6. Ibid., 46.
7. New York *Times*, November 22, 1861; Weisberger, *Reporters*, 186.
8. Weisberger, *Reporters*, 188; 177–178.
9. *Missouri Republican*, November 16, 1861.
10. Andrews, *North Reports*, 49.
11. Charleston *Mercury*, April 22, 1861.
12. Chicago *Times*, February 17, 1862.
13. Andrews, *North Reports*, 29.
14. William Shanks, "How We Get Our News," *Harper's New Monthly Magazine* (May 1867), 519.
15. Starr, *Bohemian Brigade*, 233.
16. Shanks, "How We Get Our News," 519.
17. Andrews, *North Reports*, 192.
18. New York *Tribune*, February 15, 1863.
19. Andrews, *North Reports*, 432; 434.
20. New Orleans *Daily Crescent*, October 30, 1861.
21. Franc B. Wilkie, *Walks Around Chicago, 1871–1881. And Army and Miscellaneous Sketches* (Chicago: 1882), 43–45.
22. New York *Times*, October 3, 1861.
23. Cincinnati *Commercial*, March 2, 1863.
24. Richardson, *Secret Service*, 271.
25. Junius Henri Browne, *Four Years in Secessia* (New York: Arno Press, reprint 1970), 84–85.
26. New York *Times*, October 30, 1862.
27. Charleston *Daily Courier*, July 21, 1863.
28. Reprinted in the New York *Times*, April 13, 1862; Starr, *Bohemian Brigade*, 114.
29. Columbus (Georgia) *Sun*, February 17, 1863.

Chapter 11: Washington

1. Andrews, *North Reports*, 50.
2. Cincinnati *Commercial*, October 25, 1861.
3. Starr, *Bohemian Brigade*, 68.
4. Ibid.
5. New York *Times*, November 11, 1861.
6. Starr, *Bohemian Brigade*, 76; Leech, *Reveille*, 299; Weisberger, *Reporters*, 138.
7. Starr, *Bohemian Brigade*, 78.
8. Ibid.
9. Andrews, *North Reports*, 57.
10. Moore, *Rebellion Record*, vol. 4, Diary, 28.

11. Act of February 3, 1862.
12. Moore, *Rebellion Record*, vol. 4, Diary, 40.
13. Starr, *Bohemian Brigade*, 85.
14. Moore, *Rebellion Record*, vol. 4, Diary, 67.
15. Andrews, *North Reports*, 194.
16. Starr, *Bohemian Brigade*, 83.
17. Weisberger, *Reporters*, 222–223; Chicago *Tribune*, February 1, 1862.
18. London *Times*, November 8, 1862.
19. Mobile *Evening News*, September 22, 1862.
20. Patricia Faust, ed., *Historical Times Illustrated Encyclopedeia of the Civil War* (New York: Harper Perennial, reprint 1991), 493.
21. Weisberger, *Reporters*, 87.
22. Ibid., 89.
23. Chicago *Times*, March 26, 1862.
24. Leech, *Reveille*, 123.
25. Starr, *Bohemian Brigade*, 94.
26. Moore, *Rebellion Record*, vol. 4, Documents, 306–307.
27. New York *Tribune*, March 15, 1862.
28. Weisberger, *Reporters*, 192.
29. Nathaniel Hawthorne, "Chiefly about War Matters," *Atlantic Monthly* 10 (July 1862), 43–61.

Chapter 12: Command and Control

1. James G. Smart, ed., *A Radical View: the "Agate" Dispatches of Whitelaw Reid. 1861–1865* (Memphis: Memphis State University Press, 1976), vol. 1, 190.
2. Starr, *Bohemian Brigade*, 119; Robert Debs Heinl Jr., ed., *Dictionary of Military and Naval Quotations* (Annapolis: United States Naval Institute, 1966), 258.
3. James G. Randall, "The Newspaper Problem in its Bearing Upon Military Secrecy During the Civil War," *American Historical Review* 23 (January 1918), 303–323; Starr, *Bohemian Brigade*, 39.
4. Starr, *Bohemian Brigade*, 197.
5. Andrews, *North Reports*, 711.
6. Andrews, *South Reports*, 303–304.
7. New York *Herald*, April 10, 1862.
8. Crozier, *Yankee Reporters*, 220.
9. Cincinnati *Gazette*, April 15, 1862; note the similarity to Junius Browne's "eyewitness" account of Pea Ridge, page 130.
10. Starr, *Bohemian Brigade*, 103.
11. Ibid., 104.
12. Ibid., 104; 102.

13. Ibid., 95–96.
14. Crounse, "Army Correspondent," *Harper's New Monthly Magazine* (October 1863), 628.
15. Moore, *Rebellion Record*, vol. 4, Diary, 82.
16. Crounse, "Army Correspondent," *Harper's New Monthly Magazine* (October 1863), 628–629.
17. Moore, *Rebellion Record*, vol. 5, Diary, 6.
18. New York *Herald*, May 10, 1862.
19. Weisberger, *Reporters*, 103.
20. Smart, *Radical View*, 193–194.
21. Ibid., 194–195
22. Ibid., 195.
23. Ibid., 195.
24. New York *Times*, May 26, 1862.
25. New York *World*, June 13, 1862.
26. Andrews, *North Reports*, 188.
27. Charles Carleton Coffin, *Four Years of Fighting: A Volume of Personal Observation with the Army and Navy. from the first Battle of Bull Run to the Fall of Richmond* (Boston: Ticknor and Fields, 1866), 99.

Chapter 13: The Summer of '62

1. The full dispatch is reproduced in Moore, *Rebellion Record*, vol. 5, Documents, 466–472.
2. Memphis *Appeal*, May 22, 1862.
3. Andrews, *North Reports*, 202.
4. Moore, *Rebellion Record*, vol. 5, Documents, 481; Cincinnati *Commercial*, June 7, 1862.
5. Andrews, *South Reports*, 191.
6. Ibid.
7. New York *Times*, June 16, 1862.
8. Moore, *Rebellion Record*, vol. 12, Documents, 356.
9. Ibid., 356.
10. Ibid., 357.
11. Ibid.
12. Ibid., 358.
13. Ibid., 358–359.
14. Weisberger, *Reporters*, 233.
15. Andrews, *North Reports*, 689.
16. New York *World*, July 2, 1862.
17. New York *Herald*, July 2, 1862.
18. Weisberger, *Reporters*, 193.
19. Andrews, *North Reports*, 215–216.

20. Moore, *Rebellion Record*, vol. 12, Documents, 251.
21. Crozier, *Yankee Reporters*, 257.
22. Andrews, *South Reports*, 118–119.
23. Ibid., 194.
24. Pollard, *Southern History*, 360.
25. Andrews, *South Reports*, 192–193.
26. Ibid., 193.
27. Atlanta *Confederacy*, July 21, 1862.
28. Richmond *Dispatch*, June 16, 1862.
29. Andrews, *South Reports*, 237.
30. Montgomery *Daily Advertiser*, August 11, 1862.
31. Andrews, *South Reports*, 236.
32. George W. Smalley, *Anglo-American Memories* (New York: G. P. Putnam's Sons, 1911), 134.
33. Cincinnati *Commercial*, January 14, 1863.
34. Starr, *Bohemian Brigade*, 129.
35. Smalley, *Memories*, 134; Starr, *Bohemian Brigade*, 130.
36. Starr, *Bohemian Brigade*, 130.
37. Ibid., 132.
38. Moore, *Rebellion Record*, vol. 6, Poetry and Incidents, 10, 31.
39. Richmond *Dispatch*, September 17, 1862.
40. Moore, *Rebellion Record*, vol. 12, Documents, 755.
41. Ibid.
42-1. *War of the Rebellion: A Compilation of the Official Records of the Union and Confederate Armies* (Washington: U.S. Government Printing Office, 1880–1901), Series 1, vol. 16, Pt. 1: Reports, 936–937.
42-2. Andrews, *South Reports*, 242.
43. Ibid., 253.
44. Ibid.
45. Philadelphia *Press*, July 31, 1862.
46. Weisberger, *Reporters*, 150–151
47. Moore, *Rebellion Record*, vol. 12, Documents, 477.
48. General Order 19, Washington, February 22, 1862.
49. Moore, *Rebellion Record*, vol. 5, Rumors and Incidents, 26.
50. Smalley, *Memories*, 138–139.
51. Ibid., 142.
52. Ibid., 146–147.
53. Starr, *Bohemian Brigade*, 141.
54. George Washburn Smalley, "Chapters in Journalism," *Harper's New Monthly Magazine* 89 (August 1894), 428–429.
55. Smalley, *Memories*, 149.
56. Ibid., 148–149.
57. Starr, *Bohemian Brigade*, 144.

58. New York *Tribune*, September 19, 1862.
59. Ibid.
60. Starr, *Bohemian Brigade*, 148; Richardson, *Secret Service*, 286; Henry Villard, *Memoirs*, 335.
61. Boston *Journal*, September 17, 1862.
62. New York *World*, Richmond *Enquirer*, Charleston *Courier*, Savannah *Republican*. Full text of each in Moore, *Rebellion Record*, vol. 5, Documents, 472–476.
63. Mobile *Daily Advertiser and Register*, September 25, 1862.
64. Charleston *Daily Courier*, September 11, 1862.
65. Memphis *Daily Appeal*, October 13, 1862.
66. Charleston *Daily Courier*, September 11, 1862.
67. Mobile *Daily Advertiser and Register*, October 2, 1862.
68. New York *Tribune*, October 27, 1862, October 30, 1862.
69. Moore, *Rebellion Record*, vol. 12, Documents, 655.

Chapter 14: A Matter of Color

1. Savannah *Republican*, reprinted in Moore, *Rebellion Record*, vol. 1, 44.
2. Moore, *Rebellion Record*, vol. 12, 255–256.
3. Memphis *Appeal*, July 31, 1861.
4. Indiana *Journal*, October 5, 1861.
5. Weisberger, *Reporters*, 265.
6. Baltimore *American*, January 16, 1861.
7. New York *Tribune*, May 23, 1863.
8. New York *Times*, June 2, 1863.
9. Chicago *Times*, April 21, 1864.
10. Villard, *Memoirs*, vol. 1, 213; Boston *Journal*, August 1, 1862; Weisberger, *Reporters*, 198, 234; Smart, *Radical View*, 102.
11. London *Times*, November 8, 1862.
12. Weisberger, *Reporters*, 154, 262; Andrews, *North Reports*, 297.
13. Butler's 1892 *Autobiography*, quoted in Jay M. Shafritz, *Words on War* (New York: Prentice Hall, 1990), 61.
14. New York *Times*, June 2, 1861, as quoted in Moore, *Rebellion Record*, vol. 1, Documents, 313.
15. New York *Tribune*, May 31, as quoted in Moore, *Rebellion Record*, vol. 1, Documents, 314.
16. Moore, *Rebellion Record*, vol. 2, Documents, 437.
17. Ibid., 493.
18. Louisville *Journal*, August 3, 1861.
19. Moore, *Rebellion Record*, vol. 12, 754.
20. Ibid.
21. Ibid.

22. Chicago *Times*, April 28, 1862.
23. Ohio *Statesman*, August 2, 1861; Weisberger, *Reporters*, 163, 166.
24. George Alfred Townsend, *Campaigns of a Non-Combatant and his Romaunt Abroad during* the War (Alexandria: Time-Life Books, 1982; reprint of 1866 edition), 146.
25. Weisberger, *Reporters*, 165.
26. Ibid.
27. Philadelphia *Press*, May 21, 1862.
28. New York *Times*, June 2, 8, 1862.
29. Weisberger, *Reporters*, 207–209.
30. Ibid., 209.
31. Cincinnati *Enquirer*, December 5, 1862; *Missouri Republican*, February 19, 1862.
32. Weisberger, *Reporters*, 155.
33. Ibid., 156.
34. New York *Tribune*, September 20, 1861.
35. Weisberger, *Reporters*, 159.
36. Ibid., 270.
37. Smart, *Radical View*, 71–73.
38. James M. McPherson, *The Negro's Civil War* (New York: Ballantine Books, 1991), 166.
39. Ibid., 165–166.
40. New York *Tribune*, August 20, 1862.
41. Hale, *Greeley*, 262–263.
42. Ibid., 263.
43. Moore, *Rebellion Record*, vol. 5, Documents, 475.
44. Hale, *Greeley*. 265; Wayne County (Ohio) *Democrat*, February 19, 1863.
45. Chicago *Times*, October 4, 1862; New York *Herald*, November 8, 1862; Chicago *Tribune*, November 19, 1862.
46. Richmond *Examiner*, October 1, 1862; Moore, *Rebellion Record*, vol. 5, Diary, 89.
47. London *Times*, dateline October 7, 1862.
48. London *Times*, dateline November 5, 1862.
49. Wayne County (Ohio) *Democrat*, January 6, 1863.
50. Smart, *Radical View*, 87–90.
51. McPherson, *Negro's Civil War*, 176.
52. Ibid., 221.

Chapter 15: The Press Reports a Battle: Fredericksburg, I

1. Andrews, *North Reports*, 319; Richardson, *Secret Service*, 303.
2. *Harper's Weekly*, November 15, 1862.

3. Richardson, *Secret Service*, 306; Villard, *Memoirs*, vol. 1, 350; Andrews, *North Reports*, 318; *Army Navy Journal*, reprinted in the New York *Times*, December 19, 1862; Starr, *Bohemian Brigade*, 164.

4. London *Times*, October 7, 1862.

5. William Marvel, *Burnside* (Chapel Hill and London: University of North Carolina Press, 1991), 159.

6. Villard, *Memoirs*, 347; Starr, *Bohemian Brigade*, 194.

7. Andrews, *North Reports*, 705.

8. New York *Tribune*, December 13, 1862.

9. Moore, *Rebellion Record*, vol. 11, Documents, 2.

10. Andrews, *North Reports*, 321.

11. Moore, *Rebellion Record*, vol. 5, Diary, 10.

12. Ibid., 68.

13. London *Times*, December 30, 1862.

14. Andrews, *South Reports*, 222–223; Philadelphia *Inquirer*, November 18, 1862.

15. New York *Times*, November 27, 1862.

16. London *Times*, letter of November 30, 1862.

17. New York *Times*, dateline, December 9, 1862.

18. *Harper's Weekly*, December 27, 1862.

19-1. Moore, *Rebellion Record*, vol. 6, Documents, 95.

19-2. Ibid., 96.

20. New York *Times*, December 12, 1862; Moore, *Rebellion Record*, vol. 6, 97; Andrews, *North Reports*, 324.

21. Andrews, *South Reports*, 227; Richmond *Inquirer*, December 12, 1862.

22. Pollard, *Southern History*, 540.

23. Moore, *Rebellion Record*, vol. 6, Documents, 101.

24. New York *Times*, December 15, 1862.

25. Moore, *Rebellion Record*, vol. 6, Documents, 97.

26. New York *Times*, December 12, 1862.

27. Moore, *Rebellion Record*, vol. 6, Documents, 249.

28. New York *Times*, December 15, 1862.

29. Ibid., December 16, 1862.

30. Moore, *Rebellion Record*, vol. 6, Documents, 97–98.

31. Ibid., 97.

32. New York *Times*, December 15, 1862.

33. Moore, *Rebellion Record*, vol. 6, Documents, 98.

34. New York *Tribune*, December 15, 1862.

35. Moore, *Rebellion Record*, vol. 6, Documents, 107.

36. London *Times*, January 23, 1863.

37. Richmond *Examiner*, December 12, 1862; Richmond *Dispatch*, December 12, 1862.

38. London *Times*, January 23, 1863.

39. Andrews, *South Reports*, 224.
40. London *Times*, January 23, 1863.

Chapter 16: The Press Reports a Battle: Fredericksburg, II

1. Moore, *Rebellion Record*, vol. 6, Documents, 98.
2. Ibid., 99.
3. Moore, *Rebellion Record*, vol. 6, Documents, 105.
4. New York *Times*, December 17, 1862.
5. Moore, *Rebellion Record*, vol. 6, Documents, 99.
6. Ibid.
7. New York *Times*, December 17, 1862.
8. Moore, *Rebellion Record*, vol. 6, Documents, 103.
9. Ibid., 100.
10. London *Times*, January 23, 1863.
11. Ibid.
12. Moore, *Rebellion Record*, vol. 6, Documents, 99.
13. Ibid.
14. London *Times*, January 23, 1863.
15. Villard, *Memoirs*, vol. 1, 389.
16. Ibid., 390–391.
17. London *Times*, January 23, 1863.
18. Ibid.
19. Ibid.
20. New York *Times*, December 15, 1862.
21. Moore, *Rebellion Record*, vol. 11, Documents, 9.
22. New York *Times*, December 17, 1862.
23. Ibid.
24. Ibid.
25. Ibid.
26. Andrews, *North Reports*, 335.
27. London *Times*, January 23, 1863.
28. Richard Barksdale Harwell, *Confederate Reader* (New York: Mallard Press, 1991; reprint of 1957 edition), 144.
29. Moore, *Rebellion Record*, vol. 6, Documents, 100; New York *Times*, December 17, 1862; Moore, *Rebellion Record*, vol. 6, Documents, 107.
30. London *Times*, January 23, 1863.
31. Moore, *Rebellion Record*, vol. 6, Documents, 107.
32. New York *Herald*, December 17, 1862.
33. New York *Times*, December 17, 1862.
34. New York *Tribune*, December 18, 1862.
35. Moore, *Rebellion Record*, vol. 6, Documents, 93.

36. Richardson, *Secret Service*, 306.
37. New York *Times*, December 21, 1862.
38. *Harper's Weekly*. December 27, 1862.
39. Starr, *Bohemian Brigade*, 168.

Chapter 17: The Other War

1. Crozier, *Yankee Reporters*, 305.
2. Michael Fellman, *Citizen Sherman* (New York: Random House, 1995), 90.
3. Andrews, *North Reports*, 115. This is one of at least three versions of the conversation. The others are in Whitelaw Reid, *Ohio in the War* (Columbus, 1893), vol. 1, 61; and the Cincinnati *Commercial*, September 26, 1861.
4. Fellman, *Citizen Sherman*, 94.
5. Villard, *Memoirs*, vol. 1, 212.
6. *Frank Leslie's Illustrated Newspaper*, December 21, 1861.
7. Moore, *Rebellion Record*, vol. 5, Documents, 318–319.
8. Andrews, *North Reports*, 377.
9. New York *Times*, January 18, 1863.
10. Moore, *Rebellion Record*, vol. 6, 318.
11. Crozier, *Yankee Reporters*, 295–296.
12-1. Ibid., 301.
12-2. Ibid.
13. Starr, *Bohemian Brigade*, 178.
14. Ibid., 178–179.
15. Ibid. 178.
16. Crozier, *Yankee Reporters*, 300; Starr, *Bohemian Brigade*, 178; M. A. D. W. Howe, *Home Letters of General Sherman* (New York, 1909), 238.
17. Andrews, *North Reports*, 379
18. Fellman, *Citizen Sherman*, 129.
19. Richardson, *Secret Service*, 320.
20. Ibid., 320–323.
21. Fellman, *Sherman*, 129; Crozier, *Yankee Reporters*, 304.
22. Crozier, *Yankee Reporters*, 305.
23. *Missouri Democrat*, January 18, 1863. (Full text may be found in Moore, *Rebellion Record*, vol. 6, 310–319.
24. Ibid.
25. Ibid.
26. Weisberger, *Reporters*, 111.
27. Andrews, *North Reports*, 383.
28. New York *Herald*, March 14, 1863.

29. Moore, *Rebellion Record*, vol. 11, Documents, 29; Andrews, *North Reports*, 552.
30. Andrews, *North Reports*, 614–615.
31. Ibid., 614–619.

Chapter 18: Transitions, 1863

1. Robert E. Denney, *The Civil War Years* (New York: Sterling Publishing, 1992), 257–258.
2. Andrews, *North Reports*, 339.
3. Ibid., 340.
4. Noah Brooks, *Washington in Lincoln's Time* (New York, 1895), 52.
5. New York *Times*, February 12, 1863; Andrews, *North Reports*, 359.
6. Starr, *Bohemian Brigade*, 195.
7. Ibid., 195–196.
8. Ibid., 196.
9. Gideon Welles, *The Diary of Gideon Welles* (Boston and New York: Houghton Mifflin Company, 1911), 348.
10. Smalley, *Memories*, 158; Starr, *Bohemian Brigade*, 200.
11. Smalley, *Memories*, 160.
12. Andrews, *South Reports*, 303–304.
13. Andrews, *North Reports*, 411.
14. Ibid., 384.
15. Ibid., 384.
16. Ibid., 714.
17. Starr, *Bohemian Brigade*, 281.
18. Ibid., 283–286.
19. New York *Times*, June 12, 1863.
20. Starr, *Bohemian Brigade*, 184.
21. Browne, *Four Years*, 231–238; Richardson, *Secret Service*, 337–345.
22. Browne, *Four Years*, 238.
23. Richardson, *Secret Service*, 421; Starr, *Bohemian Brigade*, 188.
24. Starr, *Bohemian Brigade*, 190.
25. Richardson, *Secret Service*, 421–422.
26. Ibid.
27. Starr, *Bohemian Brigade*, 192.
28. New York *Times*, June 16, 1862.
29. London *Times*, letter of November 21, 1862.
30. Washington *Morning Chronicle*, May 13, 1863.
31. Rev. H. M. Field, *Bright Skies and Dark Shadows*, 286; quoted in Henderson, Colonel G. F. R., *Stonewall Jackson and the American Civil War* (Longmans, Green and Co.: London, New York, Toronto. Authorized American Edition 1949).

32. Neeley, et al., *Confederate Image*, 108.
33. Ibid., 113–114.
34. Ibid., 114.
35. Ibid., 114–115.
36. Harwell, *Confederate Reader*, 191–193.

Chapter 19: The Poet as Historian, I

1. Henry Kyd Douglas, "Stonewall Jackson in Maryland," *Century Magazine*, June 1886, 287.
2. Whitman Bennett, *Whittier, Bard of Freedom* (Chapel Hill: University of North Carolina Press, 1941), 271.
3. Ibid., 254; Edmund Wilson, *Patriotic Gore* (New York: Oxford University Press, 1952), 470–471.
4. Lenoir Chambers, *Stonewall Jackson* (New York: William Morrow, 1959), 194.
5. Francis F. Browne, ed., *Bugle Echoes* (Boston: White Stokes and Allen, 1889), 124.
6. *Battles and Leaders of the Civil War*, vol. 2, 620.
7. John B. Pickard, ed., *Letters of John Greenleaf Whittier* (Cambridge, Massachusetts: Belknap Press of Harvard University Press, 1975), 46.
8. Ibid.
9. Philadelphia *Times*, July 21, 1886.
10. Ibid.
11. *Century*, September 1888, 197.
12. Harris, "Role of Newspapers," 79.
13. Charles Osborne, *Jubal: The Life and Times of General Jubal A. Early, CSA. Defender of the Lost Cause* (Chapel Hill: Algonquin Books of Chapel Hill, 1992), 118–119.
14. Chambers, *Stonewall Jackson*, 199.
15. Henry Kyd Douglas, *I Rode with Stonewall* (Chapel Hill: University of North Carolina Press, 1940), 152.
16. Ibid.
17. Osborne, *Jubal*, 125.
18. Andrews, *South Reports*, 206.
19. Chambers, *Stonewall Jackson*, 194.

Chapter 20: Watershed

1. Moore, *Rebellion Record*, vol. 7, Diary, 10; New York *Times*, July 1, 1863.
2. Andrews, *North Reports*, 413.
3. Ibid., 431.

4. Welles, *Diary*, 357.
5. Andrews, *North Reports*, 429.
6. Smart, *Radical View*, vol. 2, 62.
7. New York *Times*, July 6, 1863.
8. Andrews, *North Reports*, 481.
9. Cincinnati *Gazette*, December 2, 1863.
10. Philip Knightley, *The First Casualty* (New York and London: Harcourt Brace Jovanovich, 1975), 22.
11. *Frank Leslie's*, November 21, 1863.
12. Ibid.
13. *Harper's Weekly*, November 21, 1863.
14. Weisberger, *Reporters*, 168, 169.
15. Philadelphia *Inquirer*, May 27, 1864.
16. Horace Porter, *Campaigning with Grant* (New York: Mallard Press, 1991), 83–84.
17. Crozier, *Yankee Reporters*, 394.
18. Andrews, *North Reports*, 547.
19. New York *Times*, July 14, 1864.
20. Ibid.
21. Andrews, *North Reports*, 734.

Chapter 21: The Poet as Historian, II

1. Browne, *Bugle Echoes*, 242–243.
2. Philip H. Sheridan, *Personal Memoirs of P. H. Sheridan, General, United States Army* (1888. Reprint, 2 vols. in 1, with an introduction by Jeffly D. Wert, New York: Da Capo Press, 1992), viii.
3. New York *Times*, September 21, 1864.
4. Andrews, *North Reports*, 602.
5. *Macmillan's Magazine* 15 (August 1904), 306.
6. *The Independent*, vol. 53, 2398.
7. Andrews, *South Reports*, 420.
8. Ibid., 419–420.
9. Ibid., 420.
10. Ibid., 424.
11. New York *Times*, October 21, 1864.
12. Ibid., 421.
13. *Harper's Weekly*, October 11, 1864.
14. *Battles and Leaders*, vol. 4, 513.
15. Starr, *Bohemian Brigade*, 332.
16. Andrews, *North Reports*, 606–607.
17. New York *Times*, October 22, 1864.
18. John Fleischman, "The Object at Hand," *Smithsonian* 27:8 (November 1996), 30.

19. Starr, *Bohemian Brigade*, 330.
20. Sheridan, *Memoirs*, vol. 2, 318–319.
21. Ibid., 319.
22. Ibid., 322–323.
23. Ibid., 329; Thomas A. Lewis, *Guns of Cedar Creek.* (New York: Harper & Row, 1988), 248.
24. Sheridan, *Memoirs*, 329.
25. Pollard, *Southern History*, 408.
26-1. Ibid., 409.
26-2. Lewis, *Cedar Creek* 258.
27. Andrews, *South Reports*, 424.
28. Lewis, *Cedar Creek*, 249.
29. Sydney H. Kasper, "Rienzi's Story," *Civil War Times Illustrated* 29 (January 1989), 25.
30. New York *Herald*, November 7, 1864.
31. Sheridan, *Memoirs*, vol. 1, 96.

Chapter 22: Endgame

1. Coffin, *Four Years of Fighting*, 511–512.
2. Andrews, *South Reports*, 426–427.
3. Richmond *Dispatch*, January 2, 1865; Meridian (Mississippi) *Daily Clarion*, January 2, 1865.
4. Andrews, *South Reports*, 426.
5. Richmond *Enquirer*, October 18, 1864; November 4, 1864.
6. Alfred Hoyt Bill, *The Beleaguered City: Richmond, 1861–1865* (New York: Alfred A. Knopf, 1946), 258; Richmond *Whig*, November 9, 1864.
7. Moore, *Rebellion Record*; Pollard, *Southern History*, vol. 11, 475–476.
8. McPherson, *Negro's Civil War*, 248; James M. McPherson, *Battle Cry of Freedom: The Civil War Era* (New York: Oxford University Press, 1988), 836; 835.
9. Quoted in Coffin, *Four Years of Fighting*, 516.
10. Richmond *Whig*, February 20, 1865.
11. Ibid., February 23, 1865.
12. McPherson, *Battle Cry*, 834.
13. Pollard, *Southern History*, 473; Coffin, *Four Years of Fighting*, 517.
14. Pollard, *Southern History*, 464–467.
15. Ibid., 467.
16. Coffin, *Four Years of Fighting*, 519.
17. R. J. M. Blackett, *Thomas Morris Chester, Black Civil War Correspondent* (New York: Da Capo Press, paperback of 1989 Louisiana State University Press edition), 291.
18. Ibid., 303.

19. Ibid., 313.
20. Coffin, *Four Years of Fighting*, 508; Smart, *Radical View*, vol. 2, 197.
21. Coffin, *Four Years of Fighting*, 511–512.
22. Richmond *Whig*, April 4, 1865.
23. George Alfred Townsend, *Campaigns of a Non-Combatant, and his Romaunt Abroad during the War* (1866. Reprint, Alexandria: Time-Life Books, 1982), 345.
24. Andrews, *South Reports*, 500.
25. New York *World*, April 4, 1865; New York *Herald*, April 4, 1865.
26. New York *Tribune*, April 4, 1865.
27. Townsend, *Campaigns*, 347.
28. Andrews, *North Reports*, 637.
29. McPherson, *Battle Cry*, 852.
30. Harwell, *Confederate Reader*, 370.
31. Neeley, et al., *Confederate Image*, 82.
32. New York *Herald*, May 15, 1865.
33. Neeley, et al., *Confederate Image*, 93, 95.
34. Ibid., 94.
35. *Frank Leslie's*, June 3, 1865; New York *Herald*, May 23, 1865; Neeley, et al., *Confederate Image*, 94.
36. Coffin, *Four Years of Fighting*, 516.
37. Edward Pollard, *The Lost Cause: A New Southern History of the War of the Confederates* (1866. Reprint, Freeport, New York: Books for Libraries Press, 1970), 729, 740; Edward Pollard, *The Lost Cause Regained* (1868. Reprint, Freeport, New York: Books for Libraries Press, 1970), 14.

Chapter 23: Coda

1. Randall, "Newspaper Problem," 303.
2. James Parton, "The New York *Herald*," *North American Review* 102 (April 1866), 373–419.
3. New York *Herald*, April 7, 1865.
4. *Century* 28 (October 1884), 943–944.
5. Rollin G. Osterweis, *The Myth of the Lost Cause. 1865–1900* (Hamden, Connecticut): Archon Books, 1973), 67–68.
6. Browne, *Four Years*, 15.
7. Sherman, *Memoirs*, vol. 2, 408.
8. Crounse, "Army Correspondent," 633.
9. Randall, "Newspaper Problem," 303.
10. Marvin Kalb, guest on CNBC "Hardball," July 2, 1998; Lt. Gen. Bernard Trainer, USMC (Ret.), guest on MSNBC, July 2, 1998.

Selected Bibliography

NEWSPAPERS

Newspaper sources are cited in the text and were reviewed in various libraries and depositories, especially the Library of Congress, the Western Reserve Historical Society, Florida Atlantic University, the University of Akron and, via the World Wide Web, the University of Virginia.

BOOKS AND ARTICLES

Adams, George Worthington. *Doctors in Blue, The Medical History of the Union Army in the Civil War*. New York: Morningside, 1952.

Andrews, J. Cutler. *The North Reports the Civil War*. Pittsburgh: University of Pittsburgh Press, 1955.

————. *The South Reports the Civil War*. Princeton: Princeton University Press, 1970.

Andrews, Peter. "The Media and the Military." *American Heritage* 42/4 (July/August 1991): 78–85.

Babcock, Havilah. "The Press and the Civil War." *Journalism Quarterly* 6 (March 1929): 1–5.

Ballard, C. K. "Cheers for Jefferson Davis." *American History Illustrated* 16 (May 1981): 8–15.

Bennett, Whitman. *Whittier, Bard of Freedom*. Chapel Hill: University of North Carolina Press, 1941.

Bigelow, Donald Nevius. *William Conant Church and the Army and Navy Journal*. New York: Columbia University Press, 1952.

Bill, Alfred Hoyt. *The Beleaguered City: Richmond, 1861–1865*. New York: Alfred A. Knopf, 1946.

Blackett, R. J. M., ed. *Thomas Morris Chester: Black Civil War Correspondent; His Dispatches from the Virginia Front*. Baton Rouge: Louisiana State University Press, 1989.

Boatner, Mark M. III. *The Civil War Dictionary*. New York: Vintage Civil War Library, 1991.

Bowman, John S., ed. *The Civil War Day by Day*. New York: Barnes & Noble, 1989.

Browne, Francis F., ed. *Bugle Echoes*. Boston: White Stokes and Allen, 1889.

Browne, Junius Henri. *Four Years in Secessia*. Hartford: O. D. Case and Company, 1865.

Butler, Benjamin Franklin. *Autobiography and Personal Reminiscences of Major General Benj. F. Butler; Butler's Book*. Boston: A. M. Thayer & Co., 1892.

Carlson, Oliver. *The Man Who Made News: James Gordon Bennett*. New York: Duell, Sloan and Pearce, 1942.

Chambers, Lenoir. *Stonewall Jackson*. New York: William Morrow, 1959.

Chesnut, Mary Boykin. *A Diary from Dixie*. Boston: Houghton Mifflin, 1949.

Coffin, Charles Carleton. *Four Years of Fighting: A Volume of Personal Observation with the Army and Navy, from the first Battle of Bull Run to the Fall of Richmond*. Boston: Ticknor and Fields, 1866.

——. *Redeeming the Republic*. New York and London: Harper and Brothers, 1889.

Congdon, Charles Taber. *Tribune Essays: Leading Articles Contributed to the New York Tribune from 1857 to 1863; with an Introduction by Horace Greeley*. 1869. Reprint, Freeport, New York: Books for Libraries Press, 1971.

Crawford, Martin. *William Howard Russell's Civil War: Private Diary and Letters, 1861–1862*. Athens and London: University of Georgia Press, 1992.

Crounse, Lorenzo Livingston. "The Army Correspondent." *Harper's New Monthly Magazine* 27 (October 1863): 627–638.

Crozier, Emmet. *Yankee Reporters*. New York: Oxford University Press, 1956.

Dana, Charles Anderson. *Recollections of the Civil War* (New York, 1898).

Davis, Burke. *They Called Him Stonewall*. New York and Toronto: Rinehart & Co., 1934.

Denney, Robert E. *The Civil War Years: A Day-by-Day Chronicle in the Life of a Nation*. New York: Sterling, 1992.

Douglas, Henry Kyd. *I Rode with Stonewall*. 1899. Reprint, Chapel Hill: University of North Carolina Press, 1940.

Eisenschiml, Otto, and Ralph Newman. *The Civil War: The American Iliad as told by Those Who Lived It*. New York: Mallard Press, 1991.

Fahrney, Ralph Ray. *Horace Greeley and the Tribune in the Civil War*. Cedar Rapids: The Torch Press, 1936.

Farwell, Byron. *Stonewall.* New York and London: W. W. Norton & Company, 1992.

Faust, Patricia L., ed. *Historical Times Illustrated Encyclopedia of the Civil War.* New York: Harper & Row, 1986.

Fellman, Michael. *Citizen Sherman.* New York: Random House, 1995.

Fermer, Douglas. *James Gordon Bennett and the New York Herald: A Study of Editorial Opinion in the Civil War Era, 1854–1867.* New York: St. Martin's Press, 1986.

Fishel, Leslie H., Jr., and Benjamin Quarles. *The Negro American: A Documentary History.* New York: William Morrow & Company, 1967.

Fleischmann, John. "The Object at Hand." *Smithsonian Magazine* (November 1996): 28–30.

Hale, William Harlan. *Horace Greeley, Voice of the People.* New York: Harper & Brothers, 1950.

Harris, Brayton. "The Role of Newspapers in the Civil War." *Civil War* 15 (December 1988): 5–86.

Harwell, Richard B., ed. *The Civil War Reader.* New York: Mallard Press, 1991.

Hawthorne, Nathaniel. "Chiefly about War Matters." *Atlantic Monthly* 10 (July 1862): 43–61.

Henderson, Colonel G. F. R. *Stonewall Jackson and the American Civil War.* London, New York and Toronto: Longmans, Green and Co., 1949.

Hoole, William Stanley. *Vizetelly Covers the Confederacy.* Tuscaloosa, Alabama: The Confederate Publishing Company, 1957.

Johnson, Robert Underwood, and Clarence Clough Buel, eds. *Battles and Leaders of the Civil War.* 4 vols. New York: The Century Company, 1884–1888.

Kasper, Sydney H. "Rienzi's Story." *Civil War Times Illustrated* 27 (January 1989): 20–25.

Knightley, Phillip. *The First Casualty. From the Crimea to Vietnam: The War Correspondent as Hero, Propagandist, and Myth Maker.* New York and London: Harcourt Brace Jovanovich, 1975.

Knox, Thomas Wallace. *Camp-Fire and Cotton-Field: Southern Adventure in Time of War. Life with the Union Armies and Residence on a Louisiana Plantation* (Philadelphia and Cincinnati, 1865).

Kouwenhover, John A. *Adventures of America, 1857–1900; A Pictorial Record from Harper's Weekly.* New York and London: Harper & Brothers, 1938.

Lande, Nathaniel. *Dispatches from the Front.* New York: Henry Holt, 1995.

Leech, Margaret. *Reveille in Washington, 1860–1865.* New York and London: Harper & Row, 1941.

Lewis, Thomas A. *Guns of Cedar Creek.* New York: Harper & Row, 1988.

McPherson, James M. *Battle Cry of Freedom: The Civil War Era*. New York: Oxford University Press, 1988.

———. *The Negro's Civil War: How Blacks Felt and Acted During the War for the Union*. New York: Ballantine Books, 1991.

Marvel, William. *Burnside*. Chapel Hill and London: University of North Carolina Press, 1991.

Miers, Earl Schenck. *The General Who Marched to Hell*. New York: Alfred A. Knopf, 1951.

Moore, Frank, ed. *The Rebellion Record, A Diary of American Events, with Documents, Narratives, Illustrative Incidents, Poetry, etc.* 12 vols. 1861–1868. Reprint, New York: Arno Press, 1977.

Morse, John T., Jr., ed. *The Diary of Gideon Welles, Secretary of the Navy under Lincoln and Johnson*. 3 vols. Boston and New York: Houghton Mifflin Co., 1911.

Mullen, Robert W. *Blacks in America's Wars: The Shifts in Attitudes from the Revolutionary War to Vietnam*. New York: Anchor Foundation, 1973.

Neely, Mark E., Jr., Henry Holtzer, and Gabor S. Boritt. *The Confederate Image: Prints of the Lost Cause*. Chapel Hill and London: University of North Carolina Press, 1987.

Nevins, Allan, ed. *American Press Opinion: Washington to Coolidge*. Boston and New York: D. H. Heath and Company, 1928.

Osborne, Charles C. *Jubal: The Life and Times of General Jubal A. Early, CSA; Defender of the Lost Cause*. Chapel Hill: Algonquin Books of Chapel Hill, 1992.

Osterweis, Rollin G. *The Myth of the Lost Cause, 1865–1900*. Hamden, Connecticut: Archon Books, 1973.

Paine, Albert Bigelow, *A Sailor of Fortune, Personal Memoirs of Captain B. S. Osbon* (New York, 1906).

Perkins, Howard Cecil. *Northern Editorials on Secession*. 2 vols. 1942. Reprint, Gloucester, Massachusetts: Peter Smith, 1964.

Pickard, John B., ed. *Letters of John Greenleaf Whittier*. Cambridge, Massachusetts: Belknap Press of Harvard University Press, 1975.

Pollard, Edward A. *The Lost Cause*. 1866. Reprint, Freeport, New York: Books for Libraries Press, 1970.

———. *The Lost Cause Regained*. 1868. Reprint, Freeport, New York: Books for Libraries Press, 1970.

———. *Southern History of the War*. 1866. Reprint (2 vols. in 1), New York: Fairfax Press, 1990.

Pollard, James E. *The Presidents and the Press*. New York: Macmillan, 1947.

Poore, Benjamin Perley. "Washington News." *Harper's New Monthly Magazine* 48 (January 1874): 225–236.

Porter, Horace. *Campaigning with Grant.* 1906. Reprint, New York: Mallard Press, 1991.

Pratt, Fletcher. *Civil War in Pictures.* New York: Henry Holt and Company, 1955.

Randall, James Garfield. "The Newspaper Problem in Its Bearing upon Military Secrecy during the Civil War." *American Historical Review* 23 (January 1918): 303–323.

————. "Federal Generals and a Good Press." *American Historical Review* 39 (January 1934): 280–289.

Redpath, James. *The Roving Editor; or, Talks with the Slaves in the Southern States.* New York: A. A. Burdick, 1859.

Reynolds, Donald E. *Editors Make War: Southern Newspapers in the Secession Crisis.* Nashville: Vanderbilt University Press, 1970.

Richardson, Albert Deane. *The Secret Service, the Field, the Dungeon, and the Escape.* Hartford: American Publishing Company, 1865.

Rideing, William H. "The Metropolitan Newspaper." *Harper's New Monthly Magazine* 56 (December 1877): 43–59.

————. "The Rise and Fall of the War-Correspondent." *Macmillan's Magazine* 90 (August 1904): 301–310.

Robotham, Tom. *Civil War Album.* New York: Smithmark, 1992.

Russell, William Howard. *My Diary, North and South.* 2 vols. London: Bradbury and Evans, 1863.

Sears, Louis M. "The London Times' American Correspondent in 1861; Unpublished Letters of William H. Russell in the First Year of the Civil War." *Historical Outlook* 16 (October 1925): 251–257.

Seitz, Don Carlos. *The James Gordon Bennetts, Father and Son, Proprietors of the New York Herald.* Indianapolis: Bobbs-Merrill, 1928.

Shanks, William Franklin Gore, *Personal Recollections of Distinguished Generals* (New York, 1866).

————. "How We Get Our News." *Harper's New Monthly Magazine* 34 (March 1867): 511–522.

Sheridan, Philip H. *Personal Memoirs of P. H. Sheridan, General, United States Army.* 1888. Reprint (2 vols. in 1), with an introduction by Jeffry D. Wert, New York: Da Capo Press, 1992.

Sherman, William Tecumseh. *Memoirs of General William T. Sherman.* 2d ed., rev. and cor. New York: D. A. Appleton and Company, 1875.

Smalley, George Washburn. *Anglo-American Memories.* New York and London: G. P. Putnam's Sons, 1911.

————. "Chapters in Journalism." *Harper's New Monthly Magazine* 89 (August 1894): 426–435.

————. "Notes on Journalism." *Harper's New Monthly Magazine* 97 (July 1898): 213–223.

Smart, James G., ed. A Radical View: the "Agate" Dispatches of Whitelaw Reid, 1861–1865. 2 vols. Memphis: Memphis State University Press, 1976.

Starr, Louis M. Bohemian Brigade, Civil War Newsmen in Action. 1954. Reprint, with a foreword by James Boylan, Madison: University of Wisconsin Press, 1987.

Taylor, Marie Hansen, and Horace E. Scudder. Life and Letters of Bayard Taylor. 2 vols. (Boston, 1895).

Thompson, Robert Means, and Richard Wainwright, eds. Confidential Correspondence of Gustavus Vasa Fox, Assistant Secretary of the Navy, 1861–1865, 2 vols. (New York, 1920).

Thorndike, Rachel Sherman, ed. The Sherman Letters, Correspondence between General and Senator Sherman from 1837 to 1891. 1894. Reprint, New York: Da Capo Press, 1969.

Townsend, George Alfred. Campaigns of a Non-Combatant, and his Romaunt Abroad during the War. 1866. Reprint, Alexandria: Time-Life Books, 1982.

Villard, Henry. Memoirs of Henry Villard, Journalist and Financier 1835–1900. 2 vols. Reprint, New York: Da Capo Press, 1969.

War of the Rebellion: A Compilation of the Official Records of the Union and Confederate Armies. 128 vols. Washington, D.C: U.S. Government, 1880–1901.

Weisberger, Bernard A. Reporters for the Union. Boston: Little, Brown & Company, 1953.

Wilkie, Franc Bangs. Pen and Powder. Boston: Ticknor and Fields, 1888.

———. Walks about Chicago, 1871–1881. And Army and Miscellaneous Sketches. Chicago: Belford, Clarke, 1882.

Williams, George Forrester. "Bennett, Greeley and Raymond, A Glimpse of New York Journalism Twenty-five Years Ago." Journalist 4 (October 2, 1886): 1–2.

———. "Important Services Rendered by War Correspondents." Independent 54 (January 23, 1902): 210–212.

———. "Lights and Shadows of Army Life." Century Magazine 28 (October 1884): 803–819.

Wilson, Edmund. Patriotic Gore. New York: Oxford University Press, 1962.

Winters, John D. The Civil War in Louisiana. Baton Rouge and London: Louisiana State University Press, 1963.

Wolseley, Garnet, and James A Rawley, eds. The American Civil War, an English View. Charlottesville: University Press of Virginia, 1964.

Wykoff, George S. "Charles Mackay: England's Forgotten Civil War Correspondent." South Atlantic Quarterly 26 (January 1927): 50–62.

Young, John Russell, *Around the World with General Grant*. 2 vols. (New York, 1879).

Young, May Dow Russell, ed. *Men and Memories, Personal Reminiscences by John Russell Young*. 2 vols. (New York and London, 1901).

Index

Abolition (abolitionists), 24, 26, 35, 37, 100, 110, 196, 202, 304; NY Tribune on, 5, 19; Radicals on, 15; and Lincoln's first inauguration, 22; Southern newspapers forbidden to discuss, 49; as invaders of Virginia, 56, 58; "abolition generals," 144, 166, 171, 190; seeking "revolution," 176; and the cause of the war, 187; the "abolition press," 188; 189; "Prayer of Twenty Millions," 199, 200; agreed outcome of the war, 316

Act of February 3, 1862, 141

Act of July 17, 1862 ("Treason" Act), 105

Adams, George W. "Shad," 122

Albany *Evening Journal*, 51, 82, 84

Alexander, Peter W., 151, 183, 187, 266, on Brandy Station, 257; on drunkenness, 293, 300; on Confederate plans to enlist blacks, 304

Alexandria (LA) *Constitutional*, 109

"Angel of Marye's Heights," 228

Antietam, Battle of, 161, 179, 182–184, 201, 274, 314

Associated Press, 7, 8, 64, 74, 75, 106, 107, 127, 139, 143, 155, 165, 208, 256

Athena (AL) *Union Banner*, 109

Atlanta *Daily Southern Confederacy*, 132, 169

Atlantic Monthly, 147, 269

Augusta *Daily Constitutionalist*, 134

Bagby, George W., 15, 110, 111, 122

Baltimore *American*, 22, 58, 162; editor arrested, 165; on Bull Run, 82; racist views of, 189

Baltimore *Exchange*, 98

Baltimore *South*, 98, 103

Baltimore *Sun*, 55, 271

Bangor (ME) *Democrat*, 98

Bangor *Union*, 54

"Barbara Frietchie," 267–275

Barnum, Phineas T., 11, 99

"Battle above the Clouds," 280

"Battles and Leaders of the Civil War," 271, 320

Beauregard, Gen. P. G. T., 56, 58, 60, 71, 72, 104, 152, 160, 169, 174, 320; at Fort Sumter, 43, 44; at Bull Run, 75–80; excludes journalists, 160; as postwar author, 320

Benjamin, Secretary of War Judah P., 152

Bennett, James Gordon: begins New York *Herald*, 4; on country editors, 15; Russell's view of, 31; shifts allegiance, 46; post-war brag, 319

Bennett, James Gordon, Jr., 46, 319

Bible ploy, 7, 127, 128, 279, 293

Bickham, William, 157, 171

Big Bethel, 57

Black Republicans, 16, 22

Black seamen, 205

Black troops: Hunter's regiments, 197; enlistment authorized (North), 198; in

Militia service, 202; Negro Regiment Bill, 202, 203; Southern attempts at intimidation of, 203; Fort Pillow, 204; Southern plans for, 304–306; first to enter Richmond, 307, 308

Blair, Maj. Gen Frank, 245

Bodman, Albert H., 122

Booth, John Wilkes, 324

Boston *Atlas*, 4

Boston *Herald*, 9, 122

Boston *Journal*, 16, 24, 38, 78, 80, 139, 144, 153, 155, 157, 160, 182, 190, 306, 308; on Bull Run, 80; praises McClellan, 177; at Fredericksburg, 216, 219;

Boston *Post*, 26, 80

Boston *Transcript*, 68, 69

Bowles, Samuel, 3

Bragg, Braxton, 174, 191, 289; discipline criticized, 169; accused of security violation, 170; excludes journalists, 170

Bridgeport (CT) *Advertiser and Farmer*, 99

Brigham, Charles, 27

Brooklyn Eagle, 98, 267

Brooks, Noah, 254

Browne, Francis F., 271

Browne, Junius, 29, 30, 123, 262; unethical behavior of, 123; on Buell, 190; creates fake report, 130; held hostage, 262–263; on proper role of the war correspondent, 320

Brownlow, William G. "Parson," 109, 111–113

Bryant, William Cullen, 267

Buell, Maj. Gen. Don Carlos, 190, 191, 247

Buffalo *Commercial Advertiser*, 41

Buffalo *Courier*, 100

Bull Run, first Battle of, 67–87

Bull Run, Second Battle of, 171

Burns, George H., 68

Burnside, Maj. Gen Ambrose E.: suppresses newspapers, 106; at Antietam, 179, 181; 182; assumes command of Army of the Potomac, 205; on Hooker, 208; Fredericksburg, 205–238; accepts blame for defeat, 237, 238; "mud march," 253

Butler, Maj. Gen Benjamin F. 65, 66, 126, 194, 250; opinion of reporters, 63; in New Orleans, 103–105; on "contraband of war," 192

Byington, Aaron Homer, 278, 279

Cadwallader, Sylvanus: special relationship with Grant, 259–260; at Chattanooga, 280, 281; hired by Herald, 283; at Appomattox, 313; post-war career of, 319

California *Star*, 103

Cameron, Secretary of War Simon, 59, 69, 93, 102, 122, 138–140, 192, 193, 239–241

Canton (Ohio) *Stark County Democrat*, 98

Carpenter, George Rice, 275

Caucasian, 106

Cedar Creek, Battle of, 305

Censorship, ii, 48–50, 63–65, 85–86, 103, 138, 141–145; "Treason Act",105; 57th Article of War, 125; use of codes to avoid, 150–152; parole in lieu of, 185, 186, in later wars, 323

Century, 273, 320

Chancellorsville, Battle of, 151

Chapman, Frank, 128, 152, 279

Charleston *Courier*, 50, 61, 120; on Bull Run, 77; on Antietam, 183; on Winchester, 293

Charleston *Mercury*, 35, 52, 61, 62, 65, 78, 110, 111, 121, 123, 267, 305; on anonymity, 30; against enlistment of blacks, 303

Chase, Salmon P., 258, 259

Chenery, Thomas, 2

Chesnut, Mary, 266

Chester, Thomas Morris, 14, 308, 309

Chicago *Democrat*, 23

Chicago *Journal*, 111

Chicago *Times*, 16, 106, 122, 124, 145, 151, 166, 197, 242, 249, 259, 281, 318; field staff, 125; support of McClellan, 167; on abolition generals, 190; on Buell, 191; racism of, 194; reaction to Emancipation Proclamation, 201; on Sherman's General Order 8, 242

Chicago *Tribune*; 9, 19, 54, 122, 142, 143, 160; security violation, 62; on Russell,

90; turns away from Fremont, 102; on "West Pointers," 143; on Buell, 190; on fears of black migration; on capture of Jefferson Davis, 314

Chickamauga, 289

Chickasaw Bayou, 243, 244, 248, 258

Cincinnati *Commercial*: on unethical behavior, 129; on Washington press corps, 137; on "newly-made officers," 157; denigrates McClellan, 177; on Buell, 196; on intelligent contraband, 196; at Fredericksburg, 205–238; and Sherman's "insanity," 240, 241; on Gettysburg Address, 290

Cincinnati *Enquirer*, 16, 41, 64; on Buell, 191; on "intelligent contrabands," 196

Cincinnati *Gazette*: on Shiloh, 153; on Buell, 191; on Black troops, 198, 203; on "Battle above the Clouds," 280

Cincinnati *Press*, 86

Civil War, origins of, 22

Civil War Society, iii

Clark, Walter A., 228

Codes, used by journalists, 151

Coffin, Charles Carleton, 237, 326; at Shiloh, 153, 157, 160; on Buell, 190; at Gettysburg, 288; on Confederate efforts to enlist blacks, 316; in Richmond, 318–320; post-war career of, 329

Colburn, Richard, 130; at Shiloh, 157; on Halleck's nickname, 159

Cologne (Virginia) *Gazette*, 166

Columbia *South Carolinian*, 303

Columbus *Sun*, 134, 175

Committee on the Conduct of the War, 147, 152, 164

Concord (NH) *Democratic Standard*, 55, 100

Confiscation Act of 1861, 198

Conscription, exemptions from, 115

Constitutional Gazetteer, 105

Contraband of war, 192–194

Cook, Capt. John Esten, 210

Copperhead press, 16

Copperplate engravings, 13

Courier and Enquirer, 7

Courts martial: of B. S. Osbon, 250–251; of E. F. DeNyse, 250; of Thomas Knox, 243–249

Cox, Jacob F., 124

Crapsey, Edward, 284, 285

Crimean War, 1854–56, 2

Cross Keys, Battle of, 162

Crounse, L. L., 151, 155, 156, 309

Cumberland (Virginia) *Alleghanian*, 98

Curran, Christopher, iii

Dana, Charles A.: managing editor of the *Tribune*, 13; assistant secretary of war, 14; argues against censorship, 65, 66; on Bull Run, 80; sent to observe Grant, 259; tries to block newsmen from Richmond, 310; post-war career of, 318

Davis, Bancroft, 30, 75

Davis, Jefferson, at Bull Run, 77; favors enlistment of blacks, 305; capture of, 313–315; paroled, 315; press policy of, 321

Davis, Theodore, 37, 38

Day Book, 41, 46, 47, 55, 98, 100

De Fontaine, Felix Gregory, 44

Democratic papers, view of abolition, 189

Democrats, 16, 47, 189, 190, 203, 287

DeNyse, Edwin F., 250

Detroit *Free Press*, 214

Dickens, Charles: satirizes American newspapers, 17; invents term "war correspondent," 18; Pickwick's advice, 47

Douglas, Henry Kyd, 271, 274

Draft riots, 280

Dubuque (IA) *Herald*, 105, 106

Dunn, William, 203

Early, Jubal, 273, 293

Eastern State Journal, 98

Easton (PA) *Sentinel*, 98

Election of 1860, 22

Election of 1864, 287, 295, 301

Ellis, Garrison, iii

Ellsworth, Col. Ephraim, 56

Emancipation Proclamation, 200

Evening *Day Book*, 47, 98

Ewell, Lt. Gen. Richard, 307

Farragut, Rear Admiral David, 104, 287

Fayetteville *Observer*, 115

Fayetteville *Telegraph*, 115

"Fifteen-minute" rule, 127
Fifty-Seventh Article of War, 125
Forney, John, 156; secretary of the U.S. Senate, 142; on Battle of Fredericksburg, 235; petitions Lincoln on status of Knox, 247
Forsyth, John; and Confederate delegation, 26; and Russell, 37; joins Bragg in Kentucky, 175
Fort Donelson, 130
Fort Henry, 151
Fort Sumter, 43
Fox, Assistant Secretary of the Navy Gustavas; pledges "exclusives" for the Herald, 141; engineers Osbon court martial, 251
Frank Leslie's Illustrated Newspaper; founded 1855, 12; at Fredericksburg, 210; and Sherman's "insanity," 241; on Gettysburg Address, 282; on Cedar Creek, 297; and capture of Davis, 315
Franklin, Maj. Gen. William, 208, 211, 223–225, 228, 247
Fredericksburg, Battle of, 205–238
Freeman's Journal, 98, 106
Frémont, Maj. Gen. John Charles, 101, 102, 123; issues emancipation order, 196
Fugitive Slave Act, 192
Fulton, Charles C., 165

Galveston Civilian and Gazette, 110
Galveston Union, 110
Gay, Sidney, 127, 262; managing editor, NY Tribune, 14; sends Smalley to assess Hooker, 257; post-war career of, 318
General Order 3, 195
General Order 57, 253
General Order 67, 85, 125
Gettysburg Address, 281, 282
Gettysburg, Battle of, 278, 279
Godkin, Lawrence, 1
Grant, Lt. Gen. Ulysses S., 119, 122, 143, 190, 291, 292, 305, 307, 312, 313, 315; at Cairo, 150; at Shiloh, 154; on employment of contrabands, 193; and Sherman, 241–244; attitude toward the press, 244; on status of Knox, 247;

248; accused of being drunk, 258, 259; and Cadwallader, 259, 260; verbal portrait of, 260–261; at Chatanooga, 280; promoted lieutenant general, 283; in the Wilderness, 284; banished Swinton, 285; press policy of, 321
Greeley, Horace: establishes New York Tribune, 5; as politician, 6; Russell's view of, 31; on Bull Run, 81; proposes armistice, 83; Prayer of Twenty Millions, 199; guarantees bail for Jefferson Davis, 315; as presidential candidate, 315
Greensboro Alabama Beacon, 109
Grey, T. C; and the "Bible ploy," 279, 293
Gulf War, 323, 324
Gunn, Thomas Butler, 126

Hale, David, 3, 4, 7, 17,
Hale, E. J., 115
Halleck, Maj. Gen. Henry W.: excludes journalists, 149, 157, 171; issues Field Order 54, 157; issues General Order 3, 193; on contrabands, 193; urges Hooker to expell journalists, 258
Halstead, Murat, 63; at Fredericksburg, 211, 216, 223, 224, 229, 230; on Sherman's "insanity," 240, 241; on "drunken" Grant, 258, 259
Hammond, Surgeon General William, 163
Hanscom, Simon P., 140
Harper's New Monthly Magazine, 119
Harper's Weekly Journal of Civilization, 20, 35, 37, 80, 121, 156, 294, 317; founded, 1857, 12; on Russell, 38; on Bull Run, 80, 84; on Burnside, 213; at Fredericksburg, 210, 211, 238; on Gettysburg Address, 282; as inspiration for "Sheridan's Ride," 297
Harrisburg Patriot and Union, 105
Harrisburg Telegraph, 23
Harrisonburg (VA) Rockingham Register and Advertiser, 115, 294
Haverhill (MA) Essex County Democrat, 100
Hendren, A. B., 109

Highland *Democrat*, 98
Hill, Adams Sherman, 171; post-war career, 318
Hillsborough (NC) Recorder, 115
Hoe Lightning, 11
Holmes, Oliver Wendell, 29, 147
Homer, Winslow, 14, 121
Hooker, Maj. Gen. Joseph, 151; at Antietam, 179, 180; origin of nickname "Fighting Joe," 208; on McClellan, 208; disliked by Burnside, 208; cautioned by Lincoln, 250; replaces Burnside, 253; complains of newspaper leaks, 254; issues General Order 48, 256; reports of erratic behavior, 257; replaced by Meade, 258; at Chattanooga, 280
House Committee on the Judiciary, 144
Howard, F. Key, 98
Howard, Joseph; newspaper hoax, 106
Hudson, Fredrick, 13, 139
Hunt, Maj. Thomas H., 220
Hunter, Maj. Gen. David, 197
Hunterdon *Democrat*, 98

Illustrations, techniques of, 11
Indianapolis *Sentinel*, 100
Ives, Malcolm, 140, 141

Jackson, Gen. Thomas J. "Stonewall," 168; origin of nickname, 78; at Fredericksburg, 211; characterized, 264–266; and "Barbara Frietchie," 267, 270,–272, 274
Jackson, President Andrew, 198
Jefferson, Thomas, 187, 189
Jerseyville (NJ) *Democratic Journal*, 106
Johnson, Bushrod; past indiscretions, 130
Johnston, Gen. Joseph, 60, 80, 254; excludes journalists, 152; at Battle of Seven Pines, 162
Journal of Commerce, 3, 4, 41, 46, 98, 106, 155

Kasson, John A., 142
Kautz, Maj. Gen. August Valentine, 309
Kelley, William D., 203
Kendall, George; in Mexican War 1846–48, 1

Key, Maj. John, 157, 176
Kimball, Ambrose L., 100
King, Adm. Ernest J.; press policy of, 149
Knightley, Philip, 280, 281
Knox, Thomas: assigned to edit Memphis *Argus*, 114; court-martial of, 244–246; post-war career of, 317
Knoxville *Daily Register*, 113, 131, 235
Knoxville *Whig*, 109, 111–113
Knoxville *Whig and Rebel Ventilator*, 113
Korean conflict, 323

Lawley, Francis, 207, 210, 220, 221, 229, 230, 232, 235, 260, 264
Lee, Gen. Robert E., 168; at Seven Days' Campaign, 167; plants stories in Richmond papers, 168; issues proclamation, 174; at Fredericksburg, 210–237; described, 210; alerted of attack by newspaper reports, 250; invades Pennsylvania, 256; favors enlistment of blacks, 304, 305
Lewis, Thomas A., 299, 300
Lexington (MO), siege of, 101
Lincoln, Abraham: declines to support Greeley for senate, 6; house divided speech, 22; first meeting with Russell, 32; impact of inauguration, 25, 25; cancels Frémont's emancipation order, 196; declines offer of black regiments from Indiana, 198; response to "Prayer of Twenty Millions," 200; on status of Knox, 254; cautions Hooker, 260; Gettysburg Address, 281, 282; description of Sheridan, 290; on Grant, 292; visits Richmond, 310; last public speech, 313; press policy, 321
Literacy rate, 9
London *Illustrated News*, 11, 37, 211
London *Morning Star*, 90
London *News*, 2; on Southern prowess, 53; on mood of slaves, 195
London *Spectator*, 172
London *Times*: assigns correspondent to Crimean War, 2; sends Russell to America, 30; on "West Pointers," 143; on "skedaddle," 172; on Buell, 191; reaction to Emancipation Proclamation, 202; on Burnside, 213; at

Fredericksburg, 210, 220, 232, 235, 237, 260, 264; on Gettysburg Address, 281, 282. *See also* entries for *Times* corespondents W. H. Russell, Bancroft Davis, Francis Lawley, and Charles MacKay.
Long, Francis C., 128, 293
Longstreet, Maj. Gen. James, 162
Los Angelos, 103
Louisville *Courier*, 100, 109
Louisville *Journal*, 172
Lynchburg (VA) *Republican*, 132, 293
Lynchburg *Virginian*, 266

Mackay, Charles, 143, 201
Macmillan's Magazine, 291
Macon (MO) *Register*, 113
Mahoney, D. A., 105
Mallory, Robert, 198
Managing editor, defined, 13
Manassas, Battles of: *see* Bull Run
Manchester (England) *Examiner*, 84
Martin Chuzzlewit, 17
Maryland *News Sheet*, 115
Mauch Chunk (PA) *Carbon Democrat*, 98
McClellan, Maj. Gen George Brinton: assumes command after Bull Run, 85; dubbed "young Napoleon," 85; praises Herald, 140; as radicals favorite villain, 145; exhortation to troops, 146; complains of security violations, 161; at Batle of Seven Pines, 162; accused of mistreatment of wounded, 163; at Seven Days' Campaign, 167; compared with George Washington, 177; unique genius of, 177; removed from command, 184; presidential candidate, 287
McClernand, Maj. Gen. John A., 241–243, 247
McCormick, Richard, 2, 68
McCullagh, Joe, 14, 190
McDowell, Brig. Gen Irwin, 60, 68, 69, 71, 80, 84, 85, 91, 166, 209
Meade, Maj. Gen George Gordon, 223, 257, 258; temper of, 283; accuses reporter of libel, 283; Presidential aspirations, 284
Mechanicsville, action at, 133

Medill, Joseph, 143
Meigs, Quartermaster-General Montgomery, 60, 185, 280
Melville, Herman, 300
Memphis *Appeal*, 24, 57, 115; on Antietam, 183 on "abolition" as the cause of the war, 188; on Fredericksburg, 210
Merritt, Maj. Gen. Wesley, 294
Mexican War of 1846–48, 1, 22
Mississippian, 103
Missouri *Democrat*, 16, 19, 190, 248
Missouri *Republican*, 16, 123, 196, 249,
Mobile *Daily Tribune*, 110
Mobile *Evening News*, 144
Mobile *Register*, 26, 37, 63, 76, 175, 257, 317; on Bull Run, 77, 78; criticizes Davis, 115; advice to correspondents, 131; on Antietam, 175; on Battle of Winchester, 293
Mobile *Telegraph*, 52
Montgomery *Confederation*, 24
Montgomery *Daily Advertiser*, 169
Morse, Samuel F. B., 6
Mullaly, John, 105
Mulligan, Col. James A., 101, 128
Mumford, William B., 103
My Diary North and South, 31, 33, 34, 37, 38, 64, 71, 85, 89, 91, 95, 154, 257

Nast, Thomas, 14
National Intelligencer, 62, 63
National Zeitung, 98
Negro Soldier Law of the Confederacy, 306
Negroes, 21, 54, 194, 195, 198, 202, 203, 249, 304, 305, 309, 311; as "contraband of war," 192; as soldiers, 197
Newark (New Jersey) *Daily Advertiser*, 25
Newark *Evening Journal*, 98
New Brunswick *Times*, 98
New Haven *Palladium*, 99
New Orleans *Bee*, 24, 51
New Orleans *Crescent*, 1, 29, 62, 77, 104
New Orleans *Delta*, 104
New Orleans *Picayune*, 1, 5, 55, 69, 121; on censorship, 49; on Bull Run, 77
New Orleans *True Delta*, 76, 104
New York *Illustrated News*, 12

New York *Day Book*, 47, 55, 100
New York *Evening Post*, 2, 79, 182, 318
New York *Express*, 41, 55
New York *Herald*, 1, 16, 100, 102, 114,
127, 128, 141, 246, 247; founded, 4;
managing editor, 13; and trial of John
Brown, 20; on slavery, 21; as Northern champion of the South, 41;
attacked by mobs, 45, 46; at Bull Run,
71, 72, 74, 75; field staff, 125; on
Wilkeson, 139; as supporter of
McClellan, 145, 167; scooped at
Antietam, 182; on Buell, 191; racism
of, 194; denigrates Hunter, 197; on
McClellan's "farewell," 205; at
Fredericksburg, 210; on Sherman's
"insanity," 244; "Grant for President,"
283; supports McClellan in 1864
election, 301; scooped at Appomat-
tox, 313; on the capture of Richmond,
311; on capture of Jefferson Davis,
314, 315; post-war history of, 319
New York *Herald Tribune*, 320
New York *Illustrated News*, 210
New York *Metropolitan Record*, 105
New York *Post*, 26
New York *Sun*, 14, 267, 318
New York *Sunday Mercury*, 155
New York *Times*: founded, 5; on
"treason" of NY *Herald*, 45; on
Russell, 92, 96; on Wilkeson, 139; on
Special Order 54, 158; on Battle of
Cross Keys, 162; scooped at Antietam,
182; on "abolition" as the cause of the
war, 188; racist comment on black
troops, 199; on McClellan's "farewell,"
205; on Burnside, 207; at Fredericksburg, 210, 211, 213, 215, 216, 218,
232, 233, 237, 238; accuses Sherman
of improprieties and negligence, 243,
249; "portrait" of Grant, 260; on
specious reporting, 277; at Gettysburg,
279; confronted by mob, 289; on
Gettysburg Address, 282; on Cedar
Creek, 296; on the capture of
Richmond, 311
New York *Tribune*: founded, 5; managing
editor, 13; in Kansas (1855–56), 19;
and trial of John Brown, 20; on

slavery, 21; on the social habits of W.
H. Russell, 38; on Fort Sumter, 44;
urges military action, 56; creates
"Forward to Richmond" slogan, 60;
field staff, 125; on censorship, 142; on
"West Pointers," 143; dislike of
McClellan, 145, 155, 163, 176; at
Fredericksburg, 215, 216, 225; on
censorship, 142; security violation of,
150; on Shiloh, 154; on Antietam,
161; on Battle of Cross Keys, 162; on
McClellan's retreat, 166; racist slip-
up, 190; on Buell, 190; on "intelligent
contrabands," 195; supports Frémont's
emancipation order, 197; Prayer of
Twenty Millions, 200; reaction to
Emancipation Proclamation, 201;
attacked by mob, 280; and "Sheridan's
Ride," 287; on the capture of
Richmond, 311; scores beat on
surrender at Appomattox, 313; post-
war history of, 318, 319
New York *World*, 16, 19, 25, 26, 64, 98,
106, 122, 155, 157, 251, 257, 29; at
Bull Run, 73, 76; on censorship, 142;
on arrest of an editor, 165; praises
McClellan, 182; on Cedar Creek, 295;
on the capture of Richmond, 311
Newark *Evening Journal*, 98
Newbern (NC) *Progress*, 114
Newbould, Thomas M., 256
Newcomb, James P., 110
Nightingale, Florence, 2
North American Review, 317
North Carolina *Standard*, 304
Northern Democrats, 16
Northern Pacific Railroad, 329

Ohio *Statesman*, 194
Oregon *Democrat*, 103
Osbon, Bradley Sillick, 250–251
Osborne, Charles, 273
Osterweis, Roland G., 320
Ould, Robert, 262–264
Our Whole Union, 113

Page, Charles A., 133, 208, 309
Paige, Nathaniel, 176
Painter, Uriah: at Bull Run, 73–75;

unethical behavior, 123; testifies against McClellan, 164; captured, 173; discovers plan for invasion of Maryland, 173; on Gettysburg, 278

Palmetto Flag, 46

Parole in lieu of censorship, 155

Parton, James, 317

Pasteur, Louis, 164

Patterson, Brig. Gen. Robert, 60, 67, 80, 84, 100

Paul, E. A., 297

Pea Ridge, Battle of, 130

Peace Democrats, 16

Peoria *Daily Transcript*, 51

Perryville, Battle of, 132, 191

Petersburg *Daily Express*, 293

Pfeiff's dog, 153

Philadelphia *Bulletin*, 100

Philadelphia *Inquirer*, 11, 14, 15, 126, 128, 163; on Shiloh, 153, 155; at Fredericksburg, 210, 211; at Gettysburg, 278

Philadelphia *Morning Pennsylvanian*, 8

Philadelphia *Press*, 14, 54, 60, 67, 97, 102, 157, 165, 195, 240, 278; on Bull Run, 80; praises McClellan, 176; racist report, 195; assessment of Fredericksburg, 234; hires black journalist, 308

Philadelphia *Times,* 272

Photography, 11

Pillow, Maj. Gen. Gordon, 33, 111, 112

Pittsburg Landing, 152

Plainfield (NJ) *Gazette*, 98

Plympton, Florus, 239, 240

Pollard, Edward A.: pledges "reticence," 168; on Yankee barbarity, 213; captured, 263, 264; reports enlistment of black troops, 306; predicts the future, 326; on retributions of history, 306

Pollard, John A., 275

Poore, Benjamin Perley, 38, 144, 177,

Porter, Adm. David Dixon, 245

Porter, Brig. Gen Fitz-John, 145, 247

Postmasters, guidance to, 142

Potter, Col. R. B., 228

"Prayer of Twenty Millions," 199, 200

Prentice, George D., 101

Press Association of the Confederate States of America, 8

Press freedom, 149

Press policies of U.S. military in other wars, 334

Price, Sterling, 101, 129

Protestant Episcopal Church in the Confederate states, 188

Pseudonyms, use of, 256

Quaker guns, 146, 160, 223

Quantrell, Mary S., 273, 275

Racism, iii, 17, 189; General Order 3, 193, 194; of Democratic newspapers, 194

Radicals, 15, 16, 143–145, 190, 191

Ramsay, Charles G., 101

Randall, James , 150

Rawlins, Col. John, 150, 247, 260

Raymond, Raymond, Henry J., 5, 6, 128, 139, 254, 280; at Bull Run, 69–74

Read, Thomas Buchanan, 287

Redpath, James, 19

Reid, Samuel Chester, 121

Reid, Samuel G., 170

Reid, Whitelaw: on Shiloh, 153; argues against Field Order 54, 157; denigrates McClellan, 177; on Buell, 191; reports congressional debate on black troops, 197, 203; accuses Meade of cowardice, 284; visits Richmond, 309, 310; post-war career of, 318

Reilly, Frank W., 133

Republican Party, 5, 16, 101

Republicans, 15, 23, 187, 189–191

Rhett, Edmund, 35, 52

Rhett, R. B., 110

Richardson, Albert Deane, 47, 48, 54, 101, 128, 129, 182, 247; Southern tour, 28–30; on Frémont, 102; assigned to edit Memphis Argus, 114; unethical behavior, 122; on Brig. Gen. Jacob F. Cox, 124; on access to sources, 149; at Antietam, 179; assaulted at McClellan's "farewell," 206, 207; on Burnside, 207, 238; captured and held hostage, 262–264; post-war career of, 318

Richmond *Dispatch*, 62, 169, 220; on

Bull Run, 77; on reporter's duties, 121; description of troops, 133; security violation of, 151, 168; on Battle of Seven Pines, 162; on invasion of Maryland, 173; on "contraband of war," 195; at Fredericksburg, 216, 220; on Battle of Winchester, 293; dubs Sheridan "Chief of the Barn Burners," 294; on Cedar Creek, 300; urges confidence in future of the Confederacy, 303, 307

Richmond Enquirer, 25, 48, 56, 58, 62, 63; on the "Wide Awakes," 22; on Lincoln's inauguration, 26; praises New York Herald, 41; defends Richmond papers, 162; on Antietam, 183; on Yankee plans for liberated slaves, 187; at Fredericksburg, 213, 219, 221, 223, 237; favors enlistment of blacks, 304

Richmond Examiner, 25, 51, 55, 56, 201, 263; criticizes Davis, 110; criticizes Bragg, 175; denigrates Lee, 168; reaction to Emancipation Proclamation, 201; at Fredericksburg, 220; on poor quality of cavalry, 294; argues against enlistment of blacks, 304

Richmond Sentinel, 307

Richmond Whig: on censorship, 49; reaction to Emancipation Proclamation, 201; at Fredericksburg, 210; on Battle of Winchester, 293; on Cedar Creek, 300; argues against enlistment of blacks, 304, 305; gets new "management," 311

Rienzi, 301, 302

Riggin, Col. John, 150

Robinson, Joe, 14

Roosevelt, Lt. Col. Theodore, 323

Rosecrans, Brig. Gen William S., 86, 167, 171, 280

Russell, William Howard, 152, 182; in Crimean War, 2; given U. S. assignment, 30; on Bennett, Greeley, and New York papers, 31, 32; on Mr. and Mrs. Lincoln, 32; on Gen. Pillow, 33, 34; assessment of volunteer soldiers, 34; on slave auction, 34; on Southern politics and enmity toward the North, 34, 35; and Harper's Weekly, 35; and Theodore Davis, 37, 38; on Southern manpower, 54; and Bull Run, 68, 70, 71, 72, 74, 78, 79, 80–96; on New York Tribune and Bull Run, 82; ridiculed for Bull Run report, 91; on Secretary of War Stanton, 93; returns to England, 95; alleged gold speculation, 123; on Burnside, 207

Sacramento Union, 254

Salaries, 121

Salter, George, 43

San Antonio Alamo Express, 110

Sanford, E. S. 142, 155, 167

Savannah Republican, 48, 49, 57, 59, 60, 62–65, 71, 72, 81, 82, 187, 192, 278, 293, 300; on Bull Run, 76; on Southern Illustrated News, 116; on Antietam, 183

Scott, Lt. Gen Winfield, 60; press policy, 64

Screws, Wallace, 169, 170, 317

Security violations, 57, 61, 63, 150, 156, 161, 162, 168, 170, 250, 258

Sedgwick, Ellery, 179

Seilheimer, George O., 272, 273

Seven Days' Campaign, 164

Seward, William H.: secretary of state, 6; refuses to meet Confederate delegation, 26; on secession, 32; favors compromise over combat, 144; recommends delay in Emancipation Proclamation, 200

Seymour, Horatio, 107

Shanks, William F., 125, 317, 318

Sharpsburg (Battle of Antietam), 183

Shaw, William, 71

Sheridan, Maj. Gen. Philip: described, 290, 291; at Winchester, 291; dubbed "Chief of the Barn Burners," 294; the "ride" at Cedar Creek, 295–297

"Sheridan's Ride," 289, 290

Sherman, Sen. John, 246

Sherman, Maj. Gen William Tecumseh, 115, 190; meets Russell, 92; employment of contrabands, 193; personal history, 239; and Florus Plympton, 239, 240; and "insanity," 240, 241,

244, 248, 249; General Order 8, 242;
assault on the mail bags, 243; and
Knox court martial, 244–246; accused
of incompetence, 258; on Richardson's capture, 262; view on journalists, 321
Shiloh, battle of, 152, 153; press contingent at, 154
Short hand, 6
Slaughter, Frank, 216
Slavery, 5, 15, 16, 22, 23, 35, 49, 143–
145, 176, 191, 195, 196, 202, 204,
303, 310; attitudes toward blacks, 20;
NY Herald view, 21; NY Tribune view,
21; as cause of war, 187–189; as basis
of Confederate government, 187; as
God's plan, 188; confiscation act, 192,
193; "Prayer of Twenty Millions," 199,
200; Emancipation Proclamation, 201;
arguments against using slaves as
soldiers, 304; key element in the post-
war "Lost Cause," 316
Slaves: as "contraband of war," 192;
armed in the War of 1812, 198
Smalley, George, 31; on Battle of Cross
Keys, 162; replaces Wilkeson, 171,
172; at Antietam, 179–182; criticizes
McClellan, 182; investigates Hooker,
257, 258; post-war career of, 317
Smithsonian Museum of American
History, 302
Southern Associated Press, 8
Southern Democrats, 16
Southern Illustrated News, 13, 116, 117;
on Battle of Fredericksburg, 235;
eulogizes Stonewall Jackson, 266
Southern Literary Messenger, 20, 25; on
Southern Illustrated News, 117; on
Stonewall Jackson, 265
Southworth, Emma D. E. N., 272
Spanish-American War, 323
Springfield Republican, 3
St. Louis Democrat, 102, 153
St. Louis Evening News, 101
Staats Zeitung, 98
Stanton, Edwin M., 150, 156, 157, 161,
163–167, 176, 185, 237, 254, 290; and
Russell, 93–95, 99; appointed
secretary of war, 140; and Ives, 140,

141; tightens censorship, 141; dislike
of McClellan, 143, 145, 163, 166, 167;
refuses passes for newsmen, 283, 310;
and capture of Davis, 314
Stedman, E. C., 68, 121, 145, 318
Stereotype process, 11
Stillson, Jerome Bonaparte, 295, 296, 317
Stuart, J. E. B., 152, 173, 210, 257
Sturgis, Brig. Gen. Sam, 101
Sumner, Maj. Gen Edwin, 208, 211, 228,
247
Suppression of newspapers; North, 97–
107; South, 109–117
Swinton, William: on Brig. Gen. Jacob F.
Cox, 124; on solider's attitudes, 132;
on Burnside, 213; unethical behavior
of, 284, 285; post-war career of, 318
Sypher, Josiah, 151, 184, 256, 257

Taggart, J. H., 128
Taylor, Bayard, 120, 146
Taylor, James, 300
Taylor, Lt. Gen. Richard, 313
Telegraph: invention, 6; tariffs, 6; fifteen
minute system, 7; growth of, 8;
Buchanan comments on, 8; censorship
of, at Washington, 64. See also Bible
ploy
Thomas, Adj. Gen. Lorenzo, 102
Timrod, Henry, 126, 274
Townsend, George Alfred, v, 156; on
quality of Herald field staff, 126;
racism of, 194; on "by-lines," 256;
reports from Richmond, 312, 313;
post-war career of, 318
Transatlantic cable, 8
Treason Act of July 17, 1862, 105
Tripler, Dr. Charles, 163
Twiggs, Maj. Gen. David E., 28

Uncle Tom's Cabin, 21
Utica (NY) Observer, 54

Vicksburg Times, 117
Vicksburg Whig, 48
Vicksburg, siege of, 134
Vietnam, 323
Villard, Henry: origins, 14; carries
Herald's pledge to Lincoln, 46; at Bull

Run, 73, 75; at Shiloh, 154, 159; on
Buell, 190; on Burnside, 207; on
Hooker, 208; Fredericksburg "adven-
ture," 209, 230, 231; assaulted by
Wilkeson, 238; and Sherman's
"insanity," 241; post-war career of, 318
Violence against newspapers, 98
Virginia *Sentinel*, 49
Vizetelly, Frank, 96, 152, 210

Wadesborough (NC) *Argus*, 115
Walker, Secretary of War LeRoy Pope, 63
Wallace, Brig. Gen Lew, 114
War correspondents: origins, 1; general
data, 14; pay scales, 14; pseudonyms,
15; in the field, 119; on military staff,
123; in Washington, 137; in disrepute,
159; proper role of, 320; Sherman's
views, 321
Warren *Journal*, 98
Warren, Fitz-Henry; as *Tribune* Washing-
ton bureau chief, 57; denies responsi-
bility for Bull Run, 83; president of
Osbon court martial, 251
Washburne, Elihu B., 73, 283
Washington *Chronicle*, 142, 253, 265
Washington *Constitution*, 26
Washington press corps, 137
Webb, Charles Henry, 162, 264
Weisberger, Bernard, 189
Welles, Gideon, 257, 263, 278,
West Chester (PA) *Jeffersonian*, 98
West Pointers, 143–145, 159
White, Horace, 142
Whitely, *Herald* Washington bureau
chief, 176
Whitman, Walt, 267
Whittier, James Greenleaf, 267–276
Wickliffe, Charles A., 198
Wide Awakes, the, 22

Wikoff, Henry, 139
Wilkeson, Samuel, 200, 231, 256, 277,
279; advocates anonymity, 15;
describes field work, 120; unethical
behavior, 122; as NY *Tribune*
Washinton bureau chief, 138–140;
congressional testimony of, 144; on
McClellan's retreat, 166; on "intelligent contrabands," 196; assaults
Villard, 238; shifts to NY *Times*, 238;
and Sherman's "insanity," 240, 241; at
Gettysburg for NY *Times*, 277, 299;
return to *Tribune*, 283; poses "Meade
for President" conundrum, 285; post-
war career of, 318
Wilkie, Franc; unethical behavior, 122;
feud with Richardson, 128, 133; at
Shiloh, 153, 158; racism of, 190;
accuses Sherman of negligence, 249;
description of Grant, 260 post-war
career of, 318
Williams, George Forrester: Southern
tour, 27; and Sheridan, 291; and
Lincoln, 292; in Richmond, 310
Williamsburg, honors after the Battle of,
177
Wilmington *Journal*, 168
Wilson, Edmund, 269
Wilson, Maj. Gen. James H. 180, 314
Winchester, Battle of, 291, 296
Wing, Henry, 313
Woodcut illustrations, 11
Wooster (OH) Wayne County *Democrat*,
201
World War I and World War II, 323

Yonkers *Herald*, 98
Young, John Russell, at Bull Run, 69; 80;
arrested, 142; hires black correspondent, 308; postwar career of, 318